WJEC/Eduqas

Religious Studies
for A Level Year 2 & A2

Buddhism

Nick Heap with Richard Gray
and Paula Webber

Series Editor: Richard Gray

Illuminate
Publishing

Published in 2019 by Illuminate Publishing Ltd, PO Box 1160, Cheltenham, Gloucestershire GL50 9RW

Orders: Please visit www.illuminatepublishing.com
or email sales@illuminatepublishing.com

British Library Cataloguing-in-Publication Data

A catalogue record for this book is available from the British Library

ISBN 978-1-911208-49-5

Printed by Cambrian Printers, Aberystwyth

07.19

The publisher's policy is to use papers that are natural, renewable and recyclable products made from wood grown in sustainable forests. The logging and manufacturing processes are expected to conform to the environmental regulations of the country of origin.

Every effort has been made to contact copyright holders of material reproduced in this book. If notified, the publishers will be pleased to rectify any errors or omissions at the earliest opportunity.

This material has been endorsed by WJEC/Eduqas and offers high quality support for the delivery of WJEC/Eduqas qualifications. While this material has been through a WJEC/Eduqas quality assurance process, all responsibility for the content remains with the publisher.

WJEC/Eduqas examination questions are reproduced by permission from WJEC/Eduqas

Series editor: Richard Gray
Editor: Geoff Tuttle
Design and Layout: EMC Design Ltd, Bedford

Acknowledgements

Cover Image: Romolo Tavani / Shutterstock.com

Image credits:

p. 1 Romolo Tavani / Shutterstock.com; **p. 6** Physics_joe; **p. 8** Gaid Kornsilapa / Shutterstock.com; **p. 9** Stefano Ember / Shutterstock.com; **p. 10** (right) OohhoT / Shuitterstock.com; **p. 10** (left) Ko Backpacko / Shutterstock.com; **p. 11** infjustice; **p. 12** (top) nicepix / Shutterstock.com; **p. 12** (bottom) Jesus Sanz; **p. 13** hoksurefee; **p. 14** Garuna Liu / Shutterstock.com; **p. 17** Miki Stuido; **p. 18** Vassamon Anansukkasem / Shutterstock.com; **p. 19** nuttavut sammongkoi / Shutterstock.com; **p. 20** Phuong D. Nguyen / Shutterstock.com; **p. 22** Bibliotheque nationale de France / Public domain; **p. 25** Little Grow; **p. 27** Likoper; **p. 28** Quick Shot; **p. 30** (top) Sergey Nivens; **p. 30** (bottom) Josh Cornish; **p. 33** anek.soowannaphoom; **p. 36** NotionPic; **p. 42** vchal; **p. 43** ananaline; **p. 44** Business stock; **p. 46** Saraunyu L / Shutterstock.com; **p. 47** Courtesy Plum Village; **p. 48** tartanparty; **p. 51** Mazur Travel / Shutterstock.com; **p. 53** Hung Chung Chih; **p. 54** Skreidzeleu; **p. 55** Ian_Stewart / Shutterstock.com; **p. 56** Fotos593 / Shutterstock.com; **p. 59** Juan R. Velasco / Shutterstock.com; **p. 60** Microgen; **p. 61** Fabio Alcini; **p. 62** judyjump; **p. 64** 663highland / Creative Commons; **p. 65** Public domain; **p. 68** Zum Wong; **p. 69** (top) Everett – Art; **p. 69** (bottom left) PhOkin / Creative Commons; **p. 69** (bottom right) Attila Jandl / Shutterstock.com; **p. 70** Nichiren / Public domain; **p. 73** Manuel Ascanio; **p. 75** Tensho Shubun / Shokoku-ji Temple / Public domain; **p. 78** PhotoLizM; **p. 80** (top) Public domain; **p. 80** (bottom) Art Directors & TRIP / Alamy Stock Photo; **p. 81** Hyuougushi / Hideyuki KAMON from National Museum, Delhi, India, Creative Commons; **p. 83** (top) 5wH9zu7ONK1zOw at Google Cultural Institute / Public domain; **p. 83** (bottom) R Adam Engle / Public domain; **p. 86** Dinodia Photos / Alamy Stock Photo; **p. 90** Public domain; **p. 91** Artem Kutsenko; **p. 92** Wellcome Collection gallery (2018-03-27): https://wellcomecollection.org/works/yanq6vxb CC-BY-4.0; **p. 93** ottmarliebert.com / Creative Commons; **p. 94** Jambu Lava / Shutterstock.com; **p. 95** CHOTE BKK; **p. 96** DrewHeath / Creative Commons; **p. 100** ABIR ROY BARMAN; **p. 102** Public domain; **p. 104** Akuppa John Wigham from Newcastle upon Tyne / Creative commons Attribution 2.0 Generic license; **p. 105** Dayodaya / Creative Commons Attribution-Share Alike 20. Uported licence; **p. 107** Dusit Wongwattanakul; **p. 108** worldclassphoto; **p. 109** Japanese Traditions, Tokyobling; **p. 110** Bpilgrim / Creative Commons Attribution-Share Alike 2.5 Generic license; **p. 112** Photo Dharma from Sadao, Thailand / Creative Commons Attribution 2.0 Generic license; **p. 121** The Print Collector / Alamy Stock Photo; **p. 122** Heritage Image Partnership Ltd / Alamy Stock Photo; **p. 125** ITN / Shutterstock; **p. 127** Matyas Rehak / Shutterstock.com; **p. 129** Jack 1956 / Creative Commons CC0 1.0 Universal Public Domain Dedication; **p. 132** Hanabusa Itcho / Public domain; **p. 136** Gibson Green / Alamy Stock Photo; **p. 138** Anandajoti Bhikkhu / Creative Commons Attribution 2.0 Generic license; **p. 139** Photo Dharma fromPenang, Malaysia / Creative Commons Attribution 2.0 Generic license; **p. 141** Gakuro / Creative Commons Attribution -Share Alike 3.0 Unpported license; **p. 143** myself / Creative Commons Attribution-Share Alike 3.0 Unported license; **p. 144** John Hill / Creative Commons Attribution-Share Alike 4.0 International license; **p. 147** Gakuro / Creative Commons Attribution-Share Alike 3.0 Unported license; **p. 149** Jazon88 / Creative Commons Attribution-Share Alike 3.0 Unported license; **p. 154** Antoine Taveneaux / Creative Commons Attribution-Share Alike 3.0 Unported, 2.5 Generic, 2.0 Generic and 1.0 Generic license; **p. 156** GNU Free Documentation License, Version 1.2; **p. 157** Bernard Gagnon / GNU Free Documentation License, Version 1.2; **p. 159** Liz Highleyman / Creative Commons Attribution 2.0 Generic license; **p. 160** Colonel Warden / Creative Commons Attribution-Share Alike 3.0 Unported license; **p. 163** Creative Commons Attribution-Share Alike 3.0 Unported license; **p. 165** Sutra Nualpradid / Shutterstock.com; **p. 167** Mari Smith / Creative Commons Attribution 2.0 Generic license; **p. 168** eveleen; **p. 169** Everett Historical; **p. 170** Alizada Studios; **p. 175** Michael Bruns from Lippstadt, Deutschland / Creative Commons Attribution 2.0 Generic license; **p. 178** Creative Commons Attribution-Share Alike 3.0 Unported license; **p. 183** avesun; **p. 187** Sean Pathasema / Birmingham Museum of Art; **p. 188** Eystein Hanssen / NTB / PA Images

Contents*

*The order of contents follows the Eduqas Specification. The WJEC **order** of contents is slightly different but the contents are exactly the same.

About this book

With the new A Level in Religious Studies, there is a lot to cover and a lot to do in preparation for the examinations at A Level. The aim of these books is to provide enough support for you to achieve success at A Level, whether as a teacher or a learner, and build upon the success of the Year 1 and AS series.

Once again, the Year 2 and A2 series of books is skills-based in its approach to learning, which means it aims to continue combining coverage of the Specification content with examination preparation. In other words, it aims to help you get through the second half of the course whilst at the same time developing some more advanced skills needed for the examinations.

To help you study, there are clearly defined sections for each of the AO1 and AO2 areas of the Specification. These are arranged according to the Specification Themes and use, as far as is possible, Specification headings to help you see that the content has been covered for A Level.

The AO1 content is detailed but precise, with the benefit of providing you with references to both religious/philosophical works and to the views of scholars. The AO2 responds to the issues raised in the Specification and provides you with ideas for further debate, to help you develop your own critical analysis and evaluation skills.

Ways to use this book

In considering the different ways in which you may teach or learn, it was decided that the books needed to have an inbuilt flexibility to adapt. As a result, they can be used for classroom learning, for independent work by individuals, as homework, and they are even suitable for the purposes of 'flipped learning' if your school or college does this.

You may be well aware that learning time is so valuable at A Level and so we have also taken this into consideration by creating flexible features and activities, again to save you the time of painstaking research and preparation, either as teacher or learner.

Features of the books

The books all contain the following features that appear in the margins, or are highlighted in the main body of the text, in order to support teaching and learning.

Key terms of technical, religious and philosophical words or phrases

> **Key terms**
>
> Pitaka: basket for storage of the original Buddhist texts

Quickfire questions simple, straightforward questions to help consolidate key facts about what is being digested in reading through the information

> **quickfire**
>
> 1.1 What is the Tipitaka and how did it get its name?

Key quotes either from religious and philosophical works and/or the works of scholars

> **Key quote**
>
> None of the Buddha's early teachings is rejected by the Mahayana, although they are sometimes reinterpreted in radical ways (Keown)

Study tips advice on how to study, prepare for the examination and answer questions

Study tip

The Cornell Note Taking System is an active method of working with information from lessons, books, audio or visual media, visits and visiting speakers. It helps you before, during and after lessons and is an excellent tool for revision. You can find lots of advice on how to use this method effectively on the Internet.

AO1 Activities that serve the purpose of focusing on identification, presentation and explanation, and developing the skills of knowledge and understanding required for the examination

AO1 Activity

Using the advice in the study tip above create (and use) a mind map entitled the structure and content of the Pali Canon.

AO2 Activities that serve the purpose of focusing on conclusions, as a basis for thinking about the issues, developing critical analysis and the evaluation skills required for the examination

AO2 Activity

As you read through this section try to do the following:
1. Pick out the different lines of argument that are presented in the text and identify any evidence given in support.

Glossary of all the key terms for quick reference.

Specific feature: Developing skills

This section is very much a focus on 'what to do' with the content and the issues that are raised. They occur at the end of each section, giving 12 AO1 and 12 AO2 activities that aim to develop particular skills that are required for more advanced study at Year 2 and A2 stage.

The Developing skills for Year 2 and A2 are grouped so that each Theme has a specific focus to develop and perfect gradually throughout that Theme.

AO1 and AO2 answers and commentaries

The final section has a selection of answers and commentaries as a framework for judging what an effective and ineffective response may be. The comments highlight some common mistakes and also examples of good practice so that all involved in teaching and learning can reflect upon how to approach examination answers.

Richard Gray
Series Editor
2019

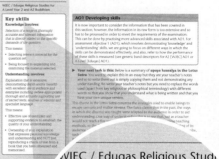

WJEC / Eduqas Religious Studi
A Level Year 2 and A2 Buddhism

Key skills
Knowledge involves:

Selection of a range of (thorough accurate and relevant informati that is directly related to the demands of the question.

T1 Religious figures and sacred texts

This section covers AO1 content and skills

Specification content

The Tipitaka.

Key terms

Abhidhamma Pitaka: third part of the Pali Canon of scriptures made up of the philosophical discourses and commentaries of later scholars

Canon: a collection of scriptures that holds authority

Pali: an ancient Indian language

Pitaka: basket for storage of the original Buddhist texts

Sutta Pitaka: second part of the Pali Canon of scriptures containing stories and teachings of the Buddha

Tipitaka: Pali Canon (three baskets, made up of the Vinaya Pitaka, the Sutta Pitaka and the Abhidhamma Pitaka); the corpus of scripture held to be authoritative by Theravada Buddhists

Vinaya Pitaka: the first part of the Pali Canon containing the rules and regulations for the discipline of the community of monks and nuns

quickfire

1.1 What is the Tipitaka and how did it get its name?

D: The Pali Canon: its role in Buddhism as a whole

The Pali Canon or Tipitaka

The Pali Canon, or Tipitaka, is a large collection of scriptures, written in the ancient Indian language of Pali. The Pali Canon contains teachings of the Buddha and are the oldest complete collection of surviving Buddhist scriptures. They hold authority within Theravada Buddhism and also within some other Buddhist schools such as Tibetan Buddhism.

Initially the teachings of the Buddha had been handed down orally through a variety of Indian dialects, although this by no means suggests that the transmission was unreliable. Research has demonstrated that ancient techniques for transmission of oral literature in Indian religions such as Hinduism and Buddhism guaranteed a high level of accurate retention.

The first written version of the Pali Canon is thought to have been compiled in Sri Lanka in the 1st century BCE. The word Tipitaka translates as 'three baskets' and refers to the original storage of the texts, written on long stitched-together leaves and organised within three discrete baskets according to the nature of the information the texts contained. The three sections, or 'baskets' (pitaka), were named the Vinaya Pitaka, the Sutta Pitaka and the Abhidhamma Pitaka.

Study tip

The Cornell Note Taking System is an active method of working with information from lessons, books, audio or visual media, visits and visiting speakers. It helps you before, during and after lessons and is an excellent tool for revision. You can find lots of advice on how to use this method effectively on the Internet.

AO1 Activity

As you work through the information in the section on the Pali Canon, use the Cornell Note Taking Method to help build your knowledge and understanding.

Pali Canon

The authority of the Vinaya for the Theravada sangha

In both Sanskrit and Pali, the term Vinaya means 'discipline'. The Vinaya Pitaka, basket of discipline, contains within it the Patimokka, the rules and regulations governing the monastic sangha. The authority of the Vinaya carries most force within the unique setting of a monastic order as this was its original purpose. The monastic setting is usually demarcated by a sima (boundary) that surrounds the temple or monastery. Although the Vinaya is specific to monks and nuns, anyone who enters the boundaries of the monastic setting, such as lay Buddhist visitors or those on retreat, are subject to its authority.

In all there are 227 rules for bhikkhus (monks) and 311 for bhikkhunis (nuns). This code of conduct was thought to have been introduced by the Buddha but developed as the sangha grew during the Buddha's ministry. An enlightened monk called Upali is thought to have recited the rules whilst arhats present at the council agreed their accuracy. For further information on the Vinaya and Patimokka see pages 38–42 from the A Level Year 1 and AS book, *Buddhism* (Illuminate Publishing, 2017) Theme 1 Section C *Buddhist texts as sources of wisdom and authority*.

This association with the Buddha and his leading disciples gives the Vinaya Pitaka a place of importance and authority in Theravada Buddhism and within some Mahayana traditions. The Vinaya rules were passed down through oral tradition and were eventually written in Pali in the Vinaya Pitaka at the Fourth Council (1st century BCE). At that time the rules were also recorded in other languages. An early sect of Buddhism, the Dharmaguptaka, left a written record of the Vinaya. This is the version of the monastic rules followed by most Mahayana monastic orders today. Tibetan Buddhists also have their own Vinaya, which developed in another early school of Buddhism.

Study tip

It is important not to learn about sacred texts from secondary sources only. Explore the scriptures themselves. This can increase your interest in, and understanding of, Buddhism and of the A Level Buddhism course as a whole. Don't forget to include references to sacred texts in examination answers.

AO1 Activity

Access an online version of the Vinaya Pitaka from the Pali Canon and choose:

1. Five rules that seem reasonable for the members of the sangha to follow.
2. Five rules that you find more difficult to understand or seem irrelevant in the 21st century.

As a class, or in small groups, share and discuss your findings. Some questions to consider might include:

- Why might it have been important to include these rules?
- Would they be useful in enabling the monastic sangha to live in harmony?
- How might these rules help bhikkhus or bhikkhunis on their path to enlightenment?

Specification content
The authority of the Vinaya for the Theravada sangha.

Key terms

Dharmaguptaka: one of the eighteen early schools of Buddhism

Patimokka: the 227 rules of the Buddhist community of monks to be found in the Vinaya; nuns have 311

Sima: a boundary that surrounds the temple or monastery

Upali: one of the ten chief disciples of the Buddha who recalled all of the rules of the Vinaya

Study tip

Terminology used in the study of Buddhism comes from a number of languages and because of this there are often alternative spellings for terms. In general, it is best to use Pali terms in the context of Theravada Buddhism and Sanskrit terms in the context of Mahayana Buddhism. There are, however, occasions when the context is indeterminate or Sanskrit is preferred; for example, on occasions in the Specification. For this reason, any legitimate spelling of terms will be accepted from students in answering a question and students do not have to determine whether the term is Sanskrit or Pali.

Study tip

It is important to use key terms correctly and in context throughout your examination. Spelling these correctly is important. Think of creative ways in which you can learn key terms. You might want to make some flash cards or keep an A–Z vocabulary book where you collect key terms and definitions throughout the course. Chunking words into syllables and saying them aloud is a good method of learning. You could use the look, cover, write and check method. When you think you have mastered the terms, try asking a friend or family member to test you.

quickfire

1.2 How many rules are there for bhikkhus (monks) and how many for bhikkhunis (nuns)?

Key terms

Bhikkhu: monk

Bhikkhuni: nun

Dasa sila: ten precepts taken by monks and nuns

Suttavibhanga: the first book of the Theravadin Vinaya Pitaka

As disagreement within the sangha grew, people approached the Buddha with accounts of misconduct, and the rules were created to address each situation. For example, the rule for **bhikkhus** and **bhikkhunis** regarding abstinence from sexual intercourse is said to have arisen as a result of the discovery of contact between bhikkhus and their ex-wives. The development of a code of conduct was important because the main goal of Buddhism is nibbana (nirvana), and conflict and misdemeanours would be detrimental to this ultimate goal. The Vinaya Pitaka contains guidance on how to settle disputes as well as the sanctions for those who commit offences. Clarke and Thompson point out that this provides a useful 'emphasis that the rules are all grounded on the realities of life'. Through the Vinaya we are able to build up a picture of what life was like within the early monastic sangha. This same way of living for the monastic sangha has been preserved within Theravada Buddhism to this day.

Yasothon, Thailand – May 2017: Gilded wooden boxes containing Pali manuscripts exhibited inside ho trai or the library of Tipitaka (Pali Canon) located at Wat Mahathat Temple.

AO1 Activity

Write a short paragraph to explain why the Vinaya was formed and how it benefitted the early sangha.

The Vinaya Pitaka contains the following sections:

- The **Suttavibhanga**, which contains the Patimokka which are the rules of discipline and training for monks and nuns. The **dasa sila** are the most important of these rules and are to be followed by all ordained bhikkhus and bhikkhunis. These ten rules were eventually expanded into 227 rules for bhikkhus and 311 rules for bhikkhunis. The Patimokka rules include a list of possessions members of the monastic community were allowed to own: three robes, an alms bowl, a razor, a needle, a girdle, and a water strainer. There are rules within this section which outline the protocol for alms rounds and the requirement that no solid food be consumed after noon. There is to be no storing of food to eat later, which makes sense in light of the Buddha's teaching on the Middle Way that avoids greed. The Suttavibhanga lists eight categories of wrongdoing for monks and nuns including the four **parajikas**, which rule against sexual intercourse, stealing, murder and falsely declaring supernatural powers. If these rules are broken then the bhikkhu or bhikkhuni can be expelled from the monastic sangha. If other rules in this section are broken, the consequences would include a meeting of the sangha to deal with the consequences: penance, forfeiture, confession or a public admission that the action has happened. This section also contains rules for training bhikkhus and bhikkhunis, as well as rules for settling legal disputes. Monks and nuns cannot plead ignorance if they have broken a rule as they still have to accept the consequences of their actions. For example, they cannot claim that they did not know that a drink contained alcohol. If this had been consumed, it would still require confession, and ignorance would be no defence. Another example might be that confession is made if a meal is consumed after noon even if the monk or nun has lost track of the time.

- In the second section, the **Khandhaka**, you will find an account of the Buddha's life after his enlightenment, as well as stories about prominent disciples. This section also gives an account of the first two Buddhist Councils. Guidance on monastic etiquette and manners are also discussed in this section. Ritual procedures for initiation and ordination, as well as guidance on the organisation of the sangha can be found in this section. Also, the format of the **uposatha days**; the organising of retreats, dress codes; rules around food; medicine and caring for the sick; and how to deal with division amongst sangha members. From this we can see that the rules of the Vinaya are often very practical. Familiarity with the rules is reinforced amongst monks and nuns as they are regularly recited during the uposatha ceremonies at every new and full moon. This provides one way of preserving the dharma and discipline. Following the recitation of each rule, confessions of the breaking of the rule takes place.

- The third section of the Vinaya is the **Parivara.** This provides a summary of the rules and valuable guidance on how to observe the Vinaya. It is mostly used in monastic training to instruct and examine bhikkhus and bhikkhunis.

The authority of the Vinaya for the Theravada sangha, therefore, appears to carry normative force. That is, it directs an individual's behaviour within the monastic environment in two ways: (1) through their daily interaction with others; and, (2) for their own spiritual path and development. It is important not to see the term 'authority' in terms of Buddhists scriptures as directly related to some form of ultimate, overall metaphysical control or controller. The authority the Vinaya carries within the Theravada sangha is more a practical distillation of tried and tested

Key terms

Khandhaka: the second section of the Vinaya Pitaka containing stories about the Buddha's Awakening and rules of etiquette for the monastic sangha

Parajikas: the 'defeats' or behaviour that forces disrobing and expulsion from the monastic order

Parivara: the third section of the Vinaya Pitaka containing a summary of the Vinaya rules

Uposatha days: days of renewed commitment to the dharma, often occurring on full moon

quickfire

1.3 Which four rules result in expulsion from the order if they are broken?

Key quote

It is possible, I think, to identify four particular concerns in the Buddhist monastic rules as set out in the Vinaya: (1) the unity and cohesion of the Sangha, (2) the spiritual life, (3) the dependence of the Sangha upon the wider community, and (4) the appearance of the Sangha in the eyes of that community. **(Gethin)**

A sangha in Burma/Myanmar: the Patimokka rules govern daily life.

ways that bring success in the monastic setting. The correct or right way, then, becomes the best possible way. It is more a case that what the Vinaya brings is the wisdom essential for spiritual success. The various prohibitions and warnings can therefore be seen as positive keys to unlocking the fetters of attachment that can lead to suffering and falling away from the path.

Novice monks observing the Vinaya rules for initiation.

A Burmese Buddhist monk reading from the Tipitaka.

quickfire

1.4 What sections is the Vinaya divided into?

quickfire

1.5 Name two things that could happen if you break the rules.

quickfire

1.6 How is the Parivara used?

AO1 Activity

Make a table to show the types of rules to be found in the Vinaya. Explain how they support the monastic sangha.

Type of rule	Support to the monastic sangha

AO1 Activity

Write down as many answers to the following question as you can think of in two minutes: Why is the Vinaya Pitaka important to Buddhists? Share your ideas with another person or a small group and add to your own answers. Whole class discussion should follow. This activity will also provide you with some lines of reasoning for AO2 style essays.

Specification content

The wider authority and significance of the Sutta Pitaka.

The wider authority and significance of the Sutta Pitaka

The Pali Suttas are collections of discourses attributed to the Buddha and some of his early disciples. They were said to have been recited at the First Council by Ananda, the Buddha's most dedicated disciple. Richard Gombrich suggests that the corresponding Sanskrit term *sūkta* means 'something that is well said'. This term was traditionally used to refer to the ancient Indian Vedic texts. Gombrich points out that, in using this term, early Buddhists were 'claiming a status on a par with the Vedas for the utterances of the Buddha' (cited in Gethin). Throughout the scriptures the phrase 'Thus I have heard' is used repetitively to add authority to the texts, indicating that they had been passed down from those witnessing the teachings of the Buddha himself. Sutta, meaning 'thread', highlights the idea that there is a connection running through the different teachings of the Buddha. Sarah Shaw describes them as being like a tapestry, or rich embroidery, because of the repetition and cross-referencing of the teachings.

They are seen as **Buddha vacana**, 'the word of the Buddha'. However, Gethin points out that the use of this formula at the beginning of a text is not necessarily an indication that it was actually uttered by the Buddha in person, but by monks and nuns who had been his disciples, some of them from long after his death. Therefore, the phrase is used as a way of giving authority to the account and even if it is not directly related to the Buddha, it is often acknowledged as an indirect affirmation of his words. The basic teachings of the Buddha found in the Suttas include the Four Noble Truths and the Eightfold Path. Two of the most popular scriptures contained in the Suttas are the Dhammapada and the Jataka Tales.

As such, the Sutta Pitaka does suggest a wider audience than a monastic setting and radiates a different kind of authority, that of the **Buddha sasana** (teaching or doctrine of the Buddha). This means that it extends to all Buddhists and should be accessible to all people. The Sutta Pitaka is widely used as a source of wisdom and guidance for Buddhist living, and spiritual, moral and practical advice can be extracted from it.

The discourses, or dialogues, contained within the Suttas are collected together into five sections:

1. The Digha Nikaya, which is the longest of the discourses. It contains 34 sermons including themes such as false teachings; the ascetic lifestyle; the view that animal sacrifice and self-mortification are bad actions; the twelve links of causation, the Buddha's parinirvana, four types of meditation, why the Buddha refused to talk about God; and the teaching on the duties of a householder.

2. The Majjhima Nikaya is a thematic collection of medium-length discourses. Included here are 152 sermons with themes such as the Buddha's Awakening or enlightenment; his renunciation and spiritual quest; advice on meditation given by the Buddha to Rahula about meditation; his past life stories; the Noble Eightfold Path; and the Four Noble Truths; the characteristics of an arahat; and **Pratekya-Buddhas**.

3. The Samyutta Nikaya, which is an anthology of 'Kindred sayings' or 2889 short discourses on subjects such as the Noble Eightfold Path and the Four Noble Truths; the twelve nidanas (links of causation); the five skandhas; the levels of jhanas and nibbana.

4. The Anguttara Nikaya contains 2308 short sayings or 'Gradual Sayings' on topics such as karma; one Buddha; meditation on loving-kindness (metta-bhavana); the five mental hindrances; and monastic duties.

Key terms

Buddha sasana: teaching or doctrine of the Buddha

Buddha vacana: the words or sayings of the Buddha

Pratekya-Buddha: literally 'a lone buddha', 'a buddha on their own' or 'a private buddha', is one of three types of enlightened beings according to some schools of Buddhism. A Buddha who reaches enlightenment and does not go on to teach

quickfire

1.7 Where are the discourses of the Buddha to be found and what is the term for 'the word of the Buddha'?

An ancient statue of Lord Buddha giving a sermon in Nakhon Nayok province, Thailand. The Suttas are seen as Buddha vacana.

5. Within the Khuddaka Nikaya you find a collection of the shortest texts. This is thought to have been added to the Tipitaka at a later date. It is made up of 15 ancient literary texts, including the Dhammapada and Jatakas. This literature, which is often made up of poetry, includes the Four Noble Truths; the Three Refuges; loving kindness; the famous parable of the blind men and the elephant; the account of the temptations of Mara; teachings on rebirth; and accounts of the past lives of the Buddha.

Despite not being in chronological order, the fragmented account of Siddhartha Gautama's life (Siddhattha Gotama) – often referred to as the 'historical Buddha' – is interwoven throughout the Suttas. The Buddha used examples from his earlier life, or lives, to illustrate his teachings and, therefore, a fairly full picture of his life can be built up by readers of the Sutta Pitaka. The key events in his life, his birth; the Four Sights; the Great Departure; The Awakening or Enlightenment; his First Sermon and his Death (parinirvana) are those celebrated within Buddhist festivals, pilgrimage, art and literature today. The key events of the life of the Buddha are often given a hagiographical reading. For more information see pages 13–20 from the A Level Year 1 and AS book, *Buddhism* (Illuminate Publishing, 2017) Theme 1 Section A *Buddhist texts as sources of wisdom and authority.*

Thai mural of the life of the Buddha at Wat Chian Grai in Lampang, Thailand.

It is evident from the Suttas that the Buddha was skilled at adapting his teachings to suit individual people. His audiences included housewives, farmers and Brahmin priests. Sarah Shaw suggests that this gives a 'wide ranging and human appeal' to the Suttas of the Digha Nikaya. Once again, this re-affirms the wider authority and appeal of the Sutta Pitaka. In a sense the Sutta Pitaka contains the earliest examples of how the Buddha used **upaya kosalla** (Pali 'skilful means'), a term often associated with Mahayana Buddhism and the Lotus Sutra (Sanskrit upaya kausalya – see later). However, it may be useful to remember that the Buddha's original reaction to his Awakening was that the Dhamma could not be easily communicated when he stated, 'Those dyed in lust, wrapped in darkness, will never discern this abstruse Dhamma which goes against the worldly stream, subtle, deep, and difficult to see.' It was the Hindu god **Brahma** who encouraged the Buddha to deliver the discourses we now have in the Suttas of the Pali Canon.

The Dhammapada, 'path of Truth', is a collection of sayings of the Buddha, believed to be gathered directly by his closest disciples and contained in 423 verses. This is probably the most well-known part of the Sutta Pitaka. According to Richard Gray it is thought to be a 'filtered version of the Buddha's teachings from the Pali Canon'. It does not contain the stories, parables and explanation of teachings and instructions that are typically contained within the rest of the Sutta Pitaka, and yet its teachings are no less profound or practical. It is easily memorised and its authority and appeal is such that it is used extensively by Theravadins, as well as being highly regarded by Buddhists of some Mahayana schools. Moreover, many lay Buddhists would have a copy of the Dhammapada in their homes. It is

The Buddha teaches the path to nirvana.

used by the laity as a source of inspiration and a practical guide for living and it is chanted as a formula for protection or during times of trouble. Buddhists seek the wisdom of the Buddha as guidance when they read it. It 'elucidates the path of the Dhamma, the path to enlightenment' according to J. Fowler. Therefore, the teachings contained within the Dhammapada are ultimately aimed at the cessation of dukkha.

Dating from approximately 300 BCE to 400 CE the Jatakas consist of a collection of over 500 anecdotes and fables told by the Buddha about experiences within his previous lives. The setting for the stories is the city of Benares in India. As the protagonist, the Buddha appears as an array of colourful characters depicted in both human and animal forms. He is regarded as the greatest storyteller. When he narrates his past lives he refers to himself as the bodhisattva, or a Buddha-to-be. He chooses the best stories to explain puzzling situations. For example, he is seen as a monkey who makes himself into a bridge in order to save his troop. The Buddha-to-be is frequently seen as the hero of these, often humorous, tales. However, he is never depicted as a woman in the Jatakas that have been collected together in the Pali Canon. In the Jatakas he often performs acts of selflessness and embodies the virtues that are the focus of the tale. The last ten highly venerated Jataka tales have morality and the Ten Perfections (generosity, virtue, renunciation, wisdom, energy, patience, truthfulness, resolution, loving kindness and equanimity) at their heart. There is an emphasis upon cultivating the Perfections in order to achieve good karma and ultimately Buddhahood. The Jatakas reinforce the Buddhist doctrine of rebirth and, perhaps show a stronger connection within the stories between one life and the next than is put forward in the notion of anatta. On the surface, the Jataka stories appear to have very little to do with Buddhist philosophy; however, lay Buddhists are particularly attracted to them and they have shaped the beliefs of Buddhists today. During festivals, such as Vesak, tales are often re-enacted. The Jatakas also remain a source of authority for sermons and religious teachings. In predominantly Buddhist countries such as Thailand, Laos, Cambodia and Burma/Myanmar a rich array of artwork is based on the Jatakas. Additionally, the Jatakas are often used as media for teaching morality to children and have been used as inspiration for many cartoons, some of which are now available on the Internet.

Sculptures of characters from the Jatakas

The relevance of the Abhidhamma for the commentarial development of Buddhism

The Abhidhamma Pitaka contains philosophical teachings which reveal the Buddhist perspective on the world and reality. Tradition has it that the Buddha taught the Abhidhamma to his mother in a heaven realm, thus giving authority to this section of the Pali Canon. Divided into seven sections, it is referred to

quickfire

1.8 What is the Dhammapada and how is the Dhammapada organised?

Key quotes

Rouse yourself, be diligent, in Dhamma faring well. Who dwells in Dhamma's happy in this birth and the next. (Dhammapada Chapter 13:167)

Driven by fear, people run for security to mountains and forests, to sacred spots and shrines. But none of these can be a safe refuge, because they cannot free the mind from fear.

Take refuge in the Buddha, the dharma, and the sangha, and you will grasp the Four Noble Truths: suffering, the cause of suffering, the end of suffering, and the Noble Eightfold Path that takes you beyond suffering.

That is your best refuge, your only refuge. When you reach it all sorrow falls away. (Dhammapada 14:188–192)

quickfire

1.9 What are the Jataka tales?

Specification content

The relevance of the Abhidhamma for the commentarial development of Buddhism.

as the 'higher Dhamma' and is thought to be more appropriate for use by the
more learned monks of the sangha. As such it is used less amongst the laity.
These teachings are not those of the historical Buddha and are thought to be
a later addition to the Canon, probably added at the Third Council in the 3rd
century BCE. Gethin argues that the Abhidhamma simply continues 'the process
of systematisation already evident in the Nikayas' of the Pali Canon and that
'commentary and interpretation had always formed part of Buddhism' (Gethin).
What sets the Abhidhamma apart from the Vinaya and the Suttas is that both of
the other sections of the Tipitaka
are commentaries on situations
that have arisen, whereas the
Abhidhamma 'is the Buddha's
teaching stated in bare and
general terms without reference
to any particular circumstances'
(Gethin).

*Yangon, Burma/Myanmar: the Buddhist Ordination Hall at
Mahapasana Cave where Tipitaka examinations take place.*

The Abhidhamma Pitaka
describes the process of
samsara, thus enabling the
reader to gain an insight into
reality. Richard Gombrich
describes the Abhidhamma
as 'a scholastic elaboration of
doctrine, especially as regards
the analysis of mind'. It discusses
issues such as **dhammas**; the
need to avoid constructing the
idea of 'self' or 'my', which are
not reality; different types of
personalities; and **causation**. Paul Williams tells us that the Abhidhamma is
concerned with 'unravelling the dynamic nature of things and explaining how the
world nevertheless hangs together'. He suggests that the Abhidhamma provides
a description of the dhammas, or building-blocks that make up the world we
experience, and that these also relate to morality and the path to liberation. It could
be suggested, therefore, that the deeply philosophical writings of the Abhidhamma
offer the reader an insight into absolute reality.

quickfire

1.10 What is contained in the
Abhidhamma Pitaka?

Study tip

Make mind maps throughout your course. They can act as excellent revision
tools. Mind maps help you to process and recall information, as well as to make
connections between the various elements of the course. Try to make them
as informative as possible. Use words, numbers, lines, illustrations and colour.
This will help you to remember the information contained in them. Don't just
file the mind map away once it is created, keep revisiting it regularly to keep
the information fresh in your mind. Think of ways that you might use the mind
map to expand on the information contained within it. For example, you might
compose a list of 'why' questions from it to enhance your AO2 skills.

AO1 Activity

Using the advice in the study tip above create (and use) a mind map entitled
the structure and content of the Pali Canon.

The importance of the Pali Canon as a source of wisdom

In the UK, the Pali Text Society was set up by T. W. Rhys Davids in1881 'to foster and promote the study of Pali texts'. The Canon was translated into the English language, making it more accessible. Academic interest in the Pali language and scriptures grew. Today translations, in a number of languages, are available for anyone to read on the Internet. It is not unusual today to see quotations from the historical Buddha (unfortunately sometimes incorrect) or from the Dhammapada on the Internet and social media sites. But this source of wisdom has not been accessible worldwide until recent times.

As Buddhist teachings become accessible, more people have engaged with its philosophy and practices. Thus, the influence of the Pali Canon as a source of wisdom to Buddhists in the UK, as well as in other countries throughout the world, has strengthened. Its practical advice for practitioners, e.g. on how to meditate and follow the dharma, remains central to Buddhists today.

The Pali Canon provides an insight into the core teachings of Buddhism, including the teachings of the historical Buddha on the Four Noble Truths and the Noble Eightfold Path. It is a source of wisdom for Theravadins who believe it contains all the teachings needed to guide them toward achieving nibbana. The texts are memorised by Theravadin monks and recited during ceremonies and meditations. It is tradition within Theravada Buddhism to see the Pali Canon as depicting the original Buddhism. As such it is seen as the word of the Buddha and carries authority as a source of wisdom.

It is the oldest written version of the historical Buddha's teachings and as such, 'even Buddhists from the Mahayana traditions accept these Pali writings as an accurate reflection ... of what Buddha taught' (Landaw and Bodian). Nevertheless, within Theravada, some Mahayana and Vajrayana schools the Pali Canon remains a central source of authority for teachings and practices, such as the Four Noble Truths, the Noble Eightfold Path, the Three Lakshanas and advice on meditation.

The custom of Sangiti, which means reciting together, is an important tradition within Buddhism. This has been the method of transmitting the dharma of the Buddha since the sangha gathered in the First Buddhist Council. The content of these recitations is now to be found within the Pali Canon. Prof. Bhikshu Satyapala tells us that in Buddhism Sangiti 'has a distinct, deeper and wider meaning and in that sense it means the recitation of the teachings of the Buddha for their collection, compilation, classification, verification, or authentication, approval and memorisation'. The practice of Sangiti continues today. Not only is it instrumental in keeping order within the monastic community but the practice also serves to ensure the continuation of the words of the Buddha in their purest and most accurate form. Indeed, the way in which the Canon has been organised is centred around this practice as it is divided up into sections depending on how it is to be recited.

Individually, the three-fold partition of the baskets allows for differentiation in how it is used as a source of wisdom. On the whole the Vinaya Pitaka is a practical source of wisdom and advice on how to follow the Buddhist path and is specifically focused on a monastic setting and for a community of practising nuns and monks. It also helps those outside the monastic boundary, on entering, to see an environment that is conducive for seeking out nibbana. In contrast, the Sutta Pitaka is more didactic, ethical, and 'historical' or 'hagiographical' in nature in that it reveals the sasana, that is, the collective teaching of the Buddha for all Buddhists. Again, the philosophical focus of the Abhidhamma Pitaka makes it a more 'specialist' and advanced pursuit for those aiming for a deeper understanding of the Buddhist teachings.

Therefore the Pali Canon holds collective importance for the whole of Buddhism as a source of wisdom; in practice, the Pali Canon is source of wisdom that has different parts catering for the different practical and spiritual needs of its adherents.

Specification content

The importance of the Pali Canon as a source of wisdom.

Key quote

Buddhism cannot be reduced to a collection of theoretical writings nor a philosophical system of thought – although both of these form an important part of its tradition. What lies at the heart of Buddhism, according to its own understanding of the matter, is dharma. (Gethin)

Key skills Theme 1

The first theme has tasks that deal with the basics of AO1 in terms of prioritising and selecting the key relevant information, presenting this and then using evidence and examples to support and expand upon this.

Key skills

Knowledge involves:

Selection of a range of (thorough) accurate and relevant information that is directly related to the specific demands of the question.

This means:

- Selecting relevant material for the question set

- Being focused in explaining and examining the material selected.

Understanding involves:

Explanation that is extensive, demonstrating depth and/or breadth with excellent use of evidence and examples including (where appropriate) thorough and accurate supporting use of sacred texts, sources of wisdom and specialist language.

This means:

- Effective use of examples and supporting evidence to establish the quality of your understanding

- Ownership of your explanation that expresses personal knowledge and understanding and NOT just reproducing a chunk of text from a book that you have rehearsed and memorised.

As you work through each section of the book, the focus will be on a variety of different aspects associated with AO1 so that you can comprehensively perfect the overall skills associated with AO1.

AO1 Developing skills

It is now important to consider the information that has been covered in this section; however, the information in its raw form is too extensive and so has to be processed in order to meet the requirements of the examination. This can be done by practising more advanced skills associated with AO1. The exercises that run throughout this book will help you to do this and prepare you for the examination. For assessment objective 1 (AO1), which involves demonstrating 'knowledge' and 'understanding' skills, we are going to focus on different ways in which the skills can be demonstrated effectively, and also, refer to how the performance of these skills is measured (see generic band descriptors for A2 [WJEC] AO1 or A Level [Eduqas] AO1).

▶ **Your task is this:** Below is a summary of **the role of the Dhammapada**. It is 211 words long. You need to use this for an answer but could not repeat all of this in an essay under examination conditions so you will have to condense the material. Discuss which points you think are the most important and then re-draft into your own summary of 100 words.

The Dhammapada, 'path of Truth', is a collection of sayings of the Buddha, believed to be gathered directly by his closest disciples and contained in 423 verses. This is probably the most well-known part of the Sutta Pitaka. According to Richard Gray, it is thought to be a 'filtered version of the Buddha's teachings from the Pali Canon'. It does not contain the stories, parables and explanation of teachings and instructions that are typically contained within the rest of the Sutta Pitaka, and yet its teachings are no less profound or practical. It is easily memorised and its authority and appeal are such that it is used extensively by Theravadins, as well as being highly regarded by Buddhists of some Mahayana schools. Moreover, many lay Buddhists would have a copy of the Dhammapada in their homes. It is used by the laity as a source of inspiration and a practical guide for living and it is chanted as a formula for protection or during times of trouble. Buddhists seek the wisdom of the Buddha as guidance when they read it. It 'elucidates the path of the Dhamma, the path to enlightenment' according to J. Fowler. Therefore, the teachings contained within the Dhammapada are ultimately aimed at the cessation of dukkha.

When you have completed the task, refer to the band descriptors for A2 (WJEC) or A Level (Eduqas) and, in particular, have a look at the demands described in the higher band descriptors towards which you should be aspiring. Ask yourself:

- Does my work demonstrate thorough, accurate and relevant knowledge and understanding of religion and belief?

- Is my work coherent (consistent or make logical sense), clear and well organised? ***(WJEC band descriptor only but still important to consider for Eduqas)***

- Will my work, when developed, be an extensive and relevant response which is specific to the focus of the task?

- Does my work have extensive depth and/or suitable breadth and have excellent use of evidence and examples?

- If appropriate to the task, does my response have thorough and accurate reference to sacred texts and sources of wisdom?

- Are there any insightful connections to be made with other elements of my course?

- Will my answer, when developed and extended to match what is expected in an examination answer, have an extensive range of views of scholars/schools of thought?

- When used, is specialist language and vocabulary both thorough and accurate?

Issues for analysis and evaluation

The relative importance of the Pali Canon in Buddhism

Today, the Vinaya continues to be a major influence mainly for the **Theravadin** and Vajrayana monastic sanghas. It informs daily life within their specific monastic communities. In other Buddhist traditions within Mahayana it is not necessarily given the same emphasis, although the monastic life is comparable in practice.

As the Vinaya is specifically for monastic living, its rules may be seen as outdated and irrelevant in today's society and so relatively unimportant for the majority of Buddhists who do not live in a monastic setting, that is, the lay community.

One widely used example of this is that it is very difficult for monks or nuns to survive today without handling money, especially in Western communities without a large Buddhist population. The alms round often does not suffice and sanghas have had to adapt in order to ensure their survival. Some Buddhist centres in the West now have to suggest a specific amount of money as **dana** in order to deliver teachings. After all, the expenses of travelling teachers need to be met. One might ask how this understandable dilemma, just one example amongst many, actually fits with the sangha rules written thousands of years ago? In this sense it could be argued that the importance of this aspect of the Pali Canon has diminished.

However, the Sutta Pitaka is important, not only to the monastic sangha but also as guidance for the laity. It is believed by Theravadins to contain the words of the Buddha or the teachings of his close disciples, thus giving it a great deal of authority. As well as teaching the path to enlightenment via key Buddhist teachings such as the Four Noble Truths, it also offers advice on many practical issues. These include subjects such as relationships; marriage; employment; handling money; and activities that may lead to addiction such as gambling. There are also positive recommendations on things such as how to use time wisely rather than idly and practices such as meditation.

Nonetheless, it is usually taught by the monks and nuns rather than being accessed directly by the laity and so there could be said to be some restrictions as to its direct importance for the laity.

Despite this, it is the one part of the Tipitaka that encapsulates all of the Buddha's teachings and biographical accounts. Whilst some of the texts in the Pali are unfamiliar to many Buddhists, the Sutta Pitaka contains the most famous of all Pali texts, i.e. the Dhammapada and the Jatakas. Thus showing how well used and respected it is. The Pali Canon is a practical guide to practices such as meditation and this has enabled the preservation of Buddhism.

Another way in which the importance of the Pali Canon is limited in terms of its readership and scholarship is the abstract and complex teaching in the Abhidhamma Pitaka. This suggests that it might only be of relevance to monks, nuns and scholars

The Patimokkha rules ensure harmony within the Sangha.

This section covers AO2 content and skills

Specification content
The relative importance of the Pali Canon as a source of wisdom.

Key terms

Dana: giving

Theravadin: an adherent of Theravada Buddhism

Key quotes

None of the Buddha's early teachings is rejected by the Mahayana, although they are sometimes reinterpreted in radical ways. (**Keown**)

It is far more common to stumble upon an isolated sentence or paragraph like a carved scene on a chipped stone, that offers a brief tantalising glimpse into his world. (**Batchelor**)

AO2 Activity

As you read through this section try to do the following:

1. Pick out the different lines of argument that are presented in the text and identify any evidence given in support.

2. For each line of argument try to evaluate whether or not you think this is strong (convincing) or weak (unconvincing).

3. Think of any questions you may wish to raise in response to the arguments.

This activity will help you to start thinking critically about what you read and help you to evaluate the effectiveness of different arguments and from this develop your own observations, opinions and points of view that will help with any conclusions that you make in your answers to the AO2 questions that arise.

Key quotes

With the arrival of Buddhism in the West ... the divide between monastic and lay practice is becoming less distinct, with many very committed and educated lay people studying scriptures in translation. (Clear Vision website)

The Pali Canon is a complex tapestry of linguistic and rhetorical styles, shot through with conflicting ideas, doctrines and images, all assembled and elaborated over about four centuries. The canon does not speak with a single voice. (Batchelor)

Old Tipitaka manuscript from Yasothon, North East Thailand

AO2 Activity

List some conclusions that could be drawn from the AO2 reasoning from the above text; try to aim for at least three different possible conclusions. Consider each of the conclusions and collect brief evidence to support each conclusion from the AO1 and AO2 material for this topic. Select the conclusion that you think is most convincing and explain why it is so. Try to contrast this with the weakest conclusion in the list, justifying your argument with clear reasoning and evidence.

who are pursuing dhamma studies at a higher level. This might suggest, therefore, that it is of limited overall importance.

The Pali Canon may also seem irrelevant to Mahayana schools such as Nichiren Buddhism who see its teachings as Upaya or 'skilful means'. Their view is that these teachings have been superseded by later texts such as the Lotus Sutra. However, it could be argued that many of the ideas in the Abhidhamma have been developed in Mahayana texts. Additionally, the Abhidhamma Pitaka continues to engage scholarly interest as a source of wisdom amongst academics as well as more advanced members of the monastic sangha.

To support this line of argument, the Clear Vision website reminds us that in-depth study of the scriptures is not essential for Buddhist practice and that many Buddhists in the world are not able to read. Indeed, the website points out that it is meditation and ethical practice that are central to self-translation.

Stephen Batchelor suggests that when reading the Pali Canon you don't often find long sections containing the biography of the historical Buddha. Batchelor argues that it is like finding a needle in a haystack when you come across any detail about his life. Despite modern research into oral traditions, Batchelor argues that when these details were handed down by the monks through the oral tradition 'no doubt, certain details were forgotten, omitted or muddled up, and doctrinal passages were elaborated and refined'. However, Batchelor goes on to say that as 'each chipped and weathered stone finds its place ... the sublime tragedy of Siddhartha Gotama's life begins to unfold before one's startled eyes'. Therefore even with all this in mind, over 2500 years after the life of the historical Buddha, the content of the Pali Canon remains a significant source of authority, information, inspiration and wisdom to Buddhists.

Some would argue, like Batchelor, that it is unlikely that the historical Buddha would ever have spoken the language of Pali and the words contained there are unlikely to be the actual words of the Buddha. Additionally, this is only a selection of the Buddha's teaching, as it would have been impossible to record everything he said over his 45-year teaching career. So it gives a piecemeal account of his life and work. Nonetheless, just because we have an 'edited' version does not necessarily diminish its status as a significant source of authority, information, inspiration and wisdom to Buddhists.

In conclusion, the Pali Canon is a vast collection of literature, and few Buddhists would sit and read it entirely. The monastic sangha are the guardians of the dharma. They interpret the scriptures and pass it on to the laity. Of course, the rules of the Vinaya and Abhidhamma Pitakas are meant for use by the monastic sangha only. The Suttas hold more relevance to Buddhists within the lay sangha, some being more often known and used than others. Some of the stories, parables, and teachings of the Buddha are very familiar, e.g. those such as the Jatakas, that are used to teach children and the refuges used to show commitment in daily practice. Sometimes parts of the Canon are recited for protection and others used to reflect on the blessings of life, e.g. the Metta Sutta on universal love. Monks learn some parts of the Canon by heart. Some parts of the Canon are chanted daily. What is evident is that the basic teachings and biographical narratives of the historical Buddha that are so familiar to Buddhists today that are sourced from the Pali Canon. The Canon is treated with the same great respect as relics of the Buddha.

Study tip

Remember there is great diversity within Buddhism with different views being held by the different schools of Buddhism. More sophisticated examination answers will reflect this. The examiner is interested in seeing that you are aware of differences within the Theravada, Mahayana and Vajrayana schools. You should also be trying to use the views of different sources of wisdom.

Remember that it is the quality and not the quantity of your writing that is important in the examination.

The significance of the Vinaya for the sangha

There can be no doubt that the rules contained in the Vinaya Pitaka have great significance for the monastic sangha and indeed many uses. The main aims for those in a monastic setting are to get rid of material attachments; prevent attachment to the three poisons; remove the ego and dukkha; and to focus on the path of **arahatship** leading to the ultimate goal of nibbana. This is arguably the most significant aspect for all Buddhists eventually, although not necessarily in this present life. So although it has a specialised focus, the Vinaya may not be 'significant' for all Buddhists here and now. The real issue here is whether or not this necessarily means that on the whole this reduces its significance in Buddhism generally?

Some could argue that it does. The Vinaya contains rules that are set in place to foster good relationships and maintain order within a monastic community setting. It is therefore not really for lay Buddhists. Although lay Buddhists may access the monastic sangha for retreats, once lay Buddhists are outside the boundary, the Vinaya rules are lapsed.

However, it could be recognised that monastics who observe the Patimokka rules become good role models for the lay community. The rules instill values indirectly into the wider Buddhist community by serving to guide the laity, remove temptation and prevent distraction. By observing the rules, monks and nuns are able to live a simple life and focus upon the Dharma, developing **prajna** and showing commitment and dedication to the Middle Way. Their influence of the wider Buddhist community is very significant in this way.

Despite this, some could argue that the rules of the Vinaya Pitaka are inherently patriarchal and therefore irrelevant and outdated within modern Buddhism. For example, in terms of the role of women in the sangha, we can see from the Vinaya that during the lifetime of the Buddha, nuns as well as monks were fully ordained. This included the Buddha's own stepmother, Mahaprajapati. However, the rules required a quorum of ordained members of the sangha to be present in order for an ordination to take place. At one point in the history of Buddhism, this quorum was not achieved and there was an insufficient number of nuns present. Thus, the lineage of nuns in the Theravada tradition was broken. It has been a long road to re-establishing the order of Buddhist nuns and still today there are stigmas attached to nuns due to certain traditional prejudices. However, some would argue that such prejudices do not in any way reflect Buddhist teaching but simply the inadequacies of some social settings and the inability of them to be truly free from the fetters of world attachments that prejudiced views bring. However, this does not explain how there is still inequality of position for women in the Theravadin sangha in terms that it is dominated by a patriarchal hierarchy and structure.

Another line of thinking would be to suggest that the perceived inequality is an outcome of the practical application of the rules of the Vinaya, rather than a reflection of the status of women within the sangha. For example, Rita Gross looks at the Pali Canon from a feminist perspective and suggests that 'the texts are ... ambiguous and contradictory regarding women than those from any other period' but that to suggest that they are misogynistic is a misinterpretation. She argues that it would be hard to argue that misogyny existed in early Buddhism and that there were cultural stereotypes about women at the time.

Therefore, the Vinaya rules are significant within Buddhism but it has been their misapplication and misinterpretation that may have caused the rise of this inequality. For example, the voices of women are lacking in the texts as they are recorded by men. Additionally, some of the misogyny within the Pali Canon might be the 'outburst of an individual frustrated monk', according to Gross. In this sense, it could be argued that it is even more significant today because it is required for all to achieve enlightenment, both male and female and equally important to iron out any misapplications.

Specification content
The significance of the Vinaya for the sangha.

Key quote

Were it not for the Vinaya and for those who continue to keep it alive to this day there would be no Buddhism. (**accesstoinsight website**)

Old Tipitaka texts in Thailand

Key terms
Arahatship: becoming an arahant (arhat (Skt)), 'noble or worthy one' who has achieved enlightenment

Prajna: wisdom

AO2 Activity

As you read through this section try to do the following:

1. Pick out the different lines of argument that are presented in the text and identify any evidence given in support.

2. For each line of argument try to evaluate whether or not you think this is strong (convincing) or weak (unconvincing).

3. Think of any questions you may wish to raise in response to the arguments.

This activity will help you to start thinking critically about what you read and help you to evaluate the effectiveness of different arguments and from this develop your own observations, opinions and points of view that will help with any conclusions.

Evidently, one of the reasons Buddhism has survived into the 21st century is due to the unbroken lineage of the ordained monastic sangha. The monastic sangha, in observing the Patimokka rules, has protected the dharma since the time of the historical Buddha. It is surely not an overestimation to suggest that Theravada Buddhism might not be such a thriving, living way of dharma practice today if it were not for the application of the Vinaya rules.

Another criticism made of the Vinaya within contemporary society often concerns the additional rules bhikkhunis are required to follow, which are mostly aimed at avoidance of sexual tension within the sangha. There has been some debate as to whether this is evidence of inequality within the sangha. However, given the position of women at the time of the historical Buddha, it was very radical for him to have allowed women to be ordained at all. It is often argued that the rules were originally put in place to protect nuns within the sangha rather than to oppress them. Nevertheless, in today's society it is argued that it is reasonable to expect gender equality and within the Theravadin monastic community there are moves to address this. For instance, within the Burmese sangha, monks now undertake to observe all 311 rules.

Denise Cush suggests that often the rules contained within the Vinaya Pitaka 'are genuinely concerned with promoting the reduction of craving and the path to nirvana' but that some are just practical and 'others seem to uphold the good image of the sangha in the eyes of the public'.

Whatever the case, in conclusion it could perhaps be argued that, as a place of refuge from suffering, the sangha needs to be disciplined in order to be conducive to the cessation of dukkha and that the collected wisdom that the Vinaya brings is a practical way of achieving this and will always be significant.

Burmese nuns meditating at Shwedagon Pagoda in Yangon, Burma/Myanmar.

Study tip

Every essay title is a problem to be solved. This means understanding – or decoding – the question. Essay titles include one or more words that give you exact instructions as to what the examiner is looking for. These key words are called 'trigger words' and indicate what skills you need to demonstrate in order to answer the question successfully. It is essential to know what the trigger words mean and what they require you to do. Essays in Religious Studies A Level usually test your knowledge and understanding (AO1) or your ability to evaluate, make judgements and assess the value of different ideas or concepts (AO2).

AO2 Activity

List some conclusions that could be drawn from the AO2 reasoning from the above text; try to aim for at least three different possible conclusions. Consider each of the conclusions and collect brief evidence to support each conclusion from the AO1 and AO2 material for this topic. Select the conclusion that you think is most convincing and explain why it is so. Try to contrast this with the weakest conclusion in the list, justifying your argument with clear reasoning and evidence.

AO2 Developing skills

It is now important to consider the information that has been covered in this section; however, the information in its raw form is too extensive and so has to be processed in order to meet the requirements of the examination. This can be done by practising more advanced skills associated with AO2. The exercises that run throughout this book will help you to do this and prepare you for the examination. For assessment objective 2 (AO2), which involves 'critical analysis' and 'evaluation' skills, we are going to focus on different ways in which the skills can be demonstrated effectively, and also, refer to how the performance of these skills is measured (see generic band descriptors for A2 [WJEC] AO2 or A Level [Eduqas] AO2).

▶ **Your task is this:** Below is a summary of two different points of view concerning **whether the Abhidhamma is useful or not**. It is 150 words long. You want to use these two views and lines of argument for an evaluation; however, to just list them is not really evaluating them. Present these two views in a more evaluative style by firstly condensing each argument and then, secondly, commenting on how effective each one is (weak or strong are good terms to start with). Allow about 200 words in total.

The Abhidhamma is very useful; it is for those who want to understand the Dhamma in greater depth and detail. It aids the development of insight into the three characteristics of existence: impermanence, unsatisfactoriness and non-self. It is useful not only for the periods devoted to formal meditation, but also during the rest of the day when Buddhists are engaged in various mundane chores. Monastics derive great benefit from the study of the Abhidhamma to help experience absolute reality.

The Abhidhamma would be of no real use to a novice monk or a lay person as it is far too advanced and complex. In this sense, within the whole scope of Buddhism, the Abhidhamma is in fact pretty useless and very rarely accessed or referred to. It is also of no real practical use for anyone other than those who are far advanced along the Buddhist path such as monks and nuns.

When you have completed the task, refer to the band descriptors for A2 (WJEC) or A Level (Eduqas) and, in particular, have a look at the demands described in the higher band descriptors towards which you should be aspiring. Ask yourself:

- Is my answer a confident critical analysis and perceptive evaluation of the issue?
- Is my answer a response that successfully identifies and thoroughly addresses the issues raised by the question set?
- Does my work show an excellent standard of coherence, clarity and organisation? **(WJEC band descriptor only but still important to consider for Eduqas)**
- Will my work, when developed, contain thorough, sustained and clear views that are supported by extensive, detailed reasoning and/or evidence?
- Are the views of scholars/schools of thought used extensively, appropriately and in context?
- Does my answer convey a confident and perceptive analysis of the nature of any possible connections with other elements of my course?
- When used, is specialist language and vocabulary both thorough and accurate?

Key skills Theme 1

The first theme has tasks that deal with the basics of AO2 in terms of developing an evaluative style, building arguments and raising critical questions.

Key skills

Analysis involves:

Identifying issues raised by the materials in the AO1, together with those identified in the AO2 section, and presents sustained and clear views, either of scholars or from a personal perspective ready for evaluation.

This means:

- That your answers are able to identify key areas of debate in relation to a particular issue
- That you can identify, and comment upon, the different lines of argument presented by others
- That your response comments on the overall effectiveness of each of these areas or arguments.

Evaluation involves:

Considering the various implications of the issues raised based upon the evidence gleaned from analysis and provides an extensive detailed argument with a clear conclusion.

This means:

- That your answer weighs up the consequences of accepting or rejecting the various and different lines of argument analysed
- That your answer arrives at a conclusion through a clear process of reasoning.

As you work through each section of the book, the focus will be on a variety of different aspects associated with AO2 so that you can comprehensively perfect the overall skills associated with AO2.

Specification content

The Heart Sutra: the philosophical content regarding the mutual identity of emptiness and form.

Key terms

Hrdaya Sutra: 'Heart Sutra' also known as the 'Heart of Perfect Wisdom Sutra' or the 'Essence of Wisdom Sutra'

Madhyamaka: Middle School, of Buddhism founded upon the teaching of Nagarjuna. This school is at the root of Mahayana Buddhism

Nagarjuna: the most well known of early Buddhist philosophers (c150–250 CE)

Prajnaparamita: meaning 'the wisdom that has gone further or beyond' or 'perfection/excellence of wisdom' and is a collection of early Buddhist scriptures from the Mahayana tradition

Sambhogakaya: the celestial or heavenly body of buddhas often existing in realms such as the Pure Land

E: The main themes and concepts in two Mahayana texts

The Prajnaparamita literature

The **Hrdaya Sutra** or 'Heart Sutra' is part of a group of ancient Mahayana Buddhist texts known as the **Prajnaparamita**. The Prajnaparamita is a library of over 40 texts containing some of the oldest Mahayana Sutras. The most popular etymology for the Sanskrit term translates prajna as 'wisdom' whereas para means 'beyond' or 'further shore' and mita is a term for 'going' or 'arriving', together meaning 'that which goes beyond' or 'reached the further shore'. Some, then, refer to the Prajnaparamita as 'the wisdom that has gone beyond'.

Donald S. Lopez, professor of Tibetan Buddhist studies, sees an alternative explanation of the word as deriving from the term parama meaning 'highest' or 'most excellent' and its substantive (noun) form paramita as meaning 'excellence' or 'perfection'. In this way, combined with prajna, the term Prajnaparamita is also usually taken to mean the 'perfection of wisdom' or 'excellence of wisdom'. Some prefer this translation, since the Sanskrit term paramita ('most excellent') is then distinguished from the end mantra, 'gate... paragate ... bodhi', meaning more literally 'enlightenment that is beyond'.

Much of the Prajnaparamita chronology and dating owes much to the work of the renowned German Buddhist scholar Edward Conze. These Sutras are thought to have been composed in the early centuries CE, although they actually developed over many centuries. The Sutras have a very complicated and much debated origin and, according to Edward Conze, have a chronology between 100 BCE and 600 CE. The Hrdaya Sutra is dated towards the end of this period.

On the one hand, they are regarded as Buddha vacana throughout Mahayana schools and so are 'divine' utterances of the still existing Buddha in his heavenly body (**sambhogakaya**). On the other hand, the earliest of the Prajnaparamita texts are often tentatively associated with the Mahasamghika school of early Indian Buddhism, a school created at the second Buddhist council and often seen as the first real evidence for the emergence of the Mahayana. Hence the notion of Mahayana Buddhism emerging from Theravada traditions is established.

The Sutras are also reflected in, and supported by, the philosophical writings of **Nagarjuna** who founded the **Madhyamaka** school of Buddhism. In particular, the mutual identity of emptiness and form that is the key focus of the Heart Sutra is also the key focus for Nagarjuna and Madhyamaka. The link is also quite complex in that the Heart Sutra is often interpreted from a Madhyamaka perspective and many of the commentaries on the Heart Sutra either use Nagarjuna or are based upon Madhyamaka ideas. For example, the Tibetan Gelug school uses the longer Heart Sutra and is dependent upon the commentary by Tsongkhapa who takes a Madhyamaka view; in Chinese Buddhism (East Asian Yogacara), Kuiji's commentary on the Heart Sutra is also from a Madhyamaka perspective.

The Heart Sutra – Prajnaparamita Hrdaya

Nagarguna and the Madhyamaka school

Many Buddhists view Nagarjuna as the most famous philosopher in Buddhism, second only to the Buddha. He has been called 'the Einstein of India', such was his influence. However, there is a lot of mystery surrounding him, as very little is known of his life and there is much debate about what he actually wrote. Nagarjuna is immensely significant for the Prajnaparamita and the Hrdaya Sutra as his commentaries on the Prajnaparamita or his specific understanding of the Sutras are the foundation for Tibetan, Chinese, Pure Land and Zen Buddhism.

It is, in general, accepted that Nagarjuna wrote several philosophical works that focused on emptiness, two levels of truth and dependent origination. The texts over which issues of authentic authorship are debated are usually the ones that contain reference to later developments in Mahayana philosophy, such as tathagatagarbha (Buddha-nature) and the bodhisattva path. For instance, the Catuhstava (Hymns) which comes very close to the later teaching of tathagatagarbha without actually using the term, appears to be the threshold beyond which the issues emerge as to authentic authorship of some of the hymns.

There are then many other works ascribed to Nagarjuna that link directly to the teachings of Mahayana Buddhism as they developed, such as emptiness, the bodhisattva path, two truths or conventional and ultimate wisdom, skilful means and the tathagata. Such works are, in general, accepted as authentic by most schools of Mahayana Buddhism. In these works Nagarjuna makes direct reference to the perfect wisdom literature and serve as commentaries to unpacking the philosophical complexities within the pages written.

Despite this, the only text by Nagarjuna that all scholars agree has authentic authorship is his **Mulamadhyamikakarikas** ('verses on the fundamentals of the Middle Way'). This is by far his most famous work and examines the teachings on **sunyata** in 27 chapters.

Why is Nagarjuna's teaching significant for our understanding of the Heart Sutra?

Nagarjuna taught that the ultimate teaching of Buddhism could be found in the emptiness teaching (sunyatavada). He was also very keen to display compatibility with the teachings of traditional Buddhism such as the Four Noble Truths, the three Lakshanas and dependent origination. This is all significant because the crucial statement in the Heart Sutra is about emptiness and what it 'is' and Nagarjuna's Mulamadhyamikakarikas in its entirety explores exactly this topic – what precisely emptiness 'is' and, 'is not'. The depth of Nagarjuna's analysis also hits at the 'heart' of the debate about the implications of the emptiness teaching that make it specifically Mahayana in nature and not just a development of Theravada Buddhism.

Some have seen Nagarjuna's Mulamadhyamikakarikas as a direct debate between Mahayana Buddhism and the Sarvastivada school of Theravada Buddhism who saw the 'dhammas' of the Abhidhamma as more static entities than that of broader Theravada. Indeed, there has been one theory raised that he was an innovative and progressive Theravada monk himself. Others see his work as firmly grounded in the Mahayana school with an aim to clarify the specific teaching of sunyata to Theravada. The latter theory tends to carry more force amongst scholars in recent times. Yet again, there are scholars who see Nagarjuna as neither Theravada nor Mahayana but situated in a transitional period in the development of Mahayana Buddhism from Theravada Buddhism.

For example, according to Stephen Bachelor, despite Nagarjuna's works often being seen as an exposition and commentary on the Prajnaparamita Sutras, it is significant that Nagarjuna does not at any time refer to them or to the

Key terms

Mulamadhyamikakarikas: 'verses on the fundamentals of the Middle Way' composed by the Indian philosopher monk Nagarjuna

Sunyata (Sanskrit); sunna or sunya (Pali): the concept that form (physical and mental notions of 'existence') is empty of inherent existence and therefore nothing exists independently, but that conversely emptiness necessitates form

Key quotes

Without a foundation in the conventional truth, the significance of the ultimate cannot be taught. Without understanding the significance of the ultimate, Liberation is not achieved. By a misperception of emptiness a person of little intelligence is destroyed ... For that reason – that the Dharma is deep and difficult to understand and to learn – the Buddha's mind despaired of being able to teach it.
(Nagarjuna)

The victorious ones have said that emptiness is the relinquishing of all views. For whomever emptiness is a view, that one has achieved nothing.
(Nagarjuna)

The Prajna Paramita, or Wonderful Wisdom, courses like a boat transporting all sentient beings across the sea of defilement to the other shore that is Nirvana.
(Grand Master T'an Hsu)

One thing we can safely say about the *Heart Sutra* is that it is completely crazy. If we read it, it does not make any sense. Well, maybe the beginning and end make sense, but everything in the middle sounds like a sophisticated form of nonsense, which can be said to be the basic feature of the *Prajnaparamita Sutras* in general. If we like the word 'no', we might like the Sutra because that is the main word it uses – no this, no that, no everything. We could also say that it is a Sutra about wisdom, but it is a Sutra about crazy wisdom.
(Karl Brunnholzl)

bodhisattva ideal and tends to see the way to enlightenment as that of arhatship. This reinforces the ideas that the Mahayana arose from Theravada through traditions such as those of the Mahasamghikas and the Lokottaravadins, and that Nagarjuna's understanding of emptiness may not have been a direct result of the Prajnaparamita but some early oral teachings from within early Indian Buddhism that were loosely connected to the later development of the Prajnaparamita literature.

The response to this from scholarship has in general been to point out that understanding the way of the liberated sage (arhat) as the path to Buddhism was meeting Theravada monks at their own level of understanding.

Whatever the case may be, scholarship has long tried to explain the lack of direct reference to the Prajnaparamita literature in Nagarjuna's works despite his writings displaying remarkable similarity to them, in particular, the Heart Sutra.

Nonetheless, it appears to be accepted that the mutual identity of emptiness and form combined with Nagarjuna's Madhyamaka exposition of this, has become the key to unlocking the significance of the Heart Sutra for the majority of Mahayana Buddhist traditions.

The Heart Sutra – Prajnaparamita Hrdaya

The Prajnaparamitahrdaya Sutra (Perfection of Wisdom Heart Sutra) is the shortest of all the Prajnaparamita Sutras and there are both shorter and longer versions of the text in existence. The Sutra has been translated into English from languages such as Sanskrit, Chinese and Tibetan. It is particularly respected by both Tibetan and Zen Buddhists. The longer Sutra is extensively studied by the various Tibetan Buddhist schools and often understood from a tantric perspective. The Heart Sutra definitely post-dates Nagarjuna, but the earliest commentary in Chinese – that by Kuiji – does give the Heart Sutra a typically Madhayamaka interpretation. Some argue that the shorter Heart Sutra was in fact a Chinese composition.

The word hrdaya, translated as 'heart', is significant in several ways. Firstly, it is obvious in that it contains the essence of the Prajnaparamita teaching, the teaching on sunyata. However, another significance drawn from it is that Prajnaparamita is not something that can be intellectually grasped but it is something that is realised in an experiential way through the 'heart'. Hence its repetitive and meditational presentation. However, it is also not a coincidence that the Heart Sutra is seen to be the quintessential statement of Mahayana Buddhism, not just because it illustrates the deep insight into emptiness, but also – as we will later see – because it provides a gateway into understanding all other specifically Mahayana teachings that differentiate Mahayana from Theravada Buddhism.

It has long been argued that the heart or core of these shorter Sutras summarises the teachings of the longer Prajnaparamita Sutras. The Heart Sutra is one of the most used texts within the Mahayana tradition, and this is not only because it is short to recite. The Heart Sutra is a deeply philosophical text bringing insight into the way things are. The Heart Sutra is full of paradoxes, which may seem nonsensical. It is, therefore, impossible to fully understand the text through the use of the intellect alone. Indeed, Brunnholzl suggests: 'When we read it, it sounds nuts, but that is actually where the wisdom part comes in'. Cush supports this view by suggesting that the Heart Sutra is the 'wisdom of the Buddhas'.

The Heart Sutra commences with Avalokitesvara (Avalokita), the bodhisattva of great compassion, contemplating Perfect Wisdom. The Sutra goes on to describe the Awakening of the bodhisattva. Avalokitesvara develops prajna through engaging in vipassana meditation. The Sutra is based upon a dialogue between Sariputra and Avalokitesvara.

The shorter Hrdaya Sutra

Homage to the Perfection of Wisdom, the Lovely, the Holy!

Avalokita, *The Holy Lord and Bodhisattva, was moving in the deep course of **the Wisdom which has gone beyond**. He looked down from on high, He beheld but five heaps, and he saw that in their **own-being** they were empty.*

*Here, Sariputra, **form is emptiness and the very emptiness is form**; emptiness does not differ from form, form does not differ from emptiness; whatever is form, that is emptiness, whatever is emptiness, that is form, the same is true of feelings, perceptions, impulses and consciousness.*

*Here, Sariputra, **all dharmas are marked with emptiness**; they are not produced or stopped, not defiled or immaculate, not deficient or complete.*

*Therefore, Sariputra, in emptiness there is no form, nor feeling, nor perception, nor impulse, nor consciousness; No eye, ear, nose, tongue, body, mind; No forms, sounds, smells, tastes, touchables or objects of mind; No sight-organ element, and so forth, until we come to: No mind-consciousness element; **There is no ignorance, no extinction of ignorance, and so forth, until we come to: there is no decay and death, no extinction of decay and death. There is no suffering, no origination, no stopping, no path. There is no cognition, no attainment and non-attainment**.*

*Therefore, Sariputra, **it is because of his non-attainmentness** that a Bodhisattva, through having relied on the Perfection of Wisdom, dwells without thought-coverings. In the absence of thought-coverings he has not been made to tremble, he has overcome what can upset, and in the end he attains to Nirvana.*

All those who appear as Buddhas in the three periods of time fully awake to the utmost, right and perfect Enlightenment because they have relied on the Perfection of Wisdom.

Therefore one should know the Prajnaparamita as the great spell, the spell of great knowledge, the utmost spell, the unequalled spell, allayer of all suffering, in truth – for what could go wrong? By the Prajnaparamita has this spell been delivered. It runs like this:

Gone, gone, gone beyond, gone altogether beyond, O what an Awakening, all-hail!

(translated by Edward Conze)

Key quotes

There is no ignorance, no extinction of ignorance, and so forth, until we come to: there is no decay and death, no extinction of decay and death. There is no suffering, no origination, no stopping, no path. There is no cognition, no attainment and non-attainment. (Heart Sutra)

Therefore, Sariputra, it is because of his non-attainmentness that a Bodhisattva, through having relied on the Perfection of Wisdom, dwells without thought-coverings. (Heart Sutra)

Here, Sariputra, form is emptiness and the very emptiness is form; emptiness does not differ from form, form does not differ from emptiness; whatever is form, that is emptiness, whatever is emptiness, that is form. (Heart Sutra)

quickfire

1.11 What do the terms Prajnaparamita and Hrdaya mean?

quickfire

1.12 Name two schools of Buddhism that use the Prajnaparamita Hrdaya.

Sariputra, one of the historical Buddha's closest disciples

Key terms

Avalokitesvara: 'He who hears the cries of the world.' The bodhisattva of compassion

Sariputra: in Theravada one of the chief disciples of the Buddha but in some texts – such as the Lotus Sutra – presented as one who is slow to grasp the Mahayana Dharma

Key quotes

All beings are thus at once form and emptiness; indeed they are 'forms of emptiness' in that it is their lack of independence and substantiality that allows them to be the interrelated processes that they are. (Davis)

Each [of the skandhas] can only inter-be with all the others. So he tells us that form is empty. Form is empty of a separate self, but it is full of everything in the cosmos. The same is true with feelings, perceptions, mental formations, and consciousness. (Thich Nhat Hanh)

Key terms

Pratityasamutpada: dependent origination

Svabhava: own-being

Study tip

The following two pages are very difficult and reflect the nature of Mahayana philosophy. The headings (1) and (2) and the main text on pages 26–8 include scholarly arguments that help to clarify the different interpretations of 'emptiness' by Theravada and Mahayana Buddhisms in general. This information may be useful to teachers and pupils who want to delve deeper. Alternatively, there are two margin summaries underneath pictures on pages 27–28 that attempt to simplify the issue without having to read through the details of the text.

As a starting point, the teachings of the Buddha, on impermanence (anicca) and no permanent self (anatta), are developed further within the Heart Sutra; as is the specific teaching of dependent origination (pratityasamutpada). The Heart Sutra explains the concept of sunyata, that **all** is empty of inherent existence (svabhava, literally 'own being'). This can be seen from the claims of Avalokitesvara in the Heart Sutra, and the starting point is reference to the five skandhas ('heaps'), that is, the traditional notion of the basic interacting constituents of an individual. The Heart Sutra begins: 'He beheld but five heaps, and he saw that **in their own-being** they were empty.'

Avalokitesvara sees that 'in emptiness there is no form, nor feeling, nor perception, nor impulse, nor consciousness'. This means that there is nothing that can claim independent existence, but only acknowledge 'existence' in relation to other things. Thus, as the skandhas are empty of own being and they do not exist independently, such is the nature of **all** existence and then a critical statement is made: 'Here, Sariputra, **all dharmas are marked with emptiness**; they are not produced or stopped, not defiled or immaculate, not deficient or complete.' No 'thing' has svabhava or own being. The notion of svabhava is thus taken beyond the 'heaps' and applied to all dharmas that constitute any kind of existence.

The 'deep insight' is indeed identified in the Heart Sutra – *'the deep course of the Wisdom which has gone beyond'* – but the insight may not be quite as it is often understood.

Many often present this insight as the realisation that things, existence, phenomena are empty of svabhava (own being) and interconnected (pratityasamutpada). Whilst it cannot be denied that this is 'deep insight' indeed, the problem with such a view is that only half the teaching is expounded, and we are only left with one half of the true paradox. Note that the Heart Sutra, as well as identifying the emptiness of things often held to be substantive, also identifies as empty the very means of realising emptiness: 'There is no ignorance, **no extinction of ignorance** … there is no decay and death, **no extinction of decay and death**. There is no suffering, **no origination, no stopping, no path** …'

Here, then, emptiness refers to both ignorance and to the means by which ignorance is destroyed by truth. This, then, is the paradox:

Our deep insight helps us to see that our conventional notions of existence that are supported by ignorance are in fact 'empty'; however, equally empty is the path by which this deep insight is attained!

The paradox appears to be we know that insight into emptiness is 'enlightening' and a 'positive' and 'spiritually uplifting' realisation. But how can it be 'positive' and 'spiritually' uplifting if it is empty? Well, the answer, according to Nagarjuna, is that **it is only because the path to nirvana (and nirvana itself) is empty that it can be a reality**: 'if all things were not empty, there would be no origination and no destruction'.

This is crucial for understanding the true difference between Theravada understandings of emptiness and the Mahayana understandings of emptiness as presented in the Heart Sutra and the writings of Nagarjuna. Therefore, as to the precise nature of this 'deeper insight' we need to clarify two things:

(1) The 'deeper insight' of Mahayana Buddhism is not just the notion of emptiness (i.e. a lack of inherent existence) because this simply reaffirms the basic Buddhist teaching of anatta.

Rupert Gethin argues that the concept of dhammas in the Abhidhamma Pitaka sets out a map for the way things are and that in the teachings of the Heart Sutra this is not to be accepted as ultimate reality. Consequently, in the Heart Sutra, all dharmas are explicitly seen as empty and lacking inherent existence. In one sense it is true that the teachings of the Prajnaparamita Hrdaya differ from the teachings of the Pali Abhidhamma texts. A popular interpretation of the Abhidhamma is that the building blocks, or **dhammas** (dharmas) from which everything is formed, tend to be viewed more as static entities in the Pali teachings. This is only one understanding and this view should also be treated with caution in relation to Theravada Buddhism.

For instance, sunnata (emptiness in Pali) is a Theravada term and is used in the Pali Canon (Samyutta Nikaya XXXV, 85). Theravada scholars such as Peter Harvey in his book *The Selfless Mind*, argue that the notion of anatta and emptiness still allows a view of the self as an 'empirical self' as opposed to a 'metaphysical self' in order to differentiate it from nihilism (the view that both not-self and emptiness mean that there is 'nothingness'). Harvey is clearly aware that from an enlightened perspective this means that the empirical self is correct interpretation of anatta and sunnata. He writes: 'It is 'emptiness' or 'void' in being free of all misinterpretation (abhinivesa) as 'Self' or 'permanent' ... The apprehension of nibbana as being a signless emptiness as 'seeing through' empty phenomena is reminiscent of Mahayana Madhyamaka school's view. Indeed, the term sunnata is defined in the Pali Dictionary and expounded in the Visuddhi Magga, the most important authoritative text in Theravada Buddhism beyond the Pali Canon.

Study tip

When learning key terms, it is useful to ask the following questions:

- Where does this word fit into my course?
- What could they ask me about this in an exam?
- What are the links to other key terms in the glossary?

In this way, the teachings of the Abhidhamma on dhammas can be interpreted as an empirical philosophical exercise with an implicit understanding of the inter-connectedness of all phenomena. Ronkin (Oxford Centre for Buddhist Studies) supports this, 'Dhammas are here psychophysical occurrences, or rather acts of conceptualisation by which the mind unites and assimilates sense data and ideas to a cognitive whole that makes sense'. He continues, 'the Abhidhammikas dhammas are *flashes of experience* that make up *world-creating processes*; the irreducible elements of encountered phenomena and the final items revealed when the analysis of conscious experience is pursued to its ultimate limit.' It is similar to a computer snapshot that attempts to capture a conventional understanding of a fleeting moment of reality in order to make sense of reality, rather than analysis of a fixed moment in time. To see the 'flash of experience' as a fixed entity is futile since reality has already moved on since the inter-action of dhammas is so fluid.

In this sense the idea of understanding the Abhidhamma Pitaka of the Pali Canon as proposing dhammas as a 'fixed state' is itself a dubious and questionable interpretation and understanding of the Abhidhamma. Indeed, Peter Harvey states in his book *An Introduction to Buddhism*:

'They are dhammas because they uphold their own nature [sabhaava]. They are dhammas because they are upheld by conditions or they are upheld "according to their own nature" (Asl.39). Here "own-nature" would mean characteristic nature, which is not something inherent in a dhamma as a separate ultimate reality but arise due to the supporting conditions both of other dhammas and previous occurrences of that dhamma. This is of significance as it makes the Mahayana critique of the Sarvastivadin's notion of own-nature largely irrelevant to the Theravada.'

What is clear is that the teaching of sunyata, that things are empty of inherent existence, lies at the heart of Theravada Buddhism, the philosophy of Nagarjuna's

ZOOM IN! *Both Theravada and Mahayana Buddhism see 'form' as 'emptiness' when they analyse the very basis of existence at the microscopic level.*

Mahdhyamaka School, and also the Heart Sutra and the rest of the Prajnaparamita literature. To be fair, Rupert Gethin also argues that the Prajnaparamita Sutras, including the Heart Sutra, present their wisdom 'not as an innovation but as a restatement of the original teaching of the Buddha'. Indeed, 'Sunyata is anicca carried to its logical conclusion', declares Christmas Humphreys who argues that 'the suchness of things is that quality by which they are one with the principle of Enlightenment'. Therefore, the most definite link to sunyata can be found in the unique teaching of anatta (no self or not self) whereby the notion of inherent substance is rejected.

Perhaps the best way to view the Hrdaya Sutra is on its own merits and not in juxtaposition to Theravada Abhidhamma. The 14th Dalai Lama explains that, 'The *existence* of things and events is not in dispute; it is the *manner in which* they exist that must be clarified.' Our mind, and the language we use to describe things, actually tricks us into thinking that things actually exist. However, because everything that exists relies on causes and conditions for it to exist, and everything is interconnected according to the teachings of the Heart Sutra, they are empty of selfhood. Cush reminds us that: 'Emptiness does not mean "nothingness", nor is it a substance out of which all things are made, it is just that nothing whatsoever has ultimate or necessary being – including *nirvana*, Buddhas, perfect wisdom and emptiness.'

So if the Heart Sutra's insights into 'emptiness' and lack of 'own being' are not the full picture of the 'deeper insight' of Mahayana Buddhism then what is?

(2) *What is the 'deeper insight' in the Heart Sutra that is specific to Mahayana Buddhism?*

What the Prajnaparamita did was to develop the notion of anatta to its logical conclusion; however, this does not just stop with the insight that everything is empty. It is interesting that often people refer to the ultimate teaching of Buddhism and the Heart Sutra as 'form is emptiness' or 'everything is empty'. Although this is true, it is only half the picture.

There is a reason that the Heart Sutra states it in the following way:

'form is emptiness **and the very emptiness is form**; **emptiness does not differ from form**, form does not differ from emptiness; whatever is form, that is emptiness, **whatever is emptiness, that is form**.'

This phrase is often just understood in terms of its first section: 'form is emptiness' as in point (1) above. Here everyone marvels in the insight that there is no ultimate inherent existence since everything is empty of essence and an explanation of what this means is explored. Such an understanding would argue that the deeper insight is the depth of this realisation in Mahayana from anatta to sunyata. However, there is nothing new or innovative in this. Both Mahayana and Theravada agree on this as we have seen above. Indeed, we are not to be distracted and indulge ourselves by basking in this insight in itself. Unfortunately, many who study the Heart Sutra tend to leave with just this very impression which is one of the reasons why Thich Nhat Hanh has recently provided a new translation of the Heart Sutra.

The Heart Sutra, the writings of Nagarjuna and the Prajnaparamita Sutras are truly, distinctively Mahayana because they are new and innovative. This innovation can be discovered through a focus on the ***implications*** of the emptiness teaching and what emerged from this was then a revelation of further specifically Mahayana Buddhist teachings. The arhat path was transformed into the bodhisattva path and through a heightened emphasis on skilful means, Buddhism was logically exposed to the masses. Wisdom and compassion were now seen as different sides of the same coin.

ZOOM OUT! *The Mahayana scriptures really go to town on the 'emptiness is form' and see the universe(s) of 'form' or existence through the perceptions that 'emptiness' brings. This means ultimately that there are no distinctions and also no restrictions as to what can 'be'. Therefore there is no distinction between samsara and nirvana, we all have Buddha-nature within us and there are a multitude of universes and Buddhas! It appears that Theravada Buddhism does not go this far.*

To sum up:

> **As we have seen, the key to the Heart Sutra seems to be the phrase, *'form is emptiness and the very emptiness is form'*. This is crucial in understanding the historical debate that Mahayana is the 'greater vehicle'.**

This clearly refers to logical implications of the mutual identity of emptiness and form ('form is emptiness') in that 'the very emptiness is form'. What is vital, crucial and central to the Heart Sutra – and this cannot be emphasised enough – is not just an acknowledgement of the fact 'form is emptiness' means, but also what it *implies*, that is, '**the very emptiness is form**'. The continuation of the Heart Sutra is not simply a case of repetition. The words are there to contemplate deeply, to meditate upon.

Through deep contemplation it is the recognition that emptiness is actually an **affirmation**, and not a negation or eradication, of the true nature of our existence; indeed, this unleashes very proactive effects. The truth of the matter is that '***the very emptiness is form***' liberates a Buddhist to realisation that emptiness does not mean 'nothingness' but quite the opposite – a wonderful fulness of form. It is an affirmation of emptiness as a reality, our reality. However, this 'affirmation of reality' is itself empty and not a view; as Nagarjuna writes, 'The Buddha's doctrine is that all is reality, unreality, both reality and unreality, and neither reality nor unreality.'

The major innovative implication of this is that if indeed there are no distinctions between dhammas, causes, effects because everything is empty of essence, then it must follow that also ***there can be no limitations*** as all boundaries and constraints have been removed. The 'ultimate' reality (or, truth) is that emptiness and form become two sides of the same coin, just like nirvana and samsara, or like perfect wisdom and compassion.

The implications of the Heart Sutra's philosophical content regarding the mutual identity of emptiness and form

An additional teaching found within Madhyamaka and the Heart Sutra is that of two truths. This is the idea that we can understand existence and non-existence in two ways: **ultimate** and **conventional**. We mostly see the world through conventional truth in that we see things as separate and diverse. So we see many tables, chairs, trees, mountains, rivers, animals and people as having substance or as existing. To see the world in this way is a conventional way of understanding, just as in Harvey's 'empirical self', or Milinda's 'mere convention' in associating a name with a 'person', or indeed the 'dhammas' in the Abhidhamma Pitaka of the Theravada tradition.

The ultimate truth is (1) that there is no separate existence (2) that there are no boundaries or restrictions evident.

O'Brien points out that it is important to see that there are two truths and 'not one truth and a lie' as conventional truth is not false. However, it is also important to understand that neither is there a hierarchy as ultimate truth reveals the conventional, making a realisation of conventional truth in no way inferior. As Nagarjuna states:

According to Koller, the reason that the Prajnaparamita Sutras try to clarify reality through philosophical paradoxes 'where teachings are non-teachings, Buddhas are non-Buddhas and nirvana is identified with samsara' is 'to coax or shock the hearer into going beyond the dualities of conventional truth' and acknowledge point (2) above. In this way both ultimate truth and conventional truth can be understood or realised.

Key quotes

Therefore, Sariputra, it is because of his non-attainmentness that a Bodhisattva, through having relied on the Perfection of Wisdom, dwells without thought-coverings. In the absence of thought-coverings he has not been made to tremble, he has overcome what can upset, and in the end he attains to Nirvana. (Heart Sutra)

Since all is empty, all is possible. (Nagarjuna)

'All is empty' should not be asserted, nor should 'all is not empty', 'all is both empty and non-empty', nor 'all is neither empty nor non-empty.' Each is maintained only in the context of conventional reality. (Nagarjuna)

Without a foundation in the conventional truth, the significance of the ultimate cannot be taught. Without understanding the significance of the ultimate, nirvana is not achieved. (Nagarjuna)

Key terms

Conventional truth: truth that operates within the empirical world and makes sense of the emptiness teaching; a way of explaining the world around us using skilful means; sometimes referred to as 'partial' or 'provisional' or 'relative' truth

Ultimate truth: an enlightened view of existence as sunyata (empty)

Our minds trick us into thinking that we have inherent existence.

quickfire

1.13 Who is Avalokitesvara?

quickfire

1.14 What does emptiness not mean?

Key quotes

To see any dharma as existing in itself is to grasp at it, to try to hold on to it, but dharmas are like dreams, magical illusions, echoes, reflected images, mirages, space; like the moon reflected in water, a fairy castle, a shadow, or a magical creation; like the stars, dewdrops, a bubble, a flash of lightning, or a cloud – they are there, but they are not there, and if we reach out for them, we find nothing to hold on to. (Gethin)

Emptiness which is conceptually liable to be mistaken for sheer nothingness is in fact the reservoir of infinite possibilities. (Suzuki)

Most grasp form and mistake it for True Existence, enduring immeasurable suffering on the Wheel of Life-and-Death. (Dharma Master Lok To)

Here we begin the true and innovative 'Mahayana' journey of discovery in that **the concept of emptiness opens up all manner of ultimate possibilities**: everyone can be enlightened; everyone has Buddha-nature (tahagatagarbha), merit can be transferred through compassion; the bodhisattva path becomes the new ideal; there are a multitude of universes (Buddha ksetras or 'fields of a Buddha'). Indeed, this implication that 'the very emptiness is form' has led to some very complex philosophies such as the Hua Yen school of Buddhism and its interpenetration teachings. Indeed, it was Nagarjuna's view that emptiness necessitates an openness to change when he wrote, 'Thanks to emptiness, **everything is possible**.' Once again, if there are no distinctions then there are no limitations.

It can be argued, then, that whilst it is important to contemplate the Prajnaparamita Hrdaya in as much detail as possible, it is also meant to be taken into the heart so that understanding gradually develops intuitively through practice, rather than merely through study alone. The Sutra is recited daily in thousands of Mahayana monasteries and temples throughout the world. The practice of chanting the Heart Sutra, as a key mantra, is of particular importance within Zen Buddhism. This often takes place twice a day in Zen monasteries. It places great emphasis upon the direct understanding of scripture and aids direct realisation or experience of interconnectedness and the momentary Awakening to the nature of reality known as nibbana in Theravada, nirvana, thusness or sukhavati (Pure Land) and satori (Zen).

Key quotes

Nagarjuna's overriding theme … is the bodhisattva's path to Buddhahood and the merit and wisdom that the bodhisattva must accumulate in order to achieve Enlightenment. By wisdom, Nagarjuna meant the perfection of wisdom, declared in the Sutras to be the knowledge of emptiness. Nagarjuna is credited with transforming the Sutras' poetic and sometimes paradoxical declarations on emptiness into a philosophical system. (Lopez)

Suddenly I saw a kind of wisdom very much like the wisdom contained in the *Heart Sutra*. You have to *see* life. You shouldn't say, life *of* the leaf, but life *in* the leaf, and life *in* the tree. My life is just Life, and you can see it in me and in the tree. (Thich Nhat Hanh)

Lantau Island, Hong Kong: Wisdom Path of Heart Sutra engraved into trunks of wood.

In recent years, the Vietnamese Zen master Thich Nhat Hanh presented a new translation of the Heart Sutra. This is because he believed that the original translations led to many misunderstandings. Thich Nhat Hanh puts forward the idea of the fullness of emptiness and re-affirms what we have discussed above (see page 29). This sounds paradoxical but by this he means that to be empty of a separate self or an own-being is actually to be full of everything else. Therefore, he argues that you should not be afraid of emptiness, as there is nothing to fear. In understanding the Heart Sutra in this way Thich Nhat Hanh is indeed emphasising 'the very emptiness is form'!

We can see again that Thich Nhat Hanh's view of 'emptiness' is a positive understanding that 'the very emptiness is form' and opens up the restrictions that ignorance to emptiness brings to a realisation that limitations have been removed. He writes:

> 'Because form is emptiness, form is possible. In form we find everything else – feelings, perceptions, mental formations, and consciousness. "Emptiness" means empty of a separate self. It is full of everything, full of life. The word "emptiness" should not scare us. It is a wonderful word.'

One possible way to express the experience of the Heart Sutra is to say that one comes full circle and ends up where one had entered but with the full appreciation and understanding that not only are things empty, but they are unashamedly, conventionally – as Thich Nhat Hanh – 'inter-be'. It is here, at this point, that ultimate insight combines with unlimited compassion for all sentient beings and this is the very basis of the bodhisattva vows in Mahayana Buddhism.

Although the Heart Sutra ends with the words 'Gate Gate Paragate Parasamgate Bodhi Svaha!' (which is translated as, 'Oh Awakening that has gone, gone, gone to the further shore, gone completely to the further shore') this goal of attainment of supreme and perfect Enlightenment, that is 'beyond' is, in fact, very much right here and right now.

AO1 Activity

Explain why Thich Nhat Hanh suggests that people should not be afraid of emptiness.

There is a famous story within Buddhism of Zen Master Tue Trung who quizzed a novice monk on his understanding of the Heart Sutra. Following a discussion about the five skandhas and emptiness, the novice said that he understood that 'There are no eyes, ears, nose, tongue, body or mind; there are no forms, sounds, smells, tastes, feelings, or objects of mind; the six consciousnesses do not exist, the eighteen realms of phenomena do not exist, the twelve links of dependent arising do not exist, and even wisdom and attainment do not exist.' The Master immediately twisted the novice's nose and asked 'if the nose doesn't exist what is hurting?'

AO1 Activity

Using the information about the Prajnaparamita Hrdaya in this chapter and other sources and having read a translation of the Sutra online:

1. Discuss in small groups what the main aims of the Prajnaparamita Hrdaya might be. Record your findings.
2. Explain why the content of Prajnaparamita Hrdaya has been described by some people as 'crazy'.
3. Explain why sunyata might not mean nothingness.

quickfire

1.15 Why is the Heart Sutra chanted twice daily in Zen monasteries?

Key quotes

To be is to inter-be. You cannot just be by yourself alone. You have to inter-be with every other thing. (Thich Nhat Hanh)

Emptiness means empty of a separate self. It is full of everything. (Thich Nhat Hanh)

There is no ignorance, no decay and death, no extinction of decay and death, no suffering, no origination of suffering, no stopping, no path. (Heart Sutra)

What the *Heart Sutra* (like all *Prajnaparamita Sutras*) does is to cut through, deconstruct, and demolish all our usual conceptual frameworks, all our rigid ideas, all our belief systems, all our reference points, including any with regard to our spiritual path. (Brunnholzl)

quickfire

1.16 What do the terms 'conventional truth' and 'ultimate truth' mean?

Key quotes

Cultivation of the Prajna Parimita, the perfected virtue of knowing truth by intuitive insight, relieves us from our suffering and helps us overcome all kinds of calamities. (Dharma Master Lok To)

This great, bright Mantra emanates unadulterated Wisdom, and its power to transcend the Threefold Realms and attain supreme Nirvana is beyond comparison. (Dharma Master Lok To)

Specification content

The parable of the burning house
in the Lotus Sutra: exemplifying the
concept of skilful means and the
provisional nature of the teachings.

Skilful means in Theravada Buddhism and Mahayana Buddhism

The concept of skilful means begins with Theravada Buddhism. In fact, it directly follows the Buddha's Awakening. Following his Awakening the Buddha realised that his insight was too deep to communicate, and he was reluctant to share his insight simply because it appeared too difficult, if not impossible, a task to perform. According to Pali scriptures, the Hindu deity Brahma pleads with the Buddha to share his insight with all sentient beings. The Buddha responds by explaining, 'Perceiving trouble, O Brahma, I did not tell people the refined, sublime Dhamma …' but it was the Buddha's consequent compassion, in seeing all beings held back by ignorance, that compelled him to deliver the Dhamma.

The Samyutta Nikaya reads:

> 'Then the Blessed One, having understood Brahma's invitation, out of compassion for beings, surveyed the world with the eye of an Awakened One. As he did so, he saw beings with little dust in their eyes and those with much, those with keen faculties and those with dull, those with good attributes and those with bad, those easy to teach and those hard, some of them seeing disgrace and danger in the other world …' (Translated by Thanissaro Bhikkhu)

However, the issue was **how** to do this. The Buddha decided on upaya kosalla (skilful means), and throughout his ministry taught people according to their spiritual capacity and needs, and also according to emotional and intellectual capacities. This solution, in its basic form, manifests throughout the early Buddhist texts initially as a progressive or 'gradual instruction' (anupubbi katha) on the Dhamma. In other words, the Buddha just delivering the teachings in a simpler form. However, as the stories and traditions surrounding Kisagotami in Pali texts support, skilful means also had a practical purpose in the Buddha's pastoral ministry.

According to Peter Nelson, the 'paradigm of "skilful means" pioneered by the Buddha in the early suttas provided a template for all future developments in Buddhist pedagogy'.

The notion of skilful means in Mahayana Buddhism (Sanskrit: **upaya kausalya**) is given a subtle twist. Mahayana Buddhism teaches that the Saddharmapundarika Sutra has superseded the Pali Canon. T'ien-t'ai, a 6th-century Chinese Buddhist, established the Lotus Sutra as the supreme scripture. Indeed, the rise of Mahayana Buddhism is often referred to as the second turning of the wheel of Dhamma whereby a more developed form of the teachings is expounded. Accordingly, the Theravada Buddhist Dhamma as a whole becomes one skilful way of advocating the ultimate insight of the Buddha and in Mahayana this is taken to a whole new level. Therefore, not just the means of teaching the Dhamma in Theravada were through skilful means but the actual Dhamma itself was a form of skilful means as expounded through the Four Noble Truths and the Eightfold Path. This was the way of the arhat; however, in Mahayana a more advanced path developed around the concept of a bodhisattva. This was in line with the teachings that Mahayana Buddhism had revealed, that all sentient beings were potential Buddhas since, from an overall perspective, there were no restrictions or limitations.

Therefore the earlier teachings of the Buddha as found in Theravada Buddhism were now provisional. It is here that a tension arises between Mahayana Buddhism as the 'greater vehicle' as opposed to the 'lesser vehicle' (Hinayana) of the Theravada. This is often centred around the debate about whether or not the isolated path of the arhat, or all-embracing path of the bodhisattva, is greater. Skilful means is therefore used by the Lotus Sutra as a parody on the 'lesser' teachings of Theravada. The term skilful means has been met before in relation to the implication of the teachings in the Heart Sutra, but it is with the Lotus Sutra that greater emphasis is given to this term within Mahayana Buddhism.

Key terms

Hinayana: term used in Mahayana Buddhism, seen in the Lotus Sutra, to describe Theravada Buddhist teachings

Upaya kausalya: skilful means in Sanskrit, delivering the Buddhist Dhamma (Dharma) to people according to their spiritual capacity and needs, and also according to emotional and intellectual capacities

The Lotus Sutra (Suddharmapundarika Sutra)

The Suddharmapundarika Sutra, 'the Sutra of the Lotus Blossom of the Wonderful Law', is often referred to simply as the Lotus Sutra. The dating of the Sutra is disputed amongst scholars. It is thought to have been compiled in approximately 200 CE; however, its oldest sections could date back as far as the first century BCE. Despite the fact that the author of the Sutra is unknown, it remains one of the most well-known and significant scriptures amongst the many within Mahayana Buddhism. Indeed, it was one of the first scriptures to refer to Mahayana as the 'Greater Vehicle'.

The Lotus Sutra is one of the most popular scriptures in China and Japan, despite it originating in India. In order to give it greater authority, it was probably translated from a local dialect into Sanskrit. The most famous Chinese version of the text was translated in approximately 406 CE. To this day, however, the Lotus Sutra has been translated into many languages, including English. Thus it has played a significant role in the spread of Mahayana Buddhism into Britain and the West. The Lotus Sutra has had a great impact upon Japanese Zen Buddhism and is the object of great devotion within Nichiren Buddhism today.

Paul Williams tells us that the Sino-Japanese tradition claims that 'the Lotus Sutra was the final teaching of the Buddha, preached immediately before he manifested his parinirvana'. It could be argued that this attaches authority to the Sutra as it is seen as words of the Buddha, 'Buddha vacana'. Whilst some schools claim that this is the teaching of the Buddha, many believe that it is not thought to have been inspired by revelation but is the direct word of Shakyamuni Buddha. As this is not the Buddha of the Theravada tradition the historicity of the Lotus Sutra is not an issue.

Key quotes

The teaching about the path that leads to nirvana was given as a preliminary teaching to encourage people to start out on the spiritual path who were not ready for the final teaching. That they were not is demonstrated by a large group of 5000 monks, nuns, laymen and laywomen who leave in disgust at this point. These represent all the Buddhists who cannot accept the Mahayana teaching. **(Cush)**

It is the Lotus Sutra alone which contains the ultimate truth of Shakyamuni's teaching, a truth which at one and the same time transcends all his earlier teachings, and yet unites them. **(Fowler)**

Key terms

Parinirvana: the final passing away into nirvana from the cycle of life, death and rebirth

Shakyamuni: a term used, mostly within Mahayana Buddhism, to refer to the Buddha, Siddhartha Gautama, and means 'sage of the Shakya'. Shakyamuni of the Lotus Sutra is also seen as the Eternal Buddha

quickfire

1.17 What is the full title of the Lotus Sutra?

quickfire

1.18 Who is Shakyamuni?

Lotus flower: a symbol of Enlightenment

Study tip

A good way to learn and remember key terms and their definitions is to record them and keep playing them back.

The great interest Mahayanists have in the Lotus Sutra outweighs the claims that there is no evidence to associate the text with Shakyamuni Buddha, Siddhartha Gautama, and that it was simply invented at a later stage. The theatrical and mythological language of the Lotus Sutra ensures that historicity is not a big issue. The opening scene sees a cosmic drama being staged as Shakyamuni Buddha addresses an audience of celestial beings, bodhisattvas, arhats, famous disciples, etc. The beautifully creative writing depicts a scene of miraculous and supernatural happenings.

1.19 What expression, frequently associated with Buddhist scriptures, adds authority to the opening of the Saddharmapundarika Sutra?

Key terms

Buddha-nature: the fundamental nature of all beings that they *are* already enlightened and essentially need to realise it

Buddhahood: the Mahayanist concept of Awakening or Enlightenment which is available to everyone

Dharmakaya: dharma body

Nirmanakaya: the emanation body of a Buddha according to the doctrine of Trikaya

Trikaya: the 'three bodies' or ways of being of the Buddha, dharmakaya, sambhogakaya and nirmanakaya

---

The opening statement of the Sutra is 'Thus I have heard'. This expression is used frequently within earlier scriptures, including the Pali Canon, to give the scriptures authority of the Buddha. Here it reinforces the authority of the Saddharmapundarika Sutra as the word of Shakyamuni Buddha. The opening scene features a sermon by Buddha at Mount Gridhrakuta (the Vulture Peak) near Rajagriha. This grounds the Sutra within a real geographical location associated with the historical Buddha, thus giving it more significance. However, the Lotus Sutra reveals that the Buddha is not in fact dead, as the Pali Canon had indicated, but is still very much alive and accessible to those who have faith.

The main themes of the Lotus Sutra

(1) Eternal Buddha and Buddhahood for all ('Buddha-nature')

The Buddha depicted in the Lotus Sutra is not Siddhartha Gautama of the Pali Canon, but the Eternal Shakyamuni. The Buddha of the Saddharmapundarika Sutra transcends time. The reason for this is that it is not possible to limit his compassion to a single human lifespan. Therefore, the Sutra describes the nature of Shakyamuni as ongoing. There is a stark difference to the view of **Buddhahood** within the Pali Canon. There Siddhartha Gautama is seen as a human example or role model who has entered parnirvana and left the dharma as a guide to those of the path to nirvana. Here in the Lotus Sutra the Eternal Buddha is seen as accessible in the here and now.

Paul Williams supports this argument when he suggests that 'whether the Buddha is literally eternal or not, the Buddha of the Lotus Sutra is, as it were, religiously eternal – for any devotee he is always there'. Merv Fowler goes a step further by suggesting that the Eternal Buddha is 'one who is both omniscient and omnipresent in the world, helping others in their quest for Enlightenment'. Denise Cush also reminds us that this Sutra promotes the idea that, out of compassion for the world, 'all beings are not called to become arhats, but to be Buddhas'. Therefore, a key message of the Lotus Sutra is that this Buddhahood is available to everyone, as the ultimate goal and that the Eternal Buddha is there to help on the way.

In order to understand the concepts of Buddha and Buddhahood within the Lotus Sutra it would be helpful to understand the Mahayana teaching of **Trikaya**, that Buddha can be manifest in three ways, **nirmanakaya**, sambhogakaya and **dharmakaya**. This teaching is implied within the Sutra, rather than fully explained, but this has certainly become a major doctrine within Mahayana Buddhism. The Buddha of the Lotus Sutra is presented as dharmakaya, or the ultimate reality which unites all things. The Eternal Buddha is beyond time, space, existence and non-existence as well as found within all beings. Indeed, the very nature of all beings is that of **Buddha-nature**. All beings are believed to be Buddhas and they need to wake up and realise this. This Awakening is Nirvana and it is said that if all beings are Buddhas, then samsara are two sides of the same coin. Nirvana is attainable here and now for everyone.

Shakyamuni is not the only Buddha to be depicted in the Lotus Sutra. In Chapter 11 in a floating stupa rising from the earth, the past Buddha Prabhetaratna appears. Indeed, he took a vow to appear whenever the Lotus Sutra is taught. This shows that 'the Lotus Sutra is not new, but its preaching is part of the ministry of every Buddha' and that 'there can be more than one Buddha existing at the same time and in the same region' (Williams). This also suggests that the teaching that the Buddha has entered parinirvana and is inaccessible is false. As Williams explains, 'Prabhetaratna is supposed to be dead, and yet here he is radiantly vigorous and apparently living inside his stupa.'

AO1 Activity

1. Using the text in the section above alongside a selection of other sources, describe the main differences between the historical Buddha and the Buddha of the Lotus Sutra.

2. From these sources of wisdom find two useful quotations that you could use in an AO1 essay and explain why you have selected them.

3. Share your findings with a partner or in a small group and discuss.

(2) One vehicle or pathway ('ekayana')

Ekayana is the idea that there is only one vehicle or 'one way', which is the way of Buddhahood. The second chapter of the Lotus Sutra, known as the Hoben, puts forward the idea that previously there were three vehicles to realising Buddhahood. Firstly there were the Sravakas, or hearers of the dharma, who would attain the status of arhat. Secondly, the Pratyekabuddhas, those who had found enlightenment themselves. And, thirdly, there were the bodhisattvas who became enlightened and went on to teach. Therefore, the three types of 'vehicle' or yana presented in the Lotus Sutra are the sravaka-yana, pratyekabuddha-yana and the bodhisattva-yana. Nevertheless, the Lotus Sutra advocates the idea that the bodhisattva way is now the only true way to enlightenment. The idea is that there is now only one way to enlightenment or Buddhahood, Ekayana, which is a superior way. The other ways are seen as Hinayana, a lesser vehicle, which were simply upaya kausalya. In fact, the notion of ideas being considered as 'one' is fundamental within the Lotus Sutra, thus it is believed that the name of the Lotus Sutra itself contains within it all truth.

(3) Skilful means ('upaya kausalya')

The notion of upaya kausalya in the Lotus Sutra concerns the strategies used to enable beings to escape samsara and realise nirvana. The Sutra claims that in the past, the ways in which the dharma was taught were adapted to the audience in order to aid understanding. One way of understanding this is to see that, just as a teacher would not teach a five year old and a twenty year old using the same teaching methods, so the dharma needs to be adapted to the level of understanding of its audience. When you are trying to explain concepts that are impossible to describe, such as the essence of nirvana, you have to vary the ways in which it is explained. It is not possible to say what nirvana is, therefore everything that is said about it should be thought of as provisional or upaya. Indeed, Michael Pye suggests that 'all Buddhist teachings are upaya – merely fingers pointing to the moon'. The Lotus Sutra also puts forward the idea that the reappearance of the Buddha at various times throughout countless eons is seen as another example of upaya. The Buddha's intention in doing this was to reveal the dharma in the best way he could, in order to lead beings to supreme enlightenment. Cush argues that in effect, the 'birth, Enlightenment and death was just a teaching device. The Buddha pretended to pass away into Nirvana, but in fact is still around, working to liberate all beings'.

Through the idea of upaya-kausalya the Lotus Sutra claims it has superiority over other Sutras. According to the principle of upaya, the Dharma does not have to be true, it is whether it helps a being towards enlightenment which decides its value. This means, of course that the Lotus Sutra itself is also provisional. Having said that, the teaching of upaya is found rarely within the Lotus Sutra, and is not thought to have been among the teachings of the historical Buddha. Nevertheless, it could be argued perhaps that the concept of upaya harks back to the parable of the raft in the Majjhima Nikaya of the Pali Canon. This is the Buddha's notion of the dharma as like a raft that gets you to Enlightenment but can then be discarded.

Key terms

Ekayana: the concept of one vehicle or 'one way' which is the way of Buddhahood

Hoben: chapter 2 of the Lotus Sutra, known as 'Expedient Means'

Pratyekabuddhas: those who had found Enlightenment themselves

Sravakas: hearers of the dharma, who would attain the status of arhat

Yana: vehicle

Key quote

The principal message of the first half of the Lotus Sutra [is] the Buddha's skilful means, the doctrine of the One Vehicle, and the complete joy of the Buddha's disciples in finding that they will, indeed must, attain Perfect Buddhahood. (Williams)

quickfire

1.20 What are the three vehicles to Enlightenment or Buddhahood?

Key quote

The Buddha teaches out of his infinite compassion for sentient beings. All teachings are exactly appropriate to the level of those for whom they were intended. Any adaptation whatsoever, provided it is animated by the Buddha's compassion and wisdom, and is suitable for the recipient, is a part of or relatively acceptable to Buddhism. The Buddha, or indeed in some contexts a Bodhisattva, is quite capable of teaching even non-Buddhist teachings if that is for the benefit of beings. (Williams)

This teaching might, therefore, be seen as a precursor to the concept of upaya. Additionally, because nirvana can never fully be expressed, all teachings could be seen as inadequate in expressing the truth and, therefore, provisional. This concept of upaya very cleverly clears up contradictions that might be found within Buddhist teachings. The Sutra justifies changing Buddhist teachings and practices to suit a particular culture and the teachings are not so much seen as the truth but are seen to be helpful in the realisation of nirvana.

(4) Compassion ('karuna')

Compassion (karuna) is a major theme in the Lotus Sutra. The Sutra condemns 'Hinayana' teachings as selfish because the goal the arhat seeks is enlightenment for himself only. From the outset the Lotus Sutra makes the point that some arhats, revealing their self-importance, leave when the Buddha starts teaching. The intention of this is to indicate that those who display such behaviour cannot be Enlightened; therefore, the arhats of Theravada Buddhism have not attained this ultimate goal. In contrast, of course is the unlimited compassion of the Eternal Shakyamuni. Nichiren Buddhists, in the hope that they will develop the compassion and realise Buddha nature will chant this phrase from the Lotus Sutra daily:

> At all times I think to myself:
> How can I cause living beings
> to gain entry into the unsurpassed way
> and quickly acquire the body of a Buddha? (From Chapter 16 Lotus Sutra)

The parables of the Lotus Sutra

The Lotus Sutra is rich with parables used to illustrate its main teachings. A selection of these are summarised and discussed below. The parable of the burning house is listed in the WJEC/Eduqas Specification and this forms the main part of the analysis below in discussing skilful means and the provisional nature of the teachings. However, there is also a very brief analysis of four other parables in order to provide further evidence and examples for the purpose of development or use in an AO2 answer.

The parable of the burning house (Chapter 3)

The parable of the burning house is found in the 'Simile and Parable' chapter of the Lotus Sutra following directly from Chapter 2, the 'Expedient Means' chapter, in which Shakyamuni Buddha makes a statement that the purpose of the Buddha's presence is to ensure that all sentient beings attain Buddhahood. The Buddha uses parables in Chapter 3 to reinforce this.

The parable is about an elderly man who owns a big, dilapidated house with only one door. One day the house catches fire. The man's children, who are playing inside are in danger of losing their lives. They don't notice the fire as they are engrossed in their games and they do not hear their father calling them to safety. In this parable the old man is said to use upaya, or skilful means, to save the lives of his beloved children. He knows them well and shouts to them that there are goat-carts, deer-carts, and bullock-carts waiting for them if they come outside. The children hear this and rush out of the house. They are saved from the fire. But when they emerge from the house, they are not greeted by the promised carts but by an even more spectacular sight of a white bullock pulling a magnificent chariot.

This parable is overflowing with allegory. The Buddha points out that there are three different paths toward enlightenment that can be undertaken. However, only one of these paths truly exists, the other two are merely used to encourage people to begin practising Buddhist teachings. In the parable, the burning house represents samsara in which all sentient beings are trapped. This is skilfully symbolised by the young children who are found trapped in the house. The reader is made aware of the peril they are in as the old man, representing the Tathagata (Buddha), does everything

The burning house symbolises the peril of samsara.

within his power to save them from the fire. This ignorance of the imminent danger of the fire represents the three poisons of greed, hatred and ignorance which, according to Buddhist teachings, keep people imprisoned in samsara. The offering of the gifts of three different carts represent the three different ways to nirvana. Finally, the reward they achieve when they finally escape the house is beyond their expectations. This is nirvana or Buddhahood.

The Lotus Sutra also discusses whether the father lied to the sons. Sariputra, the Buddha's disciple, is adamant that this is not the case. He explains that skilful means are used to get the children out of the perilous building. If the end justifies the means and the motivation is to bring about spiritual advancement, the action or teaching is moral. So, the parable of the burning house illustrates the urgent situation humankind find themselves in and how preoccupied they can be when they are in samsara; the need, therefore, to use skilful means; the idea that the teachings of Buddhism are merely provisional; and the superiority of the bodhisattva way.

Key quote

The doctrine that the Buddha remains, has not abandoned his children but is still here helping us in many infinite compassionate ways ... forms the centrepiece of the Lotus Sutra's second half. (Williams)

AO1 Activity

1. Complete a table to display the symbolism and allegory within the parable of the burning house.

Symbol	Explanation
Old man	
Burning house	
Children	
Fire	
Three carts	
Chariot and white bullock	

2. Explain how the use of upaya in the parable of the burning house might conflict with following the five precepts. Think of reasons why this might be seen as an acceptable exception to following the precept.

The parable of the prodigal son (Chapter 4)

Another well-known parable from the Lotus Sutra is that of a prodigal son who left home, became impoverished, and later became employed as a servant in the house of a kindly master. The menial work he undertook in this role represents arhatship. Prior to the death of the father, in small stages that the son could comprehend, it was eventually revealed that he was actually the son of the master. He was then given his rightful place as heir to the household. This is seen as an example of upaya, as it was thought that the son would initially be unable to cope with knowing the whole truth.

The parable of the phantom city (Chapter 7)

In this parable, a group of people, led by a wise guide, are journeying through a wilderness. They are told that there will be great treasure at the end of their journey. However, they become tired and lack the motivation to continue. The guide uses skilful means by telling they will find a city where they can stay, rest and refresh themselves. When, after resting, they feel much better, the city miraculously vanishes. The guide had created the phantom city to satisfy their needs. Once it had fulfilled its purpose, he made it vanish. They are encouraged to continue their journey by the guide who assures them that the treasure is near and, with further effort, they will find it. In this parable, the guide represents the Buddha; the group of people are his disciples; the phantom city is Buddhism; and the treasure to be found is the Buddha-nature.

The parable of the physician's sons (Chapter 16)

This parable tells of a physician who discovers that his sons have swallowed
poisonous chemicals. Some of his sons are aware enough to take the antidote
he prepared for them. However, the others are extremely confused and do not
see the urgency of the situation. The physician leaves the country, but stages his
death, in order to shock the other sons into taking the antidote. Subsequently, the
father returns home and lives happily forever after. This parable also shows use of
skilful means. Additionally, however, Japanese translations of the Sutra show the
Buddha (the physician) living for eternity, describing him as 'Father of the world,
self-born, the healer and protector of all creatures' (cited Cush). On the other hand,
Paul Williams reminds us that the Tibetan interpretation is that the Buddha's life
is 'an enormously long, but still finite length'. There is, therefore, a difference in
interpretation within Mahayana Buddhism. Japanese traditions suggest that beings
are already Buddhas and just need to realise it, whereas the Tibetan tradition
advocates the view that we will all eventually become Buddhas.

The parable of the medicinal herbs (Chapter 5)

This parable describes a vast cloud that covers the whole world. From it, rain pours
upon a great variety of plants and medicinal herbs of very different shapes and
sizes. The plants in turn grow, blossom and bear fruit. They grow from the same
ground and are watered by the same rain, yet all remain different from each other.
In the same way, the Buddha appears like the vast cloud. He teaches the dharma to
beings equally for their benefit. All beings are incredibly different but the Dharma
is the same. As the rain, is the Buddha-Dharma and is available equally to all. The
Sutra implies that the value lies in how well the audience understands the Dharma
not in the depth of the talk.

The importance of the Lotus Sutra

The Saddharmapundarika is one of the most famous scriptures within Buddhism.
Given varying degrees of authority by different Buddhist schools, its teachings
lie at the heart of Japanese, Chinese and Korean schools of Buddhism. Nichiren
Buddhists exclusively use the Lotus Sutra as a source of authority. Sections of the
Sutra are recited daily by Nichiren Buddhists. In fact it is believed that merely in
chanting its title you can realise Nirvana. Nichiren Buddhists believe that sounds
manifest what they represent. The primary practice of Nichiren Buddhists is to
chant the **daimoku**, Nam Myoho Renge Kyo 'Reverence to the Lotus Sutra, the
supreme law of life'. They believe that when they chant, the truth of the Lotus
Sutra is uttered and that in chanting the title of the Lotus Sutra they are indeed
reciting the entire Sutra. Merv Fowler explains that Nichiren Buddhists believe
that 'those who chant the title of the Lotus Sutra, even without understanding
its meaning, realise the very heart of the Lotus Sutra as well as the essence of the
Buddha's teaching'.

Nichiren Buddhists support this practice by reciting the Hoben and Juryo chapters
from the Lotus Sutra. It could be argued, therefore, that the Lotus Sutra contains
an almost magical power to save beings who have faith and show devotion. It is
believed that Buddhism encourages people to recognise that they have an infinite
potential to Awaken to Buddhahood in their lives and to enable it in the lives of
others. Nichiren Buddhism teaches that when people are aware of this, it will

Key quote

For Nichiren Buddhists, the
Lotus Sutra both encapsulates
and surpasses the teachings of
Sakyamuni, but familiarity with the
text is of no avail unless its power
is translated into practical living.
Again and again these schools make
this self-same point, again and
again it is the practice of daimoku
which translates the dynamism of
the Lotus Sutra into the dynamism
of life. (Fowler)

Key term

Daimoku: the central chant
(or mantra) of all forms of
Nichiren Buddhism

enable them to treat others with the respect they deserve; this in turn will awaken the same self-awareness within those with whom they interact. This then enables limitless self-improvement. As we have seen, from a Nichiren viewpoint, chanting the title of the Lotus Sutra provides a direct path to enlightenment, therefore, the prestigious position given to the Lotus Sutra and its paramount importance to Nichiren Buddhists is clear for all to see.

Study tip

The ability to use quotations effectively is an essential skill for all Religious Studies students. Make sure quotations you use are accurate and relevant. They can be from a variety of primary and secondary sources and should be used to enhance the content of your essay. Quotes are a useful way of exploring and providing evidence and examples to justify your point of view. You should usually provide some kind of context for the quote and comment on what's interesting about it.

The idea that the Saddharmapundarika Sutra has some kind of magical power might account for its popularity, especially as this power is available to all. To recite the Lotus Sutra in great faith can save the most depraved people, enabling their rebirth into the Pure Land. Chapter 25 tells of how Avalokitesvara saves a robber from injury because of his devotion. Women can be drawn to the teachings of the Sutra, as women are seen to advance spiritually. For example, in Chapter 12 an eight-year-old naga princess becomes a bodhisattva and preaches to Manjushri. In an instant the princess in transformed into a male and then attains Buddhahood. That it was a necessity for the girl to become male prior to attaining Buddhahood is a cause of some debate amongst those advocating feminist views within contemporary Buddhism. However, it is important to realise that this teaching would have been revolutionary during the time that the Lotus Sutra was recorded as women then would have experienced significant discrimination.

Since the Second World War there has been increased interest in the Lotus Sutra in new Japanese traditions of Buddhism, such as Sokka Gakkai and Rissho Kosei Kai. These new schools have pushed the study of the text on a global scale. Etai Yamada, the 253rd head priest of the Tendai school of Buddhism, used the Lotus Sutra as the foundation of ecumenical discussions with world religious leaders including a summit in 1987. He also encouraged the use of the Lotus Sutra as a basis for Socially Engaged Buddhism.

Nevertheless, it could be argued that the Saddharmapundarika's importance is essentially achieved because of the significance of the teachings it conveys. These have influenced the lives of Mahayanists worldwide. The scripture sets out a new view of the Buddha and of nirvana. It introduces the concepts of upaya and the bodhisattva ideal, thus emphasising the compassion of the Buddha (and bodhisattvas) for all beings. The scripture's emphasis upon the goal of recognising that all beings are Buddha and at-one with the Transcendent Buddha have become highly valued teachings within Mahayana Buddhism.

AO1 Activity

After reading the section on the Lotus Sutra close the book and write down what you consider the main points to be. This could be in a mind map or in a list.

Study tip

A Religious Studies student should always be reading. Don't just rely on one textbook. You don't have to buy them: use your local library to borrow some. They are always willing to send for relevant books and other sources for people.

Key quotes

The magical power of the Lotus Sutra has no doubt been one reason for its popularity. (Williams)

No matter how many words and phrases of the text one has committed to memory, no matter how eloquently and aptly one may be able to interpret them, if one cannot apply the teachings of the text in one's daily life and translate them into practical and concrete terms of action, then one's understanding of the Sutra is valueless. (Ikeda)

The Lotus Sutra is not a scholarly work for specialists, but a practical guide for living our lives in the here and now. The heart of the Lotus Sutra teaching, the bodhisattva way of the Great Vehicle is this: We are all bodhisattvas. We can use the Sutra, and the insight it gives us into the six paramitas, in our life every day. When we study the Sutra we do not study it just for ourselves, but for the benefit of all people. (Thich Nhat Hanh)

The *dramatis personae* of the Lotus Sutra include buddhas and *bodhisattvas* as well as humans, and its message is unequivocal: Buddhahood is for all humanity; indeed, it is humankind's natural state. The great drama played out in the Lotus Sutra finds Sakyamuni Buddha as the cosmic Buddha in human form helping others in the same path to Enlightenment that he himself treads. (Fowler)

Key term

Manjushri: one of the most important bodhisattvas in Mahayana who is the embodiment of wisdom

Key skills

Knowledge involves:

Selection of a range of (thorough) accurate and relevant information that is directly related to the specific demands of the question.

This means:

- Selecting relevant material for the question set

- Being focused in explaining and examining the material selected.

Understanding involves:

Explanation that is extensive, demonstrating depth and/or breadth with excellent use of evidence and examples including (where appropriate) thorough and accurate supporting use of sacred texts, sources of wisdom and specialist language.

This means:

- Effective use of examples and supporting evidence to establish the quality of your understanding

- Ownership of your explanation that expresses personal knowledge and understanding and NOT just reproducing a chunk of text from a book that you have rehearsed and memorised.

AO1 Developing skills

It is now important to consider the information that has been covered in this section; however, the information in its raw form is too extensive and so has to be processed in order to meet the requirements of the examination. This can be done by practising more advanced skills associated with AO1. For assessment objective 1 (AO1), which involves demonstrating 'knowledge' and 'understanding' skills, we are going to focus on different ways in which the skills can be demonstrated effectively, and also, refer to how the performance of these skills is measured (see generic band descriptors for A2 [WJEC] AO1 or A Level [Eduqas] AO1).

▶ **Your next task is this:** Below is a summary of **upaya kausalya in the Lotus Sutra**. You want to explain this in an essay but they are your teacher's notes and so to write them out is simply copying them and not demonstrating any understanding. Re-write your teacher's notes but you need to replace the words used (apart from key religious or philosophical terminology) with different words so that you show that you understand what is being written and that you have your own unique version.

This theme in the Lotus Sutra concerns the strategies used to enable beings to escape samsara and realise nirvana. The Sutra claims that in the past, the ways in which the dharma was taught were adapted to the audience in order to aid understanding. One way of understanding this is to see that, just as a teacher would not teach a five year old and a twenty year old using the same teaching methods, so the dharma needs to be adapted to the level of understanding of its audience. When you are trying to explain concepts that are impossible to describe, such as the essence of nirvana, you have to vary the ways in which it is explained. It is not possible to say what nirvana is, therefore everything that is said about it should be thought of as provisional or upaya. Indeed, Michael Pye suggests that 'all Buddhist teachings are upaya – merely fingers pointing to the moon'. The Lotus Sutra also puts forward the idea that the reappearance of the Buddha at various times throughout countless eons is seen as another example of upaya. The Buddha's intention in doing this was to reveal the dharma in the best way he could, in order to lead beings to supreme enlightenment.

When you have completed the task, refer to the band descriptors for A2 (WJEC) or A Level (Eduqas) and, in particular, have a look at the demands described in the higher band descriptors towards which you should be aspiring. Ask yourself:

- Does my work demonstrate thorough, accurate and relevant knowledge and understanding of religion and belief?

- Is my work coherent (consistent or make logical sense), clear and well organised?

- Will my work, when developed, be an extensive and relevant response which is specific to the focus of the task?

- Does my work have extensive depth and/or suitable breadth and have excellent use of evidence and examples?

- If appropriate to the task, does my response have thorough and accurate reference to sacred texts and sources of wisdom?

- Are there any insightful connections to be made with other elements of my course?

- Will my answer, when developed and extended to match what is expected in an examination answer, have an extensive range of views of scholars/schools of thought?

- When used, is specialist language and vocabulary both thorough and accurate?

Issues for analysis and evaluation

The teachings in Mahayana Sutras as representative of reality

Since the idea of 'skilful means' (teaching each individual in a way that meets their needs) is not really a major issue in relation to representing 'reality', it would be more pertinent to look at the teaching of the Prajnaparamita, in particular, the Heart Sutra and Nagarjuna.

One line of argument could be that the teachings about reality found in the Prajnaparamita, in particular, the Heart Sutra and Nagarjuna, are in fact the Buddhist perspective of reality. This involves an empirical view of the 'self' or 'essence' or 'units' as mere conventions and that, ultimately, the analysis of reality is subtler. It is grounded in the teachings of Shakyamuni Buddha, namely anicca and anatta but is expressed in its fullest form through the teachings of emptiness – the sunyatavada – as found in Prajnaparamita, in particular, the Heart Sutra and the writings of Nagarjuna. In this respect, it makes sense to those following the Buddhist path and is a perfectly sensible explanation of reality. Beyond this, some may not appreciate this subtler view of reality simply because they are unaware of the logical process it takes or the full implications of the term 'emptiness'. Nevertheless, there are those practising Buddhism who use a more conventional analysis of reality and prefer to follow more 'concrete' guidance than simply stating that everything is empty. It could be argued that following the Four Noble Truths, the Eightfold Path and practices such as dana, metta bhavana, use of **mandalas** and **malas**, or simply reciting the **nembutsu** are more realistic for the majority of Buddhists, since an analysis and true realisation of everything as empty is quite an advanced level.

However, does the Heart Sutra stand apart in its insistence on sunyata or can we see this as fully representative of reality as understood from a scientific perspective? Indeed, some may point out parallels in modern science. It is not insignificant that early in the 20th century, modern physicists rejected the idea of 'emptiness' as a description based upon their discovery of atomic particles but then later with the discovery of 'quarks' confirmed that reality may not be quite what we think it is. Indeed, the work of scientists such as Brian Greene and his books, for example his exploration of parallel universes in *The Hidden Reality*, that appeal to a wider general audience, can be compared to the emptiness teaching. In fact, years earlier Fritjof Capra had indicated parallels in science and Asian thought in his work, *The Tao of Physics*. Accordingly, the implications of understanding the universe as 'empty' has led to the talk of parallel universe and multiverses. Again, it could be argued that the notion of multiverses is no different from the inter-penetration teachings of the **Avatamsaka Sutra** (Flower Garland Sutra), in Chinese Hua Yen Buddhism: as Chapter 39 The **Gandavyuha** states: 'with Bodhisattvas as numerous as the dust motes in ineffable Buddha kshetras'. Therefore, the Heart Sutra's explanation that, because all is empty of inherent existence (svabhava) infinite possibilities consequently emerge, might be seen as consistent with a scientific understanding of reality as, for example, via particle physics and also the notion of multiverses.

In saying all this, there does seem to be a point at which a tangible theory is proposed, reaches its limits, and creative speculation takes over. Science and Buddhism can seem to be compatible in terms of their perceptions of reality to a point. This point appears the be the possibility of multiverses or multiple Buddha kshetras (Buddha fields or universes). However, to then expand upon the nature of such possibilities appears to be beyond the realms of what is proposed. Both agree 'form is emptiness' and both agree that 'the very emptiness is form', but the possibilities the latter statement opens up for Buddhists are much more speculative

This section covers AO2 content and skills

Specification content

The teachings in Mahayana Sutras as representative of reality.

Key terms

Avatamsaka Sutra: literally, 'Flower Garland' Sutra, important in East Asian Buddhism, particularly the Hua Yen school

Gandavyuha: 39th chapter of the Avatamsaka

Malas: Tibetan meditation beads

Mandala: Tibetan diagram of the cosmos for meditational focus

Nembutsu: recitation used in Pure Land Buddhism

Key quotes

Form is emptiness and the very emptiness is form. (The Hrdaya Sutra)

All is possible when emptiness is possible. (Nagarjuna)

AO2 Activity

As you read through this section try to do the following:

1. Pick out the different lines of argument that are presented in the text and identify any evidence given in support.

2. For each line of argument try to evaluate whether or not you think this is strong (convincing) or weak (unconvincing).

3. Think of any questions you may wish to raise in response to the arguments.

This activity will help you to start thinking critically about what you read and help you to evaluate the effectiveness of different arguments and from this develop your own observations, opinions and points of view that will help with any conclusions.

Is Buddhism similar to particle physics that has opened up scientific investigation as to the nature of 'reality'?

Key term

Sukhavati: the term for 'Pure Land', the Buddha kshetra of Amitabha Buddha

Key quotes

In each dust-mote of these worlds are countless worlds and Buddhas … from the tip of each hair of Buddha's body are revealed the indescribable Pure Lands … **(Avatamsaka Sutra)**

… the universe is only one component of a far grander, perhaps far stranger, and mostly hidden, reality. **(Greene)**

… all of the parallel universe proposals that we will take seriously emerge unbidden from the mathematics of theories developed to explain conventional data and observations. **(Greene)**

AO2 Activity

List some conclusions that could be drawn from the AO2 reasoning from the above text; try to aim for at least three different possible conclusions. Consider each of the conclusions and collect brief evidence to support each conclusion from the AO1 and AO2 material for this topic. Select the conclusion that you think is most convincing and explain why it is so. Try to contrast this with the weakest conclusion in the list, justifying your argument with clear reasoning and evidence.

than those of science. Taken as a whole, the Mahayana Sutras portray a universe of demons, kings, asuras, devas, celestial bodhisattvas, multiple realms; which is not representative of reality as understood in the scientific paradigm. For example, the interpenetration teaching of Chinese Hua Yen – what Chang has called 'teachings of totality' – that is, multiple Buddhas, bodhisattvas and universes of the Avatamsaka, one could argue enters the realms of fantasy at worse or imagery at best. Even the **Sukhavati** Sutra with its account of the creation of the Pure Land and other Buddha worlds does not appear to be at all representative of reality as understood in any scientific paradigm; indeed, the parallel worlds theory in quantum mechanics again suggests nothing of the specific nature of such worlds.

Nonetheless, if taken as imagery and not at face value then such concepts may be realistic as they do represent a logical relationship with 'real' Buddhist teachings. Indeed, the Sutras can be readily demythologised, for instance, to see bodhisattvas representing the working of compassion in the universe. It could also be argued that if Nagarjuna's notion of the equality and mutuality of nirvana and samsara is accepted, reality is unlikely to conform to unenlightened, discriminative thinking such as that of the scientific paradigm anyway. In fact, this opens up a new question and line of enquiry. Is there universal agreement on what we actually mean by 'reality'?

In addition, the Mahayana Sutras describe a tier of bodhisattvas whose aid can be called upon and this could be argued to detract from the real Buddhist focus on a person achieving enlightenment through their own efforts. It is, however, possible to explain this through skilful means as a conventional way of accessing the ultimate and a more realistic option for many. Whether this is sufficient to justify it as representative of reality is another matter altogether?

Another argument may be that to be fully representative of reality, there has to be some concept of origination with regard to the universe such as the Big Bang theory and this is lacking in the Mahayana Sutras. However, this is not such a strong objection if one considers the fact that the notion of origination is made unnecessary through sunyatavada (emptiness teaching). Nagarjuna even questions the notion of time (present, past and future).

If one accepts the speculative nature of Mahayana projections, then maybe a spiritual reality exists outside of the limits of empirical research? There are strong arguments that suggest 'reality' is not as we may first think from both Buddhism and science and there is much that is compatible. It does appear, however, that trying to pinpoint the precise nature of this reality is problematic. Indeed, one could go as far as to suggest that this would be attempting to answer questions that the Buddha saw as idle speculation. In the parable of the poisoned arrow (Cula-Malunkyovada Sutta), the Buddha illustrates how foolish it is to ask questions about the origins and nature of something, such as an arrow, when it is causing immediate suffering. Common sense dictates that the object of suffering is removed and then one is in a position to raise such questions; however, maybe such questions need not be asked when there is no longer any suffering?

Also, the Buddha during his teaching ministry indicated that there were many 'unfathomable', 'indeterminate' or 'unanswerable' questions - these questions run through the Pali Canon and the Buddha was indifferent when he was faced with issues that pertained to the metaphysical realm. Maybe an obsession with such matters is redundant?

Study tip

Remember that it is the quality and not the quantity of your writing that is important in the examination. At the same time, it is the correct quantity of quality that brings success! – editing and timing your answers is a good way of doing this.

Skilful means as a key to understanding Buddhism's diversity

It would be useful to identify exactly what we mean by 'Buddhism's diversity'. The most obvious understanding would be in relation to the historical, and 'denominational', division between Theravada Buddhism and Mahayana Buddhism.

If this is the case, it could be argued that skilful means is certainly a key to understanding Buddhism's diversity in terms of teachings and practices. First of all, the notion that 'delivering the Buddhist Dhamma to people according to their spiritual capacity and needs, and also according to emotional and intellectual capacities' is certainly a feature of Theravada Buddhism. Within Theravada Buddhism this explains not only the different ways in which the Buddha delivered his religious and pastoral ministry, but also the differentiation between the four-fold sangha according to spiritual capacity and needs, and also according to emotional and intellectual capacities. In short, the Buddha recognised that skilful means was required to meet all the needs of the diverse range of sentient beings he encountered: the Buddha, immediately following his Enlightenment, according to the Ayacana Sutta, 'surveyed the world ... he saw beings with little dust in their eyes and those with much, those with keen faculties and those with dull'. Thereby he always taught accordingly using skilful means. In addition, the differentiation between stages of spiritual development of lay and monastic Buddhists and the various stages on the path to arhatship, indicate a practical application of skilful means. This then does explain the diversity of teachings and practices within Theravada Buddhism. However, there is also the difference between Theravada and Mahayana Buddhism.

Indeed, from the perspective of Mahayana Buddhism it could also be argued that, as the turning of the second wheel of Dhamma, Mahayana sees Theravada Buddhism in its completeness as a provisional understanding of Buddhism using skilful means and that a more developed or 'greater' way is that of the Mahayana. Although there has always been debate and tension regarding this differentiation, it is one way of seeing how skilful means justifies and makes sense of Mahayana Buddhism, since as a later development of Buddhism its authenticity could be challenged. In seeing Mahayana as 'greater' and by advocating the bodhisattva path, skilful means is a convenient explanation. This does, then, make sense of Buddhism's diversity in this respect. For example, there are Tibetan traditions, Chinese and Japanese forms. Within each of these there are a variety of beliefs and practices ranging from Tibetan Gelugpa, Chinese and Japanese Hua Yen, Cha'n and Pure Land, Japanese Nichiren and Zen. The complexities do not cease here. For example, there are different schools of Tibetan Buddhist traditions and even within Zen there is a distinction between Rinzai and Soto.

Moreover, there has been claimed to be a third turning of the Dhamma wheel, that of Vajrayana Buddhism, which is a more esoteric, tantric expression of the Dhamma that is prevalent in Tibet, Bhutan and Nepal. This form of Buddhism differentiates itself from both Theravada and Mahayana and, according to skilful means, is the highest expression of Buddhism.

Within both Mahayana and Vajrayana there is a diversity of belief and practice, and once again, as with Theravada, that could be seen to be a practical outworking of skilful means.

However, an alternative perspective could be that such diversities are not just down to skilful means because they may not be a direct result of skilful means. It may well be that skilful means explains how there can be variations but it may be argued that it is not the case that skilful means can be the key to a full understanding of Buddhism's diversity. If this is the case, do we have an alternative explanation as to Buddhism's diversity?

Specification content

Skilful means as a key to understanding Buddhism's diversity.

How many times has the 'wheel of Dhamma' turned?

Key quote

Then the Blessed One, having understood Brahma's invitation, out of compassion for beings, surveyed the world with the eye of an Awakened One. As he did so, he saw beings with little dust in their eyes and those with much, those with keen faculties and those with dull ... (Samyutta Nikaya)

AO2 Activity

As you read through this section try to do the following:

1. Pick out the different lines of argument that are presented in the text and identify any evidence given in support.

2. For each line of argument try to evaluate whether or not you think this is strong (convincing) or weak (unconvincing).

3. Think of any questions you may wish to raise in response to the arguments.

This activity will help you to start thinking critically about what you read and help you to evaluate the effectiveness of different arguments and from this develop your own observations, opinions and points of view that will help with any conclusions that you make in your answers to the AO2 questions that arise.

Key quotes

It is like when someone points his finger at the moon to show it to someone else. Guided by the finger, that person should see the moon. If he looks at the finger instead and mistakes it for the moon, he loses not only the moon but the finger also. (**Shurangama Sutra**)

As the ignorant grasp the finger-tip and not the moon, so those who cling to the letter, know not my truth. (**Lankavatara Sutra**)

Study tip

Every good evaluation has some form of conclusion. It may be at the start, at the end or even built up through an argument by the use of intermediate conclusions. Wherever it may appear, an argument requires a conclusion.

AO2 Activity

List some conclusions that could be drawn from the AO2 reasoning from the above text; try to aim for at least three different possible conclusions. Consider each of the conclusions and collect brief evidence to support each conclusion from the AO1 and AO2 material for this topic. Select the conclusion that you think is most convincing and explain why it is so. Try to contrast this with the weakest conclusion in the list, justifying your argument with clear reasoning and evidence.

One argument against skilful means explaining the totality of Buddhist diversity could be religious, historical or cultural elements. The various 'Buddhisms' that have emerged globally have not done so in isolation. There are cultural variations within every classification of Buddhism in the Theravada, Mahayana and Vajrayana models. Tibetan Buddhism does not really exist as a single phenomenon; there is great variety within schools. The same can be said of Chinese and Japanese forms of Buddhism. The influences of indigenous worldviews as Buddhism spread means that elements of Bon are spread throughout Tibetan Vajrayana, Taoism and Confucianism throughout Chinese Buddhism and Shinto amongst Japanese Buddhism. This is just the tip of the iceberg. Social conventions and norms have also been incorporated.

Whatever the case may be, skilful means makes clear that a wide variety of techniques can achieve the purpose of enlightenment. The parable of the burning house shows that skilful means are key because it underlines how the urgency of the human condition and the distracted state of sentient beings requires a variety of vehicles to achieve enlightenment. The parable of the burning house indicates that the Buddha's teaching is provisional and this explains Buddhism's diversity in relation to both the rift between Theravada and Mahayana Buddhism but also the differences within Mahayana Buddhism in particular.

Conversely, ekayana (one path/vehicle) would seem to indicate that overall there is no diversity; indeed, all paths lead into the one same path to enlightenment. Skilful means helps elucidate the saying from the Shurangama Sutta that none of the diverse paths is the truth as such, but all are like fingers pointing to the moon.

In conclusion, what is clear is that the Buddha from the outset adapted and adopted a variety of methods to help all sentient beings achieve enlightenment, and as with the parable of the poisoned arrow, it is important that the focus remains on the destination and not on the various routes. Conversely, more mundane factors may be seen as key to Buddhism's diversity such as the focus on compassion and greater inclusion in Mahayana as opposed to more monastic Theravada but maybe this would be labouring the point too much and concentrating on the finger and thus missing the full glory of the moon?

Does your evaluation see the glory of the moon or just analyse the finger?

AO2 Developing skills

It is now important to consider the information that has been covered in this section; however, the information in its raw form is too extensive and so has to be processed in order to meet the requirements of the examination. This can be done by practising more advanced skills associated with AO2. For assessment objective 2 (AO2), which involves 'critical analysis' and 'evaluation' skills, we are going to focus on different ways in which the skills can be demonstrated effectively, and also, refer to how the performance of these skills is measured (see generic band descriptors for A2 [WJEC] AO2 or A Level [Eduqas] AO2).

▶ **Your next task is this:** Below is a brief summary of two different points of view concerning **dhammas (dharmas) and ultimate reality (sunyata)**. You want to use these two views and lines of argument for an evaluation; however, they need further reasons and evidence for support to fully develop the argument. Re-present these two views in a fully evaluative style by adding further reasons and evidence that link to their arguments. Aim for a further 100 words.

On the one hand, the teachings of the Prajnaparamita Hrdaya differ from the teachings of the Pali Abhidhamma texts in that the building blocks, or dhammas (dharmas) from which everything is formed, tend to be viewed more as static entities in the Pali teachings. Although the Abhidhamma Pitaka sets out a map for the way things are, in the teachings of the Heart Sutra this is not to be accepted as ultimate reality because ultimately everything is sunyata (empty).

On the other hand, the teaching of the Abhidhamma on dhammas is more an empirical philosophical exercise with an implicit understanding of the inter-connectedness of all phenomena. As Ronkin writes, 'Dhammas are here psychophysical occurrences, or rather acts of conceptualisation by which the mind unites and assimilates sense data and ideas to a cognitive whole that makes sense'. Therefore, an understanding of the Abhidhamma Pitaka of the Pali Canon as proposing dhammas as a 'fixed state' is dubious.

When you have completed the task, refer to the band descriptors for A2 (WJEC) or A Level (Eduqas) and, in particular, have a look at the demands described in the higher band descriptors towards which you should be aspiring. Ask yourself:

- Is my answer a confident critical analysis and perceptive evaluation of the issue?
- Is my answer a response that successfully identifies and thoroughly addresses the issues raised by the question set?
- Does my work show an excellent standard of coherence, clarity and organisation?
- Will my work, when developed, contain thorough, sustained and clear views that are supported by extensive, detailed reasoning and/or evidence?
- Are the views of scholars/schools of thought used extensively, appropriately and in context?
- Does my answer convey a confident and perceptive analysis of the nature of any possible connections with other elements of my course?
- When used, is specialist language and vocabulary both thorough and accurate?

Key skills

Analysis involves:

Identifying issues raised by the materials in the AO1, together with those identified in the AO2 section, and presents sustained and clear views, either of scholars or from a personal perspective ready for evaluation.

This means:

- That your answers are able to identify key areas of debate in relation to a particular issue
- That you can identify, and comment upon, the different lines of argument presented by others
- That your response comments on the overall effectiveness of each of these areas or arguments.

Evaluation involves:

Considering the various implications of the issues raised based upon the evidence gleaned from analysis and provides an extensive detailed argument with a clear conclusion.

This means:

- That your answer weighs up the consequences of accepting or rejecting the various and different lines of argument analysed
- That your answer arrives at a conclusion through a clear process of reasoning.

**This section covers AO1
content and skills**

Specification content

A comparison of the background
and work of the 14th Dalai Lama
and Thich Nhat Hanh: Thich Nhat
Hanh's views about compassion and
non-harming.

quickfire

1.21 What is the name of the sangha
founded by Thich Nhat Hanh?

Key terms

Dharma name: the name given to
a Buddhist during initiation into the
sangha

Dharmacharya: teacher

Order of Interbeing: Tiep Hien, is
a lay and monastic sangha founded
by Thich Nhat Hanh, which has
its headquarters at Plum Village in
Southern France

Thay: teacher

Thich Nhat Hanh: Vietnamese Zen
Buddhist Master and founder of the
Order of Interbeing

ich Nhat Hanh film Walk With Me

quickfire

1.22 What is the name of the journal in
which Thich Nhat Hanh writes and
what is the name of the documentary
about Thich Nhat Hanh?

F: The contribution made to the development of Buddhist thought by the work of contemporary Buddhist teachers

Thich Nhat Hanh's views about compassion and non-harming

The Venerable **Thich Nhat Hanh** (1926–present) is a contemporary Vietnamese Zen Buddhist Master and the founder of the **Order of Interbeing**. His birth name was Nguyen Xuan Bao, born in the Quang Ngai province, Vietnam. According to Vietnamese custom, he should be either given his full title, which he took upon entering the monastery at the age of 16, or referred to as Nhat Hanh. Thich Nhat Hanh's **dharma names** are Phung Xuan, which means 'Meeting Spring', or 'Nhat Hanh', which means 'one action'. However, his disciples affectionately call him **Thay** (teacher). He is often referred to as the most beloved Buddhist teacher in the West.

As an eminent contemporary Buddhist master and **dharmacharya**, Thich Nhat Hanh has authored over a hundred books including *The Miracle of Mindfulness*, *Peace Is Every Step* and *Being Peace*. He contributes to the journal published quarterly by the Order of Interbeing the *Mindfulness Bell*. Nhat Hanh gained support from both the Civil Rights activist Dr Martin Luther King and the famous Catholic monk and writer, Father Thomas Merton, who wrote an essay about him called 'Nhat Hanh is my Brother'. Nhat Hanh's book *Living Buddha, Living Christ* never leaves the bedside of Oprah Winfrey, who interviewed him on her television show called Soul Sunday. Thich Nhat Hanh is certainly one of the most well-known Buddhist leaders in the world, respected amongst Buddhists and non-Buddhists alike. He also has hundreds of thousands of followers on Facebook and Twitter as testament to this.

Thich Nhat Hanh is a softly spoken, eloquent orator. He has travelled extensively, sharing the dharma globally. One of his most well-known talks, on the topic of mindfulness, was given to the employees of Google. He has also delivered mindfulness training courses in Silicon Valley, which have been attended by the leaders and directors of the world's most powerful technology companies. His message to these big corporations is not how to make more money, but how to make the world a better place to live in. A documentary film, called *Walk With Me*, about the life of Thich Nhat Hanh, has screened in cinemas throughout the world. The narrator of the film, Benedict Cumberbatch, is himself a practising Buddhist. It is easy to see, therefore, that this modest Zen monk, Thich Nhat Hanh, has been very instrumental in the growth of interest in Buddhism and the practice of mindfulness globally.

AO1 Activity

As a homework activity, watch a talk or interview given by Thich Nhat Hanh online and take Cornell notes. Identify questions or points for discussion in the following lesson.

Thich Nhat Hanh felt called to be a monk at the age of seven, following the discovery of a picture of the face of the Buddha on the cover of a magazine. The happy and serene face of the Buddha made him want to radiate the same qualities. And so he entered a monastery at the age of sixteen before taking full ordination in 1949. Thich Nhat Hanh's views on compassion and non-harming as a Buddhist monk led to his exile from Vietnam in 1966 as a result of leading peaceful protest against the Communist regime and the civil war taking place. Following his exile, he made it his mission to spread the message found in Buddhism of compassion and peace (non-harming) around the world. Initially he moved to the United States. However, his home is now in **Plum Village** about 85 km east of Bordeaux, near Sainte Foy La Grande in southern France. It wasn't until 2005 that Nhat Hanh was actually given permission to return to visit his homeland of Vietnam.

Thich Nhat Hanh is probably most famous for his peace activism. Dr Martin Luther King felt strongly that Nhat Hanh's support for the promotion of peace in war-torn Vietnam deserved to be recognised, and so nominated him for the Nobel Peace Prize in 1967. Unfortunately, the prize was not awarded to anyone that year.

During that civil war, Buddhist monks were accused by their government of supporting Communism. Thich Nhat Hanh and other Buddhist monks used non-violent methods to champion their cause. In a document entitled 'Call to Peace', Thich Nhat Hanh called for 'a way to stop the war and help all Vietnamese people live peacefully and with mutual respect'. He spoke out against the government of the United States, who had become involved in the war. He met with Martin Luther King in the mid 1960s to encourage him to speak out against the Vietnam War. Thich Nhat Hanh continues to try to seek solutions to conflict through methods such as non-violent protest and dialogue. He led the Buddhist delegation in the Paris Peace Talks.

Thich Nhat Hanh's mission is **Socially Engaged Buddhism**. Nhat Hanh coined the term Engaged Buddhism in his book, *Vietnam: Lotus in a Sea of Fire*, as a response to the suffering caused by the Vietnam War. His use of the term dates back to 1954, but he acknowledges that the practice dates back much further to Tran Nhan Tong who founded the Bamboo Forest Tradition in 13th-century Vietnam. Engaged Buddhism is putting the insights, gained during mindfulness meditation and from the dharma, into practice in situations where suffering and injustice are found. Engaged Buddhism brings practical solutions to suffering in everyday life. A good example of this is that he founded the School of Youth for Social Services (SYSS), a grassroots organisation, in the early 1960s. This organisation provides education and healthcare in rural Vietnam. It also has a focus upon improving the infrastructure. Following the war, it rebuilt villages that had been bombed and resettled families who found themselves homeless.

quickfire

1.23 Why was Nhat Hanh exiled from Vietnam and where has he made his home?

Key terms

Plum Village: a retreat centre set up by Thich Nhat Hanh located in the south of France the location of the headquarters of the Order of Interbeing

Socially Engaged Buddhism: a movement many believe to have been founded by the practices of Thich Nhat Hanh (but also traced back to 13th-century Vietnam) that requires Buddhists to become involved in social issues and committed in exceptional times of confrontation, injustice and violence (it is also sometimes referred to as Engaged Buddhism)

Key quotes

I do not personally know of anyone more worthy of [this prize] than this gentle monk from Vietnam. His ideas for peace, if applied, would build a monument to ecumenism to world brotherhood, to humanity. (Martin Luther King)

If we are to change the world we need to begin with ourselves and awaken that eternal part of us where true peace resides, our own buddha nature. (Thich Nhat Hanh)

Plum Village, the retreat centre in the South of France

Specification content

Thich Nhat Hanh: a practical
interpretation of Buddhist teachings
for life in the West with reference
to Thich Nhat Hanh's emphasis on
simple practices (smiling, breathing
and walking).

quickfire

1.24 What is the main focus of the retreats
held at Plum Village and what do the
teachings of Thich Nhat Hanh focus on?

Key quotes

I dwelled mindfully on each act,
beginning as I placed down my
overnight bag in my room, boiled
water to prepare a bath, and then
put on my meditation clothes. First
I did walking meditation alone
in the woods and picked some
wildflowers and bamboo branches
for flower arrangements. Then after
a few hours of dwelling mindfully
in each act and releasing most of
my worries, I began to feel renewed.
(Sister Chan Khong)

Peace is in yourself, peace is by
walking. (Thich Nhat Hanh)

Mindfulness is the energy of being
aware and awake to the present
moment. It is the continuous
practice of touching life deeply in
every moment of daily life. To be
mindful is to be truly alive, present
and at one with those around you
and with what you are doing. We
bring our body and mind into
harmony while we wash the dishes,
drive the car or take our morning
shower. (Plum Village website)

Key term

Prasangika: a specific interpretation
of Nagarjuna's philosophy that
argues against the idea of accepting
emptiness and yet recognising some
form of conventional empirical essence
or intrinsic nature. This latter view,
rejected by Nagarjuna, is usually
associated with the Svatantrika
interpretation of the 6th-century
Indian Buddhist scholar Bhaviveka

A practical interpretation of Buddhist teachings for life (smiling, breathing and walking)

The Order of Interbeing (Tiep Hien) was founded by Thich Nhat Hanh in 1966.
This is a Buddhist lineage school, based at Plum Village in the South of France,
where Thich Nhat Hanh now lives. Plum Village is primarily a monastery for
monks and nuns. It is also an eco-friendly village that offers retreats, teaching
and events throughout the year that are attended by lay people. Thich Nhat Hanh
offers teachings twice a week during retreats, held during the winter, spring,
and autumn. These retreats focus on living mindfully following the Fourteen
Mindfulness Trainings, which are the order's interpretation of the bodhisattva
path. The teachings include a focus upon non-attachment from views, anicca,
pratityasamutpada and upaya. Mindfulness is practised each moment, as
practitioners breathe, smile, eat, walk and work, as well as when they practise
sitting in meditation. Thich Nhat Hanh teaches people to walk as if they are kissing
the earth with their feet. The aim is that the whole of life is practised mindfully and
compassionately.

Thich Nhat Hanh's Fourteen Mindfulness Trainings, which lie at the heart of the
Order of Interbeing, are formal vows taken by members of the Order. They are
seen as a guide or a teacher. The Trainings allow members to understand the
nature of Interbeing, the reality of life, which can be experienced in the here and
now. They enable people to see the interconnection between their own happiness
and that of others because there is no separate self.

The notion of 'Interbeing' is grounded in Mahayana Buddhism's foundational
understanding of the nature of existence as expounded by the Heart Sutra (see
earlier) and the principle that although 'form is emptiness' there is resurrected an
appreciation of emptiness and full and 'Inter-be-ness' of everything in the same
way 'that very emptiness is form'. This does not mean that emptiness is any kind
of underlying substance at all – this is the view Nagarjuna fought against – and is
synonymous with a **pransangika** view as advocated by Nagarjuna and the schools
within Tibetan Buddhism.

The trainings are openness; non-attachment to views; freedom of thought;
awareness of suffering; compassionate, healthy living; taking care of anger;
dwelling happily in the present moment; true community and communication;
truthful, loving speech; protecting and nourishing the sangha; right livelihood;
reverence for life; generosity; and true love.

As the Order of Interbeing has developed, hundreds of similar sanghas have been
set up throughout the World. Thich Nhat Hanh has influenced many noteworthy
students including the Buddhist nun Sister Chan Khong who was also instrumental
in helping to set up Plum Village. She now teaches and leads retreats worldwide.

Mindful walking, kissing the earth with your feet

Some examples of the many students of Nhat Hanh include the American singer songwriter Skip Ewing; Noah Levine, who found Buddhism helpful in his addiction recovery and is now a dharma teacher and writer of books including *Dharma Punx: A Memoir* and *Refuge Recovery: A Buddhist Path to Recovering from Addiction*; and Joan Halifax who is a Zen Buddhist teacher who established the Upaya Institute in New Mexico, which teaches Engaged Buddhism. These followers, along with many others, are now passing on the teachings of Thich Nhat Hanh.

Thich Nhat Hanh's philosophy has combined the teachings of Zen, Theravada with other Mahayana traditions. He also takes a variety of disciplines into account, including aspects of psychology. Thich Nhat Hanh does not believe in God, but he believes that Jesus was an enlightened teacher like the Buddha. Nhat Hanh is an advocate of following the bodhisattva path, which is a central teaching in Mahayana Buddhism. He sees this as a practical way of practising Socially Engaged Buddhism, and he has dedicated his life and work to seeking inner transformation for the sake of all other sentient beings. Nhat Hanh believes that bodhisattvas are not perfect beings but are beings on a path of developing awareness and helping others. It is his view that there is no way to happiness, but happiness is the way.

AO1 Activity

In small groups or as a class, discuss the following questions:

1. What do you think Thich Nhat Hanh might mean by 'there is no way to happiness, but happiness is the way'?
2. How might this relate to Socially Engaged Buddhism?

Thich Nhat Hanh's teaching of mindfulness meditation has been influential to many in the West. His key teaching is to live mindfully in the present moment, thus following the philosophy of Mahayana Buddhism that Awakening is found in the here and now. What could arguably be different is Thich Nhat Hanh's uncomplicated, yet profound, explanations of these Mahayanist notions. His simple practices are certainly very attractive to people in the fast-paced, 21st-century world we live in. And, Thich Nhat Hanh suggests that Nirvana can be found through these practices in the here and now as practitioners free themselves from wrong perceptions, 'Ultimate is Nirvana. It is God and it is available to us 24 hours a day' (Thich Nhat Hanh).

Thich Nhat Hanh advocates living life according to the Eightfold Path of the Buddha, as this is exactly what the world needs today. This is the practice of Engaged Buddhism, with the Five Mindfulness Trainings at its core. He has developed them in such a way that they are easily practised by the lay community and to suit people in the modern age. He made these amendments because he felt that the original precepts are being misunderstood as commandments rather than guidance towards awareness, love and compassion. The Five Mindfulness Trainings are very practical and require social engagement.

Five Mindfulness Trainings

1. Reverence for life – To protect life, to decrease violence in one-self, in the family and in society.
2. True happiness – To practise social justice, generosity, not stealing and not exploiting other living beings.
3. True love – To practise responsible sexual behaviour in order to protect individuals, couples, families and children.
4. Loving speech and deep listening – To practise deep listening and loving speech to restore communication and reconcile.
5. Nourishment and healing – To practise mindful consumption, to help us not bring toxins and poisons into our body or mind.

quickfire

1.25 What do the Fourteen Mindfulness Trainings allow members of the Order of Interbeing to understand?

Key quotes

Life can only be found in the present moment. The past is gone, the future is not yet here, and if we do not go back to ourselves in the present moment, we cannot be in touch with life. (Thich Nhat Hanh)

When bombs begin to fall on people, you cannot stay in the meditation hall all of the time. Meditation is about the awareness of what is going on – not only in your body and in your feelings, but all around you. (Thich Nhat Hanh)

Key quotes

With mindfulness, we are aware of what is going on in our bodies, our feelings, our minds and the world, and we avoid doing harm to ourselves and others. Mindfulness protects us, our families and our society. When we are mindful, we can see that by refraining from doing one thing, we can prevent another thing from happening. We arrive at our own unique insight. It is not something imposed on us by an outside authority. (Thich Nhat Hanh)

Thay has made the precepts more relevant to contemporary concerns, including the growing threat to the environment, the exploitation of developing nations by multinational corporations, and the conflict and terrorism caused by religious fanaticism. Through his worldwide influence on people who work for peace, this gentle monk, who practises the slow walking and mindful awareness that he teaches, has helped further the cause of peace and justice by embodying peace and justice himself. (Landaw and Bodian)

AO1 Activity

In 3 minutes, think of as many practical examples as you can of how the Five Mindfulness Trainings might be practised by Socially Engaged Buddhists. Share your examples with the class as part of a discussion.

Recent developments

Following his visits to Vietnam after 2005, Thich Nhat Hanh has come under criticism from the independent Unified Buddhist Church of Vietnam (UBCV). They believe Nhat Hanh's visits supported the government-sanctioned Buddhist Church of Vietnam (BCV). The government arrested and persecuted members of the UBCV, who believe Thich Nhat Hanh was working with the government by not opposing their persecution. They suggest that he should have showed his opposition. Additionally, Thich Nhat Hanh had visited a BCV monastery at Bat Nha to train his followers, but since then, he has publicly stated that the Dalai Lama should be allowed to return to Tibet. In reaction to this political statement, the Vietnamese government became hostile toward the monastic sangha at Bat Nha, physically forcing them out of the monastery. Consequently, Thich Nhat Hanh has continued to travel the world, but has not returned to Vietnam. As he has been in poorer health in recent years, it seems, perhaps, unlikely that he will ever return to the homeland he loves. In the meantime, Thich Nhat Hanh has concentrated upon adapting his teachings to suit people in Western society. For example, he teaches the Five Mindfulness Trainings, which he has adapted from the ethical guidance of the Five Precepts of the Buddha.

In 2014 Thich Nhat Hanh suffered a brain haemorrhage and has spent time in recovery since then. At the time of writing this book, he has undergone treatment in the United States and is now back at his home in Plum Village where he continues, supported by the sangha, to live mindfully and to teach the dharma. It could be suggested that Thich Nhat Hanh's legacy will be that he encouraged a practical application of Socially Engaged Buddhism, which is relevant to the contemporary world, in his attempt to enable all sentient beings to suffer less and to be happy. Through engaging in life in this way people find meaning in their lives. Nhat Hanh suggests that there is suffering and there is a way out of suffering, and that you find a great deal of joy in helping people.

Study tip

Break up any content you are trying to learn into bite-size chunks. Learning one thing at a time soon builds up when you put the pieces together. There is a well-known tip that asks: How do you eat an elephant? One bite at a time!

The Dalai Lama (1935 – present)

The current **Dalai Lama** describes himself as a simple Buddhist monk but he is admired by Buddhists and non-Buddhists throughout the world. The Dalai Lama is a Tibetan Buddhist.

The term Tibetan Buddhism is problematic because there are within the tradition further different traditions. In addition, Tibetan Buddhism as a phenomenon is not seen as purely 'Tibetan' since the lineage of transmission in **Nyingmapa** (meaning 'ancient' and the oldest school of Tibetan Buddhism) can be traced back to **Padmasambhava**, an ancient Indian tantric Mahayana monk; hence the development of mantra, mudra and mandala-based forms of practice (see p. 157ff Theme 4). In addition, the influence of the indigenous **Bon** religion is still debated (see p. 154ff Theme 4). Lately, the preferred term amongst scholars is Indo-Tibetan Buddhism; however, as long as we are aware of these issues, for ease, and in line with the Specification, we shall refer to the phenomenon as 'Tibetan Buddhism'.

His Holiness the 14th Dalai Lama gives teachings at his residence in Dharmasala, India.

The Dalai Lama is seen as the most important leader within Tibetan Buddhism and is the spiritual and political leader of the **Gelugpa** (virtuous way, also known as Kadampa) school of Tibetan Buddhism. It is also known as 'Yellow Hat' tradition. Hats in Tibetan culture often represent attitudes towards abstract concepts; the yellow hats of the Gelugpa distinguish themselves from the 'Red Hats' of the other three main Tibetan traditions, Nyingmapa, Sakyapa and Kagjugpa.

The Dalai Lama is Tenzin Gyatso. 'Tenzin' is a Tibetan term meaning 'holder of the teachings'. Gyatso is a title of respect that Dalai Lamas have in their names. It means 'ocean'. The term Dalai Lama is actually a title bestowed upon him. 'Dalai' also means 'Ocean' in Mongolian and the term '**lama**' means a guru or a teacher. Therefore, the Dalai Lama is seen as an 'Ocean of Wisdom'.

The Gelugpa tradition of Tibetan Buddhism has a focus upon ancient tantric practices from the Indian Buddhist tradition, monastic discipline and Vinaya code, as well as the crucial role of scholarship. The Dalai Lama was the political leader of the country of Tibet until he was exiled by the Chinese in the late 1950s. He lived in **Potala Palace** in Lhasa.

An important lama in Tibet does not inherit this position as a birthright. In Tibetan Buddhism it is believed that major lamas have the ability to control the processes of rebirth and reincarnate themselves; Tenzin Gyatso is seen to be the 14th incarnation of the Dalai Lama. This lineage is over 500 years old stretching back to **Tsongkhapa** (1357–1419), the founder of the Gelug tradition. The term given to a young incarnate lama is '**Tulku**' which, according to the Dalai Lama, refers to the 'emanation body of the Buddha' or nirmanakaya (for information on the 'Three Bodies' doctrine see Year 1 and AS book on *Buddhism* Illuminate Publishing p.83).

Specification content

A comparison of the background and work of the 14th Dalai Lama and Thich Nhat Hanh: The 14th Dalai Lama and the practical interpretation of Buddhist teachings for life in the West.

Key terms

Bon: original religion in Tibet prior to Buddhism

Dalai Lama: meaning 'Ocean of Wisdom' this is the title given to the reincarnated leader of Tibetan Buddhism

Gelugpa: meaning 'virtuous way' this is a sect of Tibetan Buddhism which focuses on the Vinaya rules, monastic celibacy and scholarship

Lama: guru or teacher

Nyingmapa: oldest Tibetan Buddhist tradition

Padmasambhava: an ancient Indian tantric Mahayana Buddhist monk considered by all traditions to have introduced Tibet to Buddhism

Potala Palace: the headquarters of Tibetan Buddhism and the home of the Dalai Lama before his exile from Tibet

Tsongkhapa: meaning 'the man from Onion Valley', the founder of the Gelugpa school of Tibetan Buddhism

Tulku: a reincarnated lama who is trained from a young age to pass on the teachings from a specific lineage of Tibetan Buddhism

quickfire

1.26 How does the Dalai Lama describe himself and which school of Buddhism does the Dalai Lama lead?

Key quotes

There are two ways in which someone can take rebirth after death: rebirth under the sway of karma and destructive emotions and rebirth through the power of compassion and prayer ... This is the way ordinary beings circle incessantly through existence like the turning of a wheel. (Dalai Lama)

Amongst the Tulkus of Tibet there may be those who are reincarnations of superior bodhisattvas, bodhisattvas on the paths of accumulation and preparation, as well as masters who are evidently yet to enter these bodhisattva paths. Therefore, the title of Tulku is given to reincarnate Lamas either on the grounds of their resembling enlightened beings or through their connection to certain qualities of enlightened beings. (Dalai Lama)

Superior bodhisattvas ... are able to choose their place and time of birth as well as their future parents. Such a rebirth, which is solely for the benefit of others, is rebirth through the force of compassion and prayer. (Dalai Lama)

Before exploring the notion of Tulku fully, it is important to clear up any misunderstandings with Tibetan Buddhism about rebirth and reincarnation. Buddhism teaches rebirth as opposed to reincarnation, in line with anatta and the mistaken notion of an eternally existing essence or 'soul' that transmigrates from one physical form to the next physical form between lives. Despite this, there have been suggestions that, contrary to anatta and the notion of emptiness in Mahayana, there are areas of Buddhism which hint at some ontological basis for existence. This has always been rejected by Buddhism and, as we have seen with the concept of dhamma the Abdhidhamma and the Madhayamaka debate, this is sometimes misunderstood.

Likewise with Tibetan Buddhism, some have suggested that it promotes a form of 'reincarnation'. This perception of Tibetan Buddhism has arisen firstly through a specific reading given to the Bardo Thedol (Tibetan Book of the Dead) of the Nyingmapa tradition (and accepted by the three other main traditions of Tibetan Buddhism), which is an analysis of the stages of rebirth in terms of 'consciousness' referred to as bardo (intermediate or transitional state). However, this is not a 'soul' or essence of any kind since the whole philosophy of Indo-Tibetan thought is 'grounded' in emptiness!

The second way in which this confusion has arisen is to do with a misunderstanding of the term Tulku. The concept of a Tulku is quite complicated, first of all because it needs to explain the apparent contradiction between the notion of reincarnation and anatta. Rather than trying to justify a particular view, it would be best to refer to how the Dalai Lama explains this.

The Dalai Lama firstly distinguishes between two types of rebirth (1) caused by the force of karma and negative emotions, and (2) influenced by prayer and compassion. The first type of rebirth is that of ordinary beings. The second type of rebirth is exclusive to superior spiritual beings. Within Tibetan Buddhism, therefore, this notion of rebirth is unique to the Tulku since the Tulku is seen to be a manifestation of a superior spiritual being.

The Dalai Lama explains that the Buddhas in their Sambogakaya ('enjoyment body/heavenly body' of Buddhahood) allow manifestation of themselves through the 'emanation body' which includes superior spiritual beings such as bodhisattvas:

'Hence, the ultimate physical aspect of a Buddha is the Body of Complete Enjoyment (Sambhogakaya), which is accessible to superior bodhisattvas, and has five definite qualifications such as residing in the Akanishta Heaven. And from the Body of Complete Enjoyment are manifested the myriad Emanation Bodies or Tulkus (Nirmanakaya), of the Buddhas, which appear as gods or humans and are accessible even to ordinary beings.'

According to the Dalai Lama, there are three types of nirmanakaya and the Tulku is typical of the third type – the 'Incarnate Emanation Body' – and is typically an Enlightened Being. Therefore the Tulku is a direct result of the compassion of a sambhogakaya Buddha that elects to take on rebirth through reincarnation. This is therefore the second kind of rebirth in Tibetan Buddhism and exclusive to Tulkus. As the Dalai lama writes:

'Superior bodhisattvas, who have attained the path of seeing, are not reborn through the force of their karma and destructive emotions, but due to the power of their compassion for sentient beings and based on their prayers to benefit others. They are able to choose their place and time of birth as well as their future parents. Such a rebirth, which is solely for the benefit of others, is rebirth through the force of compassion and prayer.'

The Dalai Lamas are seen to be the nirmanakaya manifestation (earthly embodiment) of the heavenly bodhisattva of great compassion (Avalokitesvara or Chenrezig). The Dalai Lama is therefore a bodhisattva, or a being that is enlightened, but who has postponed full and complete enlightenment to aid others. This is in accordance with the bodhisattva vows. Therefore, it could be argued that they would never 'enter nirvana' (parinirvana).

Whatever the case, it is believed that he has chosen to rebirth through reincarnation in order to serve humanity. The Dalai Lama, along with other important lamas, are seen to be 'actual forms of these beings'; however, Paul Williams points out that the Dalai Lama himself takes the view that lamas 'embody their virtues and have been specially blessed by them'. Wisdom and compassion are the two most important pillars in Mahayana Buddhism and these are the qualities the Dalai Lama seeks to promote. Tibetans believe anyone can be enlightened but it is not easily achieved or realised, even though nirvana is present in the here and now.

A search begins to find the new Dalai Lama at the death of a previous one who was so far down the spiritual path towards enlightenment that they were able to choose the parents of their rebirth. Dalai Lamas are usually discovered by a disciple of the previous Dalai Lama who is easily able to identify him. All Dalai Lamas have been male. But there are a few female lamas within Tibetan Buddhism. Machig Labdrong is a historical example and Jetsunma Chime Luding Rinpoche and Khandro Rinpoche (who sometimes teaches at Brynmawr Buddhist Centre) are two such contemporary examples.

When the 13th Dalai Lama passed away, the **State Oracle** predicted that the new Dalai Lama would be born in the north east near the border with China. The Regent, temporary ruler, received visions when he visited Oracle Lake. He saw a monastery, a house, juniper trees and a sequence of letters. The visions were interpreted and it was decided that Kumbum monastery must be the location of the Dalia Lama's birth, for this was also the birthplace of the great Buddhist guru Tsongkhapa who had taught the First Dalai Lama.

A group of high lamas set off in search of Tulku. Upon arrival at the village of Taktser they found two-year-old **Lhamo Thondup**, and the close friend of the previous Dalai Lama, Keusang Rinpoche was convinced that this was the child they were seeking. As a child, therefore, one of the tests Llamo Thondup had to perform in order to prove he was the Dalai Lama was identifying objects owned by his predecessor the 13th Dalai Lama. At the age of four, the Dalai Lama began to receive a special education at Potala Palace, Lhasa, Tibet.

Landaw and Bodian explain that as Dalai Lamas are already familiar with the teachings, as they had taught them themselves in a previous life, their education progresses at such a rate that they will soon be able to resume their position of spiritual leader and teacher for the benefit of all other beings. The 14th Dalai Lama was enthroned in 1940 and dressed in monk's robes and began to follow the lifestyle of a novice monk. He took on political leadership in 1950 when he was only 15 years old.

Key terms

Lhamo Thondup: the birth name of the Dalai Lama

State Oracle: a clairvoyant monk in Tibetan Buddhism

quickfire

1.27 Who predicted the place of the birth of the 14th Dalai Lama?

Potala Palace, Lhasa, Tibet

Golden statue of Chenrezig in Kathmandu, Nepal

quickfire

1.28 Who tried to persuade that 'religion is poison' and why did the world not come to the aid of Tibet?

Specification content

A comparison of the background and work of the 14th Dalai Lama and Thich Nhat Hanh: the Dalai Lama's emphasis on acts of kindness, compassion and non-harming.

As a political leader in Tibet, the Dalai Lama was expected to attend government meetings from a young age. The Chinese invasion of Tibet in 1949 placed an enormous responsibility upon this young person. Following the invasion he tried everything within his power to negotiate with the Communist Chinese government, including making a visit to Beijing in person. The Chinese tried to convert the Dalai Lama to Communism. Chairman Mao told the Dalai Lama that 'Religion is poison' and the Chinese began to strip Tibet of its own government, religion, culture and identity. The young Dalai Lama wrote to political leaders throughout the world for support. However, in the aftermath of the Second World War, most of the world just looked on without attempting to support the Tibetans in their plight. Finally, following a visit by the Dalai Lama to India in 1956, an offer of help came from the Prime Minister of India, who offered asylum to the Tibetans should war break out in Tibet.

Just days after the Dalia Lama completed his geshe degree (equivalent to a PhD in Philosophy and Divinity) in March 1959, it was discovered that the Chinese forces were to kidnap him. Thousands of Tibetans surrounded his home in an attempt to protect him. The Tibetan people begged him to leave the country. Without knowing he was safe and alive they would have had no hope for the future. Taking the advice of the State Oracle, the Dalai Lama took the decision to leave the country and head to India. His journey over the snow-capped mountains to India was arduous. From over a million Tibetans who tried to escape the brutal Chinese regime at that time, only around one hundred thousand actually reached the safety of India and other adjoining countries.

AO1 Activity

Using the information in the text and a variety of other sources answer the following questions:

1. Explain the view that the Dalai Lama is an Enlightened Being.
2. Explain the political situation in Tibet during the late 1950s.

The Dalai Lama's emphasis on acts of kindness, compassion and non-harming

Following his exile, at the invitation of the Prime Minister of India, Jawaharlal Nehru, the Dalai Lama made his new home in Dharmasala in Northern India. Landaw and Bodian suggest that the Dalai Lama was given the freedom in India to move around, to travel, to explore science and consider his own principles which were based on democracy. In 1959 he set up the Central Tibetan Administration or the Tibetan government-in-exile. He began to create policies in line with his own thinking and set up Tibet's government-in-exile based on this. Since his exile, refugees have consistently poured from Tibet into India in the hope that they might meet the Dalai Lama, or for a better life, work and education. With the assistance of international NGOs (Non-Government Organisations) and the Government of India, the Tibetan government-in-exile set up the Tibetan Children's Village (TCV) in 1972. In 2009 the Dalai Lama Institute for Higher Education was opened in Bangalore. This was the first Tibetan College in India.

The Dalai Lama has continued to constantly monitor the situation within Tibet and to raise awareness of this throughout the world. His detailed proposals for a solution to the Sino-Tibetan conflict are based upon the teachings of the historical Buddha's First Sermon. He argues that resolution should be sought through the Middle Way Approach and the Five Point Peace Plan, whereby a democratically elected government in the traditional Tibetan provinces would give autonomy to Tibetans, rather than full independence, whilst maintaining their territorial integrity for China (Jacoby and Terrone). This attempt at compromise with the People's Republic of China (PRC) has received support from the international community, but not from the PRC, who have accused the Dalai Lama of 'being dishonest, privately pressing for independence while publicly calling only for autonomy, and using religion as a pretext to pursue an otherwise political agenda' (Jacoby and Terrone).

Likewise, though the majority of Tibetans still support this policy, the Dalai Lama is under increasing criticism due to human rights violations in Tibet and the lack of progress being made with the peace negotiations (Jacoby and Terrone). The Dalai Lama announced his retirement as Head of State of the Tibetan Government in-Exile in 2011. He devolved his political power and theocracy and encouraged a secular democracy. In March 2011 Tibetans worldwide voted for their first Prime Minister (Kalon Tripa) along with 44 new members of the parliament. The Dalai Lama has repeated numerous times that 'even the continuation of the institution of the Dalai Lama himself is for the people to decide'. Indeed since 1969 the Dalai Lama has suggested that when the Tibetan people are able to govern themselves, the institution of the Dalai Lama may no longer be required. This, along with the increasing support for the Dalai Lama from the international community, has concerned the PRC, as they want to be able to control the election of the 15th Dalai Lama. That the Dalai Lama has relinquished his political authority does not, however, mean an end to the reincarnation lineage within Tibetan Buddhism. It has even been suggested that he might identify the next Dalai Lama prior to his death or even that his successor might be elected by the Tibetan people (Jacoby and Terrone). What he has confirmed is that 'he will not be reborn in a Tibet controlled by the Chinese, even if it means he is the last Dalai Lama' (Cited Harvey). Meanwhile, the Dalai Lama also continues to fight peacefully for the freedom of Tibet. He promotes global awareness of the current situation in Tibet and in 1989 he was awarded the Nobel Peace Prize for this non-violent fight.

The Dalia Lama's three main commitments include:

1. Promotion of human values – compassion, forgiveness, tolerance, contentment and self-discipline.

2. Promotion of religious harmony and understanding among the world's major religious traditions.

3. Working to preserve Tibet's Buddhist culture of peace and non-violence.

Free Tibet protesters in London March 2018

Key term

Ahimsa: the Buddhist teaching that you should harm no living thing, non-violence

Key quotes

Tibetan people regard life, any life, as something very sacred, something holy and important, so even when a small insect is killed, we immediately respond with some feeling of compassion. This remains a force in our society. (Dalai Lama)

My religion is simple. My religion is kindness. (Dalai Lama)

quickfire

1.29 Why was the Dalai Lama awarded the Nobel Peace Prize?

quickfire

1.30 Why does the Dalai Lama advocate Socially Engaged Buddhism?

Specification content

The 14th Dalai Lama and the practical interpretation of Buddhist teachings for life in the West.

Under the leadership of the Dalai Lama, Tibetan Buddhism has become a global school of Buddhism. The Dalai Lama has established monasteries within India and eventually in other parts of the world. The Dalai Lama has been an ambassador speaking in many countries around the world about the values of Buddhism including peace and non-violent conflict. He has been pivotal in facilitating the growth of Tibetan Buddhism worldwide. Jacoby and Terrone suggest that he 'is a living symbol and embodiment of deep spirituality, social engagement and altruism'. As a living teacher he is venerated in Tibetan monasteries throughout the world.

A photograph of the Dalai Lama in Thrangu Tashi Monastery in Kathmandu, Nepal

The Dalai Lama's campaigns on environmental problems led him to become the first Nobel Laureate to be acknowledged for his concerns on this. He continues to promote environmental issues worldwide. His peace plan for Tibet includes a plan for conservation within Tibet because the Chinese government have destroyed huge areas of Tibetan forests leading to flooding as far away as India as the soil from the forests is being washed into the rivers. The Dalai Lama has highlighted the effect this action has had upon wildlife as its natural habitat is destroyed. It is clear to see the teachings of Buddhism, such as ahimsa, in action in the political campaigns of the Dalai Lama. The Socially Engaged Buddhism the Dalai Lama advocates can be seen clearly when he says, 'Our planet is our house, and we must keep it in order and take care of it if we are genuinely concerned about happiness for ourselves, our children, our friends, and other beings who share this great house with us.'

The practical interpretation of Buddhist teachings for life in the West

More recently, there has been evidence that the Tibetan religion is reviving in Tibet. In exile, the Dalai Lama set up Tibetan monasteries and education throughout the world, enabling Tibetan Buddhism to flourish outside Tibet. Within just two decades Tibetan Buddhism had established more centres and groups than all other Buddhist traditions and quadrupled the number of centres in Britain (Jacoby and Terrone). The Dalai Lama believed that there should be a strong education system available for Tibetans and made it his mission to develop this whilst in exile.

The Dalai Lama seeks common ground and plays a major role in Interfaith dialogue and is respected by Buddhists and non-Buddhists alike for his great wisdom and compassion. He has worked tirelessly to establish 'warm, mutually respectful relationships with leaders, social activists, psychotherapists, artists, musicians, and countless other individuals and groups from all walks of life' (Landaw and Bodian). Advocating a compassionate and Socially Engaged Buddhism, the Dalai Lama teaches that at the heart of the dharma is that you should 'Help others if you can; but if you cannot, at least refrain from harming others'. Being a great advocate for scientific research, the Dalia Lama says that if scripture says one thing and science says another, you would have to take the scientific view. Nevertheless, he sees no conflict between Buddhism and science. He is particularly interested in studies in brain activity and considering how they can develop Buddhist philosophy on consciousness and the mind. He supports the scientific study of advanced Tibetan practitioners, who are looking at the transformative nature of spiritual practices such as meditation.

Despite pictures and photographs of the Dalai Lama being banned by the PRC in Tibet after 1996, the face of the Dalai Lama has become very familiar to people throughout the world. His cheerful character is known to millions as a result of his presence on television and in the media. He has been the subject of numerous documentaries and the central figure in major films, *Kundun* and *Seven Years in Tibet*. Well over a hundred books have been authored by him *The Art of Happiness: A Handbook for the Living*; *Beyond Religion: Ethics for a Whole World* and *Freedom in Exile: The Autobiography of the Dalai Lama*. Meanwhile in Tibet, people resisted the ban on carrying his picture by placing empty photo frames on display to show their devotion to him. At the time of his 80th birthday his images became a little more tolerated in Tibet in order to avoid potential rioting by ordinary people.

He was the recipient of the Nobel Peace Prize in 1989 for his peaceful action in support of Tibetans.

The position of the Dalai Lama on the world stage has not been without controversy. He created a media stir when he claimed that if a woman was to succeed him, she would have to be 'very, very attractive' or she would 'be not much use'. For these comments the Dalai Lama has been accused of sexism, and spokespeople for equalities organisations expressed their disappointment that this comment was made by a role model who was meant to emanate wisdom and compassion. Nevertheless, it is as a result of the efforts and leadership of the Dalai Lama that Tibetan Buddhism with its unique, rich and diverse spirituality has now become a global phenomenon. As Merv Fowler suggests, the Chinese invasion of Tibet 'proved to be the single most dramatic event which has shaped the course of Buddhism in the twentieth century' (Fowler).

Key quotes

With the ever-growing impact of science on our lives, religion and spirituality have a greater role to play reminding us of our humanity. There is no contradiction between the two. Each gives us valuable insights into the other. Both science and the teachings of the Buddha tell us of the fundamental unity of all things. This understanding is crucial if we are to take positive and decisive action on the pressing global concern with the environment. (The Dalai Lama in his Nobel Peace Prize acceptance speech)

I pray for all of us, oppressor and friend, that together we succeed in building a better world through human understanding and love, and that in doing so we may reduce the pain and suffering of all sentient beings. (The Dalai Lama in his Nobel Peace Prize acceptance speech)

Key quotes

Under his guidance, children's schools, medical facilities, handicraft centres, and other cultural organisations have been established in India (and in other countries as well). In these and countless other ways, the Dalai Lama, through his promotion, support, and encouragement, has managed to preserve the Tibetan cultural identity despite the devastating destruction and genocide. (Landaw and Bodian)

… the Dalai Lama has become the world's most widely recognised Buddhist and a revered symbol for the Buddhist virtues of wisdom, compassion, tolerance, and respect. Even people who have no interest in religion recognise and respond to his goodness, simple humanity, and humour. He has truly become a Buddhist ambassador to the world. (Landaw and Bodian)

As a Buddhist monk, my concern extends to all members of the human family and, indeed, to all sentient beings who suffer. I believe all suffering is caused by ignorance. People inflict pain on others in the selfish pursuit of their happiness or satisfaction. Yet true happiness comes from a sense of brotherhood and sisterhood. We need to cultivate a universal responsibility for one another and the planet we share. Although I have found my own Buddhist religion helpful in generating love and compassion, even for those we consider our enemies, I am convinced that everyone can develop a good heart and a sense of universal responsibility with or without religion. (The Dalai Lama in his Nobel Peace Prize acceptance speech)

quickfire

1.31 Why do Tibetan Buddhists often carry a photograph of the Dalai Lama?

Key skills

Knowledge involves:

Selection of a range of (thorough) accurate and relevant information that is directly related to the specific demands of the question.

This means:

- Selecting relevant material for the question set

- Being focused in explaining and examining the material selected.

Understanding involves:

Explanation that is extensive, demonstrating depth and/or breadth with excellent use of evidence and examples including (where appropriate) thorough and accurate supporting use of sacred texts, sources of wisdom and specialist language.

This means:

- Effective use of examples and supporting evidence to establish the quality of your understanding

- Ownership of your explanation that expresses personal knowledge and understanding and NOT just reproducing a chunk of text from a book that you have rehearsed and memorised.

AO1 Developing skills

It is now important to consider the information that has been covered in this section; however, the information in its raw form is too extensive and so has to be processed in order to meet the requirements of the examination. This can be done by practising more advanced skills associated with AO1. For assessment objective 1 (AO1), which involves demonstrating 'knowledge' and 'understanding' skills, we are going to focus on different ways in which the skills can be demonstrated effectively, and also, refer to how the performance of these skills is measured (see generic band descriptors for A2 [WJEC] AO1 or A Level [Eduqas] AO1).

▶ **Your next task is this:** Below is a brief summary of **a practical interpretation of Buddhist teachings for the West by the Dalai Lama**. You want to explain this in an essay but as it stands at present it is too brief. In order that you demonstrate more depth of understanding, develop this summary by providing examples that will help you explain it further. Aim for 200 words in total.

The Dalai Lama seeks common ground with the West and is respected by Buddhists and non-Buddhists alike for his great wisdom and compassion. He has worked tirelessly to establish 'warm, mutually respectful relationships with leaders, social activists, psychotherapists, artists, musicians, and countless other individuals and groups from all walks of life' (Landaw and Bodian). He advocates a compassionate and Socially Engaged Buddhism and the notion of ahimsa. He also is a great advocate for scientific research and sees no conflict between Buddhism and science.

When you have completed the task, refer to the band descriptors for A2 (WJEC) or A Level (Eduqas) and, in particular, have a look at the demands described in the higher band descriptors towards which you should be aspiring. Ask yourself:

- Does my work demonstrate thorough, accurate and relevant knowledge and understanding of religion and belief?

- Is my work coherent (consistent or make logical sense), clear and well organised?

- Will my work, when developed, be an extensive and relevant response which is specific to the focus of the task?

- Does my work have extensive depth and/or suitable breadth and have excellent use of evidence and examples?

- If appropriate to the task, does my response have thorough and accurate reference to sacred texts and sources of wisdom?

- Are there any insightful connections to be made with other elements of my course?

- Will my answer, when developed and extended to match what is expected in an examination answer, have an extensive range of views of scholars/schools of thought?

- When used, is specialist language and vocabulary both thorough and accurate?

Issues for analysis and evaluation

The relative success of Dalai Lama and Thich Nhat Hanh in ensuring the relevance of Buddhism in the modern world

The real issue here seems to be to what extent are the Dalai Lama and Thich Nhat Hanh expert exponents of skilful means in their presentation of Buddhism? In order to establish Buddhist principles in the modern world, there needs to be a careful application that accounts for secularisation, war, poverty, famine, technological advances and so forth. How could a message of a traditionally isolated and monastic tradition become relevant?

Regardless of how representative they are of Buddhism as a whole, it could be argued that the Dalai Lama and Thich Nhat Hanh have been successful in making Buddhism relevant in the modern world by serving as 'fingers pointing at the moon'. In other words, although there be many ways in which a monastic form of religion is not relevant to the modern world, they have still managed to succeed in sending a message of compassion to everyone in what they do and what they teach and this is, arguably, one half of the message of Mahayana Buddhism.

However, it could be contested that whilst they have done this, this does not mean they have been totally successful in differentiating what is 'Buddhist' about their approach since humanitarian and other religious figures and organisations have done the same. For example, Gandhi, Martin Luther King, Mother Teresa and movements like UNICEF, United Nations and the Red Cross. Indeed, it could also be questioned that whilst they represent Tibetan Buddhism and Vietnamese Thien (Zen), how far are the Dalai Lama and Thich Nhat Hanh successful in making the tenets of Theravada or Pure Land Buddhism relevant in the modern world? Have they been successful in promoting the diversity and richness found within Buddhist traditions worldwide? Some would argue that the Dalai Lama and Thich Nhat Hanh have only promoted a very simplistic and populist form of Buddhism that lacks philosophical depth and practical, technical substance. Their forms of Buddhism have become acceptable in the modern world simply because they present universally positive principles and have not made any attempt to present specific Buddhist teachings. This line of argument could also suggest that the beliefs of the Dalai Lama and Thich Nhat Hanh are only representative of a minority within Buddhism. They have therefore not made Buddhism as a whole, relevant in the modern world.

On the contrary, it could be argued that the Dalai Lama and Thich Nhat Hanh can be seen as outstandingly successful in making Buddhism relevant in the modern world because of the way they connect and communicate with many people and many nations regardless of nationality, ethnicity, status or gender. Moreover, they are willing to meet people where they are and not from the 'pulpit' of Buddhism.

How far has the work of the Dalai Lama affected modern China's view of Tibetan Buddhism?

This section covers AO2 content and skills

Specification content

The relative success of Dalai Lama and Thich Nhat Hanh in ensuring the relevance of Buddhism in the modern world.

Key quotes

To find solutions to the environmental crisis and violent conflicts that confront us in the 21st century, we need to seek new answers. Even though I am a Buddhist monk, I believe that these solutions lie beyond religion in the promotion of a concept I call secular ethics. (Dalai Lama)

Compassion is the radicalism of our time. (Dalai Lama)

My religion is very simple. My religion is kindness. (Dalai Lama)

AO2 Activity

As you read through this section try to do the following:

1. Pick out the different lines of argument that are presented in the text and identify any evidence given in support.

2. For each line of argument try to evaluate whether or not you think this is strong (convincing) or weak (unconvincing).

3. Think of any questions you may wish to raise in response to the arguments.

This activity will help you to start thinking critically about what you read and help you to evaluate the effectiveness of different arguments and from this develop your own observations, opinions and points of view that will help with any conclusions that you make in your answers to the AO2 questions that arise.

Key quote

There are many reasons for us to be hopeful. Recognition of universal human rights, including the right to self-determination, has expanded beyond anything imagined a century ago. There is growing international consensus in support of gender equality and respect for women. Particularly among the younger generation, there is a widespread rejection of war as a means of solving problems. Across the world, many are doing valuable work to prevent terrorism, recognising the depths of misunderstanding and the divisive idea of 'us' and 'them' that is so dangerous. (Dalai Lama)

The modern media world requires a simple message and an engaging messenger – do either the Dalai Lama or Thich Nhat Hanh fit the bill?

AO2 Activity

List some conclusions that could be drawn from the AO2 reasoning from the above text; try to aim for at least three different possible conclusions. Consider each of the conclusions and collect brief evidence to support each conclusion from the AO1 and AO2 material for this topic. Select the conclusion that you think is most convincing and explain why it is so. Try to contrast this with the weakest conclusion in the list, justifying your argument with clear reasoning and evidence.

The Dalia Lama is well known for his acceptance of science and the secular world, indeed, stating 'solutions to the environmental crisis and violent conflicts that confront us in the 21st century ... lie beyond religion in the promotion of a concept I call secular ethics'.

Nonetheless, in advocating Buddhism, just how far have the Dalai Lama and Thich Nhat Hanh engaged with and attracted attention as media celebrities rather than as advocates of Buddhism in the modern world? Their appearances on TV and in the media could be taken either way as promoting Buddhism or their own personal cause. Perhaps the latter conclusion would be harsh but it does raise the question once again of the 'type' of Buddhism they are promoting.

There is no doubt that the Dalai Lama and Thich Nhat Hanh are seen by many as the key international faces and voices of Buddhism, ensuring that it remains relevant in the modern world. Through international travel, interviews and by making themselves entirely accessible to all forms of modern media, the Dalai Lama and Thich Nhat Hanh have ensured the continuing relevance of Buddhism. As authors of numerous best-selling populist books on Buddhism, both the Dalai Lama and Thich Nhat Hanh have brought Buddhism to a mass audience including many young people. The Dalai Lama and Thich Nhat Hanh have given Buddhism a platform on the world stage in political and social matters, from issues of war and peace to the environment. They are the most well-known representatives of what Thich Nhat Hanh coined 'Socially Engaged Buddhism'.

Whilst only fully representative of their own Buddhist traditions, the Dalai Lama and Thich Nhat Hanh have been very successful in making key Buddhist teaching accessible in the modern world. The modern media world requires a simple message and an engaging messenger both of which are provided by the Dalai Lama and Thich Nhat Hanh. In particular, Thich Nhat Hanh's mild, humble and gentle manner combined with his great wisdom is of great appeal to the general masses. He presents a very down-to-earth and realistic form of Buddhism and has inspired millions through his accessible writings. His work on mindfulness is undoubtedly far-reaching and has been effective the world over. In contrast, the Dalai Lama is treated with greater formal 'reverence' due to his status claim as Tulku but also his position as spokesperson for Tibetan Buddhism and the Tibetan people in general – almost similar to a 'Royal' figure. His influence, as well as to the general masses as times, appears geared more towards dignitaries, celebrities and media sources.

Therefore, there can be absolutely no doubt that the Dalai Lama and Thich Nhat Hanh are both very recognisable figures in the modern world. We have discussed the issue of the 'types' of Buddhism they present but there is also the issue that their influence and status or recognition are two separate things; but that does not mean that what they have to say regarding Buddhism is either fully listened to or fully understood. The Dalia Lama may protest against war, conflict and the oppression and the plight of his people but have things really moved on in terms of the cause of Tibet? Thich Nhat Hanh may have been influential in promoting mindfulness worldwide but some Buddhist scholars have questioned the nature of the Western use and application of meditation as not strictly speaking reflective of the true nature of Buddhism, if distinctively Buddhist at all!

In conclusion we can see that the Dalai Lama and Thich Nhat Hanh have both enjoyed great success in promoting Buddhism to a modern audience. On the one hand, some would interpret this as a wonderful example of the application of skilful means and re-affirmation that the Buddha's message is for all times and places. On the other hand, some would be more cautious and say that a more accurate picture is that we have a diluted version of Buddhism in nature that is universally accepted. Just how far the elements of dogma and practical application of Buddhism are balanced is, however, an age-old tension within Buddhism from the forest and village-dwelling monks of ancient Sri Lanka to the universal message of a wisdom and insight that is imbued with compassion in Mahayana Buddhism.

The extent to which the Dalai Lama and Thich Nhat Hanh have developed new and innovative expressions of Buddhism

We can see from our earlier analysis and evaluation that one issue regarding the life and work of both the Dalai Lama and Thich Nhat Hanh has been to question the nature of the type of Buddhism they present to the world. It had been suggested that rather than new and innovative expressions of Buddhism, have the Dalai Lama and Thich Nhat Hanh only presented a very much simplified expression of Buddhism for the masses? The other side of the coin was to suggest that the Dalai Lama and Thich Nhat Hanh have not promoted Buddhism per se, but rather, they have used skilful means and adapted traditional Buddhism to fit in with the modern world. Here we need to consider whether or not in using skilful means the result has in fact been the emergence of a new and innovative expression of Buddhism?

One line of argument is that the Dalai Lama and Thich Nhat Hanh have only given new and innovative expressions of Tibetan Buddhism and Thien (Zen) Buddhism and, as such, they are not representative of Theravada, Pure Land or Nichiren Buddhism. In this sense they cannot have developed new and innovative expressions of Buddhism according to some. Nevertheless, this point could be contended quite easily by pointing out that firstly there is no single, unique expression of Buddhism and that to pursue the grail of a universal Buddhism is futile. This firstly, means that their own 'blends' of Buddhism can in fact be seen as unique, new and innovative. Secondly, even if they are not representative of Theravada, Pure Land or Nichiren Buddhism, this does not mean that they cannot be seen as new and innovative expressions of Buddhism.

However, the real issue for some people could be that there is a question raised as to what both the Dalai Lama and Thich Nhat Hanh present: is there very much that is actually Buddhist in what they have written and said in terms of the importance of compassion, smiling, walking and being kind? Even if this is acknowledged as vaguely Buddhist, it is hardly revolutionary and overtly distinctive.

Moreover, the Dalai Lama and Thich Nhat Hanh appear to have only developed new and innovative expressions in very small, niche areas of Buddhism; in mindfulness (possibly without a Buddhist mark to it) and in the universal principle of non-violence. On the one hand, it could be argued that Dalai Lama and Thich Nhat Hanh have simply presented selected traditional expressions of Buddhism to a modern world that is open to and familiar with such concepts: neither meditation nor pacifism are new and widely accepted. On the other hand, the Dalai Lama and Thich Nhat Hanh could be seen to have simply presented traditional expressions of Buddhism to a modern world in a new and innovative way – almost like a marketing exercise in re-packaging. Therefore, they seem like new and innovative ideas whereas in reality they are not.

An alternative line of argument could be that the interaction of the Dalai Lama and Thich Nhat Hanh with society is strictly a secular one. For example, the Dalai Lama wrote, 'I believe that to meet the challenge of our times, human beings will have to develop a greater sense of universal responsibility. Each of us must learn to work not for his or her self, family or nation, but for the benefit of all mankind. Universal responsibility is the real key to human survival.' This openly non-Buddhist statement seems to be truly innovative from a religious world view. Likewise, Thich Nhat Hanh writes, 'When we come into contact with the other person, our thoughts and actions should express our mind of compassion, even if that person says and does things that are not easy to accept. We practise in this way until we see clearly that our love is not contingent upon the other person being lovable.' This also appears to be a more secular message of tolerance.

Specification content

The extent to which the Dalai Lama and Thich Nhat Hanh have developed new and innovative expressions of Buddhism.

Study tip

Essays in Religious Studies A Level usually test your knowledge and understanding (AO1) or your ability to evaluate, make judgements and assess the value of different ideas or concepts (AO2). When approaching an AO2 answer, make sure you critically analyse and evaluate any AO1 evidence that you use.

Different face but same old story?

AO2 Activity

As you read through this section try to do the following:

1. Pick out the different lines of argument that are presented in the text and identify any evidence given in support.

2. For each line of argument try to evaluate whether or not you think this is strong (convincing) or weak (unconvincing).

3. Think of any questions you may wish to raise in response to the arguments.

This activity will help you to start thinking critically about what you read and help you to evaluate the effectiveness of different arguments and from this develop your own observations, opinions and points of view that will help with any conclusions that you make in your answers to the AO2 questions that arise.

Key quotes

When we come into contact with the other person, our thoughts and actions should express our mind of compassion, even if that person says and does things that are not easy to accept. We practise in this way until we see clearly that our love is not contingent upon the other person being lovable. (Thich Nhat Hanh)

Instead of caring for one another, we place most of our efforts for happiness in pursuing individual material consumption. We have become so engrossed in this pursuit that, without knowing it, we have neglected to foster the most basic human needs of love, kindness and cooperation. (Dalai Lama)

Walk as if you are kissing the Earth with your feet. (Thich Nhat Tanh)

People deal too much with the negative, with what is wrong. Why not try and see positive things, to just touch those things and make them bloom? (Thich Nhat Tanh)

The mission of the Mind and Life Institute is to alleviate suffering and promote flourishing by integrating science with contemplative practice and wisdom traditions. (The Mind and Life Institute)

AO2 Activity

List some conclusions that could be drawn from the AO2 reasoning from the above text; try to aim for at least three different possible conclusions. Consider each of the conclusions and collect brief evidence to support each conclusion from the AO1 and AO2 material for this topic. Select the conclusion that you think is most convincing and explain why it is so. Try to contrast this with the weakest conclusion in the list, justifying your argument with clear reasoning and evidence.

In addition, it could be argued that new and innovative expressions of Buddhism are to be found elsewhere, not in what individuals have to say, but in movements such as Triratna. Certainly, the Dalai Lama and Thich Nhat Hanh are effective communicators of Buddhism, but there is nothing new or innovative in what they have to teach in contrast to individuals like Sangharakshita. Indeed, the aim of the Triratna movement is to foster and support 'a worldwide movement of people who try to engage with the Buddha's teachings in the conditions of the modern world'.

Just how great is the achievement of either Thich Nhat Hanh and the Dalai Lama? How do we measure their success and against what?

[Indeed, this argument could be presented against either evaluation in the AO2 section.] However, some could say that in making the message of Buddhism accessible to the widest possibly global audience, have not the Dalai Lama and Thich Nhat Hanh indubitably presented a new and innovative expression of Buddhism in the same way as Triratna?

There is no doubt that Thich Nhat Hanh and the Dalai Lama have been leading proponents of a Socially Engaged Buddhism which is aimed at giving to Buddhism a new and innovative expression. New and innovative expressions of Buddhism require a new understanding of what is key to Buddhism; in terms of Socially Engaged Buddhism this message is one of praxis. Through their understanding of kindness, compassion and non-harming, this has been achieved by the Dalai Lama and Thich Nhat Hanh. However, once again the questions of injustice and social engagement are not exclusive to Zen or Tibetan Buddhism. Buddhist history is permeated with occasions of social engagement.

Another argument supporting innovation is the shift from abstract and metaphysical ideas such as karma, rebirth and even enlightenment, towards kindness, compassion and non-harm is a new and innovative expression of Buddhism for which the Dalai Lama and Thich Nhat Hanh are responsible. Once again, this is not entirely 'new' or exclusive to the teachings of the Dalai Lama and Thich Nhat Hanh. There is, however, a case for Nhat Hanh's model of 'Plum Village' being a radical departure from the traditional separation of monastery and society. It could be argued to have broken away from the exclusive monastic-village model into a more integrated system of Buddhist life. However, once again, this is not entirely new and has had much greater force with Triratna. There is also a case for the Dali Lama's unique founding of the Mind and Life Institute, which is a new and innovative engagement of Buddhism with the modern scientific world to identify the benefits of meditation. Nonetheless, the innovation is contained within a Tibetan Buddhist perspective and, albeit a worldwide phenomenon, some would suggest once again it falls foul of the criticism that it dilutes the final goal of Buddhism.

In conclusion, it cannot be denied that there are many examples of outstanding work, achievements and contributions that both the Dalai Lama and Thich Nhat Hanh have made. They have simply continued to use skilful means in providing more fingers pointing to the moon; however, it would be possible to argue from this that the purpose of their work is not to establish new and innovative forms of Buddhism but simply to engage with the ever-changing and volatile modern world around us. In this sense the starting point of our evaluation is flawed.

AO2 Developing skills

It is now important to consider the information that has been covered in this section; however, the information in its raw form is too extensive and so has to be processed in order to meet the requirements of the examination. This can be done by practising more advanced skills associated with AO2. For assessment objective 2 (AO2), which involves 'critical analysis' and 'evaluation' skills, we are going to focus on different ways in which the skills can be demonstrated effectively, and also, refer to how the performance of these skills is measured (see generic band descriptors for A2 [WJEC] AO2 or A Level [Eduqas] AO2).

▶ **Your next task is this:** Below is an argument concerning **the new and innovative expressions of Buddhism introduced by the Dalai Lama and Thich Nhat Hanh**. You need to respond to this argument by thinking of three key questions you could ask the writer that would challenge their view and force them to defend their argument.

Simply by making the message of Buddhism accessible to the widest possible global audience, have not the Dalai Lama and Thich Nhat Hanh indubitably presented a new and innovative expression of Buddhism? The shift from abstract and metaphysical ideas such as karma, rebirth and even enlightenment, towards kindness, compassion and non-harm is a new and innovative expression of Buddhism for which the Dalai Lama and Thich Nhat Hanh are responsible.

When you have completed the task, refer to the band descriptors for A2 (WJEC) or A Level (Eduqas) and, in particular, have a look at the demands described in the higher band descriptors towards which you should be aspiring. Ask yourself:

- Is my answer a confident critical analysis and perceptive evaluation of the issue?
- Is my answer a response that successfully identifies and thoroughly addresses the issues raised by the question set?
- Does my work show an excellent standard of coherence, clarity and organisation?
- Will my work, when developed, contain thorough, sustained and clear views that are supported by extensive, detailed reasoning and/or evidence?
- Are the views of scholars/schools of thought used extensively, appropriately and in context?
- Does my answer convey a confident and perceptive analysis of the nature of any possible connections with other elements of my course?
- When used, is specialist language and vocabulary both thorough and accurate?

Key skills
Analysis involves:

Identifying issues raised by the materials in the AO1, together with those identified in the AO2 section, and presents sustained and clear views, either of scholars or from a personal perspective ready for evaluation.

This means:

- That your answers are able to identify key areas of debate in relation to a particular issue
- That you can identify, and comment upon, the different lines of argument presented by others
- That your response comments on the overall effectiveness of each of these areas or arguments.

Evaluation involves:

Considering the various implications of the issues raised based upon the evidence gleaned from analysis and provides an extensive detailed argument with a clear conclusion.

This means:

- That your answer weighs up the consequences of accepting or rejecting the various and different lines of argument analysed
- That your answer arrives at a conclusion through a clear process of reasoning.

This section covers AO1 content and skills

Specification content

The development of key Buddhist traditions in Japan.

The Shitennoji Temple in Osaka built by Prince Shotoku between 574 and 622 CE.

Key quote

Japanese Buddhists of varying contexts drew upon Buddhist ideas and practices to make sense of their lives, to solve problems and to create a meaningful world – a cosmos – out of chaos. (Deal and Ruppert)

Key terms

Buddhisms: a term which reflects the view that Buddhism is not one single unified belief system as with some other world religions

Kami: the divine energy found in the natural world and divine beings which followers of Shinto practise devotion towards

Mappo: the third of three ages following the Buddha which is the age of the decay of the Dhamma

Shinto: the indigenous religion of Japan which has no single founder or sacred text and which has ritual rather than belief as its focus

A: Historical development of Japanese Buddhism

The development of key Buddhist traditions in Japan

The route of Buddhism into Japan is usually accepted to be as follows: from China, Buddhism came to Korea and then from Korea to Japan. There is much debate about when this took place but later chronicles put the date as 552 CE. In that year a royal delegation from Korea arrived in Japan with a declaration praising the Dhamma of the Buddha. This was accompanied by a gold and copper statue of Buddha, other Buddhist artefacts used in worship, and several volumes of Sutras. At that time in Japan, the main religious tradition was – and remains – Shinto. This focuses on the worship of kami, a broad term which refers to the divine and awe-inspiring energy found in a wide variety of features in the natural world. 'Kami' can also refer to individual divine beings. Shinto 'did not have a strong ethical dimension, but it had a developed appreciation of natural beauty, and a concern for ritual purity' (Harvey). From the outset, Shinto and Buddhism co-existed in harmony and aspects of each religious tradition have pervaded the other.

After its introduction into Japan, Buddhism quickly attracted followers and in 604 CE Prince Shotoku – himself a devout Buddhist – wrote a national constitution which stated that the three refuges – the Buddha, the Dhamma and the sangha – should be honoured. A unique feature of Buddhism in Japan is that it had close links, from the outset, with the ruling classes who funded the building of Buddhist temples and monasteries and the work of Buddhist monks. One result of this was that from 552 CE onwards the development of Buddhism in Japan was heavily influenced by what was happening in the area of internal politics in Japan, particularly by the feuds and wars between ruling families.

Modern scholarship into the religious traditions of the world increasingly questions the presentation of Buddhism as a single and unified system. Instead it is suggested that it is better to think of Buddhisms. This means that core Buddhist concepts such as the Four Noble Truths, the three lakshanas and the three refuges both shape, and are in turn very much shaped by, the complex mixture of indigenous culture, traditions and social norms. This applies to the variety of 'Buddhisms' found in Japan. Here, another factor was the impact made by individual Buddhist monks and their followers who travelled the country, teaching and founding sects which each had their own set of beliefs and practices.

One important concept which forms the background to the development of key Buddhist traditions in Japan is that of mappo. This refers to the third of three ages following the Buddha. The first period of one thousand years was the age of true Dhamma, the second period of one thousand years was the age of copied Dhamma, and the third period of ten thousand years was the age of mappo – the age of the decay of the Dhamma. The year when mappo began was calculated in a variety of ways by Buddhists in Japan but by the 11th century CE, social and political turmoil, natural disasters and conflict all seemed to show that the age of mappo had certainly started. 'Japanese religiosity after this time can only be understood in the context of one overriding problem – how can one be a Buddhist, how is the Buddhist religion to survive, during the Last Days – the era of cosmic and religious disaster when apparently none of the normal sources for religious inspiration can be relied upon.' (Williams)

Study tip

In order to gain a greater understanding of the key Buddhists traditions in Japan, it would be a good idea to research Japanese history in greater detail.

Buddhism became fully established in Japan in a number of temples and attached monasteries. Here, monks and nuns trained for many years studying the Dhamma and practising meditation. An important factor for a person in determining where to train and to be ordained was the **lineage** of the monastery and its teachers. This meant simply that the type of Buddhism being taught had been handed down from, and was true to, that of the main teacher or founder of the monastery. At the same time, it has to be remembered that the different Buddhisms in Japan did not develop in isolation. Monks might start being part of one tradition and then move to another tradition. They might also travel to different parts of Japan, to Korea and China. '**Networking monks** ... carried Buddhist beliefs between geographical and culture centres and peripheries.' (Deal and Ruppert)

Over the centuries the followers of different Buddhisms in Japan were often in conflict. Given the power of the temples and attached monasteries, and the allegiance which each gained from various rival feuding rulers, there was often armed conflict. One notable instance was in 1571 and the destruction of the **Enryaku-ji** temple and monastery complex with its over three thousand buildings on the mountain overlooking Kyoto. A local warlord wanted to end the power of the monks and their warrior supporters at the temple because they supported opposing clans. With an army of 30,000 men the entire complex was destroyed and some 20,000 civilians including the monks were killed.

AO1 Activity

After reading the section on 'The development of key Buddhist traditions in Japan' identify and list examples which show important background information regarding Buddhism in Japan.

This practises the AO1 skill of being able to show a thorough, accurate and relevant knowledge and understanding of religion and belief.

quickfire

3.1 In what year was Buddhism introduced to Japan?

Key terms

Enryaku-ji: the temple/monastery complex on the top of Mount Hiei which was destroyed in 1571

Lineage: the type of Buddhism being taught had been handed down from, and was true to, that of the main teacher or founder of the monastery

Networking monks: monks who carried Buddhist beliefs between geographical and culture centres and peripheries

Enryaku-ji being set on fire and monks being massacred.

Specification content

Zen, Pure Land and Nichiren.

Key quotes

Rinzai for the shogun; Soto for the peasant. (A Japanese saying)

We have seen many signs in heaven and earth: a famine, a plague, the whole country is filled with misery. Horses and cows are dying on the roadsides, and so are men, and there is no one to bury them … Look around at the misery of the age, at the decay of Buddhism. (Nichiren)

Key terms

Kamakura period of Japanese history: the period 1185–1333 which started through government by the first Shogun

Zazen: meditation which involves just sitting in the correct posture and letting go of both mind and body

Zen, Pure Land and Nichiren

Before its destruction, the Enryaku-ji temple and monastery complex had been one of the main centres of Buddhism in Japan. During the Kamakura period of Japanese history (1185–1333) the founders of three key Buddhist traditions in Japan – Zen, Pure Land and Nichiren – each had close associations with the Buddhism practised at Enryaku-ji.

Zen Buddhism had its origins with the semi-legendary monk Bodhidharma who in the 5th century CE travelled from India to China where he began teaching what became known as Ch'an Buddhism. The Chinese word 'Ch'an' and the Japanese word 'Zen' are both derived from the Sanskrit word 'dhyana' which is usually translated as meditation. Bodhidharma also founded Shao-lin monastery most widely known today for its martial arts training. His lineage continued as did the Ch'an tradition although it split into different variations. During the Kamakura period, two Japanese monks Eisai (1141–1215) and Dogen (1200–1253) travelled to China separately and returned bringing Ch'an back with them.

Returning in 1191, based on what he had studied, Eisai founded the first form of Zen known as Rinzai. In addition to meditation this cultivated martial arts, observance of ceremonial rules and defence of the state. It quickly found favour with the educated warrior and political classes.

Finding the approach of Rinzai unsatisfactory, Dogen returning from China in 1227, and based on what he had studied, founded the second form of Zen known as Soto. This rejected any dealings with politics and martial arts. Instead it upheld a life of poverty and the practice of zazen or sitting meditation. Soto became more widely popular with people in general.

Pure Land Buddhism had also had a long history in China with one of its key founders being Hui Yuan who lived in the 6th century CE. He had a vision of Amitabha Buddha and taught that meditating on Amitabha Buddha alone provided the path for enlightenment in the perfect heaven or Pure Land which Amitabha had created. Aspects of the Pure Land tradition became integrated into various Buddhisms in Japan from the 9th century CE onwards and the focus remained on Amitabha – which in Japanese is Amida.

Honen (1133–1212) had been a monk at Enryaku-ji monastery from the age of nine. He became increasingly concerned at how difficult enlightenment had become in the age of mappo even if a person were to be as he was, learned and wise in the Dhamma. Although he had distinguished himself as a scholar, he wrote: 'I am one whose eyes are blind to the truth and whose feet, paralysed, are unable to walk the Holy Path. I bitterly regret that day and night my thoughts turn in the direction of prestige and money.' Having read many Pure Land sacred texts, Honen left the monastery aged 43 to preach the Pure Land message of devotion to Amida Buddha more widely. His followers – particularly Shinran (1173–1262) – continued to develop his ideas and the Pure Land tradition thus became widely established. This 'simple and attractive teaching … offered salvation to those who could justify themselves neither by learning nor by good works'. (Eliot)

Nichiren Buddhism also emerged during the Kamakura period. Nichiren (1222–1282) had been a monk at Enryaku-ji monastery. He came from a poor background of a fishing family and became a monk at the age of eleven. His beliefs and teachings were very strongly influenced by a firm belief in the reality of the age of mappo in the country.

Nichiren appealed directly to the military government with an essay on how to bring about peace in the country and how to establish truth. He was critical of the different Buddhisms in Japan calling Zen 'the heavenly demon' and Pure Land 'Hell without interval'. It was, he argued, the duty of the government to suppress false Buddhisms and in this way bring about peace through establishing truth. That truth could be found only in the Lotus Sutra, and through faith in the Lotus Sutra which was the perfect and final truth. He wrote: 'one Scripture must be the great king of all Buddhist Scriptures'. When this happened in Japan, then peace and truth could be spread over all the world. Nichiren saw himself as a prophet and perhaps even a bodhisattva: 'I, Nichiren, am the master and lord of the sovereign, as well as of all the Buddhists of other schools.'

The subsequent history and development of Zen, Pure Land and Nichiren is complex and not linear. However, it is these three which can be identified as key Buddhist traditions in Japan.

The central practice of koans in Zen traditions

The origins of Zen are found, according to some traditions, in the story of the **Flower and Smile Sermon**. The Buddha taught the Dhamma each day but on one occasion facing the assembled sangha, he sat in silence. Everyone waited for the sermon to begin, but instead the Buddha picked a lotus and held it up saying nothing. Amongst the assembled sangha Mahakasyapa gave a subtle smile. This indicated to the Buddha that Mahakasyapa had received the Dhamma directly in a mind to mind communication. This is explained further in a saying attributed to Bodhidharma: 'A special transmission outside the sacred texts, not founded upon words and letters. Directly it points to the mind. Seeing one's own nature, one attains Buddhahood.'

For many followers of Zen, Bodhidharma's saying explains that the Buddha-nature is everyone and everything. All beings, sentient and non-sentient are the Buddha-nature. From the perspective of the Zen tradition, enlightenment takes place once this is fully grasped.

Some followers of Zen believe that sacred texts can be of help whilst others reject this completely. Some use chanting mantras and others do not. Followers of Soto tend to focus entirely on zazen – just sitting in the correct posture and letting go of both mind and body. Overall, the generally accepted pattern is that the 'special transmission' from mind to mind requires that the student of Zen has a teacher for whom enlightenment has already taken place.

The Rinzai tradition followed other practices which had their origins in Ch'an Buddhism. This approach taught that enlightenment could happen suddenly in any situation for someone who was trained. In particular it could happen when someone was exposed to a paradoxical statement breaking ordinary discursive thought. Such statements are generally called koans and many of these were written down and passed on from teacher to student over the centuries. Sometimes the koan is followed by a short poem and a commentary. Most often koans can be found in the form of a dialogue or set of questions and answers between the Zen teacher and the Zen student. Having heard the koan the student is left to contemplate it in all its aspects possibly during zazen. Further dialogue might take place with the Zen teacher but the key point is that it is left for the student to comprehend the koan.

Key quotes

Buffalo Koan: To give an example, it is like a buffalo passing through a window. Its head, horns and four legs have all passed through. Why is it that its tail cannot?

Ts'ui Yen's Eyebrows Koan: At the end of the summer retreat Ts'ui Yen said to the community, 'All summer long I've been talking to you brothers; look and see if my eyebrows are still there.' Pao Fu said, 'The thief's heart is cowardly.' Ch'ang Ch'ing said, 'Grown.' Yun Men said, 'A barrier.'

Specification content
The central practice of koans in Zen traditions.

quickfire

3.2 To which monastery can Eisai, Dogen, Honen and Nichiren be linked?

Key term

Flower and Smile Sermon: the silent sermon given by the Buddha by holding up a lotus which was recognised by Mahakasyapa who smiled

Key quotes

What Mahakasyapa understood I, alas, do not know! The story, however, indicates the direct, wordless nature of much Zen teaching, cutting through the trappings of discursive thought. (Williams)

Grass, trees, and lands are mind; thus they are sentient beings. Because they are sentient beings they are Buddha-nature. Sun, moon, and stars are mind; thus they are sentient beings; thus they are Buddha-nature. (Dogen)

Key terms

Mu Koan: the koan which asks
whether a dog has the Buddha-nature
or not

Visualisation practice: a form of
meditation which involves creating a
picture in one's mind of, for example,
the Pure Land created by Amida

Key quote

Make your whole body a mass of
doubt, and with your 360 bones and
joints and your 84,000 hair follicles,
concentrate on this one word 'Mu'.
Day and night, keep digging into it.
Don't consider it to be nothingness.
Don't think in terms of 'has' or 'has
not.' It is like swallowing a red-hot
iron ball. You try to vomit it out, but
you cannot. **(Huikai)**

quickfire

3.3 Who smiled when the Buddha held up
the lotus?

Specification content

The central practice of nembutsu in
Pure Land traditions.

'The purpose of the koan is to break the habitual thought processes of the mind; to
short-circuit our logical thinking so that pure intuition can arise.' (Baggott) Instant
enlightenment might then take place either immediately or after a period of time.

There are many examples of koans but in the Rinzai tradition the first one given to
the Zen student is the **Mu Koan** taken from a collection called 'Gateless Gate' by
the Chinese Zen Buddhist Huikai (1183–1260).

'A monk asked Master Zhaou-Zhou: "Has a dog the Buddha-nature or has it not?"
Master Zhaou-Zhou said "Mu".'

There have been many commentaries on this koan over the centuries but these
are not designed to explain it but rather to ensure that further points arise which
might then move the student beyond logic. Thus, the word 'mu' can be translated
as 'no' or 'nothing'. However, as we have seen, according to Zen Buddhism,
the Buddha-nature is all sentient beings. If that is the case then surely Master
Zhaou-Zhou should have answered 'yes' instead of 'Mu'? Why did he answer
'Mu'? Tradition states that Huikai struggled with this koan for six years before his
enlightenment took place when a woman hit him on the head with a broom.

The dog has or does not have the Buddha-nature.

Study tip

In order to gain a better understanding of koans, it would be a good idea to
research collections of koans in greater detail.

The central practice of nembutsu in Pure Land traditions

Before Honen, many Buddhist monks in Japan had incorporated devotion to
Amida Buddha alongside their other practices. Sacred texts about Amida would
be read and studied, and above all, there would be meditation which included
visualisation practice. This meant that monks would focus on creating in their
mind a spiritual vision of Amida or of the Pure Land which Amida had created.
Whilst at Enryaku-ji monastery, Honen followed this practice. However, he felt that
this was not enough, as enlightenment for him was as far away as ever.

In the age of mappo, Honen came to believe that people should rely on Amida
Buddha. When he left the monastery, Honen taught that relying on Amida did not
need to be done through studying sacred texts or visualisation.

But who is Amida Buddha? This is explained in various Pure Land Sutras. The Buddha explained that Amida was originally called Dharmakara and made 48 vows about himself and the Pure Land he would create. In each of these vows he declared that if what he vowed was not accomplished then he would not become a Buddha. In one of these vows he declared that he would not become a Buddha, unless those who called on his name even as few as ten times and entrusted themselves to him, were able to achieve rebirth in the Pure Land. From there, they could then easily achieve enlightenment or become in turn a bodhisattva or a Buddha. The Buddha concluded by stating that Amida had become a Buddha and that therefore the vows were all fulfilled.

Honen's understanding of this teaching was that by taking refuge in Amida, a person was guaranteed rebirth in the Pure Land. In order to take refuge in Amida, it was necessary to recite the nembutsu. This is a very short phrase: 'namu amida butsu' which is generally translated as 'I take refuge in Amida Buddha'.

As can be imagined, this teaching was immensely popular owing to its simplicity and to the fact that nothing else in terms of devotional practice, or even a moral life, was required. It was recorded that Honen himself recited the nembutsu sixty thousand times a day. However, there was no difference between a very devout and holy monk reciting the nembutsu and a lay person who was the worst of sinners reciting the nembutsu. The outcome would be exactly the same: rebirth in the Pure Land.

Honen did not discourage his followers from having other devotions or from studying other sacred texts. In addition, he remained a monk and a number of monks became his followers. Honen was also concerned to counter the criticism that his teaching was antinomian – it seemed to do away with the need for any rules of moral conduct at all. After all, theoretically a person could break all the dasa sila as much as they wanted as long as they then recited the nembutsu. He wrote: 'while believing that even a man guilty of the ten evil deeds and the five deadly sins may be born into the Pure Land, let us, as far as we are concerned, not commit even the smallest sins'.

One of Honen's main followers was Shinran who left the monastery of Enryaku-ji at the same time as he did. In his teaching, Shinran followed the logic of Honen's teaching with regard to the nembutsu to its logical conclusion. His followers therefore called this True Pure Land. For example, he gave up being a monk and married. This was an important step since it showed that: 'in the eyes of Amida there is no distinction between monk and laity; all can become enlightened, enlightenment is not the concern of the monastic orders alone' (Williams). In addition, Shinran discouraged his followers from studying any sacred texts or from any form of devotion other than simple recitation of the nembutsu.

Shinran did not see the need to defend his True Pure Land teaching from the accusation that it might be attractive to the worst of sinners. He even described himself as someone who 'drowned in a broad sea of lust'. For Shinran, the whole point of Amida's compassion was to save the lowest of beings who could not save themselves. Such beings might be burdened with unwholesome and unfruitful karma and general wickedness of life, all of which pointed to rebirth in the hell realm. However, all of that could be changed in an instant by calling on Amida.

Shinran concluded that people could not be saved through their own efforts. In Japanese this is called jiriki (own power). They could only be saved by calling on another power outside of themselves. In Japanese this is called tariki (other power). The only tariki that could help was that offered by Amida.

Calligraphy of the nembutsu

Key quote

By reciting Amida's name, I do not mean meditation, or reciting it as a result of studying and understanding its deep meaning. No – all I mean is simply reciting the Buddha's name, with no doubt that this will lead to rebirth in the Pure Land. (Honen)

Amida Buddha in the Pure Land

The Buddhist Wheel of Life

69

Specification content

The central practice of the daimoku
mantra in Nichiren traditions.

quickfire

3.4 What are the words of the nembutsu?

quickfire

3.5 What are the Three Great Secret Laws?

Key term

Shodai: prolonged chanting of the
daimoku

The Nichiren Gohonzon

Key quotes

When I reflect deeply on the Great
Vow …I am convinced that it was
made utterly and solely for my sake.
Bound up as I am with deep and
heavy kamma, I feel profoundly
grateful it was vowed to save the like
of me. (**Shinran**)

We can see that Nichiren … wove
the narrative of the Lotus Sutra
into his own age, reinterpreting the
absolute Buddha as an historical
actor capable of engagement with
the very conduct of the realm.
(**Deal and Ruppert**)

The central practice of the daimoku mantra in Nichiren traditions

On the one hand there was nothing particularly new in the teaching of Nichiren
since his focus was entirely on the well-established sacred text, the Lotus Sutra.
On the other hand, what was new was his teaching that the Lotus Sutra was the
only valid object of Buddhist faith in the age of mappo. His rejection of anything
else was part of his belief that, 'the disasters and violent conflicts of the day were
specifically due to the ignorant beliefs of many Buddhists' (Deal and Ruppert).

Furthermore, Nichiren believed that in the age of mappo, the Buddha-nature of
sentient beings had become so obscured that only a simplified teaching which
proclaimed the essence of the Lotus Sutra could be of use, first of all throughout
Japan and then throughout the rest of the world. This was what the cosmic and
eternal Shakyamuni Buddha as a Supreme Being required of Buddhists. Nichiren's
teaching can perhaps be best summed up by looking at the Three Great Secret
Laws for which thanks are still offered today in daily Nichiren Buddhist prayer.

The first of these is the Nichiren Gohonzon which is the object of reverence for
Nichiren Buddhists. This is a hanging calligraphic mandala originally inscribed by
Nichiren in 1279 towards which devotional chanting is directed. On the mandala
are inscribed the name of the cosmic and eternal Shakyamuni Buddha as presented
in the Lotus Sutra along with the names of other bodhisattvas and beings found
in the Sutra. The name of Nichiren is also inscribed. The third Great Secret Law is
kaidan. This may be taken to refer to the place where the Gohonzon is set up and
worshipped in a person's home or temple. Others believe it to refer to the spiritual
place within a person from which devotion flows.

It is, however, the second Great Secret Law which is the focus of our studies. This is
the daimoku which is also inscribed in the middle of the Gohonzon. The daimoku
is a short phrase which is chanted in Nichiren prayer. The term shodai refers to
prolonged chanting of the daimoku. Chanting the daimoku, especially in front of
the Nichiren Gohonzon, is the main devotional practice for Nichiren Buddhists.

The daimoku itself is: 'namu myoho renge kyo'. The word 'namu' can be translated
as 'I take refuge'. Following that 'myoho renge kyo' is the Japanese title given to
the Lotus Sutra which can be translated as 'myoho' meaning 'mystic law', 'renge'
meaning 'lotus flower' and 'kyo' meaning 'Sutra'. Putting everything together, this
can be translated as 'I take refuge in the mystic law of the Lotus Sutra'.

According to Nichiren, chanting the daimoku is all that is required of a Buddhist. It
is not necessary to read the Lotus Sutra or to study it since the very title of the Sutra
contains the essence of everything in it. As can be seen, this presents a very simple form
of Buddhism, which is what Nichiren believed was required in the age of mappo. At
the same time, given that he regarded the Lotus Sutra as the 'great King of all Buddhist
Scriptures', chanting the daimoku was for Nichiren the highest practice of Buddhism.

The Nichiren scholar Gyokei Umada explains that when looking at the Nichiren
Gohonzon and reciting the daimoku, 'heart and soul, subjectivity and objectivity
become fused into one whole, and the worshipper realises in himself the excellent
qualities of the Supreme Being, and thereby his short life is made eternal and
his limited virtue infinite … herein lies the consummation of the Nichiren Sect:
the peace of mind of all believers and religious life. The result of all this is the
realisation of the Buddha Land in the present state of existence.'

AO1 Activity

Explain how a Buddhist might respond to the following view: 'The key Buddhist
traditions in Japan are not really Buddhist.'

Explain your answer using evidence and examples from what you have read.

AO1 Developing skills

It is now important to consider the information that has been covered in this section; however, the information in its raw form is too extensive and so has to be processed in order to meet the requirements of the examination. This can be achieved by practising more advanced skills associated with AO1. The exercises that run throughout this book will help you to do this and prepare you for the examination. For assessment objective 1 (AO1), which involves demonstrating 'knowledge' and 'understanding' skills, we are going to focus on different ways in which the skills can be demonstrated effectively, and also, refer to how the performance of these skills is measured (see generic band descriptors for A2 [WJEC] AO1 or A Level [Eduqas] AO1).

▶ **Your next task is this:** Below is an outline of **the concept of mappo**. At present it has no quotations at all to support the points made. Underneath the outline are two quotations that could be used in the outline in order to improve it. Your task is to re-write the outline but make use of the quotations. Such phrases as 'according to ...', 'the scholar ... argues', or, 'it has been suggested by ...' may help.

Buddhism developed in Japan from the 6th century CE onwards. It was heavily influenced by what was happening in the area of internal politics in Japan, particularly by the feuds and wars between ruling families. The general turmoil that enveloped parts of the country was seen to be evidence of mappo. (*) Being a Buddhist during the time of the decay of the Dhamma was problematic and some Buddhists responded by trying to simplify Buddhist beliefs, teaching and practice so that people could find hope and consolation through their faith. This was the case, for example, with Nichiren. (*) He wanted to help establish peace throughout the country through upholding the Lotus Sutra.

'Japanese religiosity after this time can only be understood in the context of one overriding problem – how can one be a Buddhist, how is the Buddhist religion to survive, during the Last Days – the era of cosmic and religious disaster when apparently none of the normal sources for religious inspiration can be relied upon.' **(Williams)**

We have seen many signs in heaven and earth: a famine, a plague, the whole country is filled with misery. Horses and cows are dying on the roadsides, and so are men, and there is no one to bury them ... Look around at the misery of the age, at the decay of Buddhism. **(Nichiren)**

When you have completed the task, try to find another quotation that you could use and further extend your answer.

Key skills Theme 3
The third theme has tasks that concentrate on a particular aspect of AO1 in terms of using quotations from sources of authority and in the use of references.

Key skills
Knowledge involves:
Selection of a range of (thorough) accurate and relevant information that is directly related to the specific demands of the question.

This means:
- Selecting relevant material for the question set
- Being focused in explaining and examining the material selected.

Understanding involves:
Explanation that is extensive, demonstrating depth and/or breadth with excellent use of evidence and examples including (where appropriate) thorough and accurate supporting use of sacred texts, sources of wisdom and specialist language.

This means:
- Effective use of examples and supporting evidence to establish the quality of your understanding
- Ownership of your explanation that expresses personal knowledge and understanding and NOT just reproducing a chunk of text from a book that you have rehearsed and memorised.

Specification content

The extent to which Japanese
Buddhism is unique.

Key quote

Buddhist thought and practice
were transformed as a result of
Japanese cultural sensibilities.
The diversity of ideas, doctrines,
rituals and material culture that
comprise Japanese Buddhism is
better conceived of as multiple
Buddhism(s) deployed in different
times and places to meet a variety of
needs and purposes. These multiple
Buddhism(s) may share a family
resemblance, but it is also important
to understand the differences and
disagreements between these many
traditions. (Deal and Ruppert)

AO2 Activity

As you read through this section try to
do the following:

1. Pick out the different lines of
   argument that are presented in
   the text and identify any evidence
   given in support.

2. For each line of argument try to
   evaluate whether or not you think
   this is strong or weak.

3. Think of any questions you may
   wish to raise in response to the
   arguments.

This Activity will help you to start
thinking critically about what you
read and help you to evaluate the
effectiveness of different arguments
and from this develop your own
observations, opinions and points
of view that will help with any
conclusions that you make in your
answers to the AO2 questions
that arise.

Issues for analysis and evaluation

The extent to which Japanese Buddhism is unique

From the outset it is useful to clarify one's overall understanding of Buddhism from
a philosophical and linguistic perspective. In a book published in 1989, *Mahayana
Buddhism: The Doctrinal Foundations*, Williams presented concerns at what he
called 'an essentialist fallacy' which is particularly pervasive and deep-rooted. This
gives rise to 'the feeling that because we use the same word so there must be some
core, an essence, identified by the relevant definition'.

The 'essentialist fallacy' can be regarded as applying to Buddhism in general where,
after all, there have never been any attempts to impose orthodoxy – uniformity
and conformity in belief – and orthopraxis – uniformity and conformity in
devotional practice.

Reflecting on this issue can help to query the assumption that there is such a thing
as 'Japanese' Buddhism. Here, again, perhaps the 'essentialist fallacy' is at work.

It might be useful at this stage to bring into our assessment anicca –
impermanence – which is one of the lakshanas. As Williams pointed out, from the
outset Buddhist beliefs have always analysed 'things' so that 'unities are dissolved
into their constituent parts and true diversity is revealed'. With this in mind we can
approach the statement being fully aware that the phrase 'Japanese Buddhism' is a
linguistic unity and a construction imposed by a single naming expression.

Historical research and empirical evidence may also be seen to challenge the
assumption behind the phrase 'Japanese Buddhism'.

Some networking monks were able to travel within Japan and, more importantly,
to China and Korea. They encountered beliefs and practices which modified their
own beliefs and practices. What they had absorbed, they might well then pass
on to their students in the sangha – both monastic and lay. Those students in
turn might well modify what they received as a result of their own beliefs and
experiences. This pattern can be seen in the ways in which the type of Buddhism
practised at Enryaku-ji monastery was influential on Eisai, Dogen, Honen, Shinran
and Nichiren. Yet at the same time each 'founded' their own sects with particular
beliefs and practices.

However, it could be argued that Buddhism does present a core set of beliefs
and practices which are readily identifiable in the wide variety of Buddhisms
throughout the world. The Four Noble Truths, the Noble Eightfold Path, the Three
Refuges and the Three Lakshanas are attested to by all those calling themselves
Buddhists. Likewise, with regard to rebirth and the possibility of enlightenment.
Dhyana – meditation – is a unifying practice for all Buddhists, although its
significance and how it is manifested might vary considerably.

Furthermore, it might be argued that one can talk about 'Japanese' Buddhism. This
is because of the singular interplay of social, political and cultural forces which
shaped and formed the development of Buddhism and which were in turn shaped
and formed by Buddhism.

Looking at three key Buddhist traditions in Japan of Zen, Pure Land and Nichiren,
they are from one perspective not unique at all.

For example, the tradition of Zen Buddhism is a linear development of Cha'an
Buddhism found in China. Soto Zen and Rinzai Zen are based on schools of Cha'an
Buddhism and have a lineage which can be traced back. Zen Buddhism is also not
unique as what the teacher tries to pass on to the student is a way of achieving
enlightenment. This is precisely what Siddhartha Gautama did for six years after
the renunciation. Having achieved this under the Bodhi Tree, he passed this on to

his followers. In this sense there is nothing unique about Zen Buddhism as through the use of zazen and koans it is putting into practice meditation which is the third of the threefold trainings of the Noble Eightfold Path: samma vayama, samma sati and samma samdahi.

With regard to Pure Land Buddhism, this is not unique because Honen's motivation was karuna. He was specifically concerned at how the lowest in terms of their lack of morality might achieve rebirth anywhere else than in the hell realm. This is putting into effect the Buddhist virtue of both metta and karuna. Shinran's form of Pure Land Buddhism might appear to be unique but as Williams pointed out, the motivation for reliance on Amida and for rebirth in the Pure Land is bodhicitta and a desire to help sentient beings achieve enlightenment. This is very much in accord with the bodhisattva vow. Williams also argued that Pure Land is completely true to the philosophy of Mahayana – it is a greater vehicle 'teaching universal liberation and compassion'.

With Nichiren Buddhism, there is nothing unique because all that Nichiren applied was the general Buddhist principle of upaya – skilful means – in assisting Buddhists of his day to attain enlightenment. The Nichiren Gohonzon as a focus of devotion for Nichiren Buddhists is therefore no different from the Kamakura Daibutsu or the numerous other Buddha rupas which are used for devotion throughout the Buddhist world.

Study tip

It is vital for AO2 that you actually discuss arguments and not just explain what someone may have stated. Try to ask yourself, 'was this a fair point to make?', 'is the evidence sound enough?', 'is there anything to challenge this argument?', 'is this a strong or weak argument?' Such critical analysis will help you develop your evaluation skills.

However, it is quite possible to see in the three key Buddhist traditions in Japan of Zen, Pure Land and Nichiren aspects which make them unique.

For example, it appears to be only in Japan that Buddhist traditions became so readily identified in terms of status in society. Thus, for example, Rinzai Zen remained for many centuries the preserve of the ruling class – such as the Shoguns – whilst Soto Zen was followed much more by the general populace. It also appears to be a unique strand in that Rinzai Zen was known as a form of Buddhism strongly associated with the martial arts as in the Samurai tradition.

Furthermore, the Pure Land tradition of Honen and particularly of Shinran seem unique. This is because, by complete contrast to Theravada and much more than any other form of Mahayana Buddhism, reliance is removed from oneself and one's own efforts to achieve enlightenment or a better rebirth. In other words, jiriki (own power) is replaced by tariki (other power) as provided by Amida Buddha.

Nichiren Buddhism also appears to be unique particularly in the way in which it linked mappo and the state of Japan to its beliefs. Unlike other Buddhisms, there is a clear sense of beliefs and practices as taught by Nichiren which are accepted and those which are not. There is an entirety of focus on one sacred text, the Lotus Sutra, and on one devotional practice – chanting the daimoku. In addition, the practice of Nichiren Buddhists chanting before the Nichiren Gohonzon and treating it with devotion is very much at odds with the imagery of any other Buddhists where a Buddha or bodhisattva rupa might be used.

The three traditions in Japanese Buddhism might also appear to be unique in the way in which the lineage from student back to teacher is held in such high esteem. Hence Pure Land Buddhists focus on their link to Honen whilst True Pure Land Buddhists focus on their link to Shinran.

Key questions

Does Buddhism aim to be consistent?

If the ends of Japanese Buddhisms are the same, does it matter very much about the means?

Would Eisai, Dogen, Honen, Shinran and Nichiren have accepted each other as being authentic Buddhists?

Key quote

The emphasis in Buddhism is on the *teachings* of the Buddha(s) and the awakening of human personality that these are seen to lead to. Nevertheless, Buddhists do show great reverence to Gotama as a supreme teacher and an exemplar of the ultimate goal that all strive for. (Harvey)

The daibutsu (Great Buddha) constructed in 1252 during the Kamakura period.

AO2 Activity

List some conclusions that could be drawn from the AO2 reasoning from the above text; try to aim for at least three different possible conclusions. Consider each of the conclusions and collect brief evidence to support each conclusion from the AO1 and AO2 material for this topic. Select the conclusion that you think is most convincing and explain why it is so. Try to contrast this with the weakest conclusion in the list, justifying your argument with clear reasoning and evidence.

Specification content

The importance of koan, nembutsu
and daimoku as expressions of
Buddhist teachings.

The importance of koan, nembutsu and daimoku as expressions of Buddhist teachings

Mahayana Buddhism, as expressed in the second chapter of the Lotus Sutra, emphasised the need for upaya – skilful means. Upaya is needed to bring everyone, without exception, to enlightenment and to attain the complete wisdom of a Buddha and the compassion of a Buddha.

Taken together therefore, the koan, nembutsu and daimoku are important expressions of Buddhist teaching with regard to upaya. Each caters in its own particular way 'according to the capacities of sentient beings' (Lotus Sutra). The koan engages those who might consider themselves self-reflective and intellectual. The nembutsu might engage those with a sense of their inability to progress on the magga and who have need of tariki (other power) provided by Amida. The daimoku might engage those living busy lives for whom simple daily recitation might suffice as devotional practice.

From the perspective of upaya, it could also be argued that the koan, nembutsu and daimoku are ultimately unimportant in themselves. This approach could find backing from the parable of the raft (Majjhima Nikaya 22). The Buddha teaches: 'In the same way, monks, I have taught the Dhamma compared to a raft, for the purpose of crossing over, not for the purpose of holding onto. Understanding the Dhamma as taught compared to a raft, you should let go even of Dhammas, to say nothing of non-Dhammas.'

Arguably, the process of 'letting go' rather than 'holding onto' is of great importance. Buddhism teaches that there are three types of dukkha: dukkha-dukkha which is suffering as pain experience; virparinama-dukkha which is suffering experienced due to the changing nature of existence; sankhara-dukkha which is suffering inherent in the contingent nature of existence. The samudaya or arising of dukkha is in turn caused by tanha or craving. The Buddha teaches that the nirodha or cessation of tanha can be achieved by following the Noble Eightfold Path.

The koan is an important expression of Buddhist teaching in this area because it addresses the tanha involved with a person who has: a sense of themselves as a separate permanent being; an 'I' whose ego craves an end to dukkha; for answers to life's existential problems; for a path to happiness and for some kind of intellectual resolution. The koan breaks habitual thought processes of this type of mind in order that sudden recognition can break through so that the sense of being an 'I' with an ego is removed. True 'letting go' can then take place as the truth of anatta – no permanent self – is recognised.

The Ten Ox Herding Pictures often used to depict stages of practice in Zen Buddhism illustrate this well. The first pictures show the herder – who represents the Zen student – searching for the Ox – which represents what the student is seeking. However, by the eighth picture there is just an empty circle – no herder, no ox and no search. It is through using the koan that a Zen Buddhist can complete the task of 'letting go'.

In *Mahayana Buddhism: The Doctrinal Foundations*, Williams argued that 'letting go' is also a key part of Pure Land Buddhism particularly as taught by Shinran: 'the only meaning that can be given to the notion of egolessness, no-self, is to let go, leaving good and evil to the natural working of karmic law and surrendering wholeheartedly' to the vow made by Amida regarding rebirth in the Pure Land. In this sense, belief in anatta – no permanent self – means that logically a Buddhist cannot rely on jiriki (own power) as there is no 'own self' which has any power. This means that tariki (other power) as provided by Amida Buddha is essential.

Another way in which the nembutsu might be regarded as an important expression of Buddhist teaching is that its goal is not just rebirth in the Pure Land but rather

AO2 Activity

As you read through this section try to do the following:

1. Pick out the different lines of argument that are presented in the text and identify any evidence given in support.

2. For each line of argument try to evaluate whether or not you think this is strong or weak.

3. Think of any questions you may wish to raise in response to the arguments.

This Activity will help you to start thinking critically about what you read and help you to evaluate the effectiveness of different arguments and from this develop your own observations, opinions and points of view that will help with any conclusions that you make in your answers to the AO2 questions that arise.

it is bodhicitta and a desire to help sentient beings achieve enlightenment. That being the goal, it could also be argued that reciting the nembutsu is important in developing the Mahayana paramita (perfection) of dana – generosity towards the suffering and needs of others. This would also be true given that recitation of the nembutsu focuses on Amida and by extension on Amida's compassion for all sentient beings. This can help Pure Land Buddhists to remove from themselves conditions for unwholesome karma particularly dosa (hatred).

A development of this point might be based on arguments in *The New Buddhism* by David Brazier published in 2001. He noted the debate in Japan caused by Matsumoto Shiro and Hakamaya Norikai in the 1980s. The question they addressed was whether Japanese Buddhism based in temples and monasteries and taught by monks was 'faulty' since it appeared to be elitist and nationalistic. This would make the nembutsu and the daimoku very important Buddhist practices because they are not dependent on temples, monasteries or monks. Honen, Shinran and Nichiren were clear that recitation could be done by anyone regardless of their status or position in society. Being educated was not necessary and neither was living the type of life which was acceptable according to the norms of society.

The Ten Ox Herding pictures used in Zen Buddhism.

Whilst some might question the importance of the daimoku as an expression of Buddhist teaching, it could be argued that Nichiren was correct in his assessment of the Lotus Sutra as being the 'great king of all Buddhist Scriptures'. It is, after all, regarded by many Mahayana Buddhists as the final teaching of the Buddha. This is because of its focus on upaya – skilful means – the universal buddha-nature, the cosmic and universal Buddha and the diversity of paths leading to perfect Buddhahood. That being the case, taking refuge in the Lotus Sutra through chanting the daimoku could be seen as an entirely relevant and important Buddhist practice.

On a broader level, recitation of the nembutsu and of the daimoku could be seen as part of the Buddhist tradition regarding chanting. This is most clearly seen in Tibetan Buddhism which has sometimes been termed Mantrayana – 'Way of Mantras'. Chanting the nembutsu might help in visualisation of Amida and the Pure Land – although this is not required – whilst chanting the daimoku might help with internalising the message of the Lotus Sutra.

Again, recitation of the nembutsu and of the daimoku could be seen in the broader Mahayana context as encouraging the development of the paramita (perfection) of dhyana – one pointed concentration. Pure Land Buddhists might therefore resolve to follow the practice of Honen who recited the nembutsu sixty thousand times a day.

Furthermore, some might argue that Buddhists are still living in the age of mappo. There is a sense of what might be termed angst on an individual, national and global level. In addition, searching for authentic Dhamma – given the many Buddhist traditions in the West – can be a complex and time-consuming task. In this context it could be argued that simple recitation of the nembutsu or the daimoku are just as relevant today as they were during the Kamakura period of Japanese history.

Key skills Theme 3

The third theme has tasks that concentrate on a particular aspect of AO2 in terms of using quotations from sources of authority and in the use of references in supporting arguments and evaluations.

Key skills

Analysis involves:

Identifying issues raised by the materials in the AO1, together with those identified in the AO2 section, and presents sustained and clear views, either of scholars or from a personal perspective ready for evaluation.

This means:

- That your answers are able to identify key areas of debate in relation to a particular issue
- That you can identify, and comment upon, the different lines of argument presented by others
- That your response comments on the overall effectiveness of each of these areas or arguments.

Evaluation involves:

Considering the various implications of the issues raised based upon the evidence gleaned from analysis and provides an extensive detailed argument with a clear conclusion.

This means:

- That your answer weighs up the consequences of accepting or rejecting the various and different lines of argument analysed
- That your answer arrives at a conclusion through a clear process of reasoning.

AO2 Developing skills

It is now important to consider the information that has been covered in this section; however, the information in its raw form is too extensive and so has to be processed in order to meet the requirements of the examination. This can be achieved by practising more advanced skills associated with AO2. The exercises that run throughout this book will help you to do this and prepare you for the examination. For assessment objective 2 (AO2), which involves 'critical analysis' and 'evaluation' skills, we are going to focus on different ways in which the skills can be demonstrated effectively, and also, refer to how the performance of these skills is measured (see generic band descriptors for A2 [WJEC] AO2 or A Level [Eduqas] AO2).

▶ **Your next task is this:** Below is an evaluation of **the extent to which Japanese Buddhism is unique**. At present it has no quotations at all to support the argument presented. Underneath the evaluation are two quotations that could be used in the outline in order to improve it. Your task is to re-write the outline but make use of the quotations. Such phrases as 'according to …', 'the scholar … argues', or, 'it has been suggested by …' may help.

Some might argue that when we talk about Buddhism in general at all, we are not talking about a single religion, way of life or philosophy. Just because we call it 'Buddhism' does not make it a unified system. (*) From this perspective, all the different Buddhisms that there are, such as Japanese Buddhism, are unique. In arguing that Japanese Buddhism is unique one can also point to the radical differences between Zen, Pure Land and Nichiren. However, the ways in which these three are unique or Japanese Buddhism in general is unique can be debated. (*) It might be argued that the differences are to do with the appearance of these Buddhisms and not with fundamental beliefs.

'The feeling that because we use the same word so there must be some core, an essence, identified by the relevant definition.' **(Williams)**

'Buddhist thought and practice were transformed as a result of Japanese cultural sensibilities. The diversity of ideas, doctrines, rituals and material culture that comprise Japanese Buddhism is better conceived of as multiple Buddhism(s) deployed in different times and places to meet a variety of needs and purposes. These multiple Buddhism(s) may share a family resemblance, but it is also important to understand the differences and disagreements between these many traditions.' **(Deal and Ruppert)**

When you have completed the task, try to find another quotation that you could use and further extend your evaluation.

B: Religion and society: responses to the challenges from science

Presentations of Buddhism as avoiding 'blind faith'

The word 'faith' has a number of definitions. The *Oxford English Dictionary*, for example, defines it as 'complete trust or confidence in someone or something' and furthermore as 'strong belief in the doctrines of a religion, based on spiritual conviction rather than proof'. In some world religions, faith is given a systematic basis through creedal statements which are shared by all those belonging to the religion in question. Thus, all can use the same agreed formula: 'I believe in....'

In some ways this might be seen as 'blind faith' in that what is required – particularly if the religion has a centralised authoritarian approach – is belief which rests not on a person's own understanding or perception but on what has been handed down, taught or revealed by a sacred text or person regarded as a source of sacred wisdom and authority.

Faith, and indeed 'blind faith', may be required particularly when aspects of the religion involve the supernatural and miraculous. In such cases empirical data cannot be called upon with regard to that which is unseen, and acceptance that the laws of nature have been and can be broken is required. Often a leap of faith may be called for, whereby a person accepts the need to move beyond the rational and logical to that which cannot and can never be objectively confirmed.

In Buddhism, two words are used with regard to faith. Harvey explained that **pasada** is 'a calm and joyful faith' and **saddha** is 'soundly based faith or trustful confidence'. For many Buddhists all that is expressed is pasada which is 'inspired by the example of those who are established on the path'. By contrast, saddha is the result of listening to teaching which then leads to practice. Practice then provides partial confirmation of the teaching which leads to deeper saddha. Deeper saddha then leads on to deeper practice 'until the heart of the teaching is directly experienced'. Harvey continues by stating that when a person is awakened, they can then replace what was formerly saddha with knowledge.

What is specifically rejected in Buddhism is **amulika saddha**, which means 'blind, faith'. Instead, what is required is **akaravati saddha**, which means 'confidence based on reason and experience'.

From one perspective, the Buddha did not perform astounding supernatural miracles which resulted in amulika saddha. For example, in the story of Kisa Gotami whose only child died, the Buddha did not bring the child back to life and thereby give rise to amulika saddha. Instead the Buddha told Kisa Gotami to return to him with mustard seeds from a household where none had experienced death of family or friend. This of course she was unable to do. Having realised that no one is free of mortality she then returned to the Buddha who preached the Dhamma to her, leading to her having akaravati saddha, which led to her enlightenment.

A useful way of understanding the Buddhist approach to faith can also be found in the Alagaddupama Sutta and the Water-Snake Simile. The Buddha's teaching is in response to the issue of clinging to views and not fully grasping the Dhamma. The Buddha taught as follows: 'Suppose there were a man needing a water-snake, seeking a water-snake, wandering in search of a water-snake. He would see a large water-snake and grasp it by the coils or by the tail. The water-snake, turning around, would bite him on the hand, on the arm, or on one of his limbs, and from that cause he would suffer death or death-like suffering. Why is that? Because of the wrong-grasping of the water-snake.

This section covers AO1 content and skills

Specification content
The relationship between religion and society: respect and recognition and the ways that religious traditions view other religions and non-religious worldviews and their truth claims. Presentations of Buddhism as avoiding 'blind faith'.

Key quote

We may define 'faith' as a firm belief in something for which there is no evidence. Where there is evidence, no one speaks of 'faith'. We do not speak of faith that two and two are four or that the earth is round. We only speak of faith when we wish to substitute emotion for evidence. The substitution of emotion for evidence is apt to lead to strife, since different groups substitute different emotions. (Russell)

quickfire

3.6 What is the difference between pasada and saddha?

Key terms

Akaravati saddha: confidence based on reason and experience

Amulika saddha: blind, faith

Pasada: a calm and joyful faith

Saddha: soundly based faith or trustful confidence

Key quote

The Buddha emphasised self-reliance and the experiential testing-out of all teachings, including his own. He was well aware of the many conflicting doctrines of his day, a time of intellectual ferment. Rejecting teachings based on authoritative tradition, or mere rational speculation, he emphasised the examination and analysis of actual experience. (Harvey)

quickfire

3.7 What did the Buddha do when Kisa Gotami brought to him her dead child?

Specification content

Presentations of Buddhism emphasising the realisation of truth in experience (with reference to the Kalama Sutta v.9 & 10)

In the same way, there is the case where some worthless men study the Dhamma. Having studied the Dhamma, they don't ascertain the meaning of the Dhamma with their discernment. Not having ascertained the meaning of Dhamma with their discernment, they don't come to an agreement through pondering. They study the Dhamma both for attacking others and for defending themselves in debate. They don't reach the goal for which people study the Dhamma. Their wrong grasp of the Dhamma will lead to their long-term harm and suffering. Why is that? Because of the wrong-grasping of the Dhamma. ...Therefore, monks, when you understand the meaning of any statement of mine, that is how you should remember it. But when you don't understand the meaning of any statement of mine, then right there you should cross-question me or the experienced monks.'

The Water-Snake Simile on grasping the snake and grasping the Dhamma.

Presentations of Buddhism emphasising the realisation of truth in experience

Perhaps the most important text with regard to avoidance of amulika saddha can be found in the Kalama Sutta. According to the Sutta, the Buddha arrived in the town of Kesaputta in which lived people of the Kalama clan. There had already been a number of rival religious teachers visiting Kesaputta. Each taught and praised their own beliefs but then showed contempt for and rejected the beliefs of other religious teachers.

The Kalamas therefore ask the Buddha: 'They leave us absolutely uncertain and in doubt: which of these venerable religious teachers are speaking the truth and which ones are lying?'

The Buddha replies: 'When there are reasons for doubt, uncertainty is born.' He continues: 'Don't go by reports, by legends, by traditions, by scripture, by logical conjecture, by inference, by analogies, by agreement through pondering views, by probability, or by the thought, that this contemplative is our teacher.'

Here, the Buddha teaches that relying on religious teaching simply because it has been received and handed down is not in itself sufficient as it is second-hand knowledge. Instead a person should judge the evidence for themselves through first-hand experience of the qualities being taught by religious teachers. In a dialogue with the Kalamas, the Buddha then talks about actions which are skilful and unskilful and which lead either to harm and suffering or to welfare and . happiness. In all of this, common-sense removes doubt.

Thus, the Buddha continues: 'When you know for yourselves that, these qualities are unskilful; these qualities are blameworthy; these qualities are criticised by the wise; these qualities, when adopted and carried out, lead to harm and to suffering — then you should abandon them.'

Buddhists consider that here the Kalama Sutta shows the importance of the realisation of truth in experience which will lead to akaravati saddha. From a Western perspective this could be called an empirical approach – that knowledge is derived from investigation, observation and experience and is not just based on received assumptions. Such an approach is the basis of scientific research.

Study tip

In order to gain a greater understanding of the Kalama Sutta and of how it is recorded that the Buddha taught the Dhamma, it would be helpful to read the whole of this short Sutta which is available online.

Asian Buddhist worldviews populated with a diversity of beings and realms

The full diversity of beings and realms from the perspective of the Asian Buddhist world view depends very much on which of the Buddhisms is being assessed. Overall, they present a vast, intricate and complex amalgam of views which were in part incorporated from Hinduism and Jainism as Buddhism itself evolved and developed. In addition, the indigenous beliefs of the country in which Buddhism became established added to this diversity with gods, demons, supernatural beings, heavens and hells being incorporated into an overall belief system. Thus, any account of the diversity of beings and realms will necessarily be incomplete.

From ancient times the Asian Buddhist world view – which would have been that of the Buddha himself – considered the universe to be structured in an ordered way with different realms for rebirth. The five realms of rebirth as recorded in the Abhidhamma Pitaka are: the hell realm, the ghost realm, the animal realm, the human realm and the god realm. Three of these realms – the hell realm, the ghost realm and the god realm – clearly imply the existence of what might be termed the supernatural, i.e. a diversity of unseen realms which cannot be verified by any empirical data.

The hell realm is described in detail by the Buddha in the Devaduta Sutta. He describes how beings endowed with evil conduct at the break-up of the body after death reappear in the hell realm. Here they are taken before Yama who questions them about their evil conduct after which they suffer various gruesome punishments in different hells such as that in the Simbali Forest next to the Hot Ashes Hell, 'with trees reaching up a league, covered with thorns sixteen finger breadths long — burning, blazing, and glowing. He enters that and is made to climb up and down them. There he feels painful, racking, piercing feelings, yet he does not die as long as his evil karma is not exhausted.' These punishments continue until their evil karma is used up and they are reborn elsewhere.

An equally important world view is that the universe is made of 31 planes of existence which are divided into three realms: the realm of the formless, the realm of the form and the realm of desire. Each of these three realms is sub-divided into numerous other realms in which live a diversity of beings. This, however, is only one world out of many. 'The Buddhist view is that, taken as a totality, not only is time infinite but space too is effectively infinite. The Buddhist cosmological vision is about as vast as it is possible to conceive.' (Williams and Tribe)

quickfire

3.8 In which town did the Buddha speak to the Kalama clan?

Specification content

Asian Buddhist worldviews populated with a diversity of beings and realms.

Key quote

Buddhism is not a religion of the book, and its relationship to its scriptural record is highly ambiguous.... As emphasised in the celebrated Kalama scripture ... Buddhism enjoins seekers to rely first and foremost upon their own experience, while working all the while to deepen this and so make it a more reliable guide. (Jones)

Mount Meru, which in Buddhist cosmology was believed to be the centre of the universe.

Key quote

In 1977 I was discussing the traditional cosmology with a prominent Tibetan lama. I asked him … why it was that Mount Meru had not been discovered. We were speaking Tibetan, and his answer could be translated in two ways. The first would be, 'If one has pure karma, one can see it.' The second would be, 'If you had pure karma, you could see it'. **(Lopez)**

Key terms

Deva: supernatural godlike being living on Mount Meru

Dharmapalas: devas who protect the dharma

Jambudvipa: the continent on which human beings live

Mount Meru: the great world mountain

Overall the Buddhist universe is seen to be flat, surrounded by a vast expanse of water around which is a vast expanse of wind. At the centre of all things is the towering **Mount Meru** – the great world mountain – which is surrounded by seven concentric rings of mountains and seas beyond which lie four continents. Mount Meru has four sides of gold, silver, lapis lazuli and crystal. Human beings are to be found on only one of these continents – **Jambudvipa**.

This Buddhist flat-earth cosmology remained in place until there was exposure to, and understanding of, the Western scientific discoveries that the earth is round. Such exposure took place increasingly in the 19th century and gradually belief amongst many Buddhists in the physical reality of the flat universe and Mount Meru fell away.

Whilst some Buddhists might regard the non-human beings of the Asian Buddhist world view as belonging to mythology, for other Buddhists there is no doubt that they exist although their role is not altogether clear. 'It is a common belief amongst the Buddhist public that such deities can be influenced to grant their favours by transferring merits to them whenever meritorious deeds are performed. This belief is based on the Buddha's injunction to the deities to protect those human beings who lead a religious way of life.' (Ven K. Sri Dhammananda Maha Thera)

These protecting deities are sometimes called **Dharmapalas** which means 'protectors of the Dhamma'. These are often depicted in gruesome form as angry beings because their anger shows their willingness to protect the Dhamma and to guard Buddhists. For example, Ekajati is a female Dharmapala found in Tibetan Buddhism who is often depicted as dancing on corpses with a garland of skulls around her neck.

A useful general approach might be taken by looking at the opening of the Lotus Sutra. This gives a detailed description of the Buddha seated in meditation on Mount Gijjhakuta surrounded by a large throng including twelve thousand monks – human beings. In addition, the Sutra describes the presence of eighty thousand bodhisattvas.

Alongside these are the astasena – eight classes of non-human beings. These include **devas** who live in a hierarchy of heavenly realms above Jambudvipa. In Buddhism, devas are not gods in the way the term is understood in the West. They are invisible supernatural beings with godlike qualities which make them more powerful and longer-living than humans. They performed meritorious acts over vast periods of time and as a result they are assigned to one of the heavenly realms.

The King of the devas is Sakra who lives on the summit of Mount Meru in Tavatimsa – one of the Buddhist heavens. One supernatural miracle performed by the Buddha was his ascent to Tavatimsa where he preached the Dhamma and then returned to earth at the city of Sankassa on a ladder of jewels provided by Sakra. A shrine was later built at the spot where the Buddha's foot touched the earth after his descent.

The Lotus Sutra describes how King Sakra is seated before the Buddha along with twenty thousand devaputras – sons of devas – and the devas of the four quarters with ten thousand devaputras. Other supernatural beings include the eight naga kings. Nagas are supernatural

Ekajati a protector of the dharma in Tibetan Buddhism.

beings which take the form of snakes or dragons. They are sometimes described as protecting the Buddha and they are guardians on Mount Meru. In addition, there are thousands of kimnaras – depicted in human form with animal heads – asuras – lesser beings than devas living on the lower slopes of Mount Meru – garudas – depicted as golden winged birds and gandharvas – lesser devas.

Study tip

In order to gain a greater understanding of the diversity of beings and realms according to the Buddhist world view, it would be useful to look at images of Buddhist cosmology and of devas and dharmapalas other than those mentioned above.

The Dalai Lama's assessment of the value of science

The 14th Dalai Lama, Tenzin Gyatso, has written a great deal about science. In an article published by the *New York Times* in 2005 entitled 'Our Faith in Science', he noted that science had always fascinated him. 'As a child in Tibet, I was keenly curious about how things worked. When I got a toy, I would play with it a bit, then take it apart to see how it was put together. As I became older, I applied the same scrutiny to a movie projector and an antique automobile.'

One of the Dalai Lama's first engagements with science was with cosmology. As we have seen, Buddhist beliefs included Mount Meru and Jambudvipa in their understanding of the universe. Whilst Buddhisms in other countries such as Japan and Sri Lanka had been exposed since the 19th century and earlier to Western scientific discoveries that the earth is round, Buddhism in Tibet remained much more isolated. Thus, during his studies as a monk in the 1950s, the Dalai Lama was taught the ancient Buddhist cosmology as found in a 4th-century CE Sutta in the Abhidhamma Pitaka. However, he had already had doubts as to how reliable this might be.

In the article he describes how he had found and used an old telescope. 'One night while looking at the moon I realised that there were shadows on its surface. I corralled my two main tutors to show them, because this was contrary to the ancient version of cosmology I had been taught, which held that the moon was a heavenly body that emitted its own light. But through my telescope the moon was clearly just a barren rock, pocked with craters.'

This experience and his increasing awareness of Western views on the universe made him conclude that the cosmology he was being taught was wrong in many aspects and should be abandoned. 'If the author of that 4th-century treatise were writing today, I'm sure he would write the chapter on cosmology differently.'

The observation regarding cosmology led the Dalai Lama to make an important assessment about the relationship between science and Buddhism: 'If science proves some belief of Buddhism wrong, then Buddhism will have to change.'

Five years earlier in 2000, the Dalai Lama gave a speech entitled 'The Need and Significance of Modern Science' to abbots from the major Tibetan monastic centres of learning and to hundreds of key Tibetan monastic scholars and leaders. In the speech he announced that henceforth modern science education – particularly psychology, physics and astronomy – would form part of the Tibetan monastic curriculum.

Key term

Tenzin Gyatso: name of the 14th Dalai Lama

Specification content

The Dalai Lama's assessment of the value of science.

quickfire

3.9 Who is Sakra?

Garudas are among the astasena and are also Dharmapalas.

Key quotes

If science proves some belief of Buddhism wrong, then Buddhism will have to change. In my view, science and Buddhism share a search for the truth and for understanding reality. By learning from science about aspects of reality where its understanding may be more advanced, I believe that Buddhism enriches its own world view. (Tenzin Gyatso, 14th Dalai Lama)

The knowledge of science will be instrumental in the preservation, promotion and introduction of Buddhism to the new generation of Tibetans. Hence, it is very necessary to begin the study of science. (Tenzin Gyatso, 14th Dalai Lama)

Key terms

Buddha Bhaishajya: the Medicine Buddha

Cittamatra: the Mind Only school of Mahayana Buddhism

In his speech, the Dalai Lama explained that firstly the value of science to Tibetan Buddhism lay in the fact that it had enormously influenced in a positive way people through improving their lives. 'Developments in the field of science and technology have had positive impact on the life of people living in this world. It has directly benefited the people by helping them live a better and more comfortable life.'

In particular, the Dalai Lama argued that it was what had been regarded as the Western 'outsider's art of healing' which brought about correct diagnosis and medication rather than 'mere rituals based on teachings such as the Medicinal Tantra preached by Buddha Bhaishajya'. Buddha Bhaishajya is the Medicine Buddha in Mahayana Buddhism and is regarded as the supreme healer. Meditating on Buddha Bhaishajya is seen to be a very powerful method of bringing health and healing to oneself and others. In case of physical illness, reciting the mantra of the Buddha Bhaishajya over water and then drinking the water is seen as an important restorative.

A second point made by the Dalai Lama was that science was of value because it was 'very precise and accurate' in its analysis of 'the material world, evolution of universe, and nature of chemical substances'. This he believed would supplement and advance Buddhist observations in this area.

As an example, he cites how the treatment of time and energy from a Buddhist analysis is 'extremely gross' such as the time division of snapping one's fingers into 365 flickering instances. Again, the Buddhist analysis of atoms such as 'iron-particle, water-particle, sun-rays particle, hare-particle' does not match the sophistication of modern scientists who are able to work 'at the subtlest level possible'.

A third area identified by the Dalai Lama with regard to the value of science is a straightforward one concerning the future of Buddhism for Tibetans both inside and outside Tibet. The modern world relies on 'ceaseless effort and experimentation of science and technology, rather than mystical clairvoyance or miracle powers'. He argues therefore that it is only through bringing together science and Buddhism that 'belief and conviction' will be generated in the minds of the new generation of Tibetans particularly since they already enjoy much that modern technology has brought to them.

A fourth more philosophical point is that science is of value because it is based on empirical research, and is therefore concerned only with reality and truth. The Dalai Lama regards other religions as ideologies 'based on belief in god as the almighty creator'. In such religions, 'faith is a single-pointed devotion'. By contrast he regards Buddhism alone as combining faith with wisdom. As a result, Buddhism, unlike any other religion, is based on reality and truth. This means that science is of value because it essentially does what Buddhism is doing. On the basis of facts, logical reasoning, critical analysis, method and wisdom a solid basis is provided for progress. The Dalai Lama observes: 'On that which is void of basis, no paths can be cultivated, no goals attained. Therefore, we should look for truth wherever it is prevalent. And truth found through this approach can definitely help develop our inner mind. It will eventually help us realise the fundamental nature of how all sentient beings want happiness and do not want suffering.'

A fifth point that might be made regarding the value of science is that for the Dalai Lama it validates and upholds the teaching of Buddhism because the insights of Buddhism are giving scientific backing. In this area, the Dalai Lama refers specifically to the concepts of impermanence such that nothing truly and ultimately exists. This has always been part of the Dhamma but only recently have scientists realised the truth of the Buddhist Dhamma as they discover that 'things lack true existence' and that 'it is unfindable when closely examined and searched'. Perhaps, without themselves realising it, scientists in this way draw close to the Cittamatra – Mind Only – school of Mahayana Buddhism which also explains how phenomena are given an imaginary nature by the mind.

Finally, the Dalai Lama regards science as being of value because when it is seen how closely allied it is to Buddhism, more people will understand and embrace Buddhism. He quotes the conclusion of a seminar held with scientists: 'taking the matter of fact that science will develop greatly as it ushers into the 21st century, and if there is a religion that can develop with science, it could be none other than Buddhism'.

This overall assessment of the value of science, long-held by the Dalai Lama, led him to co-found with two other Buddhists the **Mind and Life Institute** in 1997. The mission statement of the Institute states that science provides both 'the dominant framework for investigating the nature of reality and the modern source of knowledge that could help improve the lives of humans and the planet'.

However, this approach on its own is regarded as incomplete. In addition, the founders believe that 'well-refined contemplative practices and introspective methods could, and should, be used as equal instruments of investigation — instruments that would not only make science itself more humane but also ensure its conclusions were far-reaching'. Through bringing the two together, the Mind and Life Institute sees itself as advancing 'progress in human well-being'.

Of particular interest to the Dalai Lama in this area is neuroscience and cognitive science. In other words, how the physical aspects of the brain work during meditation and the effect that this might then have on behaviour. Neurological research is a complex area and results of empirical studies need to be treated with some caution. **Neuroplasticity** is of particular interest. The term refers to the ability of the brain to generate new nerve cells and neural connections, thereby altering emotions, behaviour, and perceptions.

In an article entitled 'The Lama in the Lab', Marshall Glickman cites the eminent neuroscientist Richard Davidson who is involved in the Mind and Life Institute and who has studied depression, anxiety and phobias along with compassion, happiness and mindfulness. Using very sophisticated MRI and EEG scans, precise records are made by Davidson of changing activity in the brain. This suggests to him that meditation practice results in measurable changes in the brain leading to 'reduced anxiety, improved immune systems, and increased activity in the area of the brain associated with positive emotions such as joy, enthusiasm. and good will'.

Whilst acknowledging that this is still in its infancy, Davidson argues that such studies support the Dalai Lama's contention that together Buddhism and science can be used to 'transform the brain and body to make us happier and healthier'.

Glickman also refers to the work of psychologist Professor Paul Ekman who has studied expression, evolution and physiology of emotions. Ekman is interested in a project Cultivating Emotional Balance. The goal here is to develop a scientifically proven programme which through focus on the mind is able to reduce destructive emotions which people might harbour.

Glickman writes: 'If research can show that meditation changes brain structure in ways that increase health and happiness, the implications will be enormous. What Buddhism brings to the West is its profound understanding of the mind.'

Study tip

The Dalai Lama has written a great deal about, and given a number of interviews on, the value of science. It would be useful to research what he has had to write and to say in order to add to what has been covered here.

AO1 Activity

Explain how a Buddhist might respond to the following view: 'Science and Buddhism are incompatible.'

Explain your answer using evidence and examples from what you have read.

Santaraksita who in the 8th century CE introduced Cittamatra to Tibet.

Key terms

Mind and Life Institute: co-founded by the Dalai Lama in 1997 to bring together modern science and contemplative practice

Neuroplasticity: the ability of the brain to generate new nerve cells and neural connections, thereby altering emotions, behaviour, and perceptions

The Dalai Lama meeting with scientists.

quickpire

3.10 What did the Dalai Lama add to the Tibetan monastic curriculum in 2000?

Key skills Theme 3

The third theme has tasks that concentrate on a particular aspect of AO1 in terms of using quotations from sources of authority and in the use of references.

Key skills

Knowledge involves:

Selection of a range of (thorough) accurate and relevant information that is directly related to the specific demands of the question.

This means:

- Selecting relevant material for the question set
- Being focused in explaining and examining the material selected.

Understanding involves:

Explanation that is extensive, demonstrating depth and/or breadth with excellent use of evidence and examples including (where appropriate) thorough and accurate supporting use of sacred texts, sources of wisdom and specialist language.

This means:

- Effective use of examples and supporting evidence to establish the quality of your understanding
- Ownership of your explanation that expresses personal knowledge and understanding and NOT just reproducing a chunk of text from a book that you have rehearsed and memorised.

AO1 Developing skills

It is now important to consider the information that has been covered in this section; however, the information in its raw form is too extensive and so has to be processed in order to meet the requirements of the examination. This can be achieved by practising more advanced skills associated with AO1. For assessment objective 1 (AO1), which involves demonstrating 'knowledge' and 'understanding' skills, we are going to focus on different ways in which the skills can be demonstrated effectively, and also, refer to how the performance of these skills is measured (see generic band descriptors for A2 [WJEC] AO1 or A Level [Eduqas] AO1).

▶ **Your next task is this:** Below is a summary of **presentations of Buddhism as avoiding 'blind faith'**. At present it has no references at all to support the points made. Underneath the summary are two references to the works of scholars, and/or religious writings, that could be used in the outline in order to improve the summary. Your task is to re-write the summary but make use of the references. Such phrases as 'according to …', 'the scholar … argues', or, 'it has been suggested by …' may help. Usually a reference included a footnote but for an answer in an A Level essay under examination conditions this is not expected, although an awareness of which book your evidence refers to is useful (although not always necessary).

Faith is a word often associated with religious beliefs and teachings. It means that things are believed in for which there is no proof, such as God, heaven and hell. (*) Buddhism describes 'blind faith' as being mistaken – it is amulika saddha. Instead, the Buddha taught that experience was essential to develop akaravati saddha, which is confidence based on reason and experience. In the Water-snake Simile, for example, he states that wrong grasping of the Dhamma is dangerous and can only be avoided by thinking about things clearly, and questioning the Buddha and experienced monks to be sure of what is being taught. (*) It is this approach which is highlighted in the Kalama Sutta when the Buddha focuses on the words: 'when you know for yourselves'.

'We may define "faith" as a firm belief in something for which there is no evidence. Where there is evidence, no one speaks of "faith". We do not speak of faith that two and two are four or that the earth is round. We only speak of faith when we wish to substitute emotion for evidence. The substitution of emotion for evidence is apt to lead to strife, since different groups substitute different emotions.' **(Bertrand Russell)**

'The Buddha emphasised self-reliance and the experiential testing-out of all teachings, including his own. He was well aware of the many conflicting doctrines of his day, a time of intellectual ferment. Rejecting teachings based on authoritative tradition, or mere rational speculation, he emphasised the examination and analysis of actual experience.' **(Harvey)**

When you have completed the task, try to write another reference that you could use and further extend your answer.

Issues for analysis and evaluation

The extent to which there is a close relationship between Buddhism and science

That there is a close relationship between Buddhism and science is asserted by a number of Buddhists.

Examples of this can be seen from the 19th century. For example, the Japanese philosopher Inoue Enryo (1858–1919) founded a philosophy institute and wrote over one hundred books. His concern – which was that of many of his Buddhist contemporaries – was to defend Buddhism against the preaching of Christian missionaries whose influence was increasingly felt in Japan at that time. Inoue was 'deeply critical of Christianity as unscientific and irrational, in distinction to Buddhism, which is scientific ... Buddhism was superior to Christianity because of its congruence with scientific fact' (Deal and Ruppert).

This general approach as to Buddhism's congruence with scientific fact – in contrast to Christianity – has also been upheld in the West. In his *Buddhism and Science: A Guide for the Perplexed*, Lopez observes that for many Victorians, 'Buddhism was a tradition that saw the universe as subject to natural laws, without the need for any form of divine intervention. This led many European enthusiasts to declare Buddhism as the religion most suited to serious dialogue with Science, because both postulated the existence of immutable laws that governed the universe.'

Buddhism's apparent congruence with scientific fact is also highlighted in a quotation attributed to Einstein: 'The religion of the future will be a cosmic religion. It should transcend a personal God and avoid dogmas and theology. Covering both the natural and the spiritual, it should be based on a religious sense arising from the experience of all things, natural and spiritual as a meaningful unity. If there is any religion that would cope with modern scientific needs, it would be Buddhism.'

This highlights one of the key aspects of Buddhism which it might be argued gives it a close relationship with science: the lack of belief in a personal God. The Dalai Lama argues that religions in general are viewed as ideologies primarily because of belief in God. This he describes as 'false reification'. Reification means regarding something abstract as a material thing. Scientists therefore regard religions in general as being 'unfounded and baseless' since they 'do not see their teachings as complying to the true nature of phenomena's existence'. Since Buddhism has no belief in a personal God, it is not encumbered by false reification and so from the outset there is congruence with science.

Furthermore, Buddhism eschews belief in a creator God who is responsible for the earth and all that it inhabits. This is combined with the rejection of the soul and its immortality. In addition, the concept of prayer being answered by God, or the punishment of hell and the reward of heaven being allotted by God, are also rejected. From this perspective, Buddhism regards human life and the progression of the universe as being subject only to natural laws without any divine intervention. Such laws of the universe are those which are open to empirical research in order that they can be proven true or false. Hence, again, there is arguably a close relationship between Buddhism and science.

As we have noted, for many Buddhists the approach taken by the Buddha towards the Kalama clan in Kesaputta is one which is identifiable as a scientific one. The key phrase used by the Buddha is 'when you know for yourselves' – that is when the information gained is from empirical data and not based on what has been received or believed by others. The implication of this empirical approach is that there is an openness in Buddhism towards rejecting the old and accepting the new, when questions of truth and reality are concerned. Here, evidence is the key issue.

This section covers AO2 content and skills

Specification content

The extent to which there is a close relationship between Buddhism and science.

Key quote

The Buddha taught ... twenty-five centuries ago a scientific religion containing the highest individualistic altruistic ethics, a philosophy of life built on psychological mysticism and a cosmogony which is in harmony with geology, astronomy, radioactivity and relativity. No creator god can create an ever-changing, ever-existing cosmos. Countless billions of aeons ago the earth was existing but undergoing change, and there are billions of solar systems that had existed and exist and shall exist. (Anagarika Dharmapala speaking in 1925 quoted by Lopez)

AO2 Activity

As you read through this section try to do the following:

1. Pick out the different lines of argument that are presented in the text and identify any evidence given in support.

2. For each line of argument try to evaluate whether or not you think this is strong or weak.

3. Think of any questions you may wish to raise in response to the arguments.

This Activity will help you to start thinking critically about what you read and help you to evaluate the effectiveness of different arguments and from this develop your own observations, opinions and points of view that will help with any conclusions that you make in your answers to the AO2 questions that arise.

Key quote

A deeper dialogue between neuroscience and society – indeed between all scientific fields and society – could help deepen our understanding of what it means to be human and our responsibilities for the natural world we share with other sentient beings. (Tenzin Gyatso, 14th Dalai Lama)

Key questions

How representative is the Dalai Lama of Buddhism in general?

Does acceptance of the scientific method mean that there is therefore a close relationship between Buddhism and science?

What are the consequences of rejecting belief in Mount Meru and the supernatural realms and beings linked to it?

AO2 Activity

List some conclusions that could be drawn from the AO2 reasoning from the above text; try to aim for at least three different possible conclusions. Consider each of the conclusions and collect brief evidence to support each conclusion from the AO1 and AO2 material for this topic. Select the conclusion that you think is most convincing and explain why it is so. Try to contrast this with the weakest conclusion in the list, justifying your argument with clear reasoning and evidence.

It was empirical scientific evidence which enabled the Dalai Lama to reject the accepted Buddhist cosmology which had been taught for centuries and which he himself had studied. In his book, *The Universe in a Single Atom* he states this explicitly: 'These sizes, distances, and so forth are flatly contradicted by the empirical evidence of modern astronomy. There is a dictum in Buddhist philosophy that to uphold a tenet that contradicts reason is to undermine one's credibility; to contradict empirical evidence is still a greater fallacy. So, it is hard to take the Abhidhamma cosmology literally. My own view is that Buddhism must abandon many aspects of the Abhidhamma cosmology.'

In the same book, the Dalai Lama goes even further in supporting what might be considered the scientific method. Based on the Buddha's approach to the Kalama clan he writes: 'Although Buddhism has come to evolve as a religion with a characteristic body of scriptures and rituals, strictly speaking, in Buddhism scriptural authority cannot outweigh an understanding based on reason and experience. Just as a seasoned goldsmith would test the purity of his gold through a meticulous process of examination, the Buddha advises that people should test the truth of what he has said through reasoned examination and personal experiment. Therefore, when it comes to validating the truth of a claim, Buddhism accords greatest authority to experience, with reason second and scripture last.' This would seem to imply that for the Dalai Lama and many Buddhists, for example, belief in Mount Meru and the supernatural realms and beings linked to it, has to be rejected.

Many hold that the Buddhist concept of karma is scientific. In its essence, karma teaches that there is an unbreakable link between cause and effect. Causation appears to be a thoroughly modern and scientific concept since it can be subject to either the verification or falsification principle. This Buddhist doctrine is therefore seen as a natural law present throughout the universe when seen in a mechanistic Newtonian way.

In 1894, Thomas Huxley – a supporter of Buddhism – wrote: 'If this world is full of pain and sorrow; if grief and evil fall, like the rain, upon both the just and the unjust; it is because, like the rain, they are links in the endless chain of natural causation by which past, present, and future are indissolubly connected; and there is no more injustice in the one case than in the other. Every sentient being is reaping as it has sown; if not in this life, then in one or other of the infinite series of antecedent existences of which it is the latest term. The present distribution of good and evil is, therefore, the algebraical sum of accumulated positive and negative deserts; or, rather, it depends on the floating balance of the account.'

A further concept which some might argue shows the close relationship between Buddhism and science is that found in the Heart Sutra. In this Avalokitesvara teaches Sariputra that 'form is empty and emptiness is form'. The term for emptiness is sunyata and is a central concept in Mahayana Buddhism. It links closely with the Dalai Lama's belief that in recognising that 'things lack true existence', scientists draw close to the Cittamatra School. In *The Universe in a Single Atom* he makes this link explicit: 'To a Mahayana Buddhist there is an unmistakable resonance between the notion of emptiness and the new physics. If on the quantum level, matter is revealed as less solid and definable than it appears, then it seems to me that science is coming closer to the Buddhist contemplative insights of emptiness and interdependence.'

Kesariya is present-day Kesaputta where the Buddha addressed the Kalama clan.

Ways in which scientific world view and Buddhism are incompatible

The discovery of Buddhism within intellectual circles in the West began in the 19th century largely as a result of the British presence in India. The assessment made then was as to Buddhism having begun in India but by the 19th century no longer being present. Instead it was to be found in present day Sri Lanka, Southeast Asia and Northeast Asia.

The received opinion which dominated views then, posits an original, authentic and pure Buddhism taught by the Buddha from which Buddhism as practised over the centuries was derived. This Buddhism as practised was widely regarded as having adulterated the original, authentic and pure Buddhism of the Buddha. Theravada Buddhism was regarded as the most authentic form of Buddhism remaining – unlike Mahayana Buddhism.

Lopez maintains that it is important to understand this historical context because, he argues, the concept of there being an original, authentic and pure Buddhism derived from the historical Buddha, is an entirely Western construct created by 19th-century European scholarship. This construct is still present today. Thus, when the terms Buddhism and science are conjoined, many Buddhists and others are isolating this particular Western construct of Buddhism and making it congruent with science. In reality, it could therefore legitimately be argued that Buddhism as practised and believed in Asia is incompatible with science.

Thus, Lopez writes, 'It has generally been the case that, regardless of the differences among the various Buddhisms that have been paired with various Sciences, they share a rather spare rationality, with the vast imaginaire of Buddhism largely absent; each is a Buddhism extracted from the Buddhist universe, a universe dense with deities.'

It might also be argued that the foundation for stating that science and Buddhism are compatible is based on a simplistic interpretation of the Kalama Sutta. Bhikkhu Bodhi points this out: 'Partly in reaction to dogmatic religion, partly in subservience to the reigning paradigm of objective scientific knowledge, it has become fashionable to hold, by appeal to the Kalama Sutta, that the Buddha's teaching dispenses with faith and formulated doctrine and asks us to accept only what we can personally verify.'

Bikkhu Bodhi argues that the people of the Kalama clan are not Buddhists; what is described is their initial encounter with the Buddha. This is the context for the Buddha teaching them to not go by 'reports, by legends, by traditions, by scripture, by logical conjecture, by inference, by analogies, by agreement through pondering views, by probability, or by the thought, that this contemplative is our teacher'.

The Buddha does *not* state that this is the approach which should be adopted to the Buddhist Dhamma: he is simply giving the Kalamas general advice and good counsel about how to make choices in belief. Once they have heard him they are then moved to proclaim, 'Magnificent, lord! Magnificent ... We go to the Blessed One for refuge, to the Dhamma, and to the sangha of monks. May the Blessed One remember us as lay followers who have gone to him for refuge, from this day forward, for life.'

Arguably it is only through a very narrow and selective approach that Buddhism and science are compatible. For example, whilst belief in the physical reality of Mount Meru may have waned, that is not the same for belief in the beings which populate Mount Meru, such as the devas, nor in the realms which can be found on the top of Mount Meru, such as Tavatimsa, or the hell realms lying under the continent of Jambudvipa. The supernatural – and hence the unscientific – is woven through Buddhist thought and practice. Tavatimsa and the hell realms are

Specification content
Ways in which scientific world view and Buddhism are incompatible.

Key quote

The discourse has been described as 'the Buddha's Charter of Free Inquiry'.

It is problematic whether the sutta can support all the positions that have been ascribed to it. On the basis of a single passage the Buddha has been made out to be a pragmatic empiricist who dismisses all doctrine and faith, and whose Dhamma is simply a freethinker's kit to truth which invites each one to accept and reject whatever he likes. (Bhikkhu Bodhi)

AO2 Activity

As you read through this section try to do the following:

1. Pick out the different lines of argument that are presented in the text and identify any evidence given in support.

2. For each line of argument try to evaluate whether or not you think this is strong or weak.

3. Think of any questions you may wish to raise in response to the arguments.

This Activity will help you to start thinking critically about what you read and help you to evaluate the effectiveness of different arguments and from this develop your own observations, opinions and points of view that will help with any conclusions that you make in your answers to the AO2 questions that arise.

Key questions

To what extent can original, authentic and pure Buddhism be recovered?

Is belief in the religious supernatural ipso facto unscientific?

How far is the question of the relationship between Buddhism and science really one of whether Buddhism is a religion or not?

Key quote

The question, then, is which Buddhist doctrines can be eliminated while allowing Buddhism to remain Buddhism. Can there be Buddhism without Mount Meru? Can you play chess without the queen? Mount Meru – with its four faces of gold, silver, lapis, and crystal is a slippery slope. (Lopez)

Study tip

It is vital for AO2 that you actually discuss arguments and not just explain what someone may have stated. Try to ask yourself, 'was this a fair point to make?', 'is the evidence sound enough?', 'is there anything to challenge this argument?', 'is this a strong or weak argument?' Such critical analysis will help you develop your evaluation skills.

AO2 Activity

List some conclusions that could be drawn from the AO2 reasoning from the above text; try to aim for at least three different possible conclusions. Consider each of the conclusions and collect brief evidence to support each conclusion from the AO1 and AO2 material for this topic. Select the conclusion that you think is most convincing and explain why it is so. Try to contrast this with the weakest conclusion in the list, justifying your argument with clear reasoning and evidence.

not things which can be subject to either verification or falsification as would be required by scientific methodology.

Such narrowness and selectivity are also apparent in the focus on particular features of the Dhamma such as sunyata. The Dalai Lama notes how this concept might be congruent with quantum physics, but it is the same Dalai Lama who along with Tibetan monks practises Tantric meditation on a daily basis. Such meditation involves the entirely unscientific belief in the efficacy of using the vajra and bell, elaborate mudras and the creation and destruction of mandalas. In addition, elaborate visualisation is required when various Buddhas, bodhisattvas, devas, devaputras and the realms in which they exist are brought to mind. Part of the elaborate tantric meditation process also involves promising not to break the tantric vows which includes failing to rely on the mudra, vajra and bell and scorning gods, demigods and secret deities.

Lopez suggests that whilst researchers might focus on Buddhist meditation and what can be measured via an MRI scan, this is ignoring the basic point of meditation which the Buddha taught: 'Monks this is the direct path for the purification of being, for the surmounting of sorrow and lamentation, for the disappearance of pain and grief, for the attainment of the true way, for the realisation of nibbana.'

Concepts such as anatta and anicca might seem compatible with science, but the same cannot be said for the theological philosophy which underpins dukkha and karma leading to rebirth in the realms of samsara.

It might be argued that the incompatibility between Buddhism and science is brought into sharp focus by consideration of the avyakata – the undetermined questions.

It is recorded in the Cula-Malunkyovada Sutta that the monk Malunkyaputta was concerned with a number of issues which were 'undeclared, set aside and discarded' by the Buddha. Amongst these were questions regarding the universe. Malunkyaputta asks the Buddha: 'Lord, if the Blessed One knows that the cosmos is eternal, then may he declare to me that the cosmos is eternal. If he knows that the cosmos is not eternal, then may he declare to me that the cosmos is not eternal.' He raises the same question as to whether the universe is finite or infinite.

Rather than encouraging further research into these questions or indeed answering the questions clearly, the Buddha replies with the parable of the poisoned arrow. In this a man wounded by an arrow smeared with poison refuses to have the arrow removed until questions are answered such as who shot the arrow, what type of bow was used to shoot the arrow, what the bowstring was made of, what type of wood was used for the shaft of the arrow. The Buddha concludes that these questions are unimportant and that during the time spent asking the questions the man would die.

He applies this parable to the questions asked by Malunkyaputta and confirms: 'And what is undeclared by me? The cosmos is eternal is undeclared by me. The cosmos is not eternal is undeclared by me. The cosmos is finite is undeclared by me. The cosmos is infinite is undeclared by me.' The reason the Buddha gives for not answering these questions is that they 'are not fundamental to the holy life'.

Overall, therefore, whilst science is concerned with objective data and facts based on empirical research in order to establish truths about reality, Buddhism is only concerned with these tangentially since its goal is wholly unscientific: living the holy life and thus gaining nibbana.

AO2 Developing skills

It is now important to consider the information that has been covered in this section; however, the information in its raw form is too extensive and so has to be processed in order to meet the requirements of the examination. This can be achieved by practising more advanced skills associated with AO2. For assessment objective 2 (AO2), which involves 'critical analysis' and 'evaluation' skills, we are going to focus on different ways in which the skills can be demonstrated effectively, and also, refer to how the performance of these skills is measured (see generic band descriptors for A2 [WJEC] AO2 or A Level [Eduqas] AO2).

▶ **Your next task is this:** Below is an evaluation of **ways in which a scientific world view and Buddhism are incompatible**. At present it has no references at all to support the arguments presented. Underneath the evaluation are two references made to the works of scholars, and/or religious writings, that could be used in the evaluation in order to improve it. Your task is to re-write the evaluation but make use of the references. Such phrases as 'in his/her book … (scholar) argues that …', 'an interesting argument in support of this is made by … who suggests that …', or, 'the work of (scholar) has made a major contribution to the debate by pointing out …' may help. Usually a reference included a footnote but for an answer in an A Level essay under examination conditions this is not expected, although an awareness of which book your evidence refers to is useful (although not always necessary).

Any assessment of whether a scientific world view and Buddhism are compatible or incompatible has to recognise that since the 19th century it was customary to present Buddhism as being a scientific religion. This was based on the idea that, unlike Christianity and the other Abrahamic faiths, there is no belief required in a creator God. (*) The present Dalai Lama has emphasised that, for example, the view of cosmology in the Abhidhamma cannot be taken literally given the facts of science. However, it could be argued that this approach depends on an entirely one-sided view of Buddhism. At its core, Buddhist beliefs, teaching and practice might involve a recognition of the supernatural realm of bodhisattvas and other spiritual beings and places such as Mount Meru, which cannot be seen and which do not exist in the ordinary sense of the word. (*) Since there is no empirical evidence for any of this, it would appear that at this level Buddhism is incompatible with a scientific world view.

'The Buddha taught … twenty-five centuries ago a scientific religion containing the highest individualistic altruistic ethics, a philosophy of life built on psychological mysticism and a cosmogony which is in harmony with geology, astronomy, radioactivity and relativity. No creator god can create an ever-changing, ever-existing cosmos. Countless billions of aeons ago the earth was existing but undergoing change, and there are billions of solar systems that had existed and exist and shall exist.' **(Anagarika Dharmapala speaking in 1925 quoted by Lopez)**

'The question, then, is which Buddhist doctrines can be eliminated while allowing Buddhism to remain Buddhism? Can there be Buddhism without Mount Meru? Can you play chess without the queen? Mount Meru – with its four faces of gold, silver, lapis, and crystal is a slippery slope.' **(Lopez)**

When you have completed the task, try to write another reference that you could use and further extend your evaluation.

Key skills Theme 3

The third theme has tasks that concentrate on a particular aspect of AO2 in terms of using quotations from sources of authority and in the use of references in supporting arguments and evaluations.

Key skills
Analysis involves:

Identifying issues raised by the materials in the AO1, together with those identified in the AO2 section, and presents sustained and clear views, either of scholars or from a personal perspective ready for evaluation.

This means:

- That your answers are able to identify key areas of debate in relation to a particular issue
- That you can identify, and comment upon, the different lines of argument presented by others
- That your response comments on the overall effectiveness of each of these areas or arguments.

Evaluation involves:

Considering the various implications of the issues raised based upon the evidence gleaned from analysis and provides an extensive detailed argument with a clear conclusion.

This means:

- That your answer weighs up the consequences of accepting or rejecting the various and different lines of argument analysed
- That your answer arrives at a conclusion through a clear process of reasoning.

**This section covers AO1
content and skills**

Specification content

The relationship between religion
and society: respect and recognition
and the ways that religious traditions
view other religions and non-religious
worldviews and their truth claims.
Buddhism's frequent presentation in
the West as a secular philosophy.

*Thomas Huxley (1825–1895) who argued
that Buddhism knows no God.*

quickfire

3.11 To which monk did the Buddha explain
the parable of the poisoned arrow?

Key quote

This is the kind of freedom that
Buddhism can help anyone achieve.
When we disconnect our emotional
reactions from what happens to us,
we become free to be better workers,
better parents, better partners,
better bosses, better human beings.
(Noah Rasheta)

C: Religion and society: responses to the challenges from secularisation

Buddhism's frequent presentation in the West as a secular philosophy

Lopez argues that one of the main attractions of Buddhism to many Western
intellectuals in the 19th century was that it could be regarded as a secular
philosophy. We have already seen how for them the idea of there being a
recoverable original, authentic and pure Buddhism was very attractive. Such a
Buddhism was felt to be not that practised in Theravada or Mahayana but was
instead a secular form of Buddhism where the focus was entirely on how to live a
fulfilled life in the here and now.

We have already noted how Buddhism was attractive to the well-known Victorian
intellectual Thomas Huxley. The key point for him was that the original, authentic
and pure Buddhism was an atheistic and secular philosophical approach to life:
'A system which knows no God in the western sense; which denies a soul to man;
which counts the belief in immortality a blunder and the hope of it a sin; which
refuses any efficacy to prayer and sacrifice; which bids men look to nothing but
their own efforts for salvation; which, in its original purity, knew nothing of vows
of obedience, abhorred intolerance, and never sought the aid of the secular arm ...
and is still, with whatever base admixture of foreign superstitions, the dominant
creed of a large fraction of mankind.'

Turning to the 21st century, typical of popular contemporary presentations of
Buddhism as a secular philosophy is the work of Noah Rasheta, the founder of
Secular Buddhism.com and the Secular Buddhism podcast. In his book *Secular
Buddhism: Eastern Thought for Western Minds* he explains that for him, Buddhism is
not a religion. Instead, it is a way of life: 'not something to believe in but something
to notice and observe'. To support his approach, he quotes Thich Nhat Hanh as
saying: 'The secret of Buddhism is to remove all ideas, all concepts, in order for the
truth to have a chance to penetrate, to reveal itself.'

Citing the dialogue with Malunkyaputta and parable of the poisoned arrow,
Rasheta argues that Buddhism is not concerned in any sense at all with 'immense,
unknowable, metaphysical questions'. Instead, Buddhism is concerned with
spirituality. However, for him, this term has no religious overtones. Instead it
means two things: making a connection and finding meaning. For Rasheta, neither
of these requires what might be termed religion. Religion is what he terms a shared
conceptual belief which is entirely made by humans. Individual religious belief is
a personal conceptual belief. However, both of these fall short of what he argues
is most important: 'an experiential understanding of reality'. As a secular Buddhist
this is what he believes Buddhism offers: freedom from conceptual belief and the
possibility of an experiential understanding through understanding Buddhism as a
secular philosophy.

Rasheta's presentation of the Four Noble Truths is one which sets them in the
context of enabling people to recognise that the world is not such as their personal
conceptual beliefs may present it. The Noble Eightfold Path is there to 'serve as a
guideline for the specific areas of our lives where we can focus on becoming better
versions of ourselves'. Rasheta's secular version of meditation is to agree with
the view that 'you can make any human activity into meditation simply by being
completely with it and doing it just to do it'.

He continues by arguing that the key to understanding Buddhism as a secular philosophy is to focus on awareness – living and experiencing the present moment. To illustrate this secular philosophical approach, Rasheta relates the Zen koan of the Tiger and the Strawberry.

'There was once a man who was being chased by a ferocious tiger across a field. At the edge of the field there was a cliff. In order to escape the jaws of the tiger, the man caught hold of a vine and swung himself over the edge of the cliff. Dangling down, he saw, to his dismay, there were more tigers on the ground below him! When things seemed like they couldn't get worse, two little mice showed up and started gnawing on the vine to which he clung. He knew that at any moment he would fall to certain death. Just then, he noticed a wild strawberry growing on the cliff wall. Clutching the vine with one hand, he plucked the strawberry with the other and put it in his mouth. He never before realised how sweet a strawberry could taste.'

Buddhism as a secular philosophy focuses on awareness in living and experiencing the present moment no matter what else might be happening.

In addition, Rasheta argues that emptiness is essential to Buddhism as a secular philosophy. For him this means recognising that 'as life unfolds it doesn't mean anything. All things simply are as they are.'

For Rasheta, karma is recognising that each person is the product of a huge collocation of cause and effect and that death is part of that process. He uses the analogy of music: 'It's like recognising that there is music (life) and then there are songs (individuals). While we are songs, with a starting note (birth) and a final note (death), we were never just a song, we are music, and the music goes on.' As a secular philosophy, Buddhism is concerned with helping people recognise that they are not the labels they give to themselves and that people can and need to let go of their personal conceptual beliefs.

Stephen Batchelor: Buddhism as a rational philosophy and way of life

A far more scholarly approach to Buddhism from the secular perspective is presented by Stephen Batchelor (1953–). He is the author of a large number of books in which he outlines his view of Buddhism as a rational philosophy and way of life. He synthesises his thinking in *After Buddhism: Rethinking the Dharma for a Secular Age* published in 2015.

In a number of ways, his approach is a development and refinement of the premise put forward by Huxley. He had argued that the original, authentic and pure Buddhism had developed over time with a 'base admixture of foreign superstitions'. Batchelor's approach is to pursue an analytical approach to Buddhism in general and to the life of the historical Buddha in particular.

Batchelor interprets the word 'secular' – based on its Latin origins – as meaning 'this age' and 'this generation'. To be secular therefore means that the primary concerns are to do with 'this world – about everything that has to do with the quality of the personal, social, and environmental experience of being alive on this planet'. and sees his presentation as bringing modernity to Buddhism.

A useful analogy is to think about a very old damaged and unfinished oil painting. Over the years various painters have put their own work into it to preserve and finish it and layers of varnish have been added to protect it. Today, the work of restoration involves removing the varnish and the work of previous painters until what is revealed is the original as the artist painted it.

Study tip

Research the resources on Noah Rasheta's Secular Buddhism.com website and assess the type of Buddhism which is being presented.

Specification content

Stephen Batchelor (a Buddhist Atheist) and his presentation of Buddhism as a rational philosophy and way of life.

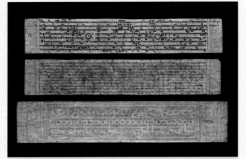

The Pali Canon which is regarded by some secular Buddhists as presenting the clearest account of the Buddha and the dharma.

Key quote

While paying heed to the different voices in the canon, I am drawn to the sceptical and pragmatic ones. They stand out as most distinctive and original in Gotama's teaching. (Batchelor)

quickfire

3.12 With which Buddhist canon of sacred text does Batchelor mainly work?

In the task of restoration, a key tool used by Batchelor is scepticism regarding Buddhist texts. He works mainly with the Pali Canon because for him, 'the very wealth of material raises serious difficulties of interpretation'. In particular he finds that they present 'conflicting ideas, doctrines and images' in addition to the work of editors and commentators. To work through these layers, Batchelor distinguishes six different 'voices' that can be found in the texts: poetic, dramatic, sceptical, pragmatic, dogmatic and mythic. He then sees his task, justified by his interpretation of the Buddha's teaching in the Kalama Sutta, to focus on two of these 'voices': the sceptical and pragmatic as being the most authentic and as representing most accurately what the Buddha taught. He in turn brings his own sceptical and pragmatic approach to Buddhism.

With regard to the life of the Buddha, a good example of this can be seen in the account whereby having been enlightened, Gotama is unsure whether to teach what he has discovered. Traditional accounts relate how the god Brahma appeared to Gotama and asked him to teach. From Batchelor's perspective this story could be seen as being shaped by the poetic, dramatic, dogmatic and mythic voices but not by the sceptical and pragmatic voices. It is not something that happened. In particular he sees it as a reminder that from the outset Buddhism developed within the social and religious norms of Brahmanism. Making Brahma appear to Gotama makes 'the dharma legitimate because it was sanctioned by God'. Supernatural elements which are related regarding the life of the Buddha belong to the mythic voices of the past: 'they originate in a long-lost enchanted world where gods and devils alike descended to earth to commune with human beings'.

A similar approach of being sceptical and pragmatic is applied to the Dhamma as a whole. Batchelor questions the typical Western approach of many 'convert' Buddhists who accept the dogmatic voice of Buddhism without query and question in a way which does not match the modern secular age in which people live. The dogmatic voice can be seen in, for example, the presentation of 'the four noble truths, the twelve links of dependent origination, the two truths, the end of suffering …elaborate theories about karma, rebirth, and nonhuman realms of existence'.

Removing the layers which have covered the Dhamma, Batchelor states that it is important to keep in mind that some utterances ascribed to the Buddha are ones which are 'determined by the common outlook of the time' and can therefore be put to one side as not being authentic. His focus is instead only on those teachings which 'cannot be derived from the world view of 5th century BCE India'.

This leads Batchelor to conclude that there are what he calls four P's which provide the basis for a rational philosophy and way of life:

1. The Principle of Conditionality

This does not have the complex meaning often ascribed to pratitya-samutpada – dependent origination. The Buddha was simply being pragmatic here and not talking about an abstract principle. Instead Batchelor interprets it as follows: 'You understand how previous choices, acts, and circumstances brought you to your current situation and which present choices and acts might lead to a less restricted and more flourishing future … The best way to know your past is to examine the quality of your present experience, and the most fruitful way to prepare for the future is to consider the quality of what you think, say, and do in response to situations here and now.'

2. The Principle of a Fourfold Task

This consists of the following:

a. To comprehend suffering
b. To let go of the arising of reactivity
c. To behold the ceasing of reactivity
d. To cultivate an eightfold path: complete view, complete thought, complete speech, complete action, complete livelihood, complete effort, complete mindfulness and complete concentration. Here, Batchelor prefers to use the world 'complete' rather than the word 'right' because the way of life he envisages means that each element of the path can become 'an integral part of a whole'.

3. The Perspective of Mindful Awareness

Mindful Awareness for Batchelor is not 'just stepping back and passively noticing what is passing before the inner eye'. It is much more about having a heightened attention to everything that is being done. Meditation finds its place in this context as it means above all being fully aware. This can be, for example, being fully aware of one's own body through 'imaginatively peeling off the skin and considering what lies inside the body'. The key point here is that through Mindful Awareness a person can develop 'an exploratory and potentially transformative relationship with the pulsing, sensitive, and conscious material of life itself'.

4. The Power of Self-Reliance

To explain this concept, Batchelor's comments regarding some of the final teaching of the Buddha can be noted. Very sick and near to death, the Buddha speaks to his closest follower: 'Therefore, Ananda, you should live as islands unto yourselves, being your own refuge, with no other refuge, with the dharma as an island, with the dharma as your refuge, with no other refuge.' The concept of being one's own refuge is advocating Self-Reliance. This means being independent of others in the sense of framing one's own life using the four P's. Thus, responses to suffering are not conditioned by reactivity. 'Gotama encourages a caring and care-full life, founded on personal responsibility and autonomy rather than on a set of rules or precepts to be applied irrespective of circumstance.'

With the four P's as the basis, Batchelor argues that an egalitarian community can be established as envisaged by the Buddha in which – unlike the situation in the world of Buddhism today – all 'are entirely equal in the training they receive in the dharma, the practices they undertake to master and understand it, and the responsibility they have in communicating its message.' He emphasises this point in his Ten Theses of Secular Buddhism in which he says of the Fourfold Task that it can be practised by: 'All human beings, irrespective of gender, race, sexual orientation, disability, nationality, and religion.' Secular Buddhists should then work within society in the type of ways encouraged by Socially Engaged Buddhism.

Key quotes

The eightfold path is a model for a centred life, which is balanced, harmonious, and integrated instead of imbalanced, discordant, and fragmented. It is not a recipe for a pious Buddhist existence in which the practitioner does everything right and gets nothing wrong. (Batchelor)

The dharma serves the needs of people at specific times and places. Each form the dharma assumes is a transient human creation, contingent upon the historical, cultural, social, and economic conditions that generated it. (Batchelor)

Stephen Batchelor: a key proponent of Secular Buddhism

quickfire

3.13 What are the four P's?

Specification content

Buddhism's frequent presentation in the West as a secular philosophy, with reference to David Brazier, who claims Buddhism is a religion.

Key quote

Looking at a Buddhist text, the Westerner seems not to notice the references to rebirth, to conversations with deities, to supernatural occurrences, to faith, to past aeons, to celestial Buddhas, and to anything else that does not fit into the modernist paradigm. (Brazier)

quickfire

3.14 What is David Brazier's Buddhist name?

David Brazier: Buddhism in the West as a religion

The year before Batchelor's *After Buddhism: Rethinking the Dharma for a Secular Age*, David Brazier (1947–) published his book *Buddhism is a Religion: You Can Believe It*. Both Batchelor and Brazier have significant backgrounds in Buddhism but Brazier's approach is the antithesis to that provided by Batchelor. In addition to being the author of a number of books on Buddhism, Brazier describes himself as a Buddhist priest and as Head of the Order of Amida Buddha. His Buddhist name is given as Dharmavidya, which means 'clear perception of what is fundamental'.

For Brazier, what is fundamental is that 'Buddhism is, has always been, and needs to continue to be understood as a religion'. He argues that in the West the type of view expounded by Huxley regarding Buddhism has gained increasing momentum particularly in the age of modernity which values secularism, humanism and materialism. For that reason, he believes that his views run 'against a currently popular trend'.

Brazier argues that making Buddhism a secular philosophy, as has happened in the West, has meant that Buddhism has been distorted so that 'only some parts of some forms' of it have been accepted, adopted and adapted. He uses the analogy of fitting an eagle into a canary cage: 'Bits stick out all over the place and the truth is that it simply will not all go in. If you were to manage to get it in you would kill it in the process.'

Rather than helping to bring Buddhism to the modern age, the process that has often taken place in the West is to practise a 'selective blindness'. The 'bits of the eagle' which will not fit in the cage are the 'devotional, supernatural and metaphysical aspects' which for Brazier are at the heart of Buddhism. Taking these away or dismissing them as 'a base admixture of foreign superstitions' means in effect that true Buddhism is destroyed in the process. Instead, Brazier suggests that Buddhists in the West should 'grow into the bigger-mindedness and bigger-heartedness that it is offering us'. He suggests that holding onto secular Buddhism is rather like being 'people who never learn to swim because they will not let go of the rail on the edge of the pool'.

As we have seen, part of the concept of Buddhism being distorted by 'a base admixture of foreign superstitions' is the belief that an original, authentic and pure Buddha can be found who is in essence a man with a rational philosophy. Brazier disputes this claim. He presents the Buddha specifically as someone who was 'a religious organiser'. Thus, for example, the order of monks is one which was not a later addition but one founded by the Buddha himself.

Buddhist monks praying in a temple.

In addition, Brazier argues that the presentation of the Buddha as a metaphysical being with supernatural gifts and abilities is one that has been accepted throughout the course of Buddhist history and is one that should still be accepted today: 'Buddha is presented by Buddhists as the teacher of the gods, which hardly bears out this reductionist contention. In fact, for Buddhists, Buddha is an eternally continuing presence in metaphysical form. In the doctrine of the Three Body (Trikaya with kaya meaning body) nature of Buddha, all three bodies are essentially metaphysical.'

In his explanation of the Trikaya nature, Brazier points out in each case the metaphysical and supernatural qualities of the Buddha and Buddhas which are presented:

a. Dharmakaya refers to the Dhamma body of the Buddha which equates to 'the unconditional love, compassion, truth and being of Buddha that pervades all existence'. This understanding of the Dharmakaya requires complete spiritual and religious enlightenment.

b. Sambhogakaya refers to enjoyment bodies. This is the way in which Buddhas appear as a result of a spiritual experience such as in a dream or a vision. Brazier describes them as being akin to angels who bring messages from the spiritual world to the mundane world. He refers, for example, to accounts of how Atisha – who is one of those credited with bringing Buddhism to Tibet – saw many sambhogakaya-Buddhas such as Tara and Maitreya in dreams and visions who encouraged him in his studies.

c. Nirmanakaya refers to transformation bodies. This refers to the fact that Buddhas can appear in any form whatsoever. Thus, ordinary-seeming people and objects can manifest Dharmakaya and in this way again the spiritual breaks through into the mundane.

The response of the secular Buddhist might be to say 'But this is just ...' Brazier states that this straightaway demonstrates another attempt to fit 'the eagle into the canary cage': 'the intention to reduce the spiritual life to factors that can be accommodated within a materialist framework'.

It is only a Western and modern obsession with 'facticity, the concrete, the historical and the psychological' which means that the focus is not on the Trikaya nature as it is everywhere else in the Buddhist world but simply on the historical Shakyamuni Buddha and attempts to rediscover his life. The East Asian tradition demonstrates that facts, the concrete, the historical and the psychological are entirely unimportant. Here, in their shrines, are Buddhas which exist in 'other dimensions and in other worlds' such as Kuan-Yin, Manjushri, Samantabhadra and Amitabha.

Brazier does not attempt to distinguish and separate the different 'voices' which Batchelor sees in Buddhist texts. Instead he highlights parts of the Pali Canon which, he argues, indicate the Buddha teaching that he had founded a religion and not a secular philosophy. One example he gives is that the Buddha was clear about the importance of worship and veneration. This is apparent in his teaching to Ananda with regard to holy places of pilgrimage. Thus, the Buddha describes the four places 'a pious person should visit and regard with sentiments of reverence' being Lumbini, Bodh Gaya, Sarnath and Kushinara.

Statue of Kuan-Yin, the holy being of compassion

Key quote

… the female form of Avalokitesvara has provided some of the most attractive stories in Buddhist folk literature and some of the most beautiful works in the world of religious art. Among the various forms of Kuan-yin, all female, we find the Kuan-yin 'Giver of Children' … or the 'Lion's Roar' Kuan-yin, seated on the back of a playful Chinese lion or the Kuan-yin 'Holder of the Lotus'. (Williams)

quickfire

3.15 What term is used for the enjoyment body of the Trikaya?

In addition, the Buddha gives instructions as to the creation of a stupa after his death because those who see it and visit it 'at the dissolution of the body, after death, they will be reborn in a heavenly realm of happiness'. Brazier argues that circumambulation of stupas – in which were Buddhist relics – whilst chanting mantras was one of the earliest forms of Buddhist devotional practices. Such circumambulation was a form of religious worship which it was believed would bring spiritual power and spiritual healing.

A useful way of understanding Brazier's approach to Buddhism as a religion is to note his presentation of the opening of the Dhammapada.

Mind runs ahead of Dharma
mind leads, mind creates.
If with impure mind
one speaks, one acts,
dukkha follows
as the wheel the hoof.
Mind runs ahead of Dharma
mind leads, mind creates.
If with pure mind
one speaks, one acts,
sukha follows
as an unfading shadow.

Three Buddha statues symbolising the Trikaya doctrine.

He distinguishes between dukkha as meaning affliction and sukha as meaning bliss. An impure mind leads to words and actions which cause a burdensome life as illustrated by the image of the cart being pulled slowly along by the ox. By contrast, the pure mind leads to words and actions which make no demands upon a person as illustrated by the shadow which follows without any effort being required.

Moral effort is clearly required to avoid having an impure mind which is full of self by avoiding words and actions which create a negative karmic effect. But how can one gain a pure mind? Brazier quotes the Buddhist story of a boy named Mattakundali. 'Mattakundali becomes sick with jaundice and is close to death. His father is wealthy but stingy. Because the father is unwilling to spend money on a doctor the boy grows more and more ill and eventually dies. The Buddha, perceiving with his divine eye the plight of the boy, appears to him before his death in a vision. The boy is joyful on seeing the Buddha and thus dies with a pure heart full of faith. Consequently, the boy is reborn in a heaven.'

This is seen as teaching that the boy experiences sukha simply because he has a pure mind full of Buddha. There is no moral effort required of him. Instead, 'with a mind full of faith in Buddha, one can die in peace. The principle ... is how East Asian people generally take the central message of Buddhism.'

Study tip

In order to gain a greater understanding of the views of Batchelor and Brazier, research their biographical backgrounds and the variety of views which they have expressed in articles and podcasts accessible on the web.

Study tip

In order to gain a greater understanding of the diversity of beings and realms according to the Buddhist world view, it would be useful to look at images of Buddhist cosmology and of devas and dharmapalas other than those mentioned above.

AO1 Activity

Explain how different Buddhists might respond to the view that faith in the Buddha brings about rebirth in one of the heaven realms.

Explain your answer using evidence and examples from what you have read.

Key quote

The story of Mattakundali was an unforgettable popular story and often Key quoted. According to this tale, each morning the Buddha entered into a trance of mahakaruna (great compassion) to survey the world to see beings who suffered most intensely and those that needed guidance as well as those ready to benefit from his teaching immediately ... Mattakundali, having seen the radiance of the Buddha was pleased, died peacefully and was born in a happier situation. (Wickremeratne)

quickfire

3.16 What does Dharmavidya mean?

Key skills Theme 3

The third theme has tasks that concentrate on a particular aspect of AO1 in terms of using quotations from sources of authority and in the use of references.

Key skills

Knowledge involves:

Selection of a range of (thorough) accurate and relevant information that is directly related to the specific demands of the question.

This means:

- Selecting relevant material for the question set

- Being focused in explaining and examining the material selected.

Understanding involves:

Explanation that is extensive, demonstrating depth and/or breadth with excellent use of evidence and examples including (where appropriate) thorough and accurate supporting use of sacred texts, sources of wisdom and specialist language.

This means:

- Effective use of examples and supporting evidence to establish the quality of your understanding

- Ownership of your explanation that expresses personal knowledge and understanding and NOT just reproducing a chunk of text from a book that you have rehearsed and memorised.

AO1 Developing skills

It is now important to consider the information that has been covered in this section; however, the information in its raw form is too extensive and so has to be processed in order to meet the requirements of the examination. This can be achieved by practising more advanced skills associated with AO1. For assessment objective 1 (AO1), which involves demonstrating 'knowledge' and 'understanding' skills, we are going to focus on different ways in which the skills can be demonstrated effectively, and also, refer to how the performance of these skills is measured (see generic band descriptors for A2 [WJEC] AO1 or A Level [Eduqas] AO1).

▶ **Your final task for this Theme is:** Below is a summary of **Buddhism's frequent presentation in the West as a secular philosophy**. You want to use this in an essay but as it stands it is undeveloped and has no quotations or references in it at all. This time you have to find your own quotations (about 3) and use your own references (about 3) to develop the answer. Sometimes a quotation can follow from a reference but they can also be used individually as separate points.

Buddhism has been presented in the West as a secular philosophy since the 19th century CE. The type of Buddhism presented tended to be a simplified form of Theravada which was seen to be authentic and pure. Today Buddhism can be seen as a secular philosophy in the sense of it being a way of life which people can choose to follow and which does not require any faith as such. Buddhism is not interested in metaphysical questions. For example, this approach views meditation as being about focusing on living fully in the here and now. Presenting Buddhism as a secular philosophy generally involves using only the Pali Canon and adopting the pragmatic approach of the Buddha himself. Buddhism in its accepted form today is therefore like an old and over-varnished oil painting which has to be restored. Once this happens, true Buddhism as a secular philosophy can be revealed.

The result will be a fairly lengthy answer and so you could then check it against the band descriptors for A2 (WJEC) or A Level (Eduqas) and in particular have a look at the demands described in the higher band descriptors towards which you should be aspiring. Ask yourself:

- Does my work demonstrate thorough, accurate and relevant knowledge and understanding of religion and belief?

- Is my work coherent (consistent or make logical sense), clear and well organised?

- Will my work, when developed, be an extensive and relevant response which is specific to the focus of the task?

- Does my work have extensive depth and/or suitable breadth and have excellent use of evidence and examples?

- If appropriate to the task, does my response have thorough and accurate reference to sacred texts and sources of wisdom?

- Are there any insightful connections to be made with other elements of my course?

- Will my answer, when developed and extended to match what is expected in an examination answer, have an extensive range of views of scholars/schools of thought?

- When used, is specialist language and vocabulary both thorough and accurate?

Issues for analysis and evaluation

The legitimacy of Western presentations of Buddhism as atheistic and secular

Specification content

The legitimacy of Western presentations of Buddhism as atheistic and secular.

One response to this issue is to argue that Buddhism has developed in such a way that it has always absorbed, adapted and adopted the beliefs of the culture in which it becomes embedded. The beliefs of the West today might be described as being post-Christian, atheistic and secular. It was for this reason that the Christian theologian Dietrich Bonhoeffer (1906–1945) argued the case for developing a 'religionless Christianity' which was fit for a completely religionless time. Another Christian theologian cited by Batchelor is Don Cupitt (1934–). He wrote: 'Religion today has to become belief less. There is nothing out there to believe in or to hope for. Religion therefore has to become an immediate and deeply felt way of relating yourself to life in general and your own life in particular.' It could be argued, therefore that developing in the West a religionless and belief less form of Buddhism is entirely legitimate.

Another response to the issue of the legitimacy of Western presentations of Buddhism as atheistic and secular, is to argue that there is nothing for such Western presentations to defend: Buddhism never was, and has never been, a 'religion' in the sense that the word is commonly understood. It has always been atheistic and secular and avoided what the Dalai Lama called 'false reification' – making the abstract material.

That this is the case is clear from the rejection of belief in one omnipotent, omniscient and omnibenevolent deity who is the creator and sustainer of all things. The key feature of the teaching of the Buddha and of Buddhism is that from the outset it separated itself from Brahmanism by rejecting belief in Brahman as the eternal and unchangeable constant reality.

Batchelor quotes the Christian theologian Paul Tillich as stating that religion is about one's 'ultimate concern'. For believers in a theistic religion – such as each of the major world religions – the 'ultimate concern' must be faith in God. Such an 'ultimate concern' cannot be found in Buddhism and therefore it is legitimate to call Buddhism atheistic and secular.

Religion also provides certainty regarding life after death. Again, it could be argued that this is not something which Buddhism seeks to do. There are a variety of views about what happens when a person dies depending on which form of Buddhism is being considered. But above all, it could be argued that the Buddha himself was non-committal. At the end of the Kalama Sutta, the Buddha describes the assurances received by those whose minds are free from hostility, ill will, undefiled and pure. The first two are:

'If there is a world after death, if there is the fruit of actions rightly and wrongly done, then this is the basis by which, with the break-up of the body, after death, I will reappear in a good destination, the heavenly world. If there is no world after death, if there is no fruit of actions rightly and wrongly done, then here in the present life I look after myself with ease — free from hostility, free from ill will, free from trouble.'

In Western Christian theology, a great deal of focus in the 19th and 20th centuries was upon trying to rediscover the historical Jesus and his teaching through a careful analysis of socio-economic, cultural, religious and historical data. In addition, textual criticism was used in this effort of reconstruction. Exactly the same approach can be identified with regard to the Buddha and his teaching. Scholars such as Batchelor propose that the original Buddha and the authentic and pure Buddhism which they have uncovered is not religious but is wholly atheistic and secular. This is therefore arguably a wholly legitimate presentation of Buddhism.

Key quote

Our old religious and moral traditions have faded away and nothing can resuscitate them … We say that the new culture is so different from anything that existed in the past that religion has to be completely reinvented. Unfortunately, the new style of religious thinking that we are trying to introduce is so queer and so new that most people have great difficulty in recognising it as religion at all. (Don Cupitt quoted by Batchelor)

AO2 Activity

As you read through this section try to do the following:

1. Pick out the different lines of argument that are presented in the text and identify any evidence given in support.

2. For each line of argument try to evaluate whether or not you think this is strong or weak.

3. Think of any questions you may wish to raise in response to the arguments.

This Activity will help you to start thinking critically about what you read and help you to evaluate the effectiveness of different arguments and from this develop your own observations, opinions and points of view that will help with any conclusions that you make in your answers to the AO2 questions that arise.

Sarnath where, with his first sermon, Ling argues the Buddha aimed to found a new civilisation.

An example of this can be seen in the research of Trevor Ling (1920–1995) whose work was influential on the ideas developed by secular Buddhists in the West. One of his books published in 1973 is entitled *The Buddha: The Social-Revolutionary Potential of Buddhism*. This gives an insight into his overall theory which is that the Buddha was not the founder of a religion and that his teaching was not religious. His teaching flourished because it was a time of economic growth and urbanisation and a time when tribal republics and autocratic monarchies were establishing their identity.

Against this background, a class of wealthy, intellectual urban individuals no longer tied to the land came to the fore asking new questions about the new type of life they were able to live. The Buddha provided them with new non-religious concepts such as anatta, which meant not focusing on the self but instead on the general welfare. He also gave them the concept of a new type of community, the sangha, where bhikkhus all shared equally in the common wealth of the society. What happened to people was not determined by superstitious religious acts and sacrifices but by the simple fact of cause and effect. The Buddha therefore offered 'the real possibility of human choice and freedom of action'. According to Ling, the Buddha was 'the discoverer, initiator, and exponent of a social, psychological and political philosophy'. This was above all rational, secular and atheistic – not religious.

Study tip

It is vital for AO2 that you actually discuss arguments and not just explain what someone may have stated. Try to ask yourself, 'was this a fair point to make?', 'is the evidence sound enough?', 'is there anything to challenge this argument?', 'is this a strong or weak argument?' Such critical analysis will help you develop your evaluation skills.

Ling stated that the focus on Buddhism as a religion is part of the 'continually recurring human religion-making tendency'. Arguably such a tendency transformed the Buddha from being the pragmatic philosopher giving a non-religious rationale to life, into a supernatural being. According to Batchelor, the Buddha's Enlightenment was not mystical or spiritual but simply his realisation that he could give up alaya – his place in life – in order to find secure tthana – ground. The tthana found by the Buddha was fully understanding the truth and existence of contingency. It was not 'gaining a privileged knowledge into some higher truth'. Siddhatta Gotama in his life 'was a dissenter, a radical, an iconoclast. He wanted nothing to do with the priestly religion of the brahmins. He dismissed its theology as unintelligible, its rituals as pointless, and the social structure it legitimised as unjust.'

In one sense, those who support the legitimacy of Western approaches to Buddhism as atheistic and secular might argue that Buddhism can be criticised in the same way that the Dalai Lama criticised other religions – it is an ideology with false reification – making the abstract material. Something of this kind can be seen with regard to karma which is taken to be a central Buddhist dogma. However, in the Sivaka Sutta, the Buddha appears to adopt a pragmatic and empirical view of the matter.

Sivaka asks whether what an individual feels in terms of present pleasure or pain is caused by what was done before. The Buddha replies that this might be so but equally it could be due to bodily condition in terms of 'bile, phlegm, internal winds, uneven care of the body and harsh treatment of the body'. The Buddha concludes: 'So any brahmans and contemplatives who are of the doctrine and view that whatever an individual feels — pleasure, pain, neither-pleasure-nor-pain — is entirely caused by what was done before — slip past what they themselves know, slip past what is agreed on by the world. Therefore, I say that those brahmans and contemplatives are wrong.'

The question of whether Buddhism is a religion

Specification content

The question of whether Buddhism is a religion.

In discussing the issue of whether Buddhism is a religion, Ling suggests that the following dilemma might be reached: 'I have a feeling that Buddhism should be included in, rather than excluded from, any survey of religions, for if it is not a religion, then what is it?' Others have designated Buddhism as a moral system without a God or as a faith without a God.

Ling contends that the earliest forms of Buddhism were not religious because they were non-theistic and in addition some forms of Buddhism particularly Theravada still appear to be non-theistic. However, at the same time theistic beliefs were very quickly incorporated into Buddhism, and other forms of Buddhism.

One example of such theistic beliefs can be found in Tibetan Buddhism. Batchelor gives a good illustration of this in discussing his experiences as a monk in Tibet in the 1970s in Dharamsala where the Dalai Lama lives in exile. As a result of a series of unfortunate events, it was believed that an evil demon was at loose and thus monks specialising in exorcism arrived and after secret rituals announced to the relief of all that 'the demon had been captured inside a triangular box, which was sealed with vajras and buried deep in the earth'. Batchelor observes: 'Most Buddhists throughout Asia are and always have been polytheists. They believe in the existence of a range of spirits and gods whose worlds intersect with our own. These entities do not have a merely symbolic existence; they are real beings with consciousness, autonomy and agency, who can grant favours if pleased and wreak havoc if offended. It is very much in our interests to keep on the right side of them. But since many of these spirits are fickle beings like ourselves, they cannot be ultimately trusted.'

Ninian Smart (1927–2001), who was instrumental in developing the field of academic religious studies as a university subject, devised a methodology which, both addresses the question of whether Buddhism is a religion and at the same time avoids the question. Instead he argued that whether a religion was theistic or non-theistic, it contained recognisable dimensions which could be found in all religions. The first three dimensions are para-historical dimensions, which means that they refer to the religious experience of believers in that religion. The remaining four dimensions are historical dimensions and refer to objective criteria which can be studied, analysed and assessed.

1. Ritual: forms and orders of ceremonies
2. Narrative: mythic stories and accounts particular of the founder of the religion
3. Experiential: experiences of devotion, liberation, awe, mystery, etc., which are both public and private
4. Social and Institutional: belief system which is shared on a smaller community level and larger societal level
5. Ethical and legal: codes regarding conduct handed down, possibly in a supernatural way, for all to follow
6. Doctrinal and philosophical: religious beliefs and teachings codified in a systematic way for believers to accept
7. Material: the sacred and supernatural elements of religious belief are manifest in objects and places which are given sacred meaning.

The Sutta most often cited in relation to the question of whether or not Buddhism is a religion is the Nibbana Sutta. On this occasion, the Buddha was teaching the monks and found them to be very receptive. For that reason, he declared: 'There is, monks, an unborn, unbecome, unmade, unfabricated. If there were not that unborn, unbecome, unmade, unfabricated, there would not be the case that escape from the born, become, made, fabricated would be discerned. But precisely because there is an unborn, unbecome, unmade, unfabricated, escape from the born, become, made, fabricated is discerned.'

Key quote

On formally becoming a Buddhist, one 'takes refuge' in the Buddha, Dharma and Sangha … But the spirits and gods are only downgraded, not abolished. They continue to play a role in one's personal and social life. This is the thought-world one finds throughout the Pali Canon. Siddhattha Gotama did not reject the existence of the gods, he marginalised them. He may have mocked their conceits but he acknowledged their presence. (Batchelor)

AO2 Activity

As you read through this section try to do the following:

1. Pick out the different lines of argument that are presented in the text and identify any evidence given in support.
2. For each line of argument try to evaluate whether or not you think this is strong or weak.
3. Think of any questions you may wish to raise in response to the arguments.

This Activity will help you to start thinking critically about what you read and help you to evaluate the effectiveness of different arguments and from this develop your own observations, opinions and points of view that will help with any conclusions that you make in your answers to the AO2 questions that arise.

Key questions

Does Buddhism really match Smart's seven dimensions of religion?

To what extent does the Nibbana Sutta actually refer to the Absolute?

If there is such a thing, how can the Absolute be known?

Key quote

The ultimately empirical and the ultimately noumenal are not graspable with words, but they are real intuitions of great moment to our actual lives. Life is lived in the in-between. In that in-between, out of the metaphysical we crystallise ideals, values, and motives.
(Brazier)

Study tip

It is vital for AO2 that you actually discuss arguments and not just explain what someone may have stated. Try to ask yourself, 'was this a fair point to make?', 'is the evidence sound enough?', 'is there anything to challenge this argument?', 'is this a strong or weak argument?' Such critical analysis will help you develop your evaluation skills.

AO2 Activity

List some conclusions that could be drawn from the AO2 reasoning from the above text; try to aim for at least three different possible conclusions. Consider each of the conclusions and collect brief evidence to support each conclusion from the AO1 and AO2 material for this topic. Select the conclusion that you think is most convincing and explain why it is so. Try to contrast this with the weakest conclusion in the list, justifying your argument with clear reasoning and evidence.

It might be argued that what Buddha is describing in the phrase 'there is an unborn, unbecome, unmade, unfabricated' is what theologians might call the Absolute. That being the case, from a certain point of view this could be seen as religious since one understanding of religion is to define it as the relationship that human beings have with the Absolute, however that Absolute is envisaged.

Kant argued that we live in the phenomenal realm of existence. This is the realm of the empirical, the ascertainable, the physical and measurable. However, our minds are able to conceive of the noumenal realm. This is the realm of the abstract, the unascertainable, the metaphysical and unmeasurable. The Absolute lies within the noumenal realm.

Brazier suggests this type of approach makes sense from the Buddhist perspective because Buddhism is 'the way that we creatures of this relative, conditional world relate to the absolute: to the unconditional, unborn, undying, that we cannot help intuiting'. The Buddhist equivalent of the noumenal realm is 'the other shore': 'It is a domain that...is completely empty (shunya) of anything empirical – no form, no sound, no taste, no smell, no touch, and not even imaginary objects. This emptiness (shunya-ta) is timeless.'

One of the titles of the Buddha is lokavid. The term means 'knower of the world' and Brazier suggests that this is entirely apt because the Buddha could see the two realms. He continues: 'This is one way of understanding what Buddhism is. Buddhism is awakening to these two domains.'

Ultimately in the discussion of Buddhism as a religion, everything depends on the person who is discussing it and what they want to see. As with the rabbit-duck illusion, some see a complex religion with everything which the word religion implies, whereas others see a fully developed rational, secular and atheistic philosophy of life. One way of understanding why this might be so, is the tension between the academic who studies the religion from the outside and the believer who follows the religion from within.

In April 1994, the Dalai Lama visited the University of Michigan for a private seminar with faculty and graduate students studying Buddhism. They gave a presentation on the origins of Mahayana according to Western scholarship. Essentially this dates the origin of Mahayana texts to the beginning of the common era and suggests that they were composed by monks and nuns. The Dalai Lama responded that 'this was something to know' which according to Lopez meant in reality that 'it did not fall into the category of what was truly worth knowing'. Lopez concluded: 'in the end, he seemed to view Buddhist practice and Buddhist scholarship (at least of the Western variety) as ultimately irreconcilable'.

The Dalai Lama continued by explaining that if he accepted what the students had told him in their survey of Western scholarship regarding Mahayana Buddhist texts, he would not be able to believe in the sambhogakaya or the dharmakaya. All that would be left would be the historical Buddha bereft of his omniscience. He concluded: 'If I believed what you told me the Buddha would only be a nice person.'

Such a tension appears in what Batchelor has to say about Buddhism as an organised religion. Here, the point is not 'to abandon all institutions and dogmas but to find a way to live with them more ironically, to appreciate them for what they are – the play of the human mind in its endless quest for connection and meaning – rather than timeless entities that have to be ruthlessly defended or forcibly imposed.'

The rabbit–duck illusion presents an ambiguous image where one thing can be seen in two ways.

AO2 Developing skills

It is now important to consider the information that has been covered in this section; however, the information in its raw form is too extensive and so has to be processed in order to meet the requirements of the examination. This can be achieved by practising more advanced skills associated with AO2. For assessment objective 2 (AO2), which involves 'critical analysis' and 'evaluation' skills, we are going to focus on different ways in which the skills can be demonstrated effectively, and also, refer to how the performance of these skills is measured (see generic band descriptors for A2 [WJEC] AO2 or A Level [Eduqas] AO2).

▶ **Your final task for this Theme is:** Below is an evaluation of **the question of whether Buddhism is a religion**. You want to use this in an essay but as it stands it is a weak argument because it has no quotations or references in it at all as support. This time you have to find your own quotations (about 3) and use your own references (about 3) to strengthen the evaluation. Remember, sometimes a quotation can follow from a reference but they can also be used individually as separate points.

Arguably Buddhism must be a religion because if it is not, what is it? After all, it shares the characteristics which other religions have such as worship and beliefs about what is good, bad, right and wrong. Some forms of Buddhism have also adopted and absorbed many indigenous beliefs about the existence of spirits and demons, which add to the sense of it being a religion. The Buddha himself, when he talks about nibbana, seems to be referring to a perfect state which is not of this world but which belongs to a different realm altogether. It could be argued that whether or not Buddhism is a religion is all a matter of perception – some people might see religion and others might see a way of life. The way in which many Buddhists regard the Buddha himself is very important here as either a historical person or as something more.

The result will be a fairly lengthy answer and so you could then check it against the band descriptors for A2 (WJEC) or A Level (Eduqas) and in particular have a look at the demands described in the higher band descriptors towards which you should be aspiring. Ask yourself:

- Is my answer a confident critical analysis and perceptive evaluation of the issue?
- Is my answer a response that successfully identifies and thoroughly addresses the issues raised by the question set?
- Does my work show an excellent standard of coherence, clarity and organisation?
- Will my work, when developed, contain thorough, sustained and clear views that are supported by extensive, detailed reasoning and/or evidence?
- Are the views of scholars/schools of thought used extensively, appropriately and in context?
- Does my answer convey a confident and perceptive analysis of the nature of any possible connections with other elements of my course?
- When used, is specialist language and vocabulary both thorough and accurate?

Key skills Theme 3

The third theme has tasks that concentrate on a particular aspect of AO2 in terms of using quotations from sources of authority and in the use of references in supporting arguments and evaluations.

Key skills

Analysis involves:

Identifying issues raised by the materials in the AO1, together with those identified in the AO2 section, and presents sustained and clear views, either of scholars or from a personal perspective ready for evaluation.

This means:

- That your answers are able to identify key areas of debate in relation to a particular issue
- That you can identify, and comment upon, the different lines of argument presented by others
- That your response comments on the overall effectiveness of each of these areas or arguments.

Evaluation involves:

Considering the various implications of the issues raised based upon the evidence gleaned from analysis and provides an extensive detailed argument with a clear conclusion.

This means:

- That your answer weighs up the consequences of accepting or rejecting the various and different lines of argument analysed
- That your answer arrives at a conclusion through a clear process of reasoning.

Specification content

The relationship between religion and society: respect and recognition and the ways that religious traditions view other religious and non-religious worldviews and their truth claims. Emphasis within Buddhism on the individual testing the teachings and staying true to experience, even if that means following a path different to Buddhism (with reference to the Kalama Sutta v. 9 & 10 and Majjhima Nikaya 56.16 – the Buddha's conversation with Upali).

Key terms

Great Renunciation: when Gotama left behind his wife, son and the palace following the Four Sights; his renunciation of the life of hedonism

Jain: the name given to the followers of Jainism – a religion focused on asceticism which developed under the leadership of Mahavira – also known as Nigantha Nataputta (c.599–527 BCE) – a contemporary of the Buddha

D: Religion and society: responses to the challenges of pluralism and diversity

Individual testing and staying true to experience in Buddhism

From a certain point of view, traditions about the life of the Buddha describe someone who is intent on finding the answers to questions through experience. Thus, having seen the Four Sights, his next step was not to seek out and discuss transcendental issues with the holy men of that time. Instead he undertook the Great Renunciation – leaving his wife, son and a life of hedonism behind. His six years of focused practice in the ascetic life were his way of individual testing into whether or not an answer to the problem of dukkha could be found through following a life of hardship, extreme yogic practices and punishment of the body. It is significant that these six years were not ones of pretending to live the ascetic life, but ones of staying true to the experience it offered until his realisation – based on his own individual testing – that they did not provide any answers at all.

In the Maha-Saccaka Sutta, the Buddha explains to Saccaka who is a **Jain**: 'My body became extremely emaciated. Simply from my eating so little, my limbs became like the jointed segments of vine stems or bamboo stems ... My backside became like a camel's hoof ... My spine stood out like a string of beads ... My ribs jutted out like the jutting rafters of an old, run-down barn.... The skin of my belly became so stuck to my spine that when I thought of touching my belly, I grabbed hold of my spine as well; and when I thought of touching my spine, I grabbed hold of the skin of my belly as well.... Simply from my eating so little, if I tried to ease my body by rubbing my limbs with my hands, the hair – rotted at its roots – fell from my body as I rubbed, simply from eating so little.'

The Buddha concluded: 'But with this racking practice of austerities I haven't attained any superior human state, any distinction in knowledge or vision worthy of the noble ones. Could there be another path to Awakening?'

It was therefore the Buddha's individual testing which enabled him to reject the path of asceticism and thus find the Middle Way. From one perspective, this type of focus on one's own experience as key, is another facet of Buddhism insofar as it upholds the concept that ultimately the individual is reliant on themselves, and that there is no other guide to be followed. Here, an important Buddhist maxim can be found in the opening of verse 160

The Buddha emaciated during his six years living as an ascetic.

of the Dhammapada: 'Atta hi attano natho' which can be translated as 'Oneself is one's own refuge'. The full verse reads:

'Oneself is one's own refuge
What other refuge could there be?
With oneself well-controlled
One obtains a refuge hard to gain.'

Self-reliance in pursuit of the path to follow might also be seen as key to understanding the Kalama Sutta. As we have already seen, the Buddha explains to the people of the Kalama clan the best approach to choosing between rival religious teachers. 'Don't go by reports, by legends, by traditions, by scripture, by logical conjecture, by inference, by analogies, by agreement through pondering views, by probability, or by the thought, that this contemplative is our teacher.' The last phrase is particularly significant: that reliance should not be placed on the basis that 'this contemplative is our teacher'. Instead the only appropriate teacher should be individual testing which, if its results are skilful, should be followed in both accepting one path and rejecting another. Thus, the Buddha concludes: 'When you know for yourselves that, these qualities are unskilful; these qualities are blameworthy; these qualities are criticised by the wise; these qualities, when adopted and carried out, lead to harm and to suffering — then you should abandon them.'

All of this links into another Buddhist concept, '**ehi-passiko**', which can be translated as 'which you can come and see'. Reasoned reflection and testing the benefits of the path are what lead to the path being followed.

It is against this general background that one can understand the significance of the Buddha's conversation with Upali. In Majjhima Nikaya 56, it is explained that Upali is a leading spokesperson for Nigantha Nataputta, which is the name given in some Buddhist Suttas to the 24th spiritual founder of Jainism, Mahivira (599–527 BCE). The Buddha and Mahivira were contemporaries and each had their own followers.

The Sutta recounts how the Jain ascetic **Digha-Tapassi** encounters the Buddha and discusses the concept of deeds being good or evil. Leaving the Buddha he then meets with Nigantha Natapputta who questions him about his encounter and commends him for upholding the Jain point of view. At this point the Jain householder Upali declares that he will take on the Buddha in debate in upholding Jain teaching: 'I will take him on in debate and drag him to and fro and round and about, like a strong man would drag a fleecy sheep to and fro and round and about!'

Digha-Tapassi advises against this, protesting that the Buddha 'is a magician. He knows a conversion magic, and uses it to convert the disciples of those who follow other paths'. However, Nigantha Natapputta sends Upali to the Buddha declaring that whilst it is *impossible* that Upali will become a follower of the Buddha, it *might be possible* that the Buddha will become a follower of Upali.

Upali debates with the Buddha and comes to the realisation of the truth of what the Buddha is teaching. Upali declares: 'Excellent, sir! Excellent! As if he was righting the overturned, or revealing the hidden, or pointing out the path to the

Key quote

In science, a theory should be tested in several ways before it can be accepted by the scientific community. The Buddha also recommended, in the Kalama Sutta, that any teaching and insight given by any teacher should be tested by our own experience before it can be accepted as the truth. **(Nhat Hanh)**

Nigantha Natapputta (Mahavira) (599–527 BCE) seated in meditation.

Key terms

Digha-Tapassi: a leading Jain ascetic and disciple of Nigantha Natapputta

Ehi-passiko: reasoned reflection and testing the benefits of the path are what lead to the path being followed – literally means 'which you can come and see'

Key quote

Buddhism is always a question of knowing and seeing, and not that of believing. The teaching of the Buddha is qualified as Ehi-Passiko, inviting you to come and see, but not to come and believe. (Rahula)

lost, or lighting a lamp in the dark so people with good eyes can see what is there, so too the Buddha has made the teaching clear in many ways.' This leads Upali to then declare that he will now be a disciple of the Buddha: 'I go for refuge to the Buddha, to the teaching, and to the mendicant Sangha. From this day forth, may the Buddha remember me as a lay follower who has gone for refuge for life.'

The Buddha's response to Upali's apparent conversion is significant since rather than accepting it immediately and then wanting to count it as a form of victory over Nigantha Nataputta which could be used to bolster his own support, the Buddha declares: 'Householder, you should act after careful consideration. It is good for well-known people such as yourself to act after careful consideration.'

As has been suggested, there is again evidence that reflection and reasoning are called for in choosing whichever path is going to be chosen. It is only after Upali again confirms his intention of going for refuge to the Buddha, that the Buddha begins to teach him, 'step by step, with a talk on giving, ethical conduct, and heaven. He explained the drawbacks of sensual pleasures, so sordid and corrupt, and the benefit of renunciation.'

Only after it is apparent that Upali understands this teaching does the Buddha continue: 'And when he knew that Upali's mind was ready, pliable, rid of hindrances, joyful, and confident he explained the special teaching of the Buddhas: suffering, its origin, its cessation, and the path.'

When Digha-Tapassi discovers what has happened he again tells Nigantha Nataputta that all of this is due to the Buddha's 'conversion magic'. Having questioned Upali himself, Nigantha Nataputta comes to the same conclusion declaring to Upali: 'You are mad, householder! You are a fool.... You have been converted by the ascetic Gotama's conversion magic!'

Upali responds by giving a simile in which he compares the doctrine of the Buddha to a new pair of garments which can be dyed, pounded in washing and pressed: 'In the same way, the doctrine of the Buddha looks fine initially – for the astute, not for fools – and it can withstand being scrutinised and pressed.' For Upali, the Buddha's 'conversion magic' is simply providing teaching that can withstand being 'scrutinised and pressed'. Upali can thus declare joining the palms of his hands in the direction of where the Buddha was staying, 'he is the Buddha, and I am his disciple'.

quickfire

3.17 What does 'Atta hi attano natho' mean?

Study tip

Research the beliefs and teachings of Jainism and establish the similarities and differences it has with Buddhism.

Specification content

Approach taken by Mahayana Buddhism: the teachings are sometimes considered to be only provisional, different upaya (skilful means) being used to suit different listeners.

The use of skilful means in Mahayana Buddhism

Following the Buddha's Awakening, accounts explain how he spent some time deciding what to do next. In the Ariyapariyesana Sutta, the Buddha wonders about teaching the Dhamma and the thought occurs to him; 'Enough now with teaching what only with difficulty I reached. This Dhamma is not easily realised by those overcome with aversion and passion. What is abstruse, subtle, deep, hard to see, going against the flow – those delighting in passion, cloaked in the mass of darkness, will not see'.

At this point, Brahma appears to him and urges him to teach declaring: 'Behold the people submerged in sorrow, oppressed by birth and ageing. Rise up, hero, victor in battle! ... Teach the Dhamma, O Blessed One: There will be those who will understand.'

The Buddha then surveys the world and concludes: 'Just as in a pond of blue or red or white lotuses, some lotuses — born and growing in the water — might flourish while immersed in the water, without rising up from the water; some might stand at an even level with the water; while some might rise up from the water and stand without being smeared by the water – so too, surveying the world with the eye of an Awakened One, I saw beings with little dust in their eyes and those with much, those with keen faculties and those with dull, those with good attributes and those with bad, those easy to teach and those hard.'

From the outset therefore, the Buddha recognised that there would be a wide diversity of people in terms of their readiness to receive the Dhamma. That being the case, he employed upaya (skilful means) to suit different listeners. As the Buddha explains in the Ariyapariyesana Sutta, the first five ascetics who had been with him until he broke his fast were readier and more apt than others for the Dhamma. Once he had convinced them to listen to him, he began his teaching in a very simple and practical way: 'I would teach two monks while three went for alms, and we six lived off what the three brought back from their alms round. Then I would teach three monks while two went for alms, and we six lived off what the two brought back from their alms round.' Thus, it was after a period of instruction that 'knowledge and vision arose in them'. As we have seen, similar upaya (skilful means) was used with Upali: the Buddha teaches him 'step by step' and only when he is ready teaches him 'the special teaching of the Buddha'.

From this perspective, the correct application of upaya (skilful means) focuses on the audience which is being taught the Dhamma. This would mean distinguishing – to use the Buddha's analogy – between those 'with little dust in their eyes and those with much'. A further development might be noted wherein the focus remains on the audience being taught the Dhamma but in addition considers the nature of the Dhamma itself and its usefulness.

In this regard, reference is often made to the parable of the raft – which is found in the Alagaddupama Sutta – to which allusion has already been made (see page 77). The Buddha explains that the Dhamma is similar to a raft, 'as having the purpose of crossing over, not the purpose of being clung to'. A man is on a dangerous shore and can see over a great expanse of water to the far shore which is 'secure and free from risk'. The lack of a ferryboat or a bridge leads him to the thought of what he should do and then the action carrying it out. 'The man, having gathered grass, twigs, branches, and leaves, having bound them together to make a raft, would cross over to safety on the other shore in dependence on the raft, making an effort with his hands and feet.'

Having crossed the water, the Buddha indicates the choice the man might make. He might reflect on the usefulness of the raft which he constructed and which helped him cross in safety, and conclude: 'Why don't I, having hoisted it on my head or carrying on my back, go wherever I like?' Alternatively, he might reflect in exactly the same way, but then conclude: 'Why don't I, having dragged it on dry land or sinking it in the water, go wherever I like?' The Buddha teaches that it is only in the second case that the man would be doing what should be done with the raft.

Whilst there are various interpretations of the parable of the raft, there does appear to be a sense in which the Buddha is stating that upaya (skilful means) is important in how the Dhamma is interpreted and used as the means to reach the far shore 'which is secure and free from risk'. Whilst it is not stated in the Parable or in the Buddha's explanation, the far shore has been interpreted as enlightenment, which is the goal of the Buddhist life. It might therefore be argued that the purpose of the Dhamma lies not so much in the Dhamma itself – it is 'not for the purpose of holding onto' – but rather in its functionality, since it can be used 'for the purpose of crossing over'.

Lotuses in a pond as described by the Buddha.

Key quote

In the same way, monks, I have taught the Dhamma compared to a raft, for the purpose of crossing over, not for the purpose of holding onto. Understanding the Dhamma as taught compared to a raft, you should let go even of Dhammas, to say nothing of non-Dhammas.
(Alagaddupama Sutta: parable of the raft)

The pratyekabuddha is described in the Khaggavisana Sutta as being like a rhinoceros who wanders alone.

Key terms

Pratyekabuddha-yana: the yana of the solitary Buddha. This refers to someone who is outside of the monastic sangha, who does not have a teacher and who, therefore, has not been taught the Dhamma

Sravaka-yana: the yana of the arhat who as a disciple been taught the Dhamma of the Buddha and who is part of the monastic sangha

The possibly provisional nature of the Dhamma which is at the very least alluded to in the parable of the raft, is much more fully developed for Mahayana Buddhists. Professor Michael Pye in his book *Skilful Means: A Concept in Mahayana Buddhism* (1978) explains: 'In Mahayana Buddhism the various forms of Buddhist teaching and practice are declared to be provisional means, all skilfully set up by the Buddha for the benefit of the unenlightened. A Buddhist who makes progress himself comes to recognise this provisional quality in the forms of his religion, and through using the means provided for him he has to learn not to be wrongly attached to them.' From this perspective, Buddhism in its totality is seen above all as a religion of upaya (skilful means) since the path provided by the Buddha is only of importance insofar as it leads to the goal.

The most developed expression of upaya can be found in the Lotus Sutra to which allusion has already been made. There is much debate about the context out of which the Lotus Sutra emerged and therefore about how its teaching on upaya (skilful means) should be interpreted. One useful way of approaching the text is to begin by recognising that, at the time of its composition, amongst the various Buddhisms which had developed, there were three yanas (vehicles) to enlightenment:

1. Sravaka-yana: the yana of the arhat who as a disciple had been taught the Dhamma of the Buddha and who is part of the monastic sangha. This might be seen as the typical Theravada path.

2. Pratyekabuddha-yana: the yana of the solitary Buddha. This refers to someone who is outside of the monastic sangha, who does not have a teacher and who, therefore, has not been taught the Dhamma. The pratyekabuddha is described in the Khaggavisana Sutta as being like a rhinoceros. This is because the rhinoceros was regarded as a solitary animal. The refrain throughout the sutta is 'wander alone like a rhinoceros'. The pratyekabuddha avoids companionship in any form and could thus declare 'unled by others, I have knowledge arisen'.

3. Bodhisattva-yana: the yana of the bodhisattva. This refers to someone who models their approach on that of the historical Buddha. It regards his innumerable previous rebirths, the development of the paramitas (perfections) and his bodhicitta – Awakened mind – which led him to act out of compassion for all sentient beings as the pattern to be followed. This long and difficult path leads to the attainment of perfect Buddhahood or to the realisation of tathagatagarbha – the buddha-nature within.

In the Lotus Sutra – which Laumakis describes as 'arguably the most important and influential Buddhist text throughout Asia' – the Buddha is seated before a huge audience including monks, nuns, deities and bodhisattvas. It is important to note that the Buddha now addresses his words to Sariputra who is seen to be the wisest and greatest of arhats who have followed the sravaka-yana. The Buddha praises the wisdom of innumerable buddhas in innumerable rebirths in the course of innumerable ages: 'Profound and immeasurable is the wisdom of the buddhas. The gate to their wisdom is hard to enter and difficult to understand. None of the sravakas and pratyekabuddhas may be capable of understanding it.'

The Buddha continues by telling Sariputra: 'After attaining Buddhahood, I expounded the teaching extensively with various explanations and illustrations, and with upaya (skilful means) led sentient beings to rid themselves of their attachments. Why is this? Because all the buddhas have attained perfect mastery of upayas (skilful means), wisdom, and insight.' It is *only* the buddhas who have understood 'this immeasurable, limitless, and unprecedented dharma' which is the saddharma – the true Dhamma.

In the verses which follow, the Buddha emphasises the point he has made by stating that even if the 'worlds of ten directions' were filled with sravakas such as Sariputra or were filled with pratyekabuddhas who during innumerable ages tried to understand the Dhamma, 'they would not understand it in the least'. The same would be true for bodhisattvas even though elsewhere in the Sutra they are regarded as being superior to sravkas and pratyekabuddhas. The Buddha concludes: 'It was I who caused them to become free from the bondage of suffering, and to attain nirvana. I have revealed the teaching of the three vehicles with the power of the upaya (skilful means) of the buddhas so as to free the sentient beings from their various human attachments.'

The Buddha teaches that the three yanas of the sravaka, the pratyebuddha and the bodhisattva were taught in the past as upaya (skilful means) most suited to people in the various stages of their understanding. The saddharma is that there is only one yana. As Lopez explains, what is being taught by the Buddha is that 'there is only one path, one vehicle (ekayana): the path to buddhahood, the buddha vehicle (buddhayana). He explains that if he had revealed this single path from the beginning, many would have felt incapable of following it. Therefore, he devised a skilful method to accommodate them, teaching a shorter and simpler path, the path to the nirvana of the arhat. Now, he is revealing that there is only one path and that that path is available to all.'

It is this teaching which is illustrated by the parable of the burning house whereby the father in effect deceives the children within the burning house with a falsehood by promising them three carts one pulled by a sheep, another by a deer and the third by an ox. Once they have escaped the house the father provides them with just a single cart into which they all climb. 'The Buddha explains that the burning house is samsara the realm of rebirth; he is the father, and the children are the sentient beings of the universe, so absorbed in the world that they ignore its dangers. Knowing the predilections and capacities of sentient beings, the Buddha lures them to various paths to escape samsara by offering them something that appeals to their limited aspirations. However, this is his skilful method.' (Lopez)

At the end of the parable of the burning house, the Buddha ask Sariputra whether the father has deceived his children or not? Sariputra replies, 'He saved their lives and did not deceive them. This is by no means a deception. Why? Because by saving their lives they obtained marvellous toys. Moreover, they were saved from the burning house by skilful means.' In this way the teachings of Buddhism can be seen as only provisional since they are all simply upaya (skilful means). The Buddha replies to Sariputra by identifying himself as the father and concludes, 'as the father of the entire world, he permanently dispels fear, distress, anxiety, ignorance, and blindness. He has attained immeasurable wisdom, insight, power, and fearlessness, as well as great transcendent powers and the power of wisdom. He has attained the perfection of upaya (skilful means) and of wisdom. With his great mercy and compassion, he incessantly and indefatigably seeks the welfare of all beings and benefits them all.' In Mahayana it is the intention of 'great mercy and compassion' which is the justification of upaya (skilful means).

Study tip

Research the beliefs and teachings of Jainism and establish the similarities and differences it has with Buddhism.

Parable of the burning house from the Lotus Sutra.

Key quote

According to this perspective, at least as it is presented in the Lotus Sutra, the Buddha adapts his teaching to the level of his hearers. Out of his compassion he gives the teaching which is appropriate to their needs. Thus, he may give one teaching at one time, and completely the opposite teaching at another. (Williams)

quickfire

3.18 Explain different ways in which the parable of the raft might be interpreted.

Specification content

Belief of many Buddhists who
consider that there is good within all
religions and they should be respected
(Edicts of Emperor Ashoka, Rock Edict
NB 7 and Rock Edict NB 12).

Emperor Ashoka: Rock Edict NB 7 and Rock Edict NB 12: is there good in all religions?

An important aspect of the story of Upali the Jain and his conversion to becoming a disciple of the Buddha is what it illuminates regarding the overall question of Buddhism and other religions.

As we have seen, one of the things which impresses Upali is that the Buddha says to him, 'Householder, you should act after careful consideration. It is good for well-known people such as yourself to act after careful consideration.' What the Buddha and his followers do *not* do is celebrate Upali's conversion as being, in some sense, a victory for Buddhism over Jainism. Thus, Upali declares: 'Now I am even more delighted and satisfied with the Buddha, since he tells me to act after careful consideration. For if the followers of other paths were to gain me as a disciple, they would carry a banner all over Nalanda, saying: "The householder Upali has become our disciple!" And yet the Buddha says "householder, you should act after careful consideration".'

In addition, the Buddha reminds Upali: 'For a long time now, householder, your family has been a well-spring of support for the Jain ascetics. You should consider giving to them when they come.' Here again, Upali is delighted because this contradicted what people had *mistakenly* quoted the Buddha as saying: 'Gifts should only be given to me, not to others. Gifts should only be given to my disciples, not to the disciples of others. Only what is given to me is very fruitful, not what is given to others. Only what is given to my disciples is very fruitful, not what is given to the disciples of others.' Even though he would no longer be a Jain, Upali understands what the Buddha has asked of him: 'the Buddha encourages me to give to the Jain ascetics'. All of this suggests that Buddhism teaches that there is good within all religions and that they should be respected.

Almost two hundred years after the death of the Buddha – by which time Buddhism had become increasingly well-established – the Mauryan dynasty was founded by Chandragupta (322–297 BCE) and he began to rule over part of what is present-day India. His son Bindusara continued the expansion and consolidation of the territory which had been conquered, and this policy was then continued by Ashoka when he succeeded his father in c. 268 BCE. He reigned until c. 232 BCE.

Key quote

In the figure of Ashoka, Buddhism found the ideal catalyst to transform it from an obscure Middle-Indian sect into a budding world religion. (Batchelor)

Key term

Mauryan dynasty: dynasty which ruled much of India from c. 321–187 BCE – Ashoka was the third ruler of this dynasty

Pillar placed by Ashoka at Lumbini in c.249 to mark his visit to the birthplace of the Buddha.

It is very difficult to piece together the events of Ashoka's life as the source material is neither extensive nor wholly reliable. What is suggested is that his succession was only secured after a period of violent warfare and that this continued into the early part of his reign. In c. 262 BCE, Ashoka and his army attacked and conquered the kingdom of Kalinga. Traditions suggest that the bloody violence involved was responsible for Ashoka's new full-hearted commitment to Buddhism, which involved the renunciation of violence and the application of Buddhist principles in the governance of his empire.

Much of Ashoka's reputation today rests upon the evidence provided by inscriptions which have been discovered on pillars, rocks and in caves found in India, Nepal, Pakistan and Afghanistan. In these, Ashoka names himself as Devanampiya Piyadasi, which can be translated as 'Beloved of the gods – He who looks on with kindness'. A number of the inscriptions appear to record Ashoka's own words rather than being official proclamations.

Summarising their content, Ven. S. Dhammika comments on what they show regarding the influence of Buddhism on Ashoka: 'He went on pilgrimages to Lumbini and Bodh Gaya, sent teaching monks to various regions in India and beyond its borders, and he was familiar enough with the sacred texts to recommend some of them to the monastic community. It is also very clear that Ashoka saw the reforms he instituted as being a part of his duties as a Buddhist.'

The effectiveness and longevity of Ashoka's reforms are not known, but he has been held up by later Buddhists as the model ruler due to his focus on compassion and respect for all life. Rock Edict NB 2, for example, declares that Ashoka 'made provision for two types of medical treatment: medical treatment for humans and medical treatment for animals. Wherever medical herbs suitable for humans or animals are not available, I have had them imported and grown. Wherever medical roots or fruits are not available I have had them imported and grown. Along roads I have had wells dug and trees planted for the benefit of humans and animals.' Another example can be found in Rock Edict NB 4 where it is declared that the 'the sound of the drum has been replaced by the sound of the Dhamma' and that the King 'promotes restraint in the killing and harming of living beings'.

Another of the striking aspects of the King's reign was his attitude to religion. As Dhammika notes, 'while he was an enthusiastic Buddhist, he was not partisan towards his own religion or intolerant of other religions. He seems to have genuinely hoped to be able to encourage everyone to practise his or her own religion with the same conviction that he practised his.' This is apparent from Rock Edict NB 7 which states: 'Devanampiya Piyadasi, desires that all religions should reside everywhere, for all of them desire self-control and purity of heart. But people have various desires and various passions, and they may practise all of what they should or only a part of it. But one who receives great gifts yet is lacking in self-control, purity of heart, gratitude and firm devotion, such a person is mean.'

A more extensive statement of this attitude can be found in Rock Edict NB 12:

'Devanampiya Piyadasi, honours both ascetics and the householders of all religions, and he honours them with gifts and honours of various kinds. But Devanampiya Piyadasi, does not value gifts and honours as much as he values this – that there should be growth in the essentials of all religions.'

Following this statement, Ashoka goes on to state that there is good within all religions and that each person of one religion should find the good in the different religious beliefs of others.

'Growth in essentials can be done in different ways, but all of them have as their root restraint in speech, that is, not praising one's own religion, or condemning the religion of others without good cause. And if there is cause for criticism, it should be done in a mild way. But it is better to honour other religions for this reason.

Key quote

Devanampiya Piyadasi speaks thus: Dhamma is good, but what constitutes Dhamma? It includes little evil, much good, kindness, generosity, truthfulness and purity. (King Ashoka Pillar Edict 2)

Key terms

Devanampiya Piyadasi: the name given to Ashoka – which can be translated as 'Beloved of the gods – He who looks on with kindness'

Rock Edict: proclamations of Ashoka inscribed on rock which have been found in India and neigbouring countries

By so doing, one's own religion benefits, and so do other religions, while doing otherwise harms one's own religion and the religions of others.

What Ashoka then outlines is a situation of what might be described as religious tolerance, dialogue and harmony:

'Whoever praises his own religion, due to excessive devotion, and condemns others with the thought "Let me glorify my own religion," only harms his own religion. Therefore, contact between religions is good. One should listen to and respect the doctrines professed by others. Devanampiya Piyadasi, desires that all should be well-learned in the good doctrines of other religions.'

When such an approach is taken, Ashoka states that each person's own religion is strengthened and not compromised by peaceful co-existence with those of another religion.

'Those who are content with their own religion should be told this: Devanampiya Piyadasi, does not value gifts and honours as much as he values that there should be growth in the essentials of all religions.... And the fruit of this is that one's own religion grows and the Dhamma is illuminated also.'

King Ashoka depicted on his chariot with his retinue on a gateway of the Sanchi Stupa.

Writing some 2500 years later, Bhikkhu Bodhi from the Theravada perspective offers similar sentiments to those of Ashoka although from a very different historical setting. This is particularly the case given that Ashoka did not have to consider the missionary and expansionist efforts of both Christianity and Islam, which arrived at later dates in India and in other parts of Asia. Bhikkhu Bodhi notes 'the adoption of an aggressive affirmation of one's own beliefs coupled with a proselytising zeal toward those who still stand outside the chosen circle of one's co-religionists' which might be found within 'the folds of the great monotheistic religions, Christianity and Islam'. That such an aggressive affirmation of belief might be found within Buddhism is recognised, but Bhikkhu Bodhi continues by stating, that 'that though there is no guarantee against the rise of a militant fundamentalism from within Buddhism's own ranks, the Buddha's teachings can offer no sanctification, not even a remote one, for such a malignant development'.

Bhikkhu Bodhi thus affirms 'the thoroughgoing tolerance and genial good' which in general Buddhism as a religion has displayed to the many religions with which it has come into contact. 'Buddhist tolerance springs from the recognition that the dispositions and spiritual needs of human beings are too vastly diverse to be

Key quotes

To the extent that a religion proposes sound ethical principles and can promote to some degree the development of wholesome qualities such as love, generosity, detachment and compassion, it will merit in this respect the approbation of Buddhists. (Bhikkhu Bodhi)

At a time when different religions were in competition for converts, Ashoka urged mutual respect and tolerance. He saw all religious traditions as contributing in some way to spiritual development.... (Harvey

encompassed by any single teaching, and thus that these needs will naturally find expression in a wide variety of religious forms.'

From one perspective this approach to other religions seems to be aligned with the principles upheld by Mahayana Buddhism based on upaya (skilful means) as discussed in the Lotus Sutra. As the Buddha declares of himself, 'He has attained the perfection of upaya (skilful means) and of wisdom. With his great mercy and compassion, he incessantly and indefatigably seeks the welfare of all beings and benefits them all.' Some Buddhists might therefore regard other religions as part of upaya (skilful means) in providing a variety of ways of escaping from this world as illustrated by the parable of the burning house. In this sense, other religions are akin to the raft in the parable of the raft insofar as their role is 'not for the purpose of holding onto' but rather as another means designed with functionality in mind – 'for the purpose of crossing over'. All of this means that it is therefore natural that some Buddhists might accept that there is good within all religions and they should be respected.

The latter point is particularly the case when in other religions ethical principles such as compassion are evident and seen to be praiseworthy. For example, karuna (compassion) is not exclusive to Buddhism as might be seen in the life and work of the Roman Catholic Saint, Mother Teresa of Calcutta (1910–1997). Her work with the impoverished, the sick and the dying on the streets of Calcutta led the 5th Samdhong Rinpoche, Lobsang Tenzin, in his role as Prime Minster of the Tibetan government in exile to state: 'She represents love without distinction and compassion for all humanity. For Tibetan Buddhism, the Mother is the incarnation of Maha Karuna immeasurable compassion.'

Dr Karma Lekshe Tsomo pursued this approach further from the Mahayana perspective and addressed the question of whether Mother Teresa of Calcutta might be regarded as a bodhisattva. Lekshe Tsomo acknowledges that in terms of religious doctrine and belief this might appear to be 'an exercise in futility, like trying to match round pegs and square holes, since the bodhisattva ideal is predicated on a set of assumptions that, as far as we know, the Catholic Mother Teresa never considered'. At the same time one conclusion reached is that it could be stated that 'when it comes to active engagement in the world of suffering and affliction, perhaps Mother Teresa is closer to the bodhisattva ideal than any Buddhist'.

As Lekshe Tsomo points out, the bodhisattva idea cannot be limited solely to Mahayana Buddhists as that would contradict the belief that the bodhisattva's compassion is both universal and impartial. In addition, the bodhisattva 'has the capacity to appear in myriad forms to benefit sentient beings'. From this perspective it might be seen as another example of upaya (skilful means): 'it stands to reason that a bodhisattva who uses Christian terminology and beliefs has the potential to reach the greatest number of people by using a language they can understand. Using this logic, it is not impossible that Mother Teresa was a bodhisattva who manifested in a Christian form to propagate the ethic of compassion.'

Study tip

Research the various stories about King Ashoka and how he has been portrayed in later Buddhist texts.

AO1 Activity

Explain how some Buddhists might apply the parable of the raft and the parable of the burning house to their understanding of other religions.

Explain your answer using evidence and examples from what you have read.

Key term

Mother Teresa of Calcutta (1910–1997): a saint of the Roman Catholic Church renowned for the compassion in action towards the impoverished, the sick and the dying shown on the streets of Calcutta

quickfire

3.19 What key points does Rock Edict NB 12 make with regard to religion?

Key skills Theme 3

The third theme has tasks that deal with the basics of AO1 in terms of prioritising and selecting the key relevant information, presenting this in a personalised way (as in Theme 1) and then using evidence and examples to support and expand upon this (as in Theme 2).

Key skills

Knowledge involves:

Selection of a range of (thorough) accurate and relevant information that is directly related to the specific demands of the question.

This means:

- Selecting relevant material for the question set

- Being focused in explaining and examining the material selected.

Understanding involves:

Explanation that is extensive, demonstrating depth and/or breadth with excellent use of evidence and examples including (where appropriate) thorough and accurate supporting use of sacred texts, sources of wisdom and specialist language.

This means:

- Effective use of examples and supporting evidence to establish the quality of your understanding

- Ownership of your explanation that expresses personal knowledge and understanding and NOT just reproducing a chunk of text from a book that you have rehearsed and memorised.

AO1 Developing skills

It is now important to consider the information that has been covered in this section; however, the information in its raw form is too extensive and so has to be processed in order to meet the requirements of the examination. This can be achieved by practising more advanced skills associated with AO1. The exercises that run throughout this book will help you to do this and prepare you for the examination. For assessment objective 1 (AO1), which involves demonstrating 'knowledge' and 'understanding' skills, we are going to focus on different ways in which the skills can be demonstrated effectively, and also, refer to how the performance of these skills is measured (see generic band descriptors for A2 [WJEC] AO1 or A Level [Eduqas] AO1).

▶ **Your task is this:** Below is a summary of **whereby many Buddhists would consider that there is good within all religions and they should be respected**. It is 150 words long. There are three points highlighted that are key points to learn from this extract. Discuss which further two points you think are the most important to highlight and write up all five points.

It is important to note that with regard to Upali the Jain, the Buddha does not try to convert him by expressing hostile views about the religion of Nigantha Nataputta. Again, as Upali himself declares, the Buddha does not celebrate Upali's conversion to Buddhism in a triumphal fashion as though Buddhism had won a contest against Jainism. He simply tells Upali to 'act after careful consideration'. The Buddha also tells Upali to continue giving to the Jain ascetics. This type of approach can be seen in the Rock Edicts of the Buddhist emperor, Ashoka, who reigned in the 3rd century BCE. In Rock Edict 7, Ashoka states that all religions should dwell everywhere because they have the same aim of self-control and purity of heart. In Rock Edict 12, he states that there should be growth in the essential of all religions which should try to learn from each other.

Now make the five points into your own summary (as in Theme 1 Developing Skills) trying to make the summary more personal to your style of writing.

Issues for analysis and evaluation

The value of experience compared to other potential sources of authority in Buddhism

One of the problems with regard to potential sources of authority in Buddhism is the sheer range of Buddhisms which might be under consideration. Thus, the source of authority for a bhikkhu in a vihara in Bangkok, Thailand following the sravaka-yana would be very different from the source of authority for a lone Buddhist following the pratyekabuddha-yana. Similarly, the source of authority for a Buddhist student studying under a lama in Tibetan Buddhism would be very different from the source of authority for a Buddhist student studying to be part of the Order of Interbeing in Plum Village, France.

However, taken overall, it might be argued that Buddhism is no different from any other world religion with regard to potential sources of authority. Thus, for example, there is the importance of tradition. Here, Theravada upholds the importance of the monastic sangha. Senior bhikkhus are regarded as being keepers of the orthodox way of living the monastic life in terms of its daily routine and rituals. They are therefore seen as the successors to a heritage passed down through the centuries from the historical Buddha himself. The variety of practices within the vihara are all aimed at unifying the monastic community under this authority whether it be in terms of reciting the Patimokka to celebrating Kathina at the end of Vassa.

The hierarchical structure of Buddhism in Thailand in the modern era is notable here given that the Sangha Supreme Council is the ultimate authority on all matters connected with Buddhism. The Sangha Supreme Council in turn is led by the Somdet Phra Sanghraja or supreme patriarch who is head of all members of the sangha.

Within Tibetan Buddhism, tradition has always given a great deal of authority to the lama who instructs those who wish to receive empowerment. For example, Choje Akong Tulku Rinpoche (1939–2013) who founded the Samye Ling Monastery in Scotland spoke about the importance of someone wanting to be a Buddhist taking refuge in the Buddha, the Sangha, the Dhamma and in the lama or Rinpoche who had opened the door to Buddhism for them. Such a lama had to belong to an unbroken lineage: 'When the teacher who gives you refuge does so in the lineage, then you can trace your own receiving of refuge, from teacher to student, right back over two and a half thousand years, from this country to Tibet, from Tibet to India, unbroken, right back to the Lord Buddha himself.'

At the same time, however, looking to tradition as a guarantee of authority is not wholly without difficulties. The Dalai Lama advised Western Buddhists to exercise caution with regard to their attitude towards their lama. Quoting a Tibetan proverb, he stated, 'A disciple must not throw himself upon a spiritual master as a dog throws itself upon a piece of meat. A disciple must not rush to place their trust immediately in a master, but must rather take the time to reflect carefully and examine the master's qualities before establishing a spiritual bond with them by receiving their teachings.'

Taking 'the time to reflect carefully' echoes the approach of the Kalama Sutta: experience is key and decisions should be made based on: 'When you know for yourselves....'

However, the problem again arises as to what that knowledge should be based upon. From the Theravada perspective, the foundation is in sacred texts which have been transmitted via oral tradition from the Buddha and then in written form to the modern day. The Pali Canon (the Vinaya, the Suttas and the Abhidhamma)

This section covers AO2 content and skills

Specification content

The value of experience compared to other potential sources of authority in Buddhism.

AO2 Activity

As you read through this section try to do the following:

1. Pick out the different lines of argument that are presented in the text and identify any evidence given in support.

2. For each line of argument try to evaluate whether or not you think this is strong or weak.

3. Think of any questions you may wish to raise in response to the arguments.

This Activity will help you to start thinking critically about what you read and help you to evaluate the effectiveness of different arguments and from this develop your own observations, opinions and points of view that will help with any conclusions that you make in your answers to the AO2 questions that arise.

Key quotes

It is preferable to receive the teachings of a master while viewing him or her first and foremost as a spiritual friend.... Little by little, if having observed them we are convinced that they are a true master, fully qualified and worthy of trust, we can follow their teachings by considering them our master. (Tenzin Gyatso, 14th Dalai Lama)

When Bodhidharma came to China, he saw that most Chinese learners did not grasp the truth of Buddhism. They merely sought it through interpretation of texts and thought of the changing phenomena all around them as real action. Bodhidharma wished to make these eager learners see that the finger pointing at the moon is not the moon itself. The real truth is nothing but one's own mind. (Guifeng Zongmi 780–841)

Key questions

To what extent does someone who follows the pratyekabuddha-yana have to be a Buddhist?

What would be the issues involved in adopting a Thai model of Buddhism with a clear structure and a Somdet Phra Sanghraja in the UK?

What does the finger pointing at the moon analogy teach about the importance of the Dhamma?

AO2 Activity

List some conclusions that could be drawn from the AO2 reasoning from the above text; try to aim for at least three different possible conclusions. Consider each of the conclusions and collect brief evidence to support each conclusion from the AO1 and AO2 material for this topic. Select the conclusion that you think is most convincing and explain why it is so. Try to contrast this with the weakest conclusion in the list, justifying your argument with clear reasoning and evidence.

have an absolute authority. The Mahayana perspective includes these as sacred texts but in addition there are other Sutras such as the Lotus Sutra believed to contain the hidden teaching of the historical Buddha which was transmitted in different ways.

The type of authority such texts might have, since they are the main conduits of the Dhamma, is again a complex one. It might be argued that these sacred texts should not be followed in a literal sense as containing absolute truths which need to be accepted wholly on the basis of faith. Here amulika saddha (blind faith) needs to be avoided in favour of akaravati saddha (confidence based on reason and experience).

Here, words from the Surangama Sutra which are widely used in Zen Buddhism might be applicable. The Buddha teaches Ananda but he fails to grasp its true meaning because he is too focused on the teaching itself. The Buddha declares: 'This is like a man pointing a finger at the moon to show it to others who should follow the direction of the finger to look at the moon. If they look at the finger and mistake it for the moon, they lose sight of both the moon and the finger. Why? Because the bright moon is actually pointed at; they both lose sight of the finger and fail to distinguish between the states of brightness and darkness.' Arguably, this analogy might be used to suggest that sacred texts are like the finger since they only point to the truth, the moon. They are not the truth in themselves.

Study tip

The skill of AO2 is all about building a credible argument through reasoning and the use of evidence and examples. Try to avoid just 'asserting' arguments by checking that your points are supported by evidence and/or examples.

Nhat Hanh links together the Finger Pointing at the Moon analogy with the parable of the raft to make what has been stated above explicit: 'The teaching is merely a vehicle to describe the truth. Don't mistake it for the truth itself. A finger pointing at the moon is not the moon. The finger is needed to know where to look for the moon, but if you mistake the finger for the moon itself, you will never know the real moon. The teaching is like a raft that carries you to the other shore. The raft is needed, but the raft is not the other shore. An intelligent person would not carry the raft around on his head after making it across to the other shore.... Use the raft to cross to the other shore, but don't hang onto it as your property. Do not become caught in the teaching. You must be able to let it go.'

The emphasis here on one's own reason and one's own personal experience always taking precedence over other potential sources of authority is certainly one which is attractive to many contemporary Buddhists, particularly those in the West who might be seen as 'convert' Buddhists. From this perspective, the saying from the Dhammapada 'Atta hi attano natho' ('oneself is one's own refuge') takes priority.

At the same time, it cannot be denied that there can be found in Buddhism aspects which point to what might be seen as authority over and above personal experience. Within the Lotus Sutra itself, for example, there are warnings to those people who might question its authority: who 'disparage this Sutra, and despise, hate, and hold grudges against the people who recite, copy, and preserve it'. Such people will suffer in the hell realm and the animal realm. Even if they succeed in being reborn in the human realm they will be: 'Tormented, hated, and despised by people, they will constantly suffer from hunger and thirst. With withered bones and flesh, they will be in anguish while living and covered with stones after death.'

The extent to which Buddhism's openness means it is in danger of losing its own identity

It might be argued that one of the strengths of Buddhism is that it provides the broadest possible scope in encompassing such a very wide diversity of beliefs including humanist Secular Buddhism and the far more elaborate forms of Tibetan Buddhism. Different forms of Buddhism root themselves in differing ways in the historical Buddha – understood and interpreted in a variety of ways – and basic tenets such as the Four Noble Truths and the Noble Eightfold Path – again understood and interpreted in a variety of ways. Added to this it might be argued that focus on teachings such as sunyata (emptiness) and upaya (skilful means) gives to Buddhism a fluidity in terms of identity which is lacking in other world religions. As we have seen, the parable of the raft and the Finger Pointing at the Moon analogy might give to Buddhist teaching a certain provisional quality which means that the boundaries of Buddhism are very porous.

An insight into this can be found in the life and legacy of Helena Blavatksy (1831–1931) and Henry Steel Olcott (1832–1907). Both had an international following in their day, particularly through bringing the beliefs of Hinduism and Buddhism to a Western audience. Both Blavatsky and Olcott worked in India and in Sri Lanka. In Sri Lanka, Olcott helped in the revival of Theravada Buddhism in the face of the opposition of Christian missionaries and is still highly regarded in Sri Lanka today. In 1880 both became the first Westerners to officially convert to Buddhism. However, the form of Buddhism which they promoted was also part of Theosophy – a new religious movement which they had founded in 1875 and which continues today. The key tenet of Theosophy is belief in a universal ancient wisdom underlying and uniting all religions once their external rituals are removed and the core beliefs uncovered.

The legacy of Blavatsky and Olcott has endured and has had its impact on some Western approaches to religion in general. Thus, Bhikkhu Bodhi notes the attraction to some of what he terms 'spiritual universalism'. He describes this as the belief that 'the major religions differ simply in so far as they are different means, different expedients, to the same liberative experience, which may be indiscriminately designated "enlightenment," or "redemption," or "God-realisation," since these different terms merely highlight different aspects of the same goal. As the famous maxim puts it: the roads up the mountain are many, but the moonlight at the top is one.' Given what has already been noted and given Buddhism's focus on the 'liberative experience' it might be argued that Buddhism, more than any other religion, is susceptible to being seen as an expression of the universal ancient wisdom shared by all religions. Bhikkhu Bodhi explains: 'From this point of view, the Buddha Dhamma is only one more variant on the "perennial philosophy" underlying all the mature expressions of man's spiritual quest. It may stand out by its elegant simplicity, its clarity and directness; but a unique and unrepeated revelation of truth it harbours not.'

At first sight, Nhat Hanh's book *Living Buddha, Living Christ* might seem to exemplify this openness of Buddhism which some might argue means that it is in danger of losing its identity. For example, Nhat Hanh explains: 'On the altar in my hermitage in France are images of Buddha and Jesus, and every time I light incense, I touch both of them as my spiritual ancestors.' He also explains how at a conference of representatives from different religions he shared in the Christian eucharist celebrated by a Catholic priest: 'Some of the Buddhists present were shocked to hear I had participated in the Eucharist, and many Christians seemed truly horrified.'

In discussing this, Nhat Hanh quotes the Second Precept of the Order of Interbeing: 'Do not think the knowledge you presently possess is changeless, absolute truth.'

Specification content
The extent to which Buddhism's openness means it is in danger of losing its own identity.

Key quote

Many think of Buddhism as a tolerant religion, one that recognises the value of all religious traditions…. This might suggest that Buddhism holds that all religions are one, that all spiritual paths lead to the same mountaintop. Nothing could be further from the truth…. Historically, all Buddhists have held that liberation from rebirth is impossible via any religion other than Buddhism. (Lopez and Buswell)

AO2 Activity

As you read through this section try to do the following:

1. Pick out the different lines of argument that are presented in the text and identify any evidence given in support.

2. For each line of argument try to evaluate whether or not you think this is strong or weak.

3. Think of any questions you may wish to raise in response to the arguments.

This Activity will help you to start thinking critically about what you read and help you to evaluate the effectiveness of different arguments and from this develop your own observations, opinions and points of view that will help with any conclusions that you make in your answers to the AO2 questions that arise.

Key questions

What would be the benefits of developing 'spiritual universalism' in the world today?

In order to be truly Buddhist, should Buddhism lose its own identity?

How far is personal experience the best way of validating a religion's claims?

Key quote

It was only later, through friendships with Christian men and women … that I have been able to touch the depths of Christianity. The moment I met Martin Luther King, Jr., I knew I was in the presence of a holy person. Not just his good work but his very being was a source of great inspiration for me. And others, less well known, have made me feel that Lord Jesus is still here with us.
(Nhat Hanh)

AO2 Activity

List some conclusions that could be drawn from the AO2 reasoning from the above text; try to aim for at least three different possible conclusions. Consider each of the conclusions and collect brief evidence to support each conclusion from the AO1 and AO2 material for this topic. Select the conclusion that you think is most convincing and explain why it is so. Try to contrast this with the weakest conclusion in the list, justifying your argument with clear reasoning and evidence.

Avoid being narrow-minded and bound to present views. Learn and practise nonattachment from views in order to be open to receive others' viewpoints'. This has to form the basis for any form of dialogue with other religions according to Nhat Hanh: 'In a true dialogue, both sides are willing to change. We have to appreciate that truth can be received from outside of – not only within – our own group. If we do not believe that, entering into dialogue would be a waste of time. If we think we monopolise the truth and we still organise a dialogue, it is not authentic.' It is for this reason that Nhat Hanh criticises Pope John Paul II (1920–2005) for insisting that Jesus is the only Son of God. The Pope had written: 'Christ is absolutely original and absolutely unique … if He were "enlightened" like Buddha, without any doubt He would not be what He is'. Nhat Hanh argues: 'This attitude excludes dialogue and fosters religious intolerance and discrimination. It does not help.'

The key feature for Nhat Hanh is personal religious experience: 'If religions are authentic, they contain the same elements of stability, joy, peace, understanding, and love. The similarities as well as the differences are there. They differ only in terms of emphasis.'

Study tip

It is vital for AO2 that you actually discuss arguments and not just explain what someone may have stated. Try to ask yourself, 'was this a fair point to make?', 'is the evidence sound enough?', 'is there anything to challenge this argument?', 'is this a strong or weak argument?' Such critical analysis will help you develop your evaluation skills.

In discussing the approach taken by Tenzin Gyatso, the 14th Dalai Lama, to other religions, Abraham Velez de Cea highlights the Dalai Lama's firm belief in religious pluralism. The diversity of spiritual inclinations and mental dispositions mean that a form of 'spiritual universalism' is wholly untenable. Rather than there being an urge to merge Buddhism through increasing openness, which leads to loss of identity, the Dalai Lama uses the analogy of medicine. 'In the same way that it does not make much sense to prescribe one medicine for all kinds of illness, the idea that there should be only one religion or only one teaching for all beings is untenable.' In addition, just as through upaya (skilful means) the Buddha gave divergent and contradictory teachings 'depending on the needs and capacity of his disciples' many religions do exactly the same as they cater for people with 'diverse mental dispositions, and diverse spiritual and philosophical inclinations'.

It might be argued that the openness of Buddhism, its recognition of the good within all religions and its respect towards them has never prevented Buddhism from maintaining its difference, its identity and even – on occasion – its superiority. Here we might return to the story of Upali's conversion. It is notable that acting on Upali's instructions his gatekeeper on seeing Digha-Tapassi the Jain approach tells him: 'Wait, sir, do not enter. From now on the householder Upali has become a disciple of the ascetic Gotama. His gate is closed to Jain monks and nuns, and opened for the Buddha's monks, nuns, laymen, and laywomen. If you require alms-food, wait here, they will bring it to you.'

Upali now no longer accords Nigantha Nataputta the respect formerly given. On hearing that the latter along with his followers has arrived at his house, Upali takes for himself the highest and finest seat within the middle gate. As the sutta notes: 'Previously, when Upali saw Nigantha Nataputta coming, he would go out to greet him and, having wiped off the highest and finest seat with his upper robe, he would put his arms around him and sit him down.'

AO2 Developing skills

It is now important to consider the information that has been covered in this section; however, the information in its raw form is too extensive and so has to be processed in order to meet the requirements of the examination. This can be achieved by practising more advanced skills associated with AO2. The exercises that run throughout this book will help you to do this and prepare you for the examination. For assessment objective 2 (AO2), which involves 'critical analysis' and 'evaluation' skills, we are going to focus on different ways in which the skills can be demonstrated effectively, and also, refer to how the performance of these skills is measured (see generic band descriptors for A2 [WJEC] AO2 or A Level [Eduqas] AO2).

▶ **Your task is this:** Below is a one-sided view concerning **the extent to which Buddhism's openness means it is in danger of losing its own identity**. It is 150 words long. You need to include this view for an evaluation; however, to just present one side of an argument or one line of reasoning is not really evaluation. Using the paragraph below, add a counter-argument or alternative line of reasoning to make the evaluation more balanced. Allow about 100 words for your counter-argument or alternative line of reasoning.

Arguably Buddhism is in danger of losing its own identity since, for example, when it was introduced in the West it was seen as part of a general ancient form of Eastern wisdom which included teachings from Hinduism. From this perspective, Buddhism fits in well with Theosophy, which is a form of spiritual universalism. It might be argued that this approach can be found in the fact that Thich Nhat Hanh explained how on his altar are images of the Buddha and of Christ and how he participated in the Christian Eucharist. The focus on religious pluralism taken by the present Dalai Lama also suggests that Buddhism could be seen as just one spiritual path amongst many others which is as good as any other. This implies that as long as there is compassion, there would be no problem with Buddhism overlapping in beliefs, teaching and practices with other religions.

Next, think of another line of argument or reasoning that may support either argument or it may even be completely different and add this to your answer. Then ask yourself:

- Will my work, when developed, contain thorough, sustained and clear views that are supported by extensive, detailed reasoning and/or evidence?

Key skills Theme 3

The third theme has tasks that deal with specific aspects of AO2 in terms of identifying key elements of an evaluative style piece of writing, specifically counter-arguments and conclusions (both intermediate and final).

Key skills

Analysis involves:

Identifying issues raised by the materials in the AO1, together with those identified in the AO2 section, and presents sustained and clear views, either of scholars or from a personal perspective ready for evaluation.

This means:

- That your answers are able to identify key areas of debate in relation to a particular issue

- That you can identify, and comment upon, the different lines of argument presented by others

- That your response comments on the overall effectiveness of each of these areas or arguments.

Evaluation involves:

Considering the various implications of the issues raised based upon the evidence gleaned from analysis and provides an extensive detailed argument with a clear conclusion.

This means:

- That your answer weighs up the consequences of accepting or rejecting the various and different lines of argument analysed

- That your answer arrives at a conclusion through a clear process of reasoning.

Specification content

Buddhism in Britain.

Key terms

Sir Edwin Arnold: author of *The Light of Asia* and thereby an influential figure in promoting Buddhism in Britain and the USA

The Light of Asia: Sir Edwin Arnold's epic poem on the early life of the Buddha and on the Dhamma published 1879

Key quote

This poetic retelling of the Buddha's life presented Gautama in such a way that satisfied the Victorians' romantic longing for spiritual fulfilment … while affirming the moral qualities of the ideal Victorian gentleman: personal detachment united with personal benevolence, uprightness, truthfulness and perseverance. (Batchelor on *The Light of Asia*)

E: Historical development of Buddhism

Buddhism in Britain

In 1879, **Sir Edwin Arnold** (1832–1904) published *The Light of Asia*. In this epic and lengthy poem, Arnold gives an account of the Buddha's life from his conception through to his Awakening and first teaching of the Dhamma. It begins with the idea that as a bodhisattva, the Buddha had been reborn and died many times before his last rebirth. Many of the episodes in the poem are ones with which most students of Buddhism are familiar. These include: Queen Maya's dream of the elephant, the prophecy of Asita, Suddhodana's attempt to keep him in the palaces, the marriage to Yashodara, the Four Sights with Channa the charioteer and the Great Renunciation. The poem also includes key parts of the Dhamma and quotations from the Dhammapada.

The poem is reminiscent of other Victorian poems in its depiction of a heroic figure and in its language and style. For example, the Buddha's walk to the Bodhi Tree is described as follows:

'Whom—as he passed into its ample shade,
Cloistered with columned dropping stems, and roofed
With vaults of glistening green—the conscious earth
Worshipped with waving grass and sudden flush
Of flowers about his feet. The forest-boughs
Bent down to shade him; from the river sighed
Cool wafts of wind laden with lotus-scents
Breathed by the water-gods.'

The Buddha's enlightenment and realisation of the Four Nobles Truths is described leading to full understanding:

'Until—greater than Kings, than Gods more glad! –
The aching craze to live ends, and life glides—
Lifeless—to nameless quiet, nameless joy,
Blessed NIRVANA—sinless, stirless rest
That change which never changes!'

Some parts of the poem are extracts from the Dhammapada – although this is not named – in Pali then followed by English translation. Thus, as the Buddha journeys he recites words from the Dhammapada verse 183:

'Sabba papassa akaranan;	Evil swells the debts to pay,
Kusalassa upasampada;	Good delivers and acquits;
Sa chitta pariyodapanan;	Shun evil, follow good; hold sway
Etan Budhanusasanan.	Over thyself. This is the Way.'

The poem concludes with the Buddha teaching Suddhodana, Yashodara and Rahula key points of the Dhamma such as the law of rebirth and kamma:

'The Books say well, my Brothers! each man's life
The outcome of his former living is;
The bygone wrongs bring forth sorrows and woes
The bygone right breeds bliss.'

The pancha sila are outlined and the Noble Eightfold Path is then explained in detail concluding with the lines:

'Enter the Path! There spring the healing streams
Quenching all thirst! there bloom th' immortal flowers
Carpeting all the way with joy! there throng,
Swiftest and sweetest hours!'

The Buddha's founding of the monastic sangha is recorded with bhikkhus described as:

'They who, as wakened eagles, soar with scorn
From life's low vale, and wing towards the Sun....'

Arnold extols the Buddha as the one who gave 'our Asia light' and who is 'Lover! Brother! Guide! Lamp of the Law!' After this peroration the poem ends with the words:

'The dew is on the lotus! – Rise, Great Sun!
And lift my leaf and mix me with the wave.
Om Mani Padme Hum, the sunrise comes!
The Dewdrop Slips Into The Shining Sea!'

Arnold's poem is illustrative of a number of general but important points regarding the historical development of Buddhism in Britain.

In the first place, it indicates that whilst at the beginning of the 19th century it was relatively mysterious and unknown in Britain, from the mid-19th century onwards key traditions about the life of the historical Buddha and key aspects of his teachings had become well-established in the mainstream of general knowledge amongst the educated middle classes.

Secondly, Arnold's use of Pali in his poem is an indication that by the latter half of the 19th century, textual studies of Buddhist manuscripts written in a variety of languages including Pali, Sanskrit and Chinese had become as accepted as similar studies into the Hebrew, Aramaic and Greek texts of the Bible. Indeed, the scholarship involved in the latter could be seen at work with the former in terms of detailed analysis and exegesis. In this context it is argued that, for example, Brian Houghton Hodgson (1801–1894) who had worked for the British East India Company was in part responsible for the growth of Buddhist studies in Europe through his acquisition of a large number of Buddhist manuscripts in Tibet which were sent back to Europe for translation.

Thirdly, the popularity of *The Light of Asia* illustrates the readiness with which many of the educated middle-class Victorian public responded to the subject matter of the Buddha and of Buddhism. The poem was printed in over one hundred editions in Britain and in the USA, and presented a widely acceptable portrait of the Buddha. For example, in Chicago at the inaugural meeting of the Parliament of World Religions in 1893, a speech by Hikkaduwe Sri Sumangala Thera (1827–1911) – a leading pioneer in the revival of Buddhism in Sri Lanka – was read. In this he declared: 'Sir Edwin Arnold's epic, *The Light of Asia* has created a popular love for the stainless and compassionate character of Gautama Buddha. Justice being done to him; his personality is seen to shine with exceptional brilliance among the figures of human history.'

Fourthly, Arnold's verse – whatever its literary merit – is full of the exotic imagery so attractive to many Victorians due to its connections with the mysterious East. This added greatly to its popularity. The Buddha and Buddhism belonged to the Oriental World rather than the Occidental (Western) World. Much of

Key quote

A way out of suffering, a path of action and optimism, an affirmation of interdependence, a condemnation of selfishness, a human pattern of heroic renunciation and compassion, and a positive, blissful goal – this was the message which The Light of Asia presented. (Harris)

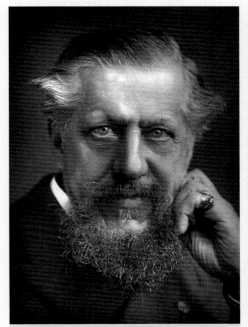

Sir Edwin Arnold, author of The Light of Asia

Key quote

The Light of Asia did more to encourage an understanding of Buddhism in the West than perhaps any other piece of writing in the latter half of the nineteenth century. (Harris)

quickfire

3.20 What is meant by 'Protestant Buddhism'?

Key term

Theosophy: an esoteric religious movement – the Theosophical Society was founded by Helena Blavatsky and Henry Olcott in 1876 with a focus is on ancient universal divine wisdom

the attraction of Buddha and of Buddhism lay in the fact that it was not seen as ordinary, everyday and mundane. Thus, the idea of hidden and secret teachings stored in inaccessible monasteries in far-flung parts of the world, imbued Buddhism with a romanticism which Christianity no longer had.

Fifthly, *The Light of Asia* presented in a positive and sympathetic way the life of a religious teacher who was not Jesus of Nazareth and whose teaching did not form Christianity. It is generally accepted in much that is written about the later Victorian period in Britain, that this was a time when traditional Christian belief was increasingly questioned by the educated middle classes and others. It is notable that Arnold's *The Light of the World* on the life of Christ published in 1891 never attained anything like the popularity of *The Light of Asia*.

Sixthly – and connected to the previous point – is an issue that relates to the parts of the poem in which the Buddha rejects the religion which Arnold describes as being that of 'the priests of Brahm' – a reference to Brahmanism or Hinduism as it was becoming known in Victorian Britain. Thus, one of Mara's daughters is described as a sorceress 'who gives dark creeds their power'. Before the Buddha dismisses her, she asks him if would dare to:

'Put by our sacred books, dethrone our gods,
Unpeople all the temples, shaking down
That law which feeds the priests and props the realms?'

In general, the Victorians in Britain had never viewed Hinduism in a particularly positive way since it was regarded as being alien, dominated by sacrifices, priests and rituals. Buddhism was seen as being a return to a pure and authentic form of belief which was devoid of any superstitions and which did not require sacrifices, priests and rituals. Indeed, some Victorians drew a parallel between Buddhism being similar to Protestantism in that just as Buddhism rejected the traditions of Brahmanism or Hinduism, Protestantism had rejected the traditions of Roman Catholicism. Buddha himself was praised as a type of Martin Luther (1483–1586) the first figure of the Protestant Reformation who had aimed to reform the religion of his time. It is notable that some also made a further distinction between what were regarded as the inferior elaborate rituals, images and traditions of Mahayana – equated with Roman Catholicism – and what was regarded as the by far superior, simpler, purer and more authentic form of Theravada Buddhism – equated with Protestantism and even sometimes called 'Protestant Buddhism' today.

Finally, the exoticism of *The Light of Asia* tapped into the increasing interest in mystical matters prevalent in the latter part of the Victorian period and beyond. As has been noted, in 1880 two of the first Westerners to officially convert to Buddhism – a year after *The Light of Asia* was published – were Helena Blavatksy (1831–1891) and Henry Steel Olcott (1832–1907). Four years before the publication of *The Light of Asia* they had founded the Theosophical Society. Blavatsky in particular formulated Theosophy as an esoteric religion which combined elements of Buddhism and Hinduism, alongside belief in

Helena Blavatsky (1831–1891), the first Western woman to be converted to Buddhism and the founder of the Theosophical Society.

the paranormal, seances, clairvoyance, clairaudience, telepathy, Spiritualism, Hermeticism and Neoplatonism. Blavatsky claimed that some of her writings were inspired by her visits to Tibetan monasteries and by messages given by mysterious Tibetan lamas.

Study tip

Research Edward Said's analysis of the term 'orientalism' and consider how applicable it might be to British understanding of Buddhism.

By the end of the 19th century and the beginning of the 20th century, there began to emerge societies based in London which were engaged in promoting Buddhism and Buddhist studies. The academic study of Buddhism was greatly enhanced by the Pali Society founded in 1881 – two years after the publication of *The Light of Asia* – by Thomas William Rhys Davids (1843–1922). As a civil servant in Sri Lanka he had developed his interest in Buddhism through the collection of manuscripts and inscriptions. Through the work of the Pali Society, the study of Pali was promoted alongside the translation of many key texts from the titpitaka into English. The Buddhist Society of Great Britain and Ireland was formed in 1907 with Rhys Davids as its first president. Through these societies, Rhys Davids and his wife Caroline Augusta Foley Rhys Davids (1857–1942) helped to promote the study of Pali in universities and also to promote the study of Theravada Buddhism. The links with Theosophy already noted may also be mentioned here as Caroline Rhys Davids was a believer in, and supporter of, Blavatsky's Theosophical Society.

One of the first British people to be ordained as a Theravada monk was **Charles Henry Allan Bennett** (1872–1923). As with many others at that time, he found his interest in Buddhism kindled following his rejection of Christianity and his reading Arnold's poem *The Light of Asia* in 1890. Again, as with many others at that time, he was initially a follower of Blavatsky's Theosophy and studied magic with his friend for some years Aleister Crowley (1875–1947) who later gained a notorious reputation for his libertine lifestyle and for his interest in the occult and black magic. Accounts suggest that Bennett moved away from Crowley's influence and in the late 1890s travelled from Sri Lanka to Rangoon in Burma. Here in 1901 he was ordained and was given the name Ananda Metteyya. He saw his mission as one of bringing Theravada Buddhism to the West and to that effect began an international Buddhist society – of which Sir Edward Arnold was the first honorary member. This society brought together a number of Buddhist scholars who contributed to the quarterly review which the society published.

In 1908 he returned to Britain to give the first Buddhist mission in the country. He remained for a year in London. During this time, he must have been a notable figure given his saffron robes, his shaven head and his absolute commitment to observing all the precepts for bhikkhus. Most of his efforts were directed at lecturing at the society, writing articles about Buddhism and officially receiving those from the society who wished to convert to Buddhism. Having returned to Rangoon, Bennett's plan was to move back to London in 1911 and there establish a permanent Theravada Buddhist community. However, what Bennett planned was not realised due to his ill health – he suffered from chronic asthma – and his poverty – he had no financial means of his own and was wholly reliant on the kindness of others. His ill health meant that he had to stop being a bhikkhu due to the hardship he imposed on himself by adhering so strictly to the rules of the Vinaya Pitaka, and in 1914 he returned to England. He had planned to join his sister in the USA but because of his illness was refused permission to board ship as it was feared that he would not survive the journey and that even if he did, would be refused entry in the USA.

By this time the international Buddhist society had ceased to function but Bennett redoubled his efforts on behalf of the Buddhist Society in London. He continued

Key quote

So may you help to render to the Western World that greatest of all services whereof it stands so sorely now in need: the spreading of the great Religion which, from the small beginning now made, will yet grow till all the thinking West stands where you stand today; and which in very fact is the sole cure for all its manifold sufferings. (Bennett)

Key term

Charles Henry Allan Bennett: one of the first people from Britain to be ordained a Buddhist monk

Key terms

Anagarika Dharmapala: regarded as the first international Buddhist missionary

Christmas Humphreys: the founder of the Buddhist Society and its president until his death in 1983

The Buddhist Society: the most influential and long-lasting of a number of Buddhist groups formed early in the 20th century officially founded in 1924

Key quote

Humphreys was a skilled organiser and writer of popular books on Buddhism, but he lacked the philosophical and linguistic skills of his German counterparts and retained a life-long commitment to the 'great principles' of Blavatsky. (Batchelor)

with the conviction that Buddhism offered the greatest hope for the West and in an editorial wrote: 'These facts, we consider, justify us in our conclusion that in the extension of this great Teaching lies not only the solution of the ever-growing religious problems of the West; but even, perhaps, the only possible deliverance of the western civilisation from that condition of fundamental instability which now so obviously and increasingly prevails.' Bennett died in 1923 and was given a Buddhist funeral by one of those he had helped convert to Buddhism. Bennett's attempts to found a Theravada Buddhist presence in London met with more success through the work of the Sri Lankan **Anagarika Dharmapala** (1864–1934) who is regarded as the first international Theravada Buddhist missionary. Again, it might be noted that Anagarika Dharmapala had close links with the Theosophical Society through the work of Olcott in Sri Lanka. Born David Hewavitharane, he took the name Anagarika Dharmapala. He was influenced by his Western education and by his travels in the West. He was notable in the role he played with regard to the revival of Buddhism in Sri Lanaka. In addition, on his visit to England he met with Sir Edwin Arnold, and he also attended the Parliament of World Religions in Chicago in 1893. Anagarika Dharmapala managed to acquire substantial financial backing and in 1926 founded the very first Buddhist vihara outside of Asia with resident bhikkhus from Sri Lanka.

In describing the development of British Buddhism, Robert Bluck writes: 'The first half of the 20th century witnessed a gradual transition from academic interest to personal involvement, though still on a small scale. The Buddha's life and teachings were increasingly seen as examples and principles to follow, and Buddhist rites of passage, together with the interest in meditation, show the beginnings of genuine Buddhist practice.'

In this development a variety of British Buddhist societies along with their publications had played their part. However, the most important of these was **the Buddhist Society** founded in 1924 by **Christmas Humphreys** (1901–1983) of which he remained as President until his death. Humphreys – a noted barrister and judge – had been a Theosophist but later converted to Buddhism although the influence of Theosophy remained. Humphreys was both wealthy and well-connected and through him the Buddhist Society was able to offer what Bluck describes as 'fine London premises, large library, lectures, classes and dissemination of Buddhist information and literature'. Humphreys was not always popular with other Buddhist groups later on as they regarded him as being too authoritarian and too conservative.

Today, the Buddhist Society presents itself as: 'a lay organisation which is one of the oldest Buddhist societies in Europe. From its inception it has not been attached to any one school of Buddhism, remaining non-sectarian in character and open in principle to the teachings of all schools and traditions.' This non-sectarian character is evident in the breadth of Buddhism which the Society has hosted in a variety of ways. From 1926 onwards, the Buddhist Society was a pioneer in having books on Buddhism published in English including articles on Buddhism in its quarterly publication *The Middle Way*. In addition, it helped in propagating Zen Buddhism through the writings of Daisetsu Teitaro Suzuki (1870–1966) – who was also a member of the Theosophist Society. Humphreys also wrote or contributed to a number of works on Buddhism including ones on meditation, the Buddhist life in general and on Zen Buddhism. When he died in 1983, he left his house in St John's Wood to the Zen Centre, London where it is now a temple in the Rinzai tradition.

Further evidence of the non-sectarian nature of the Buddhist Society can be seen in the way in which Humphreys tried to get various Buddhist groups around the world to accept his *Twelve Principles of Buddhism* written in 1945. These presented the fundamental beliefs of Buddhism in such a way as to provide what he regarded as a possible basis for one unified World Buddhism. The twelfth principle states:

'Buddhism is neither pessimistic nor "escapist", nor does it deny the existence of God or soul, though it places its own meaning on these terms .... It appeals to the West because it has no dogmas, satisfies the reason and the heart alike, insists on self-reliance coupled with tolerance for other points of view, embraces science, religion, philosophy, psychology, ethics and art, and points to man alone, as the creator of his present life and sole designer of his destiny.'

Overall, the Buddhist Society performed a key role in Britain during this period in terms of bringing together scholars, students, practising Buddhists, those interested in becoming Buddhists and in providing a centre for meditation.

Christmas Humphreys President of the Buddhist Society until his death in 1983.

Key quote

An important aspect of the Society's work is to provide a gateway for those who show a genuine interest in this ancient wisdom, and to present Buddhism in its essentials, in simple and understandable language. However, we also teach the basics of practice for those who simply wish to learn how to relax, and find some peace and tranquillity. **(Buddhist Society)**

Study tip

Research the life of Anagarika Dharmapala and try to find out about his contribution to Buddhist Modernism.

Possible reasons for the popularity of Buddhism in Britain

Trying to establish facts and figures with regard to the number of Buddhists in Britain in the *first* half of the 20th century is very difficult. Bluck records the Buddhist Society as having 1,000 members in 1964 and that, in addition, there were some 20 Buddhist groups. This suggests that since the beginning of the century in Britain there had been a relatively small but growing number of Buddhists most of whom were of white ethnicity, were educated and were middle class.

The popularity of Buddhism only grew at this time due to the decreasing popularity of the established religion of Christianity. Religious belief and practice as a uniform and expected expression of loyalty to the nation and the moral norms of society, appeared to become less attractive and less relevant. In addition, the claims of Christianity as enshrined in the institutions of the Church seemed less tenable. There was, for example, the simple fact that it was divided: the established Churches of Britain had to face the growing challenge of the Roman Catholic Church and the Nonconformist Churches and Chapels.

Another possible reason for the popularity of Buddhism was what it appeared to offer – especially in the then better-known form of Theravada – a straightforward belief system which did not require the type of faith required by Christianity. The former certainties of Christian faith seemed less secure: belief in God as creator of the universe, the six days of creation, the inerrancy of the Bible, Jesus of Nazareth being human and divine, the miracles of Jesus and the resurrection were all increasingly subject to question and doubt. In their place, Buddhism was seen to offer a philosophy of life in tune with science. There were the Four Noble Truths incorporating the Noble Eightfold Path which could lead to enlightenment. The

quickfire

3.21 What was the Buddhist name given to Charles Bennett?

Specification content

Possible reasons for the popularity of Buddhism in Britain.

Study tip

Research Buddhist groups which are active in your local area and identify to which Buddhist tradition they belong.

Key quotes

In the latter half of the twentieth century, an unprecedented number of Westerners were attracted to Buddhism. For many, it seemed to offer a safe haven from a crazy world. The prevailing attitude was 'Stop the World – I Want to Get Off', the title of a Broadway show in the 1960s. (Kraft)

The history of Buddhism in Britain sits within the context of Buddhism's changing relationship with the West and the gradual decline of Christianity. (Bluck)

law of kamma could also be seen as no more and no less than the law of causality. The moral code of the pancha sila was straightforward and the only key practice required was meditation and perhaps recitation of sacred texts.

There is also another possible reason for Buddhism's popularity in that once Christianity had been rejected, there was little by way of acceptable alternatives which might provide some form of shelter to those on a personal spiritual quest. Here Buddhism became popular – although often via Theosophy and the teachings of Blavatsky and Olcott. The route for many of the earliest British Buddhists such as Bennett and Humphreys was through the Theosophy Society. Its focus on the esoteric, orientalism, ancient wisdom, mysticism and the occult was presented in a learned and intellectually appealing way. It upheld above all that the religions of the East were superior in providing the mystical truths which could answer the individual's deepest questions and thus provide a sure spiritual home. In this way, Theosophy helped to make Buddhism popular.

Certainly, the earliest Buddhists in Britain appeared to never quite lose their Theosophical background. The Buddhist writer David Guy, for example, regards 'the influence of Theosophy' as being 'a major flaw in Humphreys' writing about Buddhism' such as in the following passage: 'Unable to teach all that had been imparted to him – owing to his pledges – though he taught a philosophy built upon the groundwork of the true esoteric knowledge, the Buddha gave to the world its outward material body and kept its soul for his Elect. This "soul", the Doctrine of the Heart, is to be found in fragments, usually mutilated, in all the Scriptures of the world. It is the ancient Wisdom to which all Arhats, Rishis, and other perfect men achieve. It has a thousand forms, yet is eternally one.'

Since the *second* half of the 20th century through to the present-day there has been a dramatic increase in Buddhism in Britain. A major cause for this increase is migration of Buddhists from countries overseas including Tibet, China, Hong Kong and Nepal. The census figures for England and Wales compiled by the Office for National Statistics suggest the following with regard to the number of those calling themselves Buddhist:

2001:   144,453   0.28% of the population
2011:   247,743   0.4% of the population

With regard to Buddhist groups in Britain, it is difficult to provide accurate data but figures based on groups which are identified by the Buddhist International Directory suggest that for the United Kingdom as a whole there are now over 700 groups. However, when considering sub-traditions of these groups, the number is probably well over 1000 as suggested by Bluck.

Another possible cause for the increase in numbers is due to the rapid changes which began to take place in Western society as a whole – and not simply in Britain – in terms of political thought, culture and social change from the 1960s onwards. Bluck describes factors such as: 'greater socio-economic mobility, further decline in church attendance and increased interest in oriental religions, an information explosion and the expansion of higher education....'

One possible reason for the popularity of Buddhism alluded to by Bluck has been the huge increase in the number of people who have been able to afford to travel to countries such as Nepal, Thailand, China, Japan and other parts of South East Asia where they can see the temples, practices and rituals of Buddhism at first hand. Since the 1960s – when world travel began to be much more affordable – this has been the case especially for young people in higher education. Such exposure to Buddhism has, for example, made images of the Buddha commonplace in hotels, bars and in homes whether used as garden sculptures or household ornaments. In addition, some people have been converted by their experience of Buddhism on their travels whilst others have returned to Britain receptive to finding out more about Buddhism.

A different possible reason for the popularity of Buddhism is the way in which for some it seemed to fit comfortably into **New Age spirituality**. Since the 1960s New Age spirituality began to develop and has continued in its appeal, particularly in terms of what it appears to offer regarding the possibility of personal mystical spiritual experiences. In addition, it did not require having to join or belong to a religious group. As a form of what might be described as 'do-it-yourself religion with a pick and mix' approach New Age spirituality could be adopted, adapted and absorbed alongside Buddhism. Thus, images of the Buddha might find a place alongside pictures of Ganesha, collections of healing gemstones, Tibetan Buddhist artwork, dream-catchers, recordings of the 'Hare Krishna' chant or 'Om Mani Padme Hum', a vegetarian or vegan diet, tarot cards and incense sticks. For some, New Age spirituality remains as the chosen form of religious expression whilst for others it provides a gateway to discovering Buddhism.

Another possible reason for the popularity of Buddhism in Britain is due to the general acceptance of meditation and the possibility of empirical evidence supporting its effectiveness. Meditation can be found in numerous guises such as when it is offered as part of mindfulness training, well-being courses, cognitive behaviour therapy, educational enhancement, counselling, etc. Whilst in these instances there is nothing religious involved, meditation has given Buddhism a great deal of positive coverage. This again might be seen in some cases as a gateway to discovering Buddhism.

The information explosion mentioned by Bluck is a further possible reason for the popularity of Buddhism in Britain given the amount of exposure that Buddhism has received. For example, following his flight from Tibet in 1959, the Dalai Lama has received continual media coverage ranging from his meetings with world politicians to his appearance on the occasion of his 80th birthday at the Glastonbury festival in 2015. Through the Internet today a huge range of Buddhist material is instantly available hence it being called 'Cyberdharma'.

Key quote

Virtually every school of Buddhism is represented online these days. There are vast treasuries of sutras and commentaries and transcribed talks, and numerous projects devoted to adding more every day. There are galleries of thangkas and mandalas; forums that invite discussion on subjects ranging from posture to politics; monks who will answer e-mailed queries about the subtle and not-so-subtle points of practice; schedules for retreat centres around the globe; and dharma talks in streaming audio and video, available at any hour. There are, in other words, myriad ways in which anyone hoping to cultivate an awakened mind can nurture the impulse. **(John House on Cyberdharma)**

Key term

New Age spirituality: the name given to a non-unified set of beliefs that developed from the 1960s onwards built on wide-ranging spiritual and philosophical beliefs such as those of the Theosophical Society

Buddhist monk on the Internet

Specification content

Distinguishing between 'heritage' Buddhism (the Buddhism of those whose relatives were born in Buddhist countries and migrated to Britain) and 'convert' Buddhism.

Key terms

'Convert' Buddhists: a term defined by Bluck as referring to 'ethnically European people in Britain who have converted to Buddhism rather than coming from an Asian Buddhist background'

Rinpoche: the honorary title given to a spiritual teacher in Tibetan Buddhism

Distinguishing between 'heritage' Buddhism and 'convert' Buddhism

The 2011 census figures for England and Wales indicates that 39.7% of Buddhists were born in Britain and that 60.3% were born outside of Britain. In terms of ethnicity, the figures from the Office for National Statistics show the following breakdown for what might be termed the three main religions of the East: Hinduism, Sikhism and Buddhism.

Mixed/multiple ethnic group:		Other ethnic group	
Hindu:	1.2%	Hindu:	1%
Sikh:	1.2%	Sikh:	9.6%
Buddhist:	4%	Buddhist:	1.5%
Asian/Asian British		White	
Hindu:	95.7%	Hindu:	1.5%
Sikh:	87.1%	Sikh:	1.8%
Buddhist:	59.7%	Buddhist:	33.8%
Black/African/Caribbean			
Hindu:	0.7%		
Sikh:	0.3%		
Buddhist:	1.1%		

What is striking about these figures is that they suggest the attraction of Buddhism to what the Office of National Statistics describes as the 'White British' group has grown and continued from the 19th century onwards in a way which has not happened with either Hinduism or Sikhism.

In describing this group, Bluck rejects the use of 'white Buddhists' in favour of **'convert' Buddhists** to describe 'ethnically European people in Britain who have converted to Buddhism, rather than coming originally from an Asian Buddhist background'. Extrapolating a number is difficult but it would seem that that there are in the region of 80,000 'convert' Buddhists.

Distinguishing between 'heritage' Buddhism and 'convert' Buddhism in Britain is a difficult task because the groups identified represent Mahayana, Vajrayana (Tibetan), Theravada and mixed non-sectarian Buddhists. However, the key differences between 'heritage' and 'convert' Buddhists might best be explained by the ways in which 'heritage' Buddhists might bring with them the cultural expression of Buddhism from their own country, whereas 'convert' Buddhists might seek to embed Buddhism within a Western and British context.

One example of 'heritage' Buddhism can be found in the area which has seen the largest increase in the number of Buddhists in recent years: Rushmoor Borough Council in Hampshire. Here, the town of Aldershot had been home to the largely Nepalese Gurkha regiment and with settlement rights in the UK granted by the government, 3.3% of the borough population are now Buddhist. This makes the borough of Rushmoor – followed by the three London boroughs of Greenwich, Kensington and Chelsea and Westminster – the area of Britain most densely populated by Buddhists.

The Buddhist Community Centre UK in Aldershot was founded in 2007 and is specifically part of the Nyingma tradition of Tibetan Buddhism. The Centre was consecrated by Khyentse Yangsi **Rinpoche** (1993–) and since then has been visited by a number of Rinpoches including Tenzin Gyatso, the 14th Dalai Lama who inaugurated the Centre in 2015 and is its patron. The Centre has two monks and reflects the 'heritage' nature of its Buddhism in having events such as empowerments with leading Rinpoches such as the Terton (revealer of spiritual treasures) Namkha Drimed Rinpoche (1938–). The recognition of the authority of the Rinpoches, the respect and reverence shown to them, the importance of their visits and the empowerment ceremonies which they alone are able to perform reflect the 'heritage' nature of its Buddhism. This can also be seen in the way that the original building has been adapted following as far as possible a traditional Tibetan model. The shrine room inside the Centre is typically Tibetan Buddhist, whilst outside there are prayer flags, prayer wheels, a rupa of the Buddha on one side of the building and a large stupa on the other. These Tibetan aspects are also to be seen in the entrance gate with the traditional two deer and the Dhamma wheel. As might be expected, Tibetan is the main language of worship.

An example of 'convert' Buddhists can be found in the Sheffield Buddhist Centre which is housed in a converted church. The visual decoration reflects a mixture of Asian and Western cultures. The Centre describes itself as being 'run by members of the **Triratna Buddhist Order**, who teach and practise a non-sectarian style of Buddhism, suitable for people living in the contemporary Western world'. It would appear that most of its members are 'convert' Buddhists. The Triratna Buddhist Order – founded by Sangharakshita formerly Dennis Lingwood (1925–2018) – describes itself as being specifically focused on engaging with the teaching of the Buddha in the modern world. Therefore, those belonging to the Order are not monks, nuns and lay people but rather 'Buddhists at varying stages of commitment and understanding'.

The type of Buddhism practised combines elements of Theravada, Mahayana and Tibetan Buddhism. The Sheffield Buddhist Centre has a Great Hall for weekday meditation and the Centre hosts Yoga and Tai Chi classes. The 'convert' Buddhist nature of the Centre can be seen in some of the events which are run including 'Gender Diverse Sheffield' which is described as 'a gathering for anyone in the Triratna community who identifies as gender diverse (e.g. non-binary, gender-fluid, trans, gender questioning)' with a focus on the Dhamma. The Centre also has a Choir, a Dads' Group and Women's Order meetings. There is a great deal of focus on meditation for beginners and on a 'Still Learning' programme for schools. Evening talks are preceded by a 'shared veggie dinner'. A past event had been the Sheffield Centre Buddhist Panto called 'Amaladin' where Amaladin's quest was to find happiness by avoiding delusion, the ugly sisters and his evil uncle Mara.

AO1 Activity

Explain the growth of Buddhism in Britain since the 19th century.

Explain your answer using evidence and examples from what you have read.

quickfire

3.22 According to the ONS Census statistics for 2011, what percentage of the population of England and Wales classify themselves as Buddhist?

Study tip

Research the nearest Buddhist groups to your area and try to find out whether they are primarily for 'convert' or 'heritage' Buddhists.

Key term

Triratna Buddhist Order: originally known as the Friends of the Western Buddhist Order, which was founded by Sangharakshita (formerly Dennis Lingwood) in 1967 in London and is a form of Buddhist modernism

The Buddhist Community Centre, Aldershot, UK

Key skills Theme 3

The third theme has tasks that deal with the basics of AO1 in terms of prioritising and selecting the key relevant information, presenting this in a personalised way (as in Theme 1) and then using evidence and examples to support and expand upon this (as in Theme 2).

Key skills

Knowledge involves:

Selection of a range of (thorough) accurate and relevant information that is directly related to the specific demands of the question.

This means:

- Selecting relevant material for the question set

- Being focused in explaining and examining the material selected.

Understanding involves:

Explanation that is extensive, demonstrating depth and/or breadth with excellent use of evidence and examples including (where appropriate) thorough and accurate supporting use of sacred texts, sources of wisdom and specialist language.

This means:

- Effective use of examples and supporting evidence to establish the quality of your understanding

- Ownership of your explanation that expresses personal knowledge and understanding and NOT just reproducing a chunk of text from a book that you have rehearsed and memorised.

AO1 Developing skills

It is now important to consider the information that has been covered in this section; however, the information in its raw form is too extensive and so has to be processed in order to meet the requirements of the examination. This can be achieved by practising more advanced skills associated with AO1. For assessment objective 1 (AO1), which involves demonstrating 'knowledge' and 'understanding' skills, we are going to focus on different ways in which the skills can be demonstrated effectively, and also, refer to how the performance of these skills is measured (see generic band descriptors for A2 [WJEC] AO1 or A Level [Eduqas] AO1).

▶ **Your next task is this:** Below is a summary of **possible reasons for the popularity of Buddhism in Britain**. It is 150 words long. This time there are no highlighted points to indicate the key points to learn from this extract. Discuss which five points you think are the most important to highlight and write them down in a list.

Buddhism's popularity in Britain is due to a number of factors. For example, what used to be the dominant religion of Christianity has since the 19th century been coming under increasing pressure due to its divisions and its resistance to accepting scientific ideas. Buddhism has become an acceptable alternative. In addition, Buddhism seems to offer more of a way of life and a rational philosophy rather than being a religion in the sense of other religions. This means that Buddhism is appealing to those who are secular and even atheists. For others, Buddhism is seen as a religion but it is different, fresh and new because it is from the East. This links with New Age spirituality and with the way in which interest in Buddhism has developed through people travelling to Buddhist countries such as Thailand and making things such as Buddha rupas very popular. Such images draw people to Buddhism.

Now make the five points into your own summary (as in Theme 1 Developing Skills) trying to make the summary more personal to your style of writing. This may also involve re-ordering the points if you wish to do so.

Issues for analysis and evaluation

The comparative significance of features which contribute to the popularity of Buddhism in Britain

This section covers AO2 content and skills

Specification content

The comparative significance of features which contribute to the popularity of Buddhism in Britain.

Arguably a first feature which contributes to the popularity of Buddhism is that it provides something which a person on a spiritual quest cannot find elsewhere. In the past in Britain, such a spiritual quest may have begun in the context of Christianity and have led a person to move through conversion from one Church to another – for example from being a member of the Church of England to becoming a Baptist. The breadth of belief and practice within British Christianity was such as to cater for many who might have felt that they needed to look elsewhere for spiritual fulfilment. Today, Buddhism provides another home for those on a spiritual quest.

A second feature concerns the type of spiritual quest which a person might be following. It is difficult to generalise here, but it may be argued that in its basic form Buddhism offers through the practice of meditation a way in which any person – regardless of, for example, their social background, ability or disability, gender, age, education, sexual orientation and race – may have a deep personal encounter with themselves and with those things which might make sense of life.

A third feature relates to the way in which British Buddhism can be seen as 'anodyne' for those who wish to follow the pratyekabuddha-yana or for those who wish to join a Buddhist group. Buddhism tends not to be a missionary religion, is non-threatening, will not provoke dissent and is inoffensive. This is particularly the case when the Socially Engaged Buddhism aspect is not present. Thus, for example, tea and biscuits or a 'veggie dinner' might be provided before a talk on the Dhamma or might follow a meditation session in much the same way that refreshments are on offer before or after meetings and services in Christian churches.

A fourth feature is that in Britain, Buddhism still retains an air of mystique. Buddhism is frequently described as 'ancient wisdom' with the implication that what has been taught and practised for over two and a half thousand years has the aura and even sanctity which such a length of time bestows upon it. This is particularly the case given its oriental origins, which some might regard as automatically superior to anything which has been previously adopted in occidental belief such as Judaism, Christianity and Islam.

A final feature with regard to British Buddhism is that it offers a person on a spiritual quest a great degree of freedom and variety in terms of what type of Buddhism they may wish to follow and the type of commitment and belief which they might need to bring. Thus, for many, becoming a Buddhist may require no significant alteration or change in their way of life. Set prayers, days and times set apart for worship, moral requirements, being part of a congregation and following the monastic life can be strictly observed by some 'convert' Buddhists or not at all by other 'convert' Buddhists. The perception of Buddhism in Britain is therefore that it can be all things to all people.

If it is the case that Buddhism can be all things to all people, then 'convert' Buddhists can usually find in a particular British Buddhist group, beliefs which correspond with their own beliefs. However, that being the case, it might be asked as to how far any particular group – no matter how popular it might be – is truly Buddhist.

In the Tittha Sutta, which is part of the Udana (6.4) in the Pali Canon, the Buddha is staying near the town of Savatthi where there were 'many contemplatives, brahmans, and wanderers of various sects ... with differing views, differing opinions, differing beliefs, dependent for support on their differing views'. In

Key quote

The lure of the mysterious East, a scholarly and reserved approach, with personal (rather than institutional) choices about what to retain or discard, all appear characteristic of a British attitude towards spiritual practice in a materialistic age. It is hardly surprising that British Buddhists have tended to be middle-class and well educated, though the emphasis of new Buddhist movements on urban centres may be encouraging a wider membership. **(Bluck)**

AO2 Activity

As you read through this section try to do the following:

1. Pick out the different lines of argument that are presented in the text and identify any evidence given in support.

2. For each line of argument try to evaluate whether or not you think this is strong or weak.

3. Think of any questions you may wish to raise in response to the arguments.

This Activity will help you to start thinking critically about what you read and help you to evaluate the effectiveness of different arguments and from this develop your own observations, opinions and points of view that will help with any conclusions that you make in your answers to the AO2 questions that arise.

Key quote

There are as many kinds of
Buddhism as there are ways the
fragmented and ever-changing
European mind has to apprehend
it.... For rationalists it means a
philological object.... For romantics
it is a fantasy object, where all is
pure and good, a justification for
one's disdain of the corrupt West.
(Batchelor)

Key questions

Which is the most important feature in
terms of the popularity of Buddhism?

To what extent would Buddhism
benefit from becoming a missionary
religion in Britain?

As Buddhism becomes more
established, in what ways do you
think its popularity will increase or
decrease?

The parable of the blind men and the elephant as taught by the Buddha.

AO2 Activity

List some conclusions that could be
drawn from the AO2 reasoning from
the above text; try to aim for at least
three different possible conclusions.
Consider each of the conclusions
and collect brief evidence to support
each conclusion from the AO1 and
AO2 material for this topic. Select
the conclusion that you think is most
convincing and explain why it is so.
Try to contrast this with the weakest
conclusion in the list, justifying
your argument with clear reasoning
and evidence.

their disputes about the Dhamma they were 'arguing, quarrelling, and disputing,
wounding one another with weapons of the mouth'. Each group claimed that only
their interpretation of the Dhamma was the correct one.

To explain the situation to his followers the Buddha gave the well-known parable
of people blind from birth being gathered around an elephant by a King. 'To some
of the blind people he showed the elephant's head, saying, "This, blind people, is
what an elephant is like." To some of them he showed the elephant's ear, saying,
"This, blind people, is what an elephant is like." To some of them he showed the
elephant's tusk ... the elephant's trunk ... the elephant's body ... the elephant's
foot ... the elephant's hindquarters ... the elephant's tail ... the tuft at the end of the
elephant's tail.'

The King then asks all the blind people if they have seen the elephant to which they
reply that they have. He then asks them to tell him what the elephant is like. Each
group of blind people having focused on just one aspect of the elephant gives a
different answer clinging on to only what they have experienced and they end by
quarrelling with each other and 'striking one another with their fists'. The Buddha
concludes with the moral of the story: 'With regard to these things, they are
attached – some contemplatives and brahmans. They quarrel and fight— people
seeing one side.'

Study tip

It is vital for AO2 that you actually discuss arguments and not just explain what
someone may have stated. Try to ask yourself, 'was this a fair point to make?',
'is the evidence sound enough?', 'is there anything to challenge this argument?',
'is this a strong or weak argument?' Such critical analysis will help you develop
your evaluation skills.

Regarding the parable of the blind men and the elephant, it might be argued that
for Buddhism in Britain, being all things to all people is positive providing that any
one group does not become 'attached' to the Buddhism of their group as being the
only correct view. As Batchelor points out: 'To fix the elephant in either space or
time is to kill her. The elephant breathes and moves – in ways one cannot foresee.'

Thus, some Buddhist groups might gain popularity for emphasising their continuity
with Theravada such as Amaravati Monastery in Hemel Hempstead opened in
1985. This is part of the Forest Sangha following in the tradition of Ajahn Chah
(1918–1992). Here, the monastic community live in accordance with the Vinaya
and the Dhamma. Alternatively, other Buddhist groups might gain popularity by
being part of Tibetan Buddhism such as the New Kadampa Tradition founded by
Geshe Kelsang Gyatso (1931–). One of its main centres is the Manjushri Kadampa
Centre at Conishead Priory in Cumbria where a Buddhist college has existed
since 1976. Other Buddhist groups might gain popularity by their links to specific
forms of Buddhism such as Zen. For example, Throssel Hole Buddhist Abbey
in Northumberland founded in 1972 follows the Serene Reflection Meditation
Tradition similar to Japanese Soto Zen. The monastic community there is part of
the Order of Buddhist Contemplatives (OBC) founded in 1978 by the Rev. Master
Jiyu-Kennett (1924–1996).

More generally, the phenomenon of the New Religious Movement (NRM) can
be noted here. An NRM is a movement which is regarded as 'new' because it has
become visible in its current form since the Second World War. It is 'religious'
because it provides a 'faith system' which gives meaning based on a spiritual
understanding of human life, its origins and its goal. Well-defined beliefs,
belonging to a group with a shared commitment and having an identity which
separates those in the group from those outside all help to make NRMs popular
with certain kinds of people. Arguably part of the popularity of some British
Buddhist groups is their status today as NRMs.

The unique nature of British Buddhism in comparison with Buddhism found in other countries

British Buddhism is a relatively recent phenomenon and trying to define its unique nature in comparison with other countries is complex. One way of looking at this issue is to consider Rev. Master Jiyu-Kennett the founder of the OBC in 1978. Due to the opposition of those wanting a more traditional form of Zen Buddhism in Britain – such as Christmas Humphreys and others in the Buddhist Society – she began her work in the West at Shasta Abbey in California, USA.

At present the OBC has temples and meditation groups in the USA, Canada, the Netherlands, Germany and Latvia. However, a large number of its temples and groups can be found in Britain where there are 25 groups and 11 temples. Meditation groups can be found in many parts of Britain including Carmarthen in Wales and Aberdeen in Scotland. The temples include Norwich Zen Buddhist Priory and Dragon Bell Temple in Okehampton.

Kennett was brought up in the Church of England, read *The Light of Asia* and converted to Buddhism as an adult. It might be argued that with Kennett – as with many other Buddhists in Britain – the sequence of being brought up as a Christian in an established Church, becoming disenchanted with its practices, beliefs and teachings and then actively choosing Buddhism adds to the unique nature of British Buddhism. This is because with regard to some 'convert' Buddhists, the Christianity of the established Church is something which shapes their Buddhism either in terms of reacting strongly against Christianity or in terms of carrying over into Buddhism with aspects of Christianity particularly in terms of practice.

The latter point can be seen in the way in which Kennett favoured the terms abbey, cloister and priory alongside abbot, abbess, prior, prioress and priest, which are all taken from the Christian monastic tradition. Kennett also adapted Zen ceremonies using the model she had been used to in the Church of England. For example, 'Feeding of the Hungry Ghosts' which takes place in July in Japan was moved to coincide with Halloween, whilst the festival of the Birth of the Buddha was moved to Christmas Day. David Kay notes: 'In this way, the cultural sensitivities of her Western disciples to Christian ritual observances were mobilised, effecting a redefinition of religious sentiment from within.'

It might be argued that using English as the medium for Buddhist teaching and practice is fundamental to what makes British Buddhism unique. Kennett translated the texts used into English and – given her background as a musician – set these to the music of Gregorian Chant as used in Christian monasteries. In addition, she composed Buddhist hymns which could be accompanied by organ music and which could be sung to the tune of hymns used in Church of England services. One of her hymns is 'Welcome Joyous Wesak Day' which includes the verse:

Joyfully we greet the coming

Of this blessed Wesak Day

Morn of our release from sorrow

Dawning of the Dhamma way!

How our hearts lift up with gladness

Unto Truth's Infinite Light

As we contemplate the freedom

In its liberating might.

The use of English as the medium for Buddhist teaching and practice is also found in other Buddhist groups. Those who belong to the New Kadampa Tradition begin every practice by reciting a prayer in English composed by Kelsang Gyatso.

Specification content

The unique nature of British Buddhism in comparison with Buddhism found in other countries.

Key quote

Traditional Christian monastic titles were used...and the responsibilities allocated ... included ... 'sacristan' and 'infirmarian'. Monastic attire was also adapted in a Christian style, the traditional Japanese kimono being replaced by the cassock, clerical shirt and dog collar of the Anglican or Catholic priest. Through these adaptations, Kennett maintained, the extraneous culture of Japan was stripped away, enabling the 'essence' of Zen to be transmitted to the West in a more suitable form. (Kay)

AO2 Activity

As you read through this section try to do the following:

1. Pick out the different lines of argument that are presented in the text and identify any evidence given in support.

2. For each line of argument try to evaluate whether or not you think this is strong or weak.

3. Think of any questions you may wish to raise in response to the arguments.

This Activity will help you to start thinking critically about what you read and help you to evaluate the effectiveness of different arguments and from this develop your own observations, opinions and points of view that will help with any conclusions that you make in your answers to the AO2 questions that arise.

Key quote

First and foremost, we are ourselves British Buddhists; we are not studying Japanese Zen, we are studying British Zen; we are not wearing Japanese robes, we are wearing British robes…. We are maintaining the spirit of Zen, at the same time expressing it in a British way. **(Kennett)**

Study tip

It is vital for AO2 that you actually discuss arguments and not just explain what someone may have stated. Try to ask yourself, 'was this a fair point to make?', 'is the evidence sound enough?', 'is there anything to challenge this argument?', 'is this a strong or weak argument?' Such critical analysis will help you develop your evaluation skills.

AO2 Activity

List some conclusions that could be drawn from the AO2 reasoning from the above text; try to aim for at least three different possible conclusions. Consider each of the conclusions and collect brief evidence to support each conclusion from the AO1 and AO2 material for this topic. Select the conclusion that you think is most convincing and explain why it is so. Try to contrast this with the weakest conclusion in the list, justifying your argument with clear reasoning and evidence.

This includes the verse:

'O Blessed One, Shakyamuni Buddha,

Precious treasury of compassion,

Bestower of supreme inner peace,

You, who love all beings without exception,

Are the source of happiness and goodness;

And you guide us to the liberating path.'

Other groups use English but for them the preservation of tradition also remains important. For example, at the Amaravati Monastery chanting is in Pali with English translation – and in English although the Pali version is always visible too. However, the chant is not set to Western music but preserves what might be regarded as the original Thai format.

It might be argued that the approach of some groups within British Buddhism to use English as the medium for Buddhist teaching and practice, and to use more Westernised and simplified forms of Buddhist art in temples and shrines is part of a growing feature of British Buddhism. One principle in following this approach is to reject what is termed 'orientalism'. Kay summarises this as 'the mechanism of defining and interpreting the East – and specifically Buddhism – through a conceptual filter that incorporates and reflects the culture and self-understanding of the West'. Kennett, for example, emphasised that it was important for Westerners to value their own customs and cultures and that Zen should be expressed in a Western way. Whilst some of Kennett's Western adaptations have been replaced, her approach of finding an essential form of Buddhism which could be transplanted into the West without the trappings of Asian culture has remained a significant model.

In an article entitled 'Is Buddhism like a Tomato?' Eva K. Neumaier-Dargyay discusses the concept of Buddhism being 'transplanted' into Germany – but her general argument is a useful one in reflecting upon Buddhism in Britain. Neumaier-Dargyay's premise is that everyone agrees that a person can purchase a tomato plant at a garden nursery and then bring it back and transplant it in their garden. In their garden it remains a tomato plant and tomatoes will grow from it. As Neumaier-Dargyay points out, there is something attractive about this metaphor: 'The idea that symbolic systems of culture can be moved and transplanted like plants or other material things is enticing. It packages complex processes rather neatly.'

Yet we have already seen in the example of Kennett and Zen Buddhism that transplanting Buddhism into the West is not as straightforward as the metaphor of the tomato plant being transplanted might imply. For example, much depends on the founder of the Buddhist group who brings Buddhism into the West. This can be a determining factor with regard to the unique nature of the Buddhism which is transplanted.

As we have noted, Kennett had her background as a Christian in the Church of England as well as her background as an accomplished musician. Thus, some might argue, the founder of the New Kadampa Tradition, Kelsang Gyatso, had his own background as a follower of the Gelug Tradition of Tibetan Buddhism but at the same time as someone who – unlike others in the Gelug Tradition such as Tenzin Gyatso the 14th Dalai Lama – had a strong devotion to the spiritual protector Dorje Shugden.

Continuing with the metaphor of the tomato plant, it might be said that much also depends on the soil into which Buddhism is planted. Regarding British Buddhism, it might be argued that it is the prevailing cultural values which have contributed to the unique nature of British Buddhism. In the same way that these values have changed since the publication of *The Light of Asia* in 1879 so they will continue to change in the foreseeable future. Arguably British Buddhism cannot remain unaffected.

The comparative legitimacy of 'convert' Buddhism with 'heritage' Buddhism

Specification content

The comparative legitimacy of 'convert' Buddhism with 'heritage' Buddhism.

From one perspective it might be argued that all forms of Buddhism are legitimate when they include looking back to the life, example and teaching of the historical Buddha. There is therefore no difference between 'convert' Buddhism and 'heritage' Buddhism – both are equally legitimate.

Batchelor quotes Nhat Hanh: 'The forms of Buddhism must change so that the essence of Buddhism remains unchanged. This essence consists of living principles that cannot bear any specific formulation.' This perspective links back to the parable of the blind men and the elephant where each one of the blind men have a grasp of the Dhamma – but only of one aspect. It might be said that their mistake is to believe that what they have hold of is the '*essence* of Buddhism' whereas they have in fact only grasped just one of the '*forms* of Buddhism'.

It might be further questioned as to whether trying to find or define the '*essence* of Buddhism' apart from 'the *forms*' in which it is found is part of what might be regarded as a Western obsession with reification – regarding something abstract as a material thing. As Lopez points out, this marked the origins of the category 'Hinduism'. A term which had its origins as 'an indigenous term for a geographical feature, the Indus River, evolved, through a series of deformations, into an abstract noun': that abstract noun 'Hinduism' has thus been reified as one of the world religions.

Lopez argues that in some ways the same can be said with regard to Buddhism, which was defined and reified in the 19th century. Since then the term has largely been 'a historical projection derived from manuscripts and block prints, texts devoted largely to a "philosophy," that had been produced and had circulated among a small circle of monastic elites.' Attempting to establish the '*essence* of Buddhism' is therefore a task which has to be approached with caution – let alone reflecting on the comparative legitimacy of 'convert' Buddhism compared with 'heritage' Buddhism. Reification would also seem to be at odds with the lakshana of anicca which teaches that nothing is permanent. Thus, the term 'Buddhism' simply refers to a functioning phenomenon – a process and not a thing.

Viewed in this way it might be argued that all Buddhism is in a sense 'convert' Buddhism. This might apply as much to Upali the Jain as to Charles Bennett who became the bhikkhu Ananda Metteyya. Whereas Upali experienced the Buddha and the Dhamma first hand, Bennett experienced it through the lens of the Theravada tradition as expressed in both Sri Lanka and Burma. Both brought to Buddhism their own religious background and upbringing and presumably as Buddhists put this into practice in how they lived their daily lives.

The question raised by Lopez appears to be a valid one: 'whether there is something called "Buddhism" apart from the local practices and institutions referred to in the West as Japanese Buddhism, Chinese Buddhism, Thai Buddhism, Korean Buddhism, Nepalese Buddhism....' One might add to that list, British Buddhism.

When Buddhism is thought of as a process and not as a thing, questions of legitimacy can be viewed in a very different way. Examples of modernist expressions of Buddhism amongst 'convert' Buddhists can be seen in the practice of the Order of Buddhist Contemplatives or in the rejection of a strict monastic sangha in favour of 'Buddhists at varying stages of commitment and understanding' in the Triratna Buddhist Order. Yet these expressions might be seen as no different in substance or form than the changes that took place in the expressions of Buddhism as the Dhamma moved through monks, nuns and Buddhist artefacts along the various trade routes from India to Sri Lanka, Tibet, China, Japan, Cambodia, Thailand and Vietnam.

From a different perspective, Batchelor, as a secular Buddhist, argues that some concepts are embedded in human beings simply due to the 'specific culture, society

Key quote

For Buddhism the range of practices and institutions encompassed by the term are in many cases so diverse as to be recognised as Buddhist only from the omniscient vantage point of the scholar. Few Theravada monks today, for example, would regard the Pure Land practice of reciting of Namu amida butsu as an efficacious Buddhist practice, much less the single practice for salvation that the Japanese master Shinran declared it to be. (Lopez)

AO2 Activity

As you read through this section try to do the following:

1. Pick out the different lines of argument that are presented in the text and identify any evidence given in support.

2. For each line of argument try to evaluate whether or not you think this is strong or weak.

3. Think of any questions you may wish to raise in response to the arguments.

This Activity will help you to start thinking critically about what you read and help you to evaluate the effectiveness of different arguments and from this develop your own observations, opinions and points of view that will help with any conclusions that you make in your answers to the AO2 questions that arise.

Key quote

Whether exposure to a modern secular world view will, over generations … alienate Asian Buddhists from their traditional beliefs and practices remains to be seen. And it is equally uncertain whether the dogmatic belief of converts will ever become sufficiently naturalised for the idea of rebirth to function in … environments that are not traditionally Buddhist. (Batchelor)

Study tip

It is vital for AO2 that you actually discuss arguments and not just explain what someone may have stated. Try to ask yourself, 'was this a fair point to make?', 'is the evidence sound enough?', 'is there anything to challenge this argument?', 'is this a strong or weak argument?' Such critical analysis will help you develop your evaluation skills.

Key questions

To what extent would a 'heritage' Buddhist and a 'convert' Buddhist really share the same world view?

How far should all Buddhist beliefs be seen as relative and impermanent?

Assess the view that 'convert' Buddhists should always adopt Buddhist names.

AO2 Activity

List some conclusions that could be drawn from the AO2 reasoning from the above text; try to aim for at least three different possible conclusions. Consider each of the conclusions and collect brief evidence to support each conclusion from the AO1 and AO2 material for this topic. Select the conclusion that you think is most convincing and explain why it is so. Try to contrast this with the weakest conclusion in the list, justifying your argument with clear reasoning and evidence.

and language' in which they grow. Everything that human beings understand about themselves and the world in which they live is then 'linguistically and socially constructed'. Due to this 'embededness' much is regarded as self-evidently true and 'it would require a determined, conscious effort to abandon and replace it with something else'.

Batchelor applies this approach to the concept of karma and reincarnation: 'Since Buddhism developed in cultures where the world view of classical India either already prevailed or had come to be accepted over a number of generations, its teachings take for granted the law of karma as a cosmogonic explanation for how things are the way they are....' For 'heritage' Buddhists therefore, karma and reincarnation are embedded and self-evident and need no further explanation or justification. On the other hand, 'convert' Buddhists face a struggle: 'You are likely to take it far more seriously than your Asian co-religionists but feel much less secure in its validity because, unlike them, you are incapable of taking it for granted.'

Might it be the case that some core Buddhist beliefs cannot be embedded in a non-Asian culture but only be preserved by 'heritage' Buddhists? If that is so perhaps the comparative legitimacy of 'convert' Buddhism could be questioned.

When discussing the process of how the Dhamma is passed on, Lopez makes a useful point regarding a key term: 'the words tradition and treason derive from the same Latin root, tradere; a passing on from one to another can also be a betrayal'. It might be argued against Nhat Hanh that the 'essence of Buddhism' does have a 'specific formulation' and that departing from that 'specific formulation' of Buddhism is 'a betrayal' of Buddhism.

To take just one example, some might believe that through establishing the monastic sangha, the Buddha provided 'a specific formulation' of Buddhism. Most Buddhists would name the sangha when they take the three Refuges – the Buddha, the Dhamma and the sangha. Given that it has been the monastic sangha which preserved and passed on the Dhamma through the centuries since the time of the Buddha, could it be said that the monastic sangha belongs to the 'essence of Buddhism'?

From the perspective of 'heritage' Buddhists this would seem to be the case given the practices which involve and which rely upon the monastic sangha – from dana being offered to gain meritorious karma, through to the celebration of Kathina at the end of Vassa. The monastic sangha having gained expertise in Buddhist practice and having proficiency regarding Buddhist texts provides the key source which ensures that lay Buddhists interpret the Dhamma in the correct way. In most 'heritage' Buddhist traditions, the monastic Sangha is accorded the greatest respect and reverence.

Whilst some 'convert' Buddhists try to follow this model in Britain, in general the monastic sangha is notable by its absence. Thus, Bluck notes that 'only 2 per cent of the convert British Buddhist community is ordained'. He also cites a number of scholars who have suggested that part of the popularity of Buddhism in the West is 'a move to egalitarianism, where the Asian hierarchy between ordained and lay people is fading'. It might be asked as to whether British 'convert' Buddhism with its suspicion of hierarchy and its emphasis on inclusivity and democratic decision making can claim that it has equal legitimacy with 'heritage' Buddhism.

'Namu amida butsu' as chanted in Pure Land practice.

AO2 Developing skills

It is now important to consider the information that has been covered in this section; however, the information in its raw form is too extensive and so has to be processed in order to meet the requirements of the examination. This can be achieved by practising more advanced skills associated with AO2. For assessment objective 2 (AO2), which involves 'critical analysis' and 'evaluation' skills, we are going to focus on different ways in which the skills can be demonstrated effectively, and also, refer to how the performance of these skills is measured (see generic band descriptors for A2 [WJEC] AO2 or A Level [Eduqas] AO2).

▶ **Your next task is this:** Below is an evaluation concerning **the comparative legitimacy of 'convert' Buddhism with 'heritage' Buddhism**. It is 150 words long. After the first paragraph there is an intermediate conclusion highlighted for you in yellow. As a group try to identify where you could add more intermediate conclusions to the rest of the passage. Have a go at doing this.

Thich Nhat Hanh raises an important point by stating that 'forms of Buddhism must change so that the essence of Buddhism remains the same'. Arguably this accepts 'convert' Buddhism, since in reality it is just another equally valid form of Buddhism. Thus, a Western Buddhist from Carlisle may have beliefs and practices shaped by her environment, education and religious experience which would be very different from those of a 'heritage' Buddhist born in Thailand. It seems therefore that the issue of 'convert Buddhism' and 'heritage' Buddhism is really only about appearances.

Conversely it might be said that only 'heritage' Buddhists can be seen as legitimate, since they share in the whole world view from which Buddhism emerged. This includes an instinctive belief in karma and rebirth which they might accept without question. Furthermore, 'heritage' Buddhists can fully understand concepts such as dukkha, for example, which cannot be easily translated into English.

When you have done this you will see clearly that in AO2 it is helpful to include a brief summary of the arguments presented as you go through an answer and not just leave it until the end to draw a final conclusion. This way you are demonstrating that you are sustaining evaluation throughout an answer and not just repeating information learned.

Key skills Theme 3

The third theme has tasks that deal with specific aspects of AO2 in terms of identifying key elements of an evaluative style piece of writing, specifically counter-arguments and conclusions (both intermediate and final).

Key skills

Analysis involves:

Identifying issues raised by the materials in the AO1, together with those identified in the AO2 section, and presents sustained and clear views, either of scholars or from a personal perspective ready for evaluation.

This means:

- That your answers are able to identify key areas of debate in relation to a particular issue

- That you can identify, and comment upon, the different lines of argument presented by others

- That your response comments on the overall effectiveness of each of these areas or arguments.

Evaluation involves:

Considering the various implications of the issues raised based upon the evidence gleaned from analysis and provides an extensive detailed argument with a clear conclusion.

This means:

- That your answer weighs up the consequences of accepting or rejecting the various and different lines of argument analysed

- That your answer arrives at a conclusion through a clear process of reasoning.

Specification content

The Buddha ordained women,
after persuasion: different views in
Buddhism about whether women can
be nuns.

Key terms

Ananda: one of the ten closest
disciples of the Buddha who was
well-known for having a good memory
and who was the Buddha's assistant
and spokesman

Cullavaga: part of the second book of
the Vinaya Pitaka containing details
about the ordination of bhikkhunis

Garudhammas: the eight chief rules
– also known as 'heavy' or 'weighty'
rules – set by the Buddha, accepted by
Maha-Pajapati-Gotami and applied to
bhikkhunis

Maha-Pajapati Gotami: the aunt
and foster-mother of the Buddha
whose life story as a bhikkhuni is
recorded in a variety of sacred texts

Tathagata: a term used by the
Buddha to describe himself and
also used by others as a title for the
Buddha; its meaning is uncertain and
sometimes translated as 'the one who
has thus gone' or 'the one who has
thus arrived'

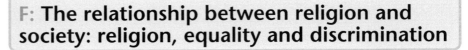

F: The relationship between religion and society: religion, equality and discrimination

Different views in Buddhism about whether women can be nuns

A key text from Theravada Buddhism regarding the role of women can be found in the second book of the Vinaya Pitaka which is named the Cullavagga. Tradition suggests that these texts along with much else of the Vinaya were compiled immediately after the death of the Buddha at the first Buddhist Council or perhaps some seventy years later at the second Buddhist Council. In the tenth chapter of the Cullavaga can be found the account of the ordination of women and subsequent teaching regarding the duties and position of bhikkhus and bhikkhunis (Buddhist monks and nuns).

The Buddha had already founded the order of bhikkhus by this time. During his travelling and preaching, he is visited by Maha-Pajapati Gotami who was his aunt and his foster-mother. When she arrives, she bows to the Buddha and then stands to one side and asks: 'It would be well, Lord, if women should be allowed to renounce their homes and enter the homeless state under the doctrine and discipline proclaimed by the Tathagata.' Simply put, she is asking that women be allowed by follow the bhikkhu path.

The Buddha rejects her request and replies: 'Enough, O Gotami! Let it not please thee that women should be allowed to do so.' This happens a second and third time and then Maha-Pajapati Gotami leaves weeping. The Buddha then travels further and again Maha-Pajapati Gotami comes to see him but this time with a group of women. She has cut off her hair and put on orange-coloured robes. She stands 'with swollen feet and covered with dust, sad and sorrowful, weeping and in tears' in the entrance porch of the hall where the Buddha is sitting.

At this point in the narrative, Ananda arrives and hearing her request goes to the Buddha and asks three times on her behalf. Each time the Buddha gives the same reply: 'Enough, Ananda! Let it not please thee that women should be allowed to do so.' After this Ananda asks the Buddha whether if women did 'renounce their homes and enter the homeless state under the doctrine and discipline' he taught they would be able to become fully enlightened as arhats. The Buddha agrees that this would be the case and Ananda therefore continues by reminding the Buddha that Maha-Pajapati Gotami was of great service to him when she fed him, gave him milk and looked after him following the death of Maya his mother. Ananda concludes: 'It were well, Lord, that women should have permission to go forth from the household life and enter the homeless state, under the doctrine and discipline proclaimed by the Tathagata.'

The Buddha replies: 'If then, Ananda, Maha-Pajapati Gotami take upon herself the Eight Chief Rules let that be reckoned to her as her initiation.' Thus, by accepting these rules, she will become a bhikkhuni. These rules are called the Eight Garudhammas and at the end of each one the Buddha declares: 'This is a rule to be revered and reverenced, honoured and observed, and her lifelong never to be transgressed.'

Maha-Pajapati Gotami seeks to become a bhikkhuni.

The Garudhammas can be summarised as follows:

1. A bhikkhuni even if she was in the order for one hundred years 'shall make salutation to, shall rise up in the presence of, shall bow down before, and shall perform all proper duties towards a bhikkhu, even if only just initiated'.

2. A bhikkhuni should not spend Vassa (the rainy season retreat) in a district where there is no bhikkhu.

3. Every two weeks a bhikkhuni should ask the sangha of bhikkhus as to the date of particular ceremonies and the time when a bhikkhu will come to give a talk.

4. At the end of Vassa (the rainy season retreat) bhikkhunis should come before the sangha of both bhikkhunis and bhikkhus for the confession of faults.

5. A bhikkhuni who has committed a fault must have this considered by the sangha of both bhikkhunis and bhikkhus.

6. After two years as a novice, a bhikkhuni is to ask for higher ordination from the sangha of both bhikkhunis and bhikkhus.

7. A bhikkhuni is on no pretext 'to revile or abuse a bhikkhu'.

8. An official warning or reprimand of bhikkhus by bhikkhunis is forbidden whereas an official warning or reprimand of bhikkhunis by bhikkhus 'is not forbidden'.

Ananda returns to Maha-Pajapati Gotami and recites to her the Garudhammas which she happily accepts: 'Just, Ananda, as a man or a woman, when young and of tender years, accustomed to adorn himself, would, when he had bathed his head, receive with both hands a garland of lotus flowers, or of jasmine flowers, or of atimuttaka flowers, and place it on the top of his head; even so do I, Ananda, take upon me these Eight Chief Rules, never to be transgressed my life long.'

In the subsequent sections of the Cullavaga, these rules are clarified and explained in greater detail. Thus, Maha-Pajapati Gotami returns to Ananda and asks whether there could be equality in terms of 'the making of salutations, the rising up in presence of another, the paying of reverence, and the performance of proper duties one towards another' between bhikkhus and bhikkhunis according to their seniority. Having heard this request from Ananda, the Buddha declares: 'This is impossible, Ananda, and unallowable, that I should so order. Even those others, Ananda, teachers of ill doctrine, allow not such conduct towards women; how much less, then, can the Tathagata allow it?' The Buddha then tells the assembled bhikkhus that for them, showing such equality of salutation to women is not allowed. Anyone who does so is guilty of a wrong action.

Elsewhere disputes between bhikkhus and bhikkhunis are brought to the Buddha for his judgment. In one, a bhikkhu on the road is struck and knocked over by a bhikkhuni. The Buddha declares this to be wrong and concludes: 'I prescribe that a bhikkhuni, O bhikkhus, on seeing a bhikkhu, should get out of the way when still at a distance, and make room for him.' Again it is explained how bhikkhunis tried to take a leadership role over bhikkhus to which the Buddha declared: 'A bhikkhuni is not, O bhikkhus, to perform any one of these official acts towards a bhikkhu. Should she do so, the act is itself invalid....' Such an action is also declared to be a wrong action.

Immediately after Maha-Pajapati Gotami accepted the Garudhammas and thus became a bhikkhuni, the Buddha explained to Ananda the negative impact that this would have on the Dhamma: 'If, Ananda, women had not received permission to go out from the household life and enter the homeless state, under the doctrine and discipline proclaimed by the Tathagata, then would the pure religion, Ananda, have lasted long, the good law would have stood fast for a thousand years. But since, Ananda, women have now received that permission, the pure religion, Ananda, will not now last so long, the good law will now stand fast for only five

Ananda, disciple of the Buddha

Key quote

Most of these additional rules are now anachronistic, and in some branches of Mahayana Buddhism they were dropped long ago. Such is the conservatism of the Buddhist tradition, however, that they remain in place in many branches of the Buddhist order to this day.
(Brazier)

Key quotes

And just, Ananda, as when the disease called blight falls upon a field of sugar-cane in good condition, that field of sugar-cane does not continue long; just so, Ananda, under whatsoever doctrine and discipline women are allowed to go forth from the household life into the homeless state, that religion does not last long. (The Buddha as quoted in Cullavaga)

Discussion of women in early Buddhism mirrored old cultural stereotypes that collided with Buddhist egalitarian principles of liberation for all beings. (Schireson)

hundred years.' (The 'homeless state' refers to living the life of a bhikkhuni in a monastic community.) The Buddha continues with a number of analogies and concludes that the Garudhammas are to be compared to 'an embankment to a great reservoir, beyond which the water should not overpass'.

These passages from the Cullavaga are of great importance with regard to different views in Buddhism about whether women can be nuns. This is an issue which has arisen for some Buddhists since the end of the 19th century. It has also become of increasing relevance in recent decades due to the impact of Western Buddhism and the influence of feminism.

In this area, the major consideration for many Buddhists is in some ways a detailed and technical one which – when simplified – is concerned with whether or not the bhikkhuni has received or can receive the higher ordination. As explained in the sixth Garudhamma, higher ordination has to be given by a sangha of bhikkhunis – each of whom has themselves received higher ordination – as well as by a sangha of bhikkhus. This is known as the dual sangha.

For some Buddhists the issue is further complicated because consideration has also to be given to the different schools of Buddhism and, above all, to the question of whether or not there is a continuous lineage of higher ordination of bhikkhunis which can be traced back from the present day to the time of the Buddha. This lineage might be one which begins in one country but – through the work of Buddhist missionaries – is then continued in another country. Taken as a whole the three recognised lineages are:

1. Theravada lineage which is found in the countries of South East Asia such as Thailand, Burma and Sri Lanka.

2. Tibetan lineage which is Tibetan/Vajrayana as found in countries such as Tibet and Mongolia.

3. Chinese lineage which is a mixture of Mahayana and Theravada as found in the countries of East Asia such as China, Korea, Taiwan and Vietnam.

With regard to the Theravada lineage, as Bhikkhu Bodhi explains: 'The last evidence for the existence of the original Bhikkhuni Sangha in a country following Theravada Buddhism dates from Sri Lanka in the 11th century.' Regarding the second, it is unclear whether higher ordination was ever carried out but only the lower ordination as a novice is found in the Tibetan lineage. It is only in the third, the Chinese lineage, that evidence of the higher ordination of bhikkhunis by the dual sangha having always been maintained can be found. However, it should be noted that for some Theravada Buddhists the Chinese lineage is not a 'pure' one but is rather a 'cross-sangha' since in the lineage there are Theravada and Mahayana bhikkhus and bhikkhunis who have been involved in the ordination process.

Focusing on the debate within Theravada, there are those who believe that women cannot be bhikkhunis. One of the arguments for this approach is that the Buddha himself was very reluctant to ordain women in the first place, and had to be persuaded by Ananda. In addition, his agreement was only given provided that the extra burden of rules in the Garudhamma were accepted. Even then, once Maha-Pajapati Gotami became a bhikkhuni, he predicted that the impact of bhikkhunis on the Dhamma would be a negative one with the 'good law' which would have lasted one thousand years now only going to last for five hundred years. The fact that the Theravada bhikkhuni sangha ceased to exist in the 11th century is one which, some might argue, proves the Buddha was correct in his reluctance and supports the view that women cannot be bhikkhunis today.

Brazier sees the Buddha's statement in the Cullavaga as to the negative impact of women being ordained on the long-term continuation of the Dhamma in a positive light which aligns with feminism. He argues: 'If we see the Buddha's agenda as being to establish a Pure Land … and if we see the dharma as the means of achieving it, then the passage can be just as well taken to mean that with women involved as well as men, the job will get done in half the time.'

Another argument is that, as laid down by the Buddha in the Cullavaga, for a woman to achieve higher ordination she has to be ordained by the dual sangha of bhikkhunis and bhikkhus. Since there has been no Theravada bhikkhuni sangha since the 11th century, this higher ordination by a dual sangha cannot now take place or ever take place in the future. Instead it is argued that women can and should accept lesser roles which might include having ordination only as a novice. In different parts of the Buddhist world there are other roles such as that of the 'mae chi' in Thailand. These are Buddhist women who might take the same precepts as a bhikkhu, wear white robes and live in communities near temples and monasteries. However, they are not regarded as being ordained.

Some Theravada Buddhist women have attempted to address this by getting ordained through the bhikkhu sangha alone. Thus bhikkhus – particularly those from the West – might be sympathetic to their cause and agree to ordain them. However, this is not something which the single bhikkhu sangha can carry out because the Buddha in the Cullavaga required ordination through a dual sangha. To further support their case, Theravada Buddhists might quote the Thai law passed by the Supreme Sangha Council in 1928 which forbids any Thai bhikkhus from ordaining women as novices and bhikkhunis.

Again, some Theravada Buddhist women have attempted to address this issue by getting ordained through a dual sangha of bhikkhunis from the Chinese lineage and Theravada bhikkhus who are sympathetic to their cause. However, the official position of Theravada Buddhism in Thailand is that this is still not recognised as the higher ordination, since the Chinese bhikkhuni lineage is not pure Theravada but is a 'cross-sangha' with a mixture of Mahayana and Theravada. Thus women who are ordained as bhikkhunis in this way are still not recognised as being ordained in the Theravada lineage.

Mae chi in Thailand

There are also those within Theravada – particularly in Sri Lanka – who do believe that women can be ordained as bhikkhunis. Returning to the Cullavaga, one general argument to support women being ordained is that much of what can be found here regarding bhikkhunis is not authentic and should not be ascribed to the Buddha himself but rather to bhikkhus who wanted to strengthen their position and authority over bhikkhunis. The words ascribed to the Buddha are therefore seen as the product of later patriarchal thinking which should be seen in that context and should not be used as a barrier to the ordination of women. One response to this approach is to argue that the Cullavaga is part of the Vinaya which is the oldest part of the Pali Canon. It cannot be regarded as being inauthentic in any sense at all: the Cullavaga is a 'frozen' text which cannot be updated and modified since this would question the very foundations of the Dhamma.

Another argument regarding the Cullavaga is to accept its authenticity as being the Dhamma of the Buddha himself, but then to explain the reasons behind his teaching as having limited relevance today. Thus, it might be argued that the Buddha's hesitation, the imposition of the Garudhammas, and his prediction regarding the negative impact of bhikkhunis on the survival of the 'good law' was due to a lack of understanding on his part since he was a man of his time. Gross argues: 'Thus it is not surprising, though it is unfortunate and causes sadness that the Buddha, in a sex-role ridden and patriarchal society, did not fully welcome women with their request to undertake an unconventional task.' It might then be argued that society has changed and that the patriarchal society of the past and its ways should be rejected. It might be said therefore, that if the Buddha were alive today, he would have no hesitation at all in ordaining women as bhikkhunis without the extra burden imposed by the Garudhammas. With that in mind women should be fully welcomed as bhikkhunis. The main response to this

Key quote

The rigidity with which the Theravada tradition wants to preserve the Dhamma and the original form, i.e. the monastic lifestyle and the legal acts prescribed for the monastic community ... aims at conserving what is believed to be the most original form of Buddhism. This endeavour is motivated by the fear of losing original meaning by a process of historical erosion, i.e. oblivion or intentional manipulation. Through the course of its history, the Theravada tradition has considered the vinaya as pivotal for safeguarding the continuity and longevity of Buddhism. (Seeger)

quickpire

3.23 What does the Buddha state after each of the Garudhammas?

Key quote

In the West, Buddhism, to varying extents, is adjusting to feminist-influenced social norms, as it has adjusted to other social norms in Asia .... In a context where people can choose between Buddhist traditions, the latter's views and practices relating to women may be a factor influencing their choice.
(Harvey)

argument is to reject it outright since it suggests that there is a limitation to the Buddha's omniscience which he gained at his enlightenment and since it questions his compassion with regard to his dealings with women.

One argument might be noted which focuses on the ordination in 2004 of Chatsumarn Kabilsingh (1944–) who became the first Thai woman to be ordained in the Theravada lineage taking the name Dhammananda. She is at present the Abbess of the only temple in Thailand where there are bhikkhunis. In order to be ordained as a bhikkhuni, she went to Sri Lanka where the bhikkhuni sangha has been revived and is gaining in acceptance and support. Her ordination involved the dual sangha of bhikkhus and bhikkhunis but the latter included those of the Chinese lineage of the bhikkhuni sangha. Dhammananda stated: 'I assure you that the ordination of Chinese nuns has its origin in a Theravada Buddhist lineage. But despite this, our Theravada tries to reject its own descendants, instead of accepting them in admiration that they have been able to remain firm and to transmit their tradition'. As we have seen the response to this by those opposed to the ordination of women as bhikkhunis would be to point to the lack of 'purity' in the Chinese lineage since it is a 'cross-sangha' with a mixture of Mahayana and Theravada. Dhammananda would therefore not be seen as a bhikkhuni since she was not ordained in the Theravada lineage.

A further argument regarding the Cullavaga is one which regards the text as entirely authentic but as one which can be explained in such a way that it does not present any hindrance to women being ordained as bhikkhunis today. Thus Harvey suggests that the Buddha's hesitation is very similar to that immediately after his enlightenment when he wondered whether he should teach the Dhamma or not: 'In both cases, he only agrees once good reasons are cited: some have "little dust in their eyes" and will understand; women can attain advanced states of insight.' It is argued that the Buddha's reluctance at that time and the imposition of the Garudhammas was simply a necessary way of protecting bhikkhunis from being exploited and of guarding against any criticism or scandal regarding sexual relations between monks and nuns. Thus the spirit of the Buddha's teaching has to be embraced which allows for the ordination of women. A general response to this might be that the spirit of the Buddha's teaching cannot be separated from what is explicitly stated in the Cullavaga.

Some argue that the text of the Cullavaga regarding the ordination of bhikkhunis has to be put into the broader context of the Buddha's other teaching. Here the Buddha makes no attempt to exclude bhikkhunis or to state that their position is secondary to that of bhikkhus. What is implicit here is that all people are offered the Dhamma to follow the path as best suited to them regardless of their gender. Bhikkhu Bodhi in support of this approach quotes the words of the Buddha about his teaching of the Four Noble Truths: 'I explained them to the bhikkhus, the bhikkhunis, the male lay followers, and the female lay followers, so that this spiritual life has become successful and prosperous, extended, popular, widespread, well proclaimed among gods and humans.' By extension therefore, women cannot be denied full access to the bhikkhuni path today on the basis of their gender. A response to this might be to assert that the detailed and explicit rules of the Cullavaga cannot be put to one side on the basis of what other texts might suggest or imply. In this way again, the debate is based on how much authority is to be given to the Pali Canon and the Vinaya pitaka in particular.

Study tip

Research the bhikkhuni sangha as found in Sri Lanka today to understand a different approach to the ordination of women as bhikkhunis.

The Lotus Sutra: the nature of Buddhahood and different views in Buddhism about whether women can attain awakening

A key text from Mahayana Buddhism regarding the belief that all equally possess the potential to attain Buddhahood can be found in the twelfth chapter of the Lotus Sutra which is entitled 'Devadatta'.

At the opening of this chapter, the Buddha recounts how an immeasurable number of years ago a king made a vow to seek 'highest enlightenment'. A sage came to him who declared, 'I possess the Mahayana teaching called the Lotus Sutra. If you faithfully follow and obey me I will expound it to you.' The king then served the sage for one thousand years: 'For the sake of the Dharma he served him diligently, making certain the sage never lacked for anything.' Ultimately, the king became a Buddha. The Buddha then states, 'The king at that time was I myself, and the sage was he who is now Devadatta'. This Devadatta will become a Buddha named Devaraja with his own world and he will enlighten innumerable sentient beings 'equal in number to the sands of the Ganges River'. Again after a period of time, 'incalculable sentient beings will attain arhatship'.

The key point of this passage in the first half of the chapter is that Devadatta is the Buddha's cousin who is described in many Buddhist texts as the epitome of evil. He tries to kill the Buddha on a number of occasions – such as when he gives alcohol to the elephant Nalagiri and goads it to attack the Buddha or tries to roll a boulder from the top of a hill to crush the Buddha. In addition, Devadatta tries to split the monastic sangha and then to take over leadership of the sangha when the Buddha becomes ill. Finally, the earth opens up under Devadatta and he falls into one of the hell realms. That even Devadatta can become a Buddha shows the universality of Buddhahood – it is open to everyone.

The Buddha calms the elephant Nalagiri with which Devadatta tried to kill him.

In the second half of the chapter, the bodhisattva Manjushri emerges from the ocean where he has been in the palace of the Dragon King. He is questioned by another bodhisattva as to how many sentient beings he managed to inspire in the Dragon King's realm. Manjushri replies, 'their number is immeasurable and incalculable' and to show this, innumerable bodhisattvas rise out of the ocean. Manjushri declares that in the ocean he only taught the Lotus Sutra. He is then asked: 'If sentient beings diligently strive to practise this Sutra, will they immediately become Buddhas or not?' To this Manjushri replies, 'Yes they will'.

At this point to illustrate the truth of what he is saying, Manjushri explains that the Dragon King's daughter – also referred to as the Naga King's daughter – is eight years old but even so: 'She instantly produced the thought of enlightenment and attained the stage of non-retrogression'. Manjushri continues by stating: 'Her virtues are perfect. Her thoughts and explanations are subtle and extensive, merciful, and compassionate. She has a harmonious mind and has attained enlightenment.' However, Manjushri is challenged by a bodhisattva who states that for the Buddha himself enlightenment was only achieved after an immeasurable period of time and that his compassion could be seen in every part of the cosmos. The bodhisattva concludes: 'It is hard to believe that this girl will instantly attain complete enlightenment.'

Specification content

The Lotus Sutra presents a range of teachings: all equally possess the potential to attain Buddhahood; the Dragon King's daughter (chapter 12) transforms into a man before attaining awakening: different views in Buddhism about whether women can attain awakening.

Key term

Devadatta: the Buddha's cousin who is presented as a figure of evil in Buddhist texts but who becomes a Buddha in the Lotus Sutra

The Bodhisattva Manjushri

Key quotes

Embedded in these stories, but often overlooked by both patriarchal and feminist interpreters, is an important insight for a Buddhist and dharmic exegesis of this motif. Dwelling in emptiness, the person who undergoes the sex change is utterly non-fixated and non-attached regarding gender. The woman is not attached to her femaleness but will leave it behind when skill-in-means to teach the dharma would be well served by a sex change. (Gross)

In these texts, the notion that a female cannot be an advanced Bodhisattva or Buddha is being played with and critically examined. It is clear that a woman can go on to become such a being. On the one hand, there is no need to transcend the female sex to reach spiritual excellence; on the other, the wise see no reason to be attached to it, by refusing to change it. (Harvey)

The Dragon King's daughter suddenly appears to them all, praises the Buddha, declares that she is enlightened and will reveal the Mahayana to save sentient beings from suffering. Sariputra – as a representative of Theravada – voices his doubts: 'You think that in no time at all you will attain the unexcelled way. This is hard to believe. Why? Because the body of a woman is filthy and impure, not a vessel for the Dharma. How could you attain unexcelled awakening? The Buddha way is long and extensive. Only after innumerable aeons of enduring hardship, accumulating good works, and thoroughly carrying out all the practices can it be reached.' Sariputra then lists five things a woman could not be, the last of which is that she cannot have the body of a Buddha.

At this, the Dragon King's daughter takes a precious jewel and offers it to the Buddha. He accepts it and she asks the bodhisattva and Sariputra whether the offering of the jewel and the acceptance of it was done quickly. They reply: 'It was done extremely quickly'. She tells them to use their holy powers and watch her become a Buddha even more quickly. The passage continues: 'Then the entire assembly saw the dragon girl instantly transformed into a male, take up bodhisattva practice, and immediately go to the world named Spotless, in the southern region, where, sitting on a precious lotus blossom, she attained impartial, proper awakening. With the thirty-two characteristics and eighty different attractive features she proclaimed the wonderful dharma to all living beings everywhere in the universe.' Sariputra, the bodhisattvas watch her from afar as countless sentient beings achieve enlightenment. The entire assembly 'silently believed and accepted this'.

The main teaching of this passage in the second part of the chapter, is that according to traditional Buddhist understanding the Dragon King's daughter is not a sentient being who should be able to achieve enlightenment on at least three counts: firstly she is only eight, secondly she is not a human being and thirdly she is female. However, according to what is described, she begins as an eight year old, becomes a bodhisattva in the next instant and immediately afterwards becomes a Buddha with the traditional thirty two characteristics ascribed to the Buddha.

The passage concerning the Dragon King's daughter is an important contributory factor to the different views in Buddhism about whether women can attain enlightenment. The focus of the discussion is on the detail in the story that 'the dragon girl instantly transformed into a male'. This would appear to suggest that full enlightenment into the bodhisattva state is something which requires being male in terms of gender identity. As Gross points out, 'it is impossible for someone with feminist sensibilities not to be slightly uncomfortable with the end of the story, especially when we know that men sometimes used this story to challenge female contemporaries who were attempting to take up positions of authority in Buddhism'.

Harvey notes that most traditions within Buddhism would teach that a female cannot attain the spiritual status of 'a Perfect and Completely Awakened One' – that is of becoming a full Buddha. This can be seen in one Mahayana text quoted by Gross where the philosopher Asanga explains why women can never be Buddhas: 'All women are by nature full of defilement and of weak intelligence. And not by one who is full of defilement and of weak intelligence is completely perfected Buddhahood attained.' The story of the Dragon King's daughter contradicts this teaching. Thus Harvey states: 'The story was not seen to show that the girl had to become a male before becoming a Buddha, but that, already having attained Buddhahood through sudden insight, she then went on to manifest a male form.'

One approach to the text is to see it in the context of other Buddhist passages where a change of sex is at issue with regard to attaining enlightenment. Here the overall view is that gender identity is ultimately only a designation which applies to the physical form of the human person and that it does not have what Harvey describes as 'fixed, inherent existence'. That the Dragon King's daughter is at one instant a female and at the next a male illustrates this point: '"Maleness" and "femaleness" are not essential ingredients of people, but relative and conditioned states or labels.'

This approach could be seen as building upon the two truths doctrine as explained in the Abhidhamma – the third part of the Tipitaka. Conventional truth is **sammuti sacca** and this refers to expressions such as 'male' and 'female' which we use for things which exist only in designation. In using these terms, conventional language is being used to speak of conventional appearance. By contrast, ultimate truth is **paramattha sacca** and this can be seen as referring to the underlying reality beneath the surface appearance. From the perspective of paramattha sacca, there is no 'male' and 'female'.

Gross develops this argument by introducing the concept of sunyata – emptiness – which might be regarded as paramattha sacca. Gross sees the story as showing that 'one should not depend on conventional signs and tokens in one's attempt to determine someone's true identity'. She places her understanding within the concept of sunyata: 'Who is this person really? Will the real Naga-princess please stand up? The real Bodhisattva? The real Buddha with the thirty-two marks? It is not that one became the other, for in emptiness, neither the Naga princess nor the bodhisattva, nor the Buddha has fixed existence.'

Connected to this, Martin Seeger presents the views of Suwanna Satha-Anand, a professor of Buddhist philosophy, on the question of 'male' and 'female' and views about attaining enlightenment. Her approach is to argue that in this context paramattha sacca is only concerned with 'the equipotentiality of awakening for men and women'. This has to take absolute priority over sammuti sacca which because of its use of designations is always subject to 'the cultural constraints of the time'. She argues that: 'the principle of [ultimate] truth over conventional truth should serve as a basis for future feminist interpretations and negotiations of the Buddhist scriptures. It should also serve as a basis for institutional decisions of the Sangha in relation to women's issues. What is at stake is not only the human rights of women, but also the philosophical universality and institutional integrity of Buddhism itself.'

Perhaps, therefore, the real focus should return to the first half of the twelfth chapter of the Lotus Sutra. The key point might be seen to be simply that any person – even the wicked Devadatta – has the potential to be a Buddha. This form of full enlightenment is a path open to all.

The Lotus Sutra is a famous text and the twelfth chapter is often used in discussion about whether women can attain awakening. However, a much earlier text called the **Therigatha**, which is found in the Sutta Pitaka in the Pali Canon, is rarely referred to even though it is one of the earliest texts describing the spiritual experience of women, having been written in the 1st century BCE following a long period of oral transmission. Therigatha might be translated as 'Verses of the Women Elders' and Gross describes these verses as being 'eloquent poems in which the women express their realisation and their penetrating insight'. It is generally assumed that the women who composed these verses were bhikkhunis who followed in the path set out by Maha-Pajapati Gotami.

The key theme of the Therigatha is that of enlightenment. For example, in the first chapter are the following verses:

'Having abandoned home I ordained,

having abandoned son, animal, dear one;

Having abandoned lust and hate,

having fully removed ignorance too;

Having pulled out craving with root,

calmed down I am, liberated.'

Key terms

Paramattha sacca: generally translated as ultimate truth or underlying reality which might be regarded as sunyata – emptiness

Sammuti sacca: generally translated as conventional truth which is conditioned by designations

Therigatha: a collection of sayings and poems written by senior bhikkhunis which is in the Pali Canon

Key quote

For many of the women who joined the nuns' order, it provided an important and liberating option…. Their songs of triumph, the Therigatha, were preserved as scriptural record by these early Buddhists. That they may be less well-known does not obviate their existence and preservation for well over two thousand years. **(Gross)**

Again in the third chapter is a dialogue between Mara and the bhikkhuni called Soma. Mara begins by questioning whether women can attain enlightenment:

'Whatever was reached by the sages, a state hard to originate;
women with two-fingered wisdom, cannot reach it.'

To this, Soma replies:

'What matters womanhood, when mind is well-restrained;
With presence of knowledge, seeing phenomena rightly with insight.
Pleasure is fully destroyed everywhere, the aggregate of darkness shattered.
Know thus O Evil One, I have destroyed you.'

Study tip

Read the whole of chapter 12 of the Lotus Sutra in order to understand its message and to see the poetic imagery used.

Rita Gross: Buddhism's commitment to the end of suffering as inherently feminist

Rita Gross (1943–2015) was a pioneer in academic studies involving feminism and comparative religion. In addition she became a Tibetan Buddhist. In much of her work she considered the relationship between religion and the stereotypes of the roles of men and women. Her book *Buddhism After Patriarchy* (1993) is regarded by many as a key work on the subject of Buddhism and feminism due to its combination of scholarship, feminist critique, and personal belief.

Gross describes her book as presenting a feminist **revalorisation** of Buddhism. On the one hand this involves revealing the 'massive undercurrents of sexism and prejudice against women' and on the other 'repairing the tradition, often bringing it much more into line with its own fundamental values and vision than was its patriarchal form'.

In examining how the stereotypes of the roles of men and women developed in Buddhism, a key term used by Gross is androcentrism, which might be defined as placing a masculine point of view at the centre of one's understanding. She describes **four levels of androcentrism** in Buddhism:

1. **First level androcentrism**: the texts and stories preserved by Buddhists whereby 'stories about men and men's statements were far more likely to be recorded than were stories about women'.

2. **Second level androcentrism**: texts and stories about women which were recorded being given second place to those about men. Here, for example, Gross notes how this happened to the Therigatha.

3. **Third level androcentrism**: Western Buddhist scholarship follows the biases of Buddhist texts and stories in presenting its version of Buddhism.

4. **Fourth level androcentrism**: contemporary Buddhism, both Asian and Western, 'is unrelenting in its ongoing androcentrism'.

These four levels of androcentrism have resulted in Buddhism as a religion which is often dominated by lay Buddhist women in terms of belief and practice but which in its institutions generally excludes women from leadership roles and from pursing their spiritual beliefs at any higher levels of studies. In addition the four levels of androcentrism mean that women are treated in Buddhism 'as exceptions to the norm that need to be regulated, explained and placed in the world'.

quickfire

3.24 What name is given to the elephant which Devadatta tries to get to kill the Buddha?

Specification content

Cultural stereotypes of the roles of men and women have no universal application within Buddhism; Buddhism's commitment to the end of suffering may be seen as inherently feminist (as indicated by Rita Gross).

Key terms

Revalorisation: the term used by Rita Gross for both critiquing the androcentric patriarchy of Buddhist texts and stories and for then repairing the Buddhist tradition

Four levels of androcentrism: four ways in which androcentrism has permeated Buddhism: preservation of male texts and stories, prioritising of male texts and stories, preserving this male bias in Western scholarship, practising this male bias in contemporary Asian and Western Buddhism

Together the four levels of androcentrism create the conditions of patriarchy. This refers to the gender hierarchy of men *over* women and the binary stereotyping of their roles as men and women. However, although Buddhism is androcentric and patriarchal, Gross does not believe that it is misogynistic. In other words there is little evidence in the texts and stories of hatred or fear of women and femininity.

Gross presents a generally accepted hypothesis that stereotypes regarding the roles of men and women had in the past been fashioned by two key 'patriarchal gender roles': economic production and human reproduction.

In the area of economic production women had become increasingly separated from control over economic production which was taken over by men. At the same time, their role 'became increasingly specialised in, limited to, and defined by their reproductive role'. As a result, clear patterns of patriarchy emerged insofar as for women, 'their realm of power and influence was within the household and extended family, the so-called private life'. Meanwhile, men moved away from the realm of private life, 'to specialise in military, economic, religious and political affairs in the so-called public realm'.

Since the Industrial Revolution in the 19th century onwards this model of patriarchy in the West has gradually faded. Thus, for example, the patriarchal division of labour based on man's greater physical strength is no longer required in the area of work since this now requires 'training, skills and intelligence' which are not gender specific. The same revolutionary change can be found in the area of human reproduction: 'The existence of birth control, much lower infant and maternal mortality rates, and a vastly increased lifespan means that women cannot focus their whole lives on reproduction....' Gross argues that this emancipation of women has meant that through their intelligence and creativity 'they take up leadership positions, in politics, religion and economics'.

The fact that the demise of patriarchy in the West and the growth of feminism has occurred at the same time as the discovery of Buddhism is regarded by Gross as an 'auspicious coincidence' which means that a feminist revalorisation of Buddhism can now take place.

Thus with regard to the stereotypes regarding the roles of men and women in Buddhism, the first part of revalorisation recognises the 'massive undercurrents of sexism and prejudice against women'. These Gross sums up as the basic assertion that 'there is some problem with the female gender'. In Buddhist texts and stories therefore: 'Women are thought to be much less likely than are men to make significant progress on the path and Buddhist men declaim on the preferability of maleness over femaleness'.

The second part of revalorisation involves 'repairing the tradition' as to the roles of men and women. This means the recognition and acceptance that in Buddhism 'being female presents no barrier to the achievement of liberation'. This position exists throughout Buddhist history and can be seen in the way in which the Dhamma is neither male nor female and that gender is ultimately irrelevant and even non-existent in Buddhist teachings. Gross also argues that texts and stories might also be found which show that 'femaleness is actually an advantage'.

Whilst this feminist revalorisation is having an impact on worldwide Buddhism, cultural stereotypes about the roles of men and women are still predominant in what Gross calls the 'the Asian homeland of Buddhism'. This can be seen even in the simplest of settings. One cultural tradition in Thailand as described by Sallie B. King is bowing as a gesture of respect: 'the lower one bows, the more one conveys one's own humility and the exalted status of the other'. Such bowing is given particularly to the monastic sangha which can be bowing low, bowing with one's knees or even bowing completely on the ground. Even members of the royal family in Thailand bow to the monastic sangha.

Rita Gross (1943–2015)

Key quote

The question, the issue, is always what to do about women, what special rules *they* would have to observe, whether or not *they* can become enlightened, whether *they* could progress as far as men on the Buddhist path. (Gross)

Key quotes

To be a feminist *is* to disagree with the socially constructed world one has inherited and to attempt to construct an alternative world. (Gross)

Women simply assumed that, if serious Buddhist practice is beneficial, then it would be beneficial for them. The Asian models were totally ignored, to the extent that it has been suggested that the single biggest difference between Asian and Western Buddhism is the active and equal involvement of women in all aspects of Buddhist practice. (Gross)

However, the key point here is that there is no bhikkhuni sangha. King observes: 'When there are only *male* bhikkhus, one realises after a while that one is living in a place in which men and women regularly bow deeply before some men, but no men ever bow that deeply before any women. This is powerful body language; though it is not so intended, it is a constant reinforcement of popular notions of the socially and karmically inferior status of women.' If the establishment of a bhikkhuni sangha in Thailand ever takes place, it might be the case that men bow deeply before women and this would then promote 'gender equality and respect'.

It might be argued that when Buddhism arrived and began to be established in the West, the governance and structure of Buddhist groups – which largely consisted of lay 'convert' Buddhists – was always male or dominated by males. Again, the type of respect shown to Buddhist religious leaders in Asia by 'heritage' Buddhists as described by King, provided the model for what was expected of Western 'convert' Buddhists. Whether the man in question be a Zen roshi from Japan, a rinpoche from Tibet or a senior bhikkhu from Thailand, the Western approach of 'convert' Buddhist women matched the cultural norm of women relating to men in a patriarchal society.

That this could be damaging became evident as King explains: 'in the 1970s and '80s a number of scandals erupted in American Zen and Tibetan practice centres involving (male) head teachers who made sexual advances or had sexual relations with female students'. Once these scandals came to light, a number of questions were raised which challenged the importation of what might be termed the cultural stereotype of patriarchal Buddhism found in some parts of Asia. King suggests that the resulting discussions necessarily focused on 'the hierarchical nature of Buddhism, the unquestioned trust in the teacher, the structure of power in Buddhist practice institutions, and the pattern of male supremacy'.

Overall Gross concludes that 'convert' Buddhists are generally free of what she describes as 'the Asian cultural patriarchal baggage' with regard to the roles of men and women. The key to this freedom is that 'Buddhist teachers are careful of the distinction between cultural habits and the dharma'. This means that Buddhist teachers 'do not want their students to become Tibetans or Japanese, but Buddhists. Most of them agree that discrimination against women is a cultural prejudice, not a Buddhist teaching.'

At the same time, Gross is critical of the unquestioning attitude of many 'convert' Buddhists in the West to the four levels of androcentrism. Although 'convert' Buddhists are generally free of what she describes as 'the Asian cultural patriarchal baggage' in terms of stereotyping the roles of men and women, they tend to be 'ignorant of Buddhism's patriarchal record'. In their approach, 'they tend to regard feminism as unnecessary in a Buddhist context and Buddhist feminists as traitors, if not heretics, who just don't understand that detachment is the heart of Buddhist teaching'.

An example of what might be understood to be androcentrism in promoting cultural stereotypes of the roles of men and women in Buddhism can be seen in the remarks of the Dalai Lama in an interview in 2015. When asked as to whether his successor could be a woman he agreed that this might be the case since a woman Dalai Lama would have 'biologically more potential to show affection and compassion'. He then continued by saying: 'If female Dalai Lama come, the face must be very very – should be very attractive'. When asked to clarify his comments, he stated: 'I mean if female Dalai Lama come, then that female must be very attractive. Otherwise, not much use'.

It might be argued that in stating that women have 'biologically more potential to show affection and compassion' the Dalai Lama was reinforcing another stereotype since scientific data and gender studies do not bear out this claim. On the other hand, it might be said that in linking the feminine with compassion, the Dalai Lama is pointing out that Buddhism's commitment to end the suffering of all sentient beings is perhaps best understood through the image of the female rather than the male bodhisattva.

For example, as Harvey notes, the male bodhisattva Avalokitesvara who is the embodiment of compassion 'gradually came to be portrayed as female' in China under the name of Kuan-yin. Harvey attributes this to the fact that 'the Chinese saw compassion as a "female" quality'. Kuan-yin came to be seen 'as an all-compassionate "mother-goddess", the most popular deity in all of China'. At the same time female bodhisattvas such as Tara in Tibet – particularly in her most popular forms as Green Tara and White Tara – is said to be the 'mother of all the Buddhas' and is 'graceful, attractive and approachable, and every ready to care tenderly for those in distress'.

In her discussion of the bodhisattva path, Gross finds that there is 'profound sympathy between Mahayana ethics and ... some of the most important insights of feminism'. The bodhisattva's commitment to the end of suffering through the practice of compassion is not one which fits easily with the androcentric approach. She considers this to be overly intellectual and concerned with separating emotions from practice. Individual autonomy and self-sufficiency are the ruling guidelines. However, the bodhisattva's commitment to the end of suffering is much better understood within the context of feminism given the view, for example, that a feminist approach begins by seeing life as fundamentally relational – thus requiring compassion. From this perspective as Gross explains: 'Women can and should feel affirmed in their mode of being, relating, and caring by the Mahayana emphasis on the centrality of such experiences to genuine spirituality.'

Gross views compassion from this feminist perspective as the spur to end suffering. She argues that whilst Buddhism has 'lofty and extremely refined teachings about compassion' this has not been put into practice in the social sphere. 'Probably most Buddhists have felt that individual transformation and enlightenment are so high a priority, and that society is so intractable and unenlightenable, that social action becomes a diversion and a waste of energy.'

Thus it is that its commitment to end suffering through the exercise of compassion suggests that Buddhism is inherently feminist. This is because when Buddhism is being true to itself 'it manifests the same vision as does feminism'.

Key quote

Compassion for those caught in an ocean of samsara, suffering all the indignities inherent in such existence, is a prime motivation for and justification of the Buddhist lifestyle. Living the eightfold path of Buddhist individual and social morality involves non-harming and working for the benefit of all sentient beings on all levels. (Gross)

Study tip

Look up images of Buddhists at worship in the West and the East and consider what these images indicate about the roles of men and women.

AO1 Activity

Give reasons some Buddhists might give for not ordaining bhikkhunis.

Explain your answer using evidence and examples from what you have read.

Giant statue of Kuan-yin in Nanshan, China

quickfire

3.25 What is the name of the best-known bodhisattva of compassion in China?

Key skills Theme 3

The third theme has tasks that deal with the basics of AO1 in terms of prioritising and selecting the key relevant information, presenting this in a personalised way (as in Theme 1) and then using evidence and examples to support and expand upon this (as in Theme 2).

Key skills

Knowledge involves:

Selection of a range of (thorough) accurate and relevant information that is directly related to the specific demands of the question.

This means:

- Selecting relevant material for the question set
- Being focused in explaining and examining the material selected

Understanding involves:

Explanation that is extensive, demonstrating depth and/or breadth with excellent use of evidence and examples including (where appropriate) thorough and accurate supporting use of sacred texts, sources of wisdom and specialist language.

This means:

- Effective use of examples and supporting evidence to establish the quality of your understanding
- Ownership of your explanation that expresses personal knowledge and understanding and NOT just reproducing a chunk of text from a book that you have rehearsed and memorised.

AO1 Developing skills

It is now important to consider the information that has been covered in this section; however, the information in its raw form is too extensive and so has to be processed in order to meet the requirements of the examination. This can be achieved by practising more advanced skills associated with AO1. For assessment objective 1 (AO1), which involves demonstrating 'knowledge' and 'understanding' skills, we are going to focus on different ways in which the skills can be demonstrated effectively, and also, refer to how the performance of these skills is measured (see generic band descriptors for A2 [WJEC] AO1 or A Level [Eduqas] AO1).

▶ **Your final task for this Theme is:** Below is a summary of **the Buddha ordaining women only after hesitation**. It is 150 words long. This time there are no highlighted points to indicate the key points to learn from this extract. Discuss which five points you think are the most important to highlight and write them down in a list.

The ordination of women by the Buddha can be found in the Pali Canon in the tenth chapter of the Cullavaga. This describes how the Buddha journeys from place to place preaching. At one place, his aunt and foster-mother Maha-Pajapati Gotama asks him three times to be ordained. The Buddha rejects her request but she returns accompanied by women who also wish to be ordained. The Buddha rejects her request but at Ananda's intercession accepts that women can be awakened/enlightened. He also accepts that Maha-Pajapati Gotama did him great service as a child. The Buddha therefore agrees to her request. However, his hesitation remains because he imposes on her and on women the eight Garudhammas, which strictly limit women's position as bhikkhunis. In addition, his hesitation can be seen in his prediction that the 'good law' of the Dhamma would now only last five hundred years rather than one thousand.

Now make the five points into your own summary (as in Theme 1 Developing Skills) trying to make the summary more personal to your style of writing. This may also involve re-ordering the points if you wish to do so. In addition to this, try to add some quotations and references to develop your summary (as in Theme 2 Developing Skills).

The result will be a fairly lengthy answer and so you could then check it against the band descriptors for A2 (WJEC) or A Level (Eduqas) and in particular have a look at the demands described in the higher band descriptors towards which you should be aspiring. Ask yourself:

- Does my work demonstrate thorough, accurate and relevant knowledge and understanding of religion and belief?
- Is my work coherent (consistent or make logical sense), clear and well organised?
- Will my work, when developed, be an extensive and relevant response which is specific to the focus of the task?
- Does my work have extensive depth and/or suitable breadth and have excellent use of evidence and examples?
- If appropriate to the task, does my response have thorough and accurate reference to sacred texts and sources of wisdom?
- Are there any insightful connections to be made with other elements of my course?
- Will my answer, when developed and extended to match what is expected in an examination answer, have an extensive range of views of scholars/schools of thought?
- When used, is specialist language and vocabulary both thorough and accurate?

Issues for analysis and evaluation

The extent to which Buddhism aligns with feminism

Firstly, it could be argued that Buddhism is not aligned with feminism because this would be aligning itself with what is sammuti sacca. From this perspective, as has been noted, gender is only a designation and is one of the skandhas. Thus, in a previous life, a woman may have been a man and a man may have been a woman. Here, there is nothing which is permanent or pertaining to paramattha sacca.

A second argument suggests that Buddhism does not align itself with feminism because its priority has always been to remove dukkha from people regardless of gender issues. As Harvey explains: 'The bottom line, from a Buddhist perspective, is whether a particular idea, attitude or practice conduces to an increase or decrease – for both men and women – in such qualities as generosity, non-attachment, calm, kindness, compassion, clarity of mind, and awareness of, and insight into, the nature of mental and physical states.'

A third point would be to assert that Buddhism cannot align itself with feminism because this implies tanha – catching hold of feminism as an ideology and refusing to let it go. As the Four Noble Truths teach, this is the cause of dukkha. Harvey points out the issue of 'dogmatic viewpoints ... both between feminists and non-feminists and within both camps'. He continues: 'this can lead to "clinging to views" – holding to particular views with attachment and indignation – which Buddhism has always been wary of, although Buddhists have not always managed to avoid it'.

A fourth way of arguing that Buddhism does not align itself with feminism is to recognise that from the outset it was rooted in a patriarchal society. Patriarchal views can be found throughout the Dhamma. Whilst the ordination of Maha-Pajapati Gotami marked a significant step in the recognition that women could achieve the same spiritual status as men, this was still framed within a clear patriarchal context as can be seen in the imposition of the Garudhammas. That patriarchal context is so interwoven with Buddhism that for Buddhism to now align itself with feminism would mean rejecting some key aspects of its reality. Gross states this point in a striking way: 'Siddartha Gautama, the Buddha, abandoned his wife and new-born infant because he was convinced that they were an obstacle to his own spiritual development. Nevertheless, he resisted women's attempts to abandon their domestic responsibilities and to seek their own spiritual development and liberation. Can a religion founded by such a man possibly serve women's interests and needs?'

From a different angle, a fifth point might be to argue that Buddhism should not align itself with feminism because the modern feminist movement is of relatively recent origin, and in particular it has its roots in Western liberal culture amongst 'convert' Buddhists. Thus, for example, the movement for the ordination of bhikkhunis in the Theravada tradition is largely a product of demands from Buddhist women living in the West. Some Eastern Buddhists and 'heritage' Buddhists in general might regard these demands as a form of cultural imperialism which implies that 'the West knows best'.

The ordination of bhikkhunis illustrates the problem of Buddhism aligning itself with feminism. One example is the controversy concerning the ordination by a dual sangha in 2009 in Australia of four women as bhikkhunis. They belonged to Ajahn Chah's Forest Sangha with its leadership based in Thailand. Many Buddhists – particularly in the West – were supportive of this move, and of Ajahn Brahm (born Peter Betts, London 1951) of Ajahn Chah's Forest Sangha – who had facilitated the ordination.

Specification content
The extent to which Buddhism aligns with feminism.

Key quote

… the enlightened one is able to change his mind after listening to sensible, contrary argument. Buddhism developed within a climate of debate and it developed its own science of logic and argument. In many quarters this appears to have been lost. The dialectics have become a sham with foregone conclusions…. A spirit of suspicion of thought and rejection of the intellect became widespread. This spirit is oppressive, anti-Buddhist and anti-enlightenment. (Brazier)

AO2 Activity

As you read through this section try to do the following:

1. Pick out the different lines of argument that are presented in the text and identify any evidence given in support.

2. For each line of argument try to evaluate whether or not you think this is strong or weak.

3. Think of any questions you may wish to raise in response to the arguments.

This Activity will help you to start thinking critically about what you read and help you to evaluate the effectiveness of different arguments and from this develop your own observations, opinions and points of view that will help with any conclusions that you make in your answers to the AO2 questions that arise.

Key questions

Should the Buddha be seen as part of the patriarchal past rather than of the post-patriarchal present?

How far might it be argued that updating Buddhist sacred texts, in order to create gender equality is essential for the survival of Buddhism?

Should aligning Buddhism with feminism as found in the West be seen as disrespectful to the history, traditions and culture of 'heritage' Buddhists?

Key quote

The siladhara training is considered to be a vehicle fully suitable for the realisation of liberation, and is respected as such within our tradition. It is offered as a complete training as it stands, and not as a step in the evolution towards a different form such as bhikkhuni ordination. (The Fifth Point of the Five Point Declaration issued by Ajahn Chah's Forest Sangha in 2009)

Study tip

It is vital for AO2 that you actually discuss arguments and not just explain what someone may have stated. Try to ask yourself, 'was this a fair point to make?', 'is the evidence sound enough?', 'is there anything to challenge this argument?', 'is this a strong or weak argument?' Such critical analysis will help you develop your evaluation skills.

AO2 Activity

List some conclusions that could be drawn from the AO2 reasoning from the above text; try to aim for at least three different possible conclusions. Consider each of the conclusions and collect brief evidence to support each conclusion from the AO1 and AO2 material for this topic. Select the conclusion that you think is most convincing and explain why it is so. Try to contrast this with the weakest conclusion in the list, justifying your argument with clear reasoning and evidence.

Ajahn Brahm was enthusiastic in his support of a bhikkhuni sangha: 'In the West, the absence of bhikkhunis is seen as a major defect of Buddhism. The lack of a female equivalent to the Theravada Buddhist monk is a big reason why many Westerners do not become Buddhists. It is my personal opinion that if we do not establish a bhikkhuni *Saṅgha*, then Buddhism will not last even another 50 years in the West!'

The response from the senior bhikkhus of the Forest Sangha was to remove Ajhan Brahm from any association with the Forest Sangha monasteries in Thailand and in the West – including the Amaravati Monastery in England. Here, as Christine Toomey explains in *The Saffron Robe: A Journey with Buddha's Daughters* published in 2015, the number of women joining the community had been increasing but none were able to receive higher ordination. Instead they only had a junior status of siladhara. Toomey quotes the testimony of Sister Candasiri: '... this was a time when real efforts towards gender equality were being made in wider western cultures, so when we began to talk about this within our monastic community it was not appreciated'.

In 2009, following discussion between the abbot of Amaravati Ajahn Sumedho (born Robert Jackman, Seattle 1934), other abbots of Forest Sangha monasteries and the Elders Council in Thailand, a Five Point Declaration was agreed. Rather than making allowance for gender equality, these points reinforced the traditional Theravada approach. Thus the first point stated that 'the most junior bhikkhu is "senior" to the most senior siladhara'. The justification given was that, 'this relationship of seniority is defined by the Vinaya, it is not considered something we can change'.

Away from Theravada, the Dalai Lama supports the higher ordination of bhikkhunis. This has been difficult to bring about within Tibetan Buddhism: Tibetan Buddhist women who choose this path have to be ordained by the dual sangha involving bhikkhunis from the Chinese lineage before continuing within the Tibetan tradition. He has suggested that in the East a gradualist approach be taken: for example, bhikkhunis come to Dharamsala and live as a bhikkhuni sangha. Over time, they might then be accepted by Tibetan bhikkhus.

In the West the Dalai Lama supports ways of combining traditional Buddhist teachings and new Western cultural forms. One example is Sravasti Abbey in Washington USA founded in 2003, by its abbess Thubten Chodron (born Cheryl Greene 1950). The abbey trains nuns and monks and is structured in a non-patriarchal manner described as 'horizontal, more collaborative, with gender equality and with seniority based on years of experience and knowledge'. Gender equality here is recognised by the Dalai Lama: 'I am glad to know that the community seeks to provide both monks and nuns with not only equal opportunity, but equal responsibility to study, practise and teach the dharma.'

Arguably it has been with new insights of feminist Buddhists that a rebalancing has begun in challenging patriarchal assumptions and interpretations which suggests that Buddhism can align itself with feminism. Brazier suggests that Buddhists who have a fixed position against the ordination of bhikkhunis, for example, should learn from the Buddha who changed his mind after hearing the view put forward by Ananda regarding the ordination of Maha-Pajapati Gotami.

Some might argue that Buddhism has always aligned itself with feminism but that this has been obscured by patriarchal attitudes – a point made by Grace Schireson in her work on women in Zen. She focuses on the Prajnaparamita Sutra which is called the 'Great Mother'. From the American perspective, rediscovering the 'Great Mother' is a new task. 'As Buddhism grows up in America, we too are growing up. We realise we can no longer imitate the practice of young Asian monks. Zen is not an Asian practice; it expresses a universal human need.'

AO2 Developing skills

It is now important to consider the information that has been covered in this section; however, the information in its raw form is too extensive and so has to be processed in order to meet the requirements of the examination. This can be achieved by practising more advanced skills associated with AO2. For assessment objective 2 (AO2), which involves 'critical analysis' and 'evaluation' skills, we are going to focus on different ways in which the skills can be demonstrated effectively, and also, refer to how the performance of these skills is measured (see generic band descriptors for A2 [WJEC] AO2 or A Level [Eduqas] AO2).

▶ **Your final task for this Theme is:** Below are listed three basic conclusions drawn from an evaluation of **the extent to which Buddhism aligns with feminism**. Your task is to develop each of these conclusions by identifying briefly the strengths (referring briefly to some reasons underlying it) but also an awareness of challenges made to it (these may be weaknesses depending upon your view).

1. Buddhism aligns with feminism because the key point about the Buddha's conversation with Maha-Pajapati Gotama was that: he accepted that women could be enlightened, he changed his mind having heard the arguments of Ananda, and he ordained women as bhikkhunis.

2. Buddhism aligns with feminism because in the West women are playing an increasingly significant part in Buddhism in terms of both participation and leadership. This has been widely accepted as a positive move by most Buddhists.

3. Buddhism aligns with feminism because it focuses on feminine characteristics and qualities such as compassion and loving kindness which can be seen in their ideal form in female bodhisattvas and Buddhas such as Kuan-Yin in China.

The result should be three very competent paragraphs that could form a final conclusion of any evaluation.

When you have completed the task, refer to the band descriptors for A2 (WJEC) or A Level (Eduqas) and in particular have a look at the demands described in the higher band descriptors towards which you should be aspiring. Ask yourself:

- Is my answer a confident critical analysis and perceptive evaluation of the issue?
- Is my answer a response that successfully identifies and thoroughly addresses the issues raised by the question set?

Key skills Theme 3

The third theme has tasks that deal with specific aspects of AO2 in terms of identifying key elements of an evaluative style piece of writing, specifically counter-arguments and conclusions (both intermediate and final).

Key skills

Analysis involves:

Identifying issues raised by the materials in the AO1, together with those identified in the AO2 section, and presents sustained and clear views, either of scholars or from a personal perspective ready for evaluation.

This means:

- That your answers are able to identify key areas of debate in relation to a particular issue
- That you can identify, and comment upon, the different lines of argument presented by others
- That your response comments on the overall effectiveness of each of these areas or arguments.

Evaluation involves:

Considering the various implications of the issues raised based upon the evidence gleaned from analysis and provides an extensive detailed argument with a clear conclusion.

This means:

- That your answer weighs up the consequences of accepting or rejecting the various and different lines of argument analysed
- That your answer arrives at a conclusion through a clear process of reasoning.

This section covers AO1 content and skills

Specification content

The relationship of Buddhism with pre-Buddhist Bon religion.

The Jowo Rinpoche dating from the 7th century CE.

Key terms

Jowo Rinpoche: statue of the Buddha in Jokhang Temple brought to Tibet in 641 CE

Bonpos: the name given to the followers of Tibet's indigenous religion, Bon

lha: good spirits or gods in Bon

Dre: evil spirits or gods in Bon

quickfire

4.1 Who is regarded as the founder of the Tibetan empire?

D: Beliefs and practices of Tibetan Buddhist traditions

The relationship of Buddhism with pre-Buddhist Bon religion

A key moment, which it might be argued symbolically marked the introduction of Buddhism to Tibet, occurred during the reign of the 33rd Tibetan Tsenpo (king) named Songtsen Gampo (ca. 617–650 CE) who is regarded as the founder of the Tibetan empire. He married a Chinese princess who brought with her in 641, as part of her dowry, a large image of the Buddha known as the **Jowo Rinpoche**, which had been sent to China from India. Tradition stated that it had been blessed by the Buddha himself. The Jowo Rinpoche was then placed in the Jokhang temple in Lhasa, where it is today one of the most revered statues for Tibetan Buddhists.

Under Songtsen Gampo, Buddhism began to be established in Tibet. However, there is continuing debate as to the existence of Buddhism in Tibet before his reign. For example, some scholars point out that Tibet had as its neighbours countries such as China, Nepal and India where Buddhism was already firmly rooted. Thus, the Jowo Rinpoche came from India to China before arriving in Tibet. It is quite possible, therefore, that Buddhist beliefs and practices had permeated Tibet at a much earlier date. In addition, scholarly debate continues as to the indigenous religion in Tibet prior to the arrival of Buddhism, which is identified as Bon.

The word 'Bon' means 'invocation' and its followers are **Bonpos**. This is a very complex area because Bonpos today generally identify three stages of Bon:

1. Old Bon – a religion of magic and rituals aimed at influencing and gaining the support of good spirits or gods known as '**lha**' and at controlling or removing evil spirits or gods known as '**dre**'. Old Bon was therefore animistic – believing that natural objects, natural phenomena, and the universe itself possess a spirit. Old Bon was also shamanistic – believing that these spirits in nature could be good or evil and could be influenced or controlled by shamans who had special powers.

2. Yungdrung Bon – founded by Shenrab Miwoche who came from a mystical land near Tibet many thousands of years ago. (The word 'yungdrung' means everlasting and its symbol is the left-turning svastika.) Shenrab Miwoche is sometimes called Buddha Shenrab and lived a life very similar to that of the historical Buddha whom he predated by thousands of years. His teaching was also Buddhist. Shenrab converted followers of Old Bon to Yungdrung Bon, which for that reason is seen by some Bonpos as a more ancient form of Buddhism than that introduced under Songtsen Gampo.

3. New Bon – the first Buddhist monastery was founded in the 8th century. Traditions state that this involved the help of the great Buddhist teacher from India Padmasambhava who showed mastery in influencing lha and controlling dre throughout Tibet. Over the following centuries, Bonpos absorbed, adapted and adopted much of the subsequent Buddhist Dhamma brought into Tibet but maintained their Bon traditions. New Bon has its own sacred texts, monasteries and religious leaders and is recognised by the Dalai Lama as one of the religious traditions of Tibet.

What was thought of as pre-Buddhist Bon had been described by scholars such as Harvey in 1990 as simply being an animistic and shamanistic 'cult of dead kings, spirit-possession, magic, and exorcism of demons and vampires, though it shares a belief in rebirth with Buddhism'.

In more recent years this view has changed as a result of further research and examination of Bon sacred texts. 'These materials provide evidence that the traditions of Tibetan Buddhism and Bon are rooted in cultural forms that have remained more or less constant in spite of Tibet's history of sectarian politics, philosophical disputes, and assimilation of non-Buddhist elements' (Petit).

Some scholars now argue that it is very difficult to identify or isolate what had been described as pre-Buddhist Bon from mainstream Tibetan Buddhism. Thus, writing in 2013, Kapstein notes that 'although Bon is often used as a designation for the pre-Buddhist Tibetan religion, the religious life of Tibet prior to the introduction of Buddhism remains poorly understood. Because the Tibetan system of writing was adopted just as Buddhism was becoming known, there are few records of early Tibetan religion in which Buddhist influences are altogether absent. From the existing texts, it is not even clear that there was a particular term regularly used to designate the pre-Buddhist Tibetan religion.'

Study tip

In order to gain a greater understanding of Bon and Tibetan Buddhism it would be a good idea to locate Tibet on a map and think about its geographical location.

Development of distinctive practices associated with Vajrayana Buddhism

The whole area of Tibetan Buddhism is highly complex and, since it is a relatively new area of academic study, there is continuing re-evaluation and re-assessment of what constitutes Tibetan Buddhism and of how it can be best explained. This applies as much to the terminology used, as to the practices associated with Tibetan Buddhism. The issue is further complicated given the huge variety of interpretations given to Tibetan Buddhist sacred texts: both the Kangyur – collection of words of the Buddha – and the Tengyur – commentaries on the sacred texts.

Whilst scholarly debate continues with regard to pre-Buddhist Bon, a general point on which there is some consensus appears to be that Bon provided Tibetan Buddhism with a dynamic view of nature and of using the senses people have been given in the mundane world as a way of entering into the supramundane. This also has to be seen against the background of religious ritual practices found in Hinduism, which were influential in the development of Buddhism in India and in Tibet. According to some, such practices might be described as Tantra, which in Tibet might also be termed Vajrayana.

It is difficult to be precise with regard to Tantra as there is no one universally agreed definition. Indeed, trying to define Tantra is something which Williams notes 'should deter the wise'. Generally, however, it may be regarded as being concerned

Key quotes

In practice, adherents of both Bon and Buddhism are equally concerned with maintaining harmony with local spirits and demons, with avoiding spiritual pollution and acquiring tokens imbued with blessings of auspicious good fortune, and with rites of passage that begin when a lama whispers a name into an infant's ear and conclude with one's departure at death. (Kapstein)

Bon doctrine, history, and practices can be found throughout Tibet, and have had a profound influence on the form of Buddhism that has taken root there, just as Buddhism in Tibet has had a profound influence on Bon. (Gardner)

Specification content

Development of distinctive practices associated with Vajrayana Buddhism.

quickfire

4.2 What does 'yungdrung' mean?

Key terms

Kangyur: collection of words of the Buddha

Tantra: practices which provide the means for becoming enlightened

Tengyur: commentaries on the sacred texts

Key quote

Tantra is an experiential and practical form of Buddhism, stressing real experience of the Buddhist goal, achieved sacramentally and symbolically. (**Cush**)

The vajra which is used extensively in Tibetan Buddhist ritual practices.

Key term

Yidam: a holy being or bodhisattva

with practices which provide the means for becoming enlightened. It is through the most advanced stages of such practices that 'a person can become a fully enlightened Buddha in one lifetime.... Hence the reputation of Tibetan Buddhism for magic and mystery! Hence also the complex iconography ... and the elaborate ritual ... of Tibetan Buddhism.' (Williams)

Tantric teachings are found in complex sacred texts, which require careful analysis and explanation since they do not make much sense on first reading. In addition, there are rituals which are kept secret and passed on to those who are initiated. All of this means that, perhaps more than other forms of Buddhism, Tibetan Buddhism stresses the overriding importance of a teacher who can guide students as they progress.

The development of the term Vajrayana for this form of Tantra is based on the usage of the vajra – originally perhaps a weapon in war which was a sceptre. The vajra became a ritual object and is used extensively in Tibetan Buddhist practices. Vajra means both 'thunderbolt' and 'diamond'. Given that 'yana' means 'vehicle', Vajrayana can therefore be understood as the diamond or thunderbolt vehicle which leads to enlightenment.

Harvey explains that the vajra was seen as a good symbol because it was 'as irresistible as a thunderbolt, suggesting the overwhelming power of the awakened mind to destroy spiritual obstacles; as hard as a diamond, suggesting the indestructible nature of the awakened mind'.

Williams describes Vajrayana as using 'magical practices for transforming mundane reality into a form most suited to help others'. One way in which this transformation is attempted is through elaborate and complex visualisation, actualisation and empowerment. This is practised in a variety of forms by the four different Tibetan Buddhist sects: Nyingmapa, Kagyupa, Sakyapa and Gelugpa.

These four sects share the same Buddhist teaching but differ in the emphasis placed on Buddhist practices. Thus, according to the Dalai Lama (who belongs to the Gelugpa sect): 'In the course of time, different lineages appeared within this complete tradition, influenced by extraordinary masters who, at different times and in different places, expressed the teachings in slightly different ways. Despite the differences between these lineages, they all incorporate the Buddha's teachings in full.'

During visualisation, practitioners might focus upon and visualise a **yidam** which has been chosen for them by their lama or teacher. Yidam refers to a deity or bodhisattva. Practitioners are supposed to be in harmony with the yidam, who would in turn act as their protector and guide. Yidams can be male or female and peaceful or angry. The anger and ferocity of some yidams is not directed to the practitioner or to people but is directed instead to illusion and all that prevents the Dhamma from taking effect in producing enlightenment in the practitioner. Yidams are not generally visualised in isolation since they are linked to and merge into other bodhisattvas and Buddhas.

During actualisation, which is a more advanced stage, practitioners are able to think of themselves as merging with, and in a sense making the yidam and the other bodhisattvas and Buddhas actual in them self.

Following these two stages, practitioners are then empowered in the same way as the yidam, bodhisattvas and Buddhas in bringing compassion to all sentient beings.

One example of visualisation, actualisation and empowerment can be found in the various commentaries on 'The Three Principal Aspects of the Path to Highest Enlightenment' written by the founder of the Gelugpa sect, Tsongkapha (1357–1419) one of whose main disciples was the first Dalai Lama Gedun Drupa.

As a preparation, practitioners might recite various mantras for purification such as 'Om vajrasattva hum' many thousands of times calling on the yidam who is the Bodhisattva Vajrasattva to purify karma, bring peace and cause enlightenment.

During the visualisation, practitioners would visualise the Buddha, bodhisattvas and their own lamas in front of themselves. They would then visualise light shining from the Buddha and think that they will obtain freedom from suffering and gain the state of perfect Buddhahood 'for the sake of all sentient beings'. They would then take refuge in their lamas, the Buddhas, the Dhamma and the sangha.

Visualisation of Tsongkapha seated on top of a jewelled tree would also take place, seeing him 'with clear white body and mouth smiling with pleasure. His wearing the three religious robes.... His two hands are performing the **mudra** of the wheel of Dhamma at his heart and stems of lotuses extend over his shoulders.'

Practitioners then need to think: 'I must attain, regardless of anything, the precious state of a completely perfect Buddha, quickly, quickly for the sake of all sentient beings.'

During the visualisation, actualisation takes place when duplicates of all the lamas and gods in front of the practitioners separate from their bodies and move to dissolve into the practitioners themselves. 'Thus, your body momentarily changes into the body of lama and Buddha. Rays of light emanate from your body transformed into lama and Buddha. By striking all the sentient beings living around you the rays of light purify their sins and obstructions.'

After this, the practitioners make prayers for empowerment to enter the path to enlightenment as quickly as possible for the sake of all sentient beings so that there may be an end to cyclical rebirth and suffering.

Using various mudras, offerings are then made by the practitioners who might also make a mandala offering in their minds. This could be based on a physical mandala which has been created, showing in symbolic form the universe with Mount Meru in the centre, all the realms and all the beings in these realms. Sometimes a mandala offering plate is also used. Practitioners might then recite prayers such as: 'Please empower me with blessings. I offer the ground anointed with incense, strewn with flowers, adorned with Meru, the four continents, Sun and Moon and visualised as a Pure Land.'

Study tip

Use bullet points to summarise the process of visualisation outlined above.

Mudra (ritual bodily movements, often hand gestures)

The word mudra means 'sign' and can refer to the gesture made by the hands of Buddha images. Mudras are also to be found in Hinduism. The mudra can often help Buddhists focus on particular aspects of the Dhamma. For example, many Buddha images have the Dhyana (meditation) mudra, which means meditation. Here, the back of the right-hand rests on the upturned palm of the other with the tips of the thumbs lightly touching. According to one interpretation, the top hand symbolises enlightenment; the bottom hand, the world of appearances. Thus, the mudra as a whole suggests the supremacy of the enlightened mind.

In Vajrayana, mudras are often used by monks during visualisation, actualisation and empowerment. In some cases, the mudra used by a monk reflects the mudra associated with their yidam or with a particular aspect of the Dhamma such as generosity, fearlessness or victory over illusion. Such mudras are generally formal in terms of having a set pattern in the way the hands are held and the fingers brought together.

quickfire

4.3 To which Tibetan Buddhist sect does the Dalai Lama belong?

Key quote

The much wider range of mudras used in tantric ritual are seen as the signs – and causes – of particular states of mind. By making various gestures, certain states of mind may be stimulated or enhanced. (Harvey)

Key term

Mudra: sign, gesture of hands made by the hands of Buddha images, ritual bodily movements

quickfire

4.4 Which yidam is referred to in the mantra 'Om vajrasattva hum'?

Specification content

Mudra (ritual bodily movements, often hand gestures).

A 12th-century seated Buddha with the Dhyana mudra.

Key terms

Mani mantra: 'om mani padme hum' ('homage to the one holding jewel and lotus)

Mantra: tool for thinking, sacred sounds

For example, in the Humkara (victory) mudra, the two hands are crossed and held as fists with the second and third fingers forming circles with the thumbs and the first and fourth fingers extended. The Humkara mudra may be used as a sign of enlightenment and the victory over cyclical rebirth.

This mudra is often associated with the bodhisattvas Vajradhara and Vajrasattva and images may show them using the vajra and tribu (bell) in their hands. In many Vajrayana practices, mudras are combined with the use of the vajra and tribu, which are held in each hand and moved in a ritualistic and precise way to channel and focus the mind's concentration during visualisation, actualisation and empowerment.

In other cases, the mudra might be seen as a way of representing the phenomenal world of the five elements: fire, air, ether, earth and water. In some practices, the thumb represents the fire and universal awareness, the index finger represents air and individual awareness, the middle finger represents the ether connecting all things, the ring finger represents the earth and the little finger represents water. As Harvey points out, mudras 'are used to amplify the efficacy of the mantras in evoking psychic forces and higher states of consciousness'.

Quite often, therefore, mudras are very elaborate and are in themselves gestures of offerings. This is well described by the English Buddhist teacher Vessantara in his first experience of Tibetan Buddhist practice. 'There were the mudras – the symbolic gestures – a dance of the hands, taking endless forms, graceful and again flowing. The hands displayed the shapes of all kinds of offerings: food and drink, flowers, lights and so on; they expressed devotion to higher forces and threat to hindering ones. They produced whole worlds to offer to the Buddhas and enlightened beings. Yet these worlds were being created always and only by the power of the mind expressed through the fingers.'

Mantra (sacred sounds)

Specification content

Mantra (sacred sounds).

Key quote

A mantra is seen as acting like a psychic key which enables a person either to have power over 'physical' things, or to visualise and communicate with a being/force whose mantra it is. (Harvey)

The word mantra comes from the Sanskrit 'man' meaning 'to think' and 'tra' meaning 'tool'. Therefore, mantra literally means 'tool for thinking'. It is believed that mantras help to purify and focus the mind. In addition, they can be used to offer devotion or thanks to the Buddha or bodhisattva. Mantras are also recited to gain spiritual protection and to nurture spiritual activity. Mantras are an essential component of Vajrayana Buddhism. This can be seen in the way that some describe Vajrayana as Mantranaya or the path of the Mantra. Again, the focus is on moving the mind from mundane, intellectual and discursive thought to the supramundane.

Whilst monks, nuns and advanced practitioners of Vajrayana may focus on a detailed examination of the meaning of each of the syllables of the mantra, it is also quite possible to recite the mantra with little understanding. This is because the actual words of the mantra are less important than the reality of the syllables uttered and the effect it is believed to have on the mind of the person chanting the mantra.

The best-known mantra in Vajrayana is sometimes referred to as the Mani mantra of the bodhisattva Chenrezig who is known by other names in the rest of Asia such as Avalokitesvara. Chenrezig is regarded as a Buddha and the present Dalai Lama Tenzin Gyatso and other leading Tibetan spiritual figures are also seen as emanations of Chenrezig.

The Mani mantra of Chenrezig is: 'om mani padme hum', which can be translated as 'homage to the one holding jewel and lotus'. The frequent chanting of these words is believed to help towards enlightenment. In addition, the mantra might be used as a prayer seeking Chenrezig's compassion, empowerment and blessings. Within Vajrayana, the focus might also simply be on the six syllables. Kapstein notes that some 'prefer to interpret its six syllables symbolically as conveying the blessings of compassion to beings inhabiting the six realms of worldly existence'.

Whilst the mantra can be chanted, the words of the mantra are also written on prayer wheels, buildings, flags and stones. All of this makes the mantra readily accessible to everyone and no special training or knowledge is required.

The Mani mantra has been analysed in a wide variety of ways with different interpretations given to each of the syllables. For example, the present Dalai Lama Tenzin Gyatso has given one commentary which can be summarised as follows:

'Om' is composed of three letters 'AUM' and represents the state of the person chanting the mantra as being impure in body, speech and mind but also represents the goal of becoming a Buddha with purity in body, speech and mind.

'Mani' means 'jewel'. Just as a jewel removes poverty so too 'the altruistic mind of enlightenment is capable of removing the poverty, or difficulties, of cyclic existence and of gaining solitary peace'.

'Padme' means 'lotus' and symbolises wisdom in recognising that there is nothing self-sufficient or substantially existent. Just as a lotus grows out of the mud but is not damaged by the mud, so the mind can grow in awareness without being held back by ignorance of the emptiness of all things.

'Hum' represents the indivisible unity of wisdom and practice as 'one undifferentiated entity'. 'Hum' is also the syllable associated with one of the Tibetan Buddhas of Wisdom, Akshobhya. Stating this at the end of the mantra indicates that what is said is 'the immovable, the unfluctuating, that which cannot be disturbed by anything'.

All of this means that for the Dalai Lama, the 'meaning of the six syllables is great and vast'. Continual recitation or sight of the Mani mantra means recognition of the reality that 'in dependence on the practice of a path which is an indivisible union of method and wisdom, you can transform your impure body, speech and mind into the pure exalted body, speech and mind of a Buddha'.

Study tip

Consolidate your knowledge by explaining in your own words why 'om mani padme hum' is important in Tibetan Buddhism.

Mandala (cosmic diagrams)

For some in the West, Vajrayana Buddhist mandalas are associated with elaborate initiation ceremonies overseen by the Dalai Lama and attended by many thousands of people, during which Kalachakra mandalas are created to the accompaniment of drums, bells, gongs and trumpets. The mandalas may be made of coloured grains of sand where each grain is painstakingly placed following a carefully measured plan. Quite often this is circular and requires highly technical knowledge and precise skill.

Whilst the word mandala literally means 'circle', when completed, the mandala is generally believed to be a two-dimensional representation of the outer universe with a huge five-floored sacred palace with the Buddhas and bodhisattvas inside representing the inner universe. There are four entrances to the palace, each of which has its own protector. The Buddhas, bodhisattvas and protectors are represented by different shapes and patterns of coloured sand. Each floor of the palace can be understood as representing a different aspect of the universe from the body on the ground floor through to the mind, wisdom and then great bliss on the top floor.

What is required of the person who wishes to be initiated is that through intense concentration they strive to visualise in front of them what the mandala represents – the entire complex of the universe, the entrances to the palace, the protectors of the entrances and the Buddhas and bodhisattvas inside. They may then strive

The mantra 'om mani padme hum' painted on stones.

Key quote

What is important about a mantra is that it has some effect (or power) beyond that of just uttering the sounds of which it is composed. Mantras may be understood as a form of ... 'performance utterance'. This is an utterance that does something, that is action as well as speech. (Williams)

quickfire

4.5 What, according to the Dalai Lama, does 'om' refer to when used in mantras?

Specification content

Mandala (cosmic diagrams).

A Kalachakra mandala made of coloured sand.

quickfire

4.6   What is Akshobhya associated with?

to visualise themselves as the Buddha or bodhisattva inside the palace. As we have noted above, this is another way in which what is found in the mundane world is used as a way of entering into the supramundane – of transforming the ordinary mind so that enlightenment may take place.

Kalachakra sand mandalas are only one type of mandala and they are impermanent, since at the end of the ceremony, the sand making up the mandala is swept up and, for example, put into a river to spread its blessings into the world. Permanent mandalas can also be painted onto cloth or used in murals on the walls of temples. Another permanent form of a mandala is the mandala offering plate. Any flat plate may serve this purpose. The mandala plate is filled with rice and when placed in a permanent shrine, it may be multi-tiered with a replica of the heavenly palace on top. It may be used in rituals as a form of a symbolic offering of the universe to the Buddha, bodhisattvas, yidams and lamas. Whilst these mandalas are material and physical structures, mandalas can also be entirely in the mind of the person engaged in the ritual and in this sense they are immaterial and mentally made constructions.

In other advanced forms of tantric practice, the practitioner's own body is viewed as either in a mandala or as a complex and intricate mandala itself. From this perspective the body is perceived as the yidam and then each component part of the body as a yidam. Lopez describes just the beginning of this process as follows: 'The monk next turns to the visualisation of the body mandala, in which thirty-seven parts of his body … are transformed into thirty-seven deities. The thirty-seven places comprise the twenty-four inner places of the body, the eight channels of the sense organs, the four channels of the heart wheel, and the indestructible drop.'

Different mandalas may have different conceptual frameworks: in some the centre of the mandala is Mount Meru as the centre of the universe with all the realms of existence depicted around it; in some what is depicted in diagrammatic form is the Pure Land of one of the Buddha universes; in some the mandala is constructed around specific bodhisattvas or yidams connected to the person meditating.

Some mandalas are constructed around the images of the five main Buddhas who are called 'conquerors of delusion and death'. The Buddha in the centre of the mandala is the specific focus for visualisation. This adds what can appear to be a further level of complexity as Cush notes: 'Thus the five main cosmic Buddhas (Vairocana, Amoghasiddhi, Amitabha, Akshobya and Ratnasambhava) are identified with the five skandhas which go to make up the human being but also with the five material elements of fire, water, earth, air and ether. The contemplation of such correspondences in the mandala is designed to help you realise the "emptiness" of all things.' A further correspondence in mandalas is that they can be representative, as Kapstein suggests, both of the 'macrocosmic universe' and 'the microcosm of the individual'.

Study tip

Research the variety of mudras, mantras and mandalas to increase your depth and breadth of knowledge in this area.

AO1 Activity

Explain how a Buddhist might respond to the following view: 'Use of the mantra is the important practice in Vajrayana Buddhism.'

Explain your answer using evidence and examples from what you have read.

AO1 Developing skills

It is now important to consider the information that has been covered in this section; however, the information in its raw form is too extensive and so has to be processed in order to meet the requirements of the examination. This can be achieved by practising more advanced skills associated with AO1. The exercises that run throughout this book will help you to do this and prepare you for the examination. For assessment objective 1 (AO1), which involves demonstrating 'knowledge' and 'understanding' skills, we are going to focus on different ways in which the skills can be demonstrated effectively, and also, refer to how the performance of these skills is measured (see generic band descriptors for A2 [WJEC] AO1 or A Level [Eduqas] AO1).

▶ **Your new task is this:** you will have to write a response under timed conditions to a question requiring an examination or explanation of **three distinctive practices associated with Vajrayana Buddhism – mudra (ritual bodily movements, often hand gestures) mandala (cosmic diagrams) and mantra (sacred sounds)**. This exercise is best done as a small group at first.

1. Begin with a list of indicative content as you may have done in the previous textbook in the series. It does not need to be in any particular order at first, although as you practise this you will see more order in your lists that reflects your understanding.

2. Develop the list by using one or two relevant quotations. Now add some references to scholars and/or religious writings.

3. Then write out your plan, under timed conditions, remembering the principles of explaining with evidence and/or examples.

When you have completed the task, refer to the band descriptors for A2 (WJEC) or A Level (Eduqas) and in particular have a look at the demands described in the higher band descriptors towards which you should be aspiring. Ask yourself:

- Does my work demonstrate thorough, accurate and relevant knowledge and understanding of religion and belief?
- Is my work coherent (consistent or make logical sense), clear and well organised?
- Will my work, when developed, be an extensive and relevant response which is specific to the focus of the task?
- Does my work have extensive depth and/or suitable breadth and have excellent use of evidence and examples?
- If appropriate to the task, does my response have thorough and accurate reference to sacred texts and sources of wisdom?
- Are there any insightful connections to be made with other elements of my course?
- Will my answer, when developed and extended to match what is expected in an examination answer, have an extensive range of views of scholars/schools of thought?
- When used, is specialist language and vocabulary both thorough and accurate?

Key skills Theme 4

The fourth theme has tasks that consolidate your AO1 skills and focus these skills for examination preparation.

Key skills

Knowledge involves:

Selection of a range of (thorough) accurate and relevant information that is directly related to the specific demands of the question.

This means:

- Selecting relevant material for the question set
- Being focused in explaining and examining the material selected.

Understanding involves:

Explanation that is extensive, demonstrating depth and/or breadth with excellent use of evidence and examples including (where appropriate) thorough and accurate supporting use of sacred texts, sources of wisdom and specialist language.

This means:

- Effective use of examples and supporting evidence to establish the quality of your understanding
- Ownership of your explanation that expresses personal knowledge and understanding and NOT just reproducing a chunk of text from a book that you have rehearsed and memorised.

Specification content

The unique nature of Vajrayana
Buddhism.

quickfire

4.7 What does the word 'yana' mean?

Key quote

Visualisation plays a central role in
tantric practice. Whether the goal
is awakening or the protection of a
locality's crops, the relevant ritual
usually requires the visualisation
of a deity or set of deities, often
located within the sacred space of a
mandala. Visualisation transforms
the world of appearances....
(Harvey)

Study tip

Make sure you understand the
different ways in which the word
'yana' appears in Buddhism: Hinayana,
Mahayana, Vajrayana, Navayana.

AO2 Activity

As you read through this section try to
do the following:

1. Pick out the different lines of
   argument that are presented in
   the text and identify any evidence
   given in support.

2. For each line of argument try to
   evaluate whether or not you think
   this is strong or weak.

3. Think of any questions you may
   wish to raise in response to the
   arguments.

This activity will help you to start
thinking critically about what you
read and help you to evaluate the
effectiveness of different arguments
and from this develop your own
observations, opinions and points
of view that will help with any
conclusions that you make in your
answers to the AO2 questions
that arise.

Issues for analysis and evaluation

The unique nature of Vajrayana Buddhism

There is much continuing and new scholarly debate about Buddhism in Tibet.
There even appears to be little agreement on some of the fundamental categories
being used.

Writing in 1990, Harvey described the Buddhism which developed in the 'lands of
Northern Buddhism' as being 'a new more powerful vehicle to salvation' which he
terms Tantrayana. He explains that 'a common term for the new movement was
Vajrayana' with another term for it being Mantrayana. Writing in 2013, Harvey no
longer uses either term but refers to tantric Buddhism and Mantranaya. Writing
in 2000, Williams explains that 'the expressions "Vajrayana Buddhism" and "tantric
Buddhism" are not synonymous. What is true of Vajrayana Buddhism is not
necessarily true of tantric Buddhism as a whole.'

Another issue is that it can seem that Vajrayana Buddhism is a term which is
treated as being synonymous with Tibetan Buddhism in that the two terms are
interchangeable. Furthermore, Vajrayana is regarded by some as a branch of
Mahayana whilst others regard it as the third main type of Buddhism in addition
to Theravada and Mahayana. A further area is as to whether Tibetan Buddhism is
really the continued flourishing of late Buddhism from India where it fell into rapid
decline in the 12th century. Judged by this approach, the tantric elements of Tibetan
Buddhism are mainly evidence of the influence of Hindu practices up until that time.

Part of the problem in the area of categorisation is that due to its geographical
location, Tibet was very much a melting pot of Buddhist practices and beliefs.
Elements of what might be regarded as Chinese Mahayana concepts can be found
alongside elements of Indian Mahayana concepts. Over the centuries, the rich
interplay between these strands and how they were understood and interpreted by
Tibetan Buddhists has created what Kapstein describes as a tradition which is a 'long,
endlessly varied, and intricately refined development within the splendid civilisation
of Tibet'.

The Dalai Lama himself describes three stages of Buddhism found in Tibet. The first
is the Shravakayana, or Fundamental Vehicle, which is the path of the Four Noble
Truths which leads to enlightenment through trainings in disciplines, concentration
and wisdom. The second is the Mahayana or Great Vehicle, which consists of six
paramitas. The third is the Vajrayana, which the Dalai Lama describes as being: 'the
vehicle of the secret mantras, which sets out the extraordinary means for realising
profound concentration through the union of mental calm and clear insight
(samatha and vipassana) and for progression through the four tantra classes'.

With some caution, it might therefore be possible to identify tantric Buddhism with
the Vajrayana Buddhism described by the Dalai Lama and suggest that this is the
predominant form of Buddhism found in Tibet. Harvey writes: 'Tibet, inheriting
Indian Buddhism in two phases from the 8th to the 12th centuries, developed a
tradition that was thoroughly tantric in complexion, with the result that all schools
of Tibetan Buddhism regard tantric Buddhism as Buddhism's highest and most
effective form.'

Taking an overview of Vajrayana, there are some features which some might argue
are unique in the sense that they are not found in other forms of Buddhism or in the
sense that are given more significance than is found in other forms of Buddhism.

One key feature in Vajrayana is the emphasis on visualisation and its associated
practices as key to enlightenment. Williams notes how this tantric practice was
reworked into the life of the Buddha in sacred texts of Vajrayana. Thus, it is related
that, whilst seated under the Bodhi Tree, the Buddha is visited by four Buddhas who
tell him that he will not gain enlightenment by just sitting in meditation. He is then

given a number of mantras to recite. Once he does this, visualisation takes place as he sees a vajra in his heart and the enlightened mind is produced and stabilised. At this point, the four Buddhas enter the vajra in his heart and he receives empowerment from their combined wisdom.

The Buddha is then truly enlightened and is given the title Vajradhatu – 'Vajra-sphere'. He is then taken to the summit of Mount Meru and placed on a lion throne whilst the four Buddhas each takes a seat at each of the four points of the compass. In this way the mandala of five Buddhas is formed. The Buddha then returns to sit under the Bodhi tree and the traditional story of his Awakening continues. Williams comments on this reworking of the usual accounts: 'Not only does it legitimise the place of tantric practice as a key part of the Buddhist path, it also provides the exemplar for tantric initiation and practice. Thus, the tantric practitioner can be seen as rehearsing the actions and experiences of the Buddha.'

Before becoming a monk in Tibet, Batchelor was taught the importance of visualisation as the 'highest class of tantra'. He was then initiated into the mandala of the yidam Yamantaka, which meant daily visualisation and recitation for life of the text describing his generation into Yamantaka: 'henceforth, every morning I would become the glorious and mighty bull-headed Yamantaka'.

In order to practise visualisation and receive empowerment, Vajrayana Buddhism insists on the importance of having a teacher – a lama. The lama is alone the one 'who gives access to tantric practice and who transmits the teachings of the various tantric scriptures' (Williams). Whilst general Buddhist Dhamma is given to all, tantric scriptures remained secret and were only communicated by the lama to those who were seen fit to be initiated. In order to be initiated, tantric empowerment is required. Batchelor explains his experience of this before becoming a monk in Tibet: 'These were secret teachings which to receive and practise one had to be empowered by a qualified tantric master, who in turn had been empowered by an unbroken lineage of teachers going back to the Buddha himself.'

A practitioner of Vajrayana would have a picture of their lama on their shrine and during visualisation would see their lama as being one with their yidam and with the Buddha. Lamas are held in such high regard because they are regarded not as ordinary human beings but as living Buddhas who had been reborn on this earth out of compassion. Practitioners have to take a vow of complete loyalty to their lama. Batchelor notes: 'I took a vow never to disparage such a teacher. To break my tantric commitment to him would result in rebirth in the worst of all possible hells. For solely through the inspiration and blessings of these extraordinary men was progress along the path to enlightenment made possible.'

Whilst Vajrayana might appear unique, it might also be argued that it has underlying connections with other forms of Buddhism. For example, in the Buddhisms of Japan such as Zen, master to pupil transmission is often a requisite. Again, Williams argues that for all its complex and baroque nature, visualisation is fundamentally underpinned by the Mahayana concept of sunyata – emptiness. The practitioner of visualisation is required to recognise that 'the individual is not a fixed entity but a changing process that is empty of ... own-existence ... or subject-object duality'.

The yidam Yamantaka, the destroyer of death.

Specification content

The centrality of practices as expressions of Buddhist ideas.

The centrality of practices as expressions of Buddhist ideas

As we have already noted, one of the distinctive features of Vajrayana Buddhism is the use made of the vajra and the tribu by the practitioner of tantra. Seen as symbols, the vajra is representative of upaya – skilful means – whilst the tribu is representative of prajna – wisdom. The two objects – the vajra and the tribu – are always used together with upaya being described as the father tantra and prajna as the mother tantra. It might be argued that in some respects, upaya covers the multitude of Buddhist practices whilst prajna covers those aspects of Buddhism which might be termed beliefs.

Bhajagovinda Ghosh cites the analogy used in Tibetan Buddhism whereby upaya is the leg and prajna is the eye. What this means is then brought out in the short parable: 'Two men set out to the city of Nirvana, but neither could make much headway because one was blind while the other was lame. Eventually they decided to join forces so the lame man climbed on the blind man's back and so they set out together with the man who had eyes pointing out the way while the man with sound legs advanced along it and thus they arrived safely in the city.' This teaches that practices and beliefs are both essential parts of the way to enlightenment.

One critique of Western approaches to Buddhism is to argue that in the West there is a tendency to focus on Buddhist beliefs and ideas, and to neglect Buddhist practices. Faure suggests that this is a result of seeing Buddhism as above all concerned with spirituality, interiority and individuality. There is in consequence a neglect, rejection or spiritualisation of Buddhist practices such as spinning prayer wheels, circumambulation of stupas and recitation of mantras. All of these have what he terms an apotropaic – designed to ward off evil – and magical – designed to procure benefits – dimension.

However, the general Western approach denies what Faure sees as true: 'that for the vast majority of its Asian followers … Buddhism is first and foremost a form of ritual'. He argues that 'the Western Buddhist elite' are reforming and transforming Buddhism into a religion fit for purpose in the modern world. 'In doing so, they are forgetting one thing: Buddhist philosophy, metaphysics, myth and ritual form an organic whole; it is impossible to dispense with one (ritual) without distorting the others.'

Whilst Faure focuses on Buddhist ritual, there are of course other ways in which it could be argued that practices such as meditation are central as expressions of Buddhist ideas. However, whilst it might be thought that meditation is a central practice for Buddhists, this is not necessarily true, as Lopez points out: 'Indeed, it is useful to recall that the vast majority of Buddhists over the course of Asian history have not practised meditation. It has traditionally been regarded as something that monks do, indeed, that only some monks do; the monastic codes make repeated reference to the needs of meditating monks, suggesting that they represented a group of specialists within the monastic order.'

One example of where Buddhist practice is central as an expression of Buddhist belief is with regard to the acquisition of merit in order to gain a good rebirth. Thus, in a number of Theravada communities, one practice is for the family to give to monks gifts of cloth for robes during festivals such as Kathina and on a daily basis to give gifts of food such as at breakfast.

A development of this practice can also be seen at Buddhist funerals. Here the belief is that merit can be transferred from the living to the dead to ensure a good rebirth for those who have died, and especially to ensure that rebirth in the realm of Hungry Ghosts is avoided.

quickfire

4.8　What is the tribu?

AO2 Activity

As you read through this section try to do the following:

1. Pick out the different lines of argument that are presented in the text and identify any evidence given in support.

2. For each line of argument try to evaluate whether or not you think this is strong or weak.

3. Think of any questions you may wish to raise in response to the arguments.

This activity will help you to start thinking critically about what you read and help you to evaluate the effectiveness of different arguments and from this develop your own observations, opinions and points of view that will help with any conclusions that you make in your answers to the AO2 questions that arise.

In the Tirokudda Sutra the Buddha teaches: 'No weeping, no sorrowing, no other lamentation benefits the dead.' Instead what benefits them is the transference of merit from the living to the dead: 'Those who feel sympathy for their dead relatives give timely donations of proper food and drink thinking: "May this be for our relatives. May our relatives be happy!"' It is through offerings to monks that the dead can benefit: 'It works for their long-term benefit and they profit immediately. In this way, the proper duty to relatives has been shown, great honour has been done to the dead, and monks have been given strength.'

This concept is summed up in a chant taken from the Tirokudda Sutra: 'As water raining on a hill flows down to the valley, even so does what is given here benefit the dead. As rivers, full of water fill the ocean full, even so does what is given here benefit the dead.'

Brazier locates practices such as transference of merit within the wider spectrum of the practice of Buddhist worship within temples and at shrines. He argues that such worship is central as it is an expression of Buddhist belief: 'Devotees make offerings of food, water, candles, incense, music, and other gifts. They kneel and prostrate. They sit with hands in the attitude of prayer. They allow the power of Buddha to enter their minds.'

Study tip

It is vital for AO2 that you actually discuss arguments and not just explain what someone may have stated. Try to ask yourself, 'was this a fair point to make?', 'is the evidence sound enough?', 'is there anything to challenge this argument?', 'is this a strong or weak argument?' Such critical analysis will help you develop your evaluation skills.

Much depends on how 'Buddhists practices' is interpreted. The phrase might include spinning a prayer wheel, reciting a mantra, joining a pacifist demonstration, practising mindfulness or circumambulation of a stupa. In one sense, each of these might not appear to be central at all in terms of expressions of Buddhist ideas. By contrast, practice and belief can be seen very closely linked in the practice of going for refuge, which is perhaps the closest to a credal formula one finds in Buddhism. Often the recitation of 'I take refuge in the Buddha, I take refuge in the Dhamma, I take refuge in the sangha' is accompanied by bowing or prostration.

Batchelor, however, takes a different approach to the word 'practices' and uses it in a much more general sense. 'I no longer think of Buddhist practice solely in terms of gaining proficiency in meditation and acquiring "spiritual" attainments.' Thus, for him 'Dharma Practice' simply consists of four tasks: to embrace suffering, to let go of reactivity, to behold the ceasing of reactivity, and to cultivate an integrated way of life.

Evidence for the centrality of this type of understanding of the term practice in Buddhism can be found in the Kalama Sutta when the Buddha stated: 'Don't go by reports, by legends, by traditions, by scripture, by logical conjecture, by inference, by analogies, by agreement through pondering views, by probability, or by the thought, that this contemplative is our teacher.'

This appears to be a rejection of beliefs per se as being central to Buddhism. Instead, the focus is on Buddhist practices and on the practical outcome that these have in life. It is only through such empirical testing that questions about the realisation of what is true can be settled. Thus, the Buddha declares 'Kalamas, when you yourselves know: "These things are good; these things are not blameable; these things are praised by the wise; undertaken and observed, these things lead to benefit and happiness", enter on and abide in them.'

Key questions

To what extent could it be argued that Buddhism as practised in the West by 'convert' Buddhists lacks any essential 'vitality'?

Does the Western focus on the practice of meditation mean that Buddhism seen as whole has been misinterpreted and misrepresented?

Which should take priority for Buddhists – upaya or prajna?

The practice of worship in a Buddhist temple.

Key quote

The core of Buddhist practice is not the pulpit and the Dharma talk … but the direct encounter between the practitioner and the spirit of Buddha, which is deemed to be eternal and universally accessible … especially so in sacred places established for the purpose. (Brazier)

AO2 Activity

List some conclusions that could be drawn from the AO2 reasoning from the above text; try to aim for at least three different possible conclusions. Consider each of the conclusions and collect brief evidence to support each conclusion from the AO1 and AO2 material for this topic. Select the conclusion that you think is most convincing and explain why it is so. Try to contrast this with the weakest conclusion in the list, justifying your argument with clear reasoning and evidence.

Key skills Theme 4

The fourth theme has tasks that consolidate your AO2 skills and focus these skills for examination preparation.

AO2 Developing skills

It is now important to consider the information that has been covered in this section; however, the information in its raw form is too extensive and so has to be processed in order to meet the requirements of the examination. This can be achieved by practising more advanced skills associated with AO2. The exercises that run throughout this book will help you to do this and prepare you for the examination. For assessment objective 2 (AO2), which involves 'critical analysis' and 'evaluation' skills, we are going to focus on different ways in which the skills can be demonstrated effectively, and also, refer to how the performance of these skills is measured (see generic band descriptors for A2 [WJEC] AO2 or A Level [Eduqas] AO2).

▶ Your new task is this: you will have to write a response under timed conditions to a question requiring an evaluation of **the unique nature of Vajrayana Buddhism**. This exercise is best done as a small group at first.

1. Begin with a list of indicative arguments or lines of reasoning as you may have done in the previous textbook in the series. It does not need to be in any particular order at first, although as you practise this you will see more order in your lists, in particular by way of links and connections between arguments.

2. Develop the list by using one or two relevant quotations. Now add some references to scholars and/or religious writings.

3. Then write out your plan, under timed conditions, remembering the principles of evaluating with support from extensive, detailed reasoning and/or evidence.

When you have completed the task, refer to the band descriptors for A2 (WJEC) or A Level (Eduqas) and in particular have a look at the demands described in the higher band descriptors towards which you should be aspiring. Ask yourself:

- Is my answer a confident critical analysis and perceptive evaluation of the issue?
- Is my answer a response that successfully identifies and thoroughly addresses the issues raised by the question set?
- Does my work show an excellent standard of coherence, clarity and organisation?
- Will my work, when developed, contain thorough, sustained and clear views that are supported by extensive, detailed reasoning and/or evidence?
- Are the views of scholars/schools of thought used extensively, appropriately and in context?
- Does my answer convey a confident and perceptive analysis of the nature of any possible connections with other elements of my course?
- When used, is specialist language and vocabulary both thorough and accurate?

Key skills

Analysis involves:

Identifying issues raised by the materials in the AO1, together with those identified in the AO2 section, and presents sustained and clear views, either of scholars or from a personal perspective ready for evaluation.

This means:

- That your answers are able to identify key areas of debate in relation to a particular issue
- That you can identify, and comment upon, the different lines of argument presented by others
- That your response comments on the overall effectiveness of each of these areas or arguments.

Evaluation involves:

Considering the various implications of the issues raised based upon the evidence gleaned from analysis and provides an extensive detailed argument with a clear conclusion.

This means:

- That your answer weighs up the consequences of accepting or rejecting the various and different lines of argument analysed
- That your answer arrives at a conclusion through a clear process of reasoning.

E: Buddhism and change: the Mindfulness Movement

Specification content

Philosophical understandings of the nature of reality and religious experience found within the contemporary Mindfulness Movement.

Philosophical understandings of the nature of reality and religious experience found within the contemporary Mindfulness Movement

Whilst there can be much debate about the origins of the contemporary Mindfulness Movement, it is generally accepted that Jon Kabat-Zinn (1944–) has had a key role in bringing it to prominence. He has been described as the godfather of the contemporary Mindfulness Movement and as the catalyst who brought contemporary Mindfulness to the West.

As explained in his books, he received his PhD in Molecular Biology from the Massachusetts Institute of Technology in 1971. His research career since then has focused on mind/body interactions for healing and on the clinical applications of mindfulness meditation training for people with chronic pain and stress-related disorders. Kabat-Zinn's work has contributed to the growth of the contemporary Mindfulness Movement into mainstream practices and institutions such as medicine, psychology, health care, schools, corporations, prisons and professional sports.

In 1979 he founded the Mindfulness-Based Stress Reduction Clinic and over the years developed what has become an internationally recognised eight-week course called Mindfulness-Based Stress Reduction (MBSR). Based on his work, Kabat-Zinn has received many awards and has been involved in founding and supporting a number of institutes focused on mind/body interactions for healing.

The focus of the MBSR course is on what might be termed meditative awareness of living moment by moment. Kabat-Zinn describes **seven attitudinal foundations** which are required of all participants in addition to commitment, self-discipline and intentionality:

1. **Non-judging**: being aware of oneself without making judgements about what arises in one's mind.
2. **Patience**: allowing things to unfold in their own time.
3. **Beginner's mind**: allowing oneself to experience things as if it were for the first time.
4. **Trust**: trusting one's own intuition and feelings during the whole process.
5. **Non-striving**: not striving to achieve a goal apart from being oneself.
6. **Acceptance**: coming to terms with things about oneself as how they are.
7. **Letting go**: not allowing our minds to hold on to thoughts and experiences.

In addition, Kabat-Zinn talks about cultivating eight 'qualities of the mind and heart':

1. **Non-harming**
2. **Generosity**
3. **Gratitude**
4. **Forbearance**
5. **Kindness**
6. **Compassion**
7. **Empathic joy**
8. **Equanimity (Calmness and Composure)**

With all of this as the basis, mindfulness practice involves sitting quietly or lying down with eyes closed in a state of meditative awareness of thoughts and

Key quote

Mindfulness is awareness that arises through paying attention, on purpose, in the present moment, non-judgementally. It's about knowing what is on your mind. (Kabat-Zinn)

Jon Kabat-Zinn (1944–) founder of the Stress Reduction Clinic.

Key terms

MBSR: Mindfulness-Based Stress Reduction

Seven attitudinal foundations: non-judging, patience, beginner's mind, trust, non-striving, acceptance, letting go

quickpire

4.9 In what year did Kabat-Zinn found the Mindfulness-Based Stress Reduction Clinic?

Key terms

Self-body-scan: observing in the mind each part of the body

Philosophical monism: mind and body are manifestations of a single entity

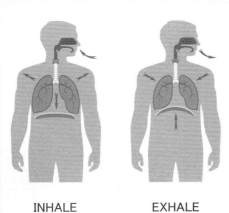

INHALE   **EXHALE**

The process of breathing, which Kabat-Zinn describes as an ally in healing.

quickpire

4.10 What does equanimity mean?

emotions as they rise and fall in the mind. A more focused self-body-scan might also take place where the person observes in their mind each part of their body.

Kabat-Zinn suggests that the key point here is that a person switches from a 'doing-mode' to a 'being-mode'. It is through this process that a person can then learn 'how to make time for yourself, how to slow down and nurture calmness and self-acceptance in yourself, learning to observe what your mind is up to from moment to moment, how to watch your thoughts and how to let go of them without getting caught up and driven by them, how to make room for new ways of seeing old problems and for perceiving the interconnectedness of things'.

The sheer amount that has been written about mindfulness can make it difficult to isolate what might be described as its philosophical understanding of the nature of reality. One of the problems here is that in the contemporary Mindfulness Movement philosophy, psychology and biology meet in assessing what might be termed the science of the mind. This makes the use of appropriate language difficult.

The underlying perception of reality which can be found in the contemporary Mindfulness Movement is highlighted in Kabat-Zinn's first book in this field entitled *Full Catastrophe Living* (1990). The word 'catastrophe' was one which was carefully chosen to be the single word that 'really captures the broad range of experiences in life that cause us distress and pain and that promote in us an underlying sense of fear, insecurity, and loss of control'. In this sense the contemporary Mindfulness Movement is directed at those who feel, at whatever level, some form of suffering or some sense of the 'disatisfactoriness' of life.

At the same time, the word 'catastrophe' is not taken to be wholly negative, since it is meant to sum up 'a supreme appreciation for the richness of life and the inevitability of all its dilemmas, sorrows, traumas, tragedies, and ironies'. Thus, the teaching of the contemporary Mindfulness Movement is meant to resonate with everyone.

In approaching the catastrophe of living, one factor that the contemporary Mindfulness Movement rejects is the philosophical dualism of Plato, Aristotle and Descartes in the sense of the mind and body being distinct and non-identical entities. Instead **philosophical monism** appears to be required. From this perspective the mind and body are manifestations of a single entity. This materialist approach suggests that all that is perceived and understood about reality is the result of physical processes.

The simplest of such physical processes is breathing. It is therefore no accident that one of the first sections of *Full Catastrophe Living* is entitled, 'The Power of Breathing: Your Unsuspected Ally in the Healing Process'. Kabat-Zinn explains the physical process of breathing: 'with each breath, we exchange carbon dioxide molecules from inside our bodies for oxygen molecules from the surrounding air. Waste disposal with each outbreath, renewal with each inbreath.'

However, it is only through focus and control of the simple physical process of breathing that a person can be enabled to develop strategies in dealing with the 'full catastrophe' of living as experienced by the mind. As a result, the mind can only then deal with physical pain and physical suffering.

Another aspect of the rejection of philosophical dualism in favour of monism can be seen in the way in which the contemporary Mindfulness Movement embraces wholeheartedly the concept of interconnectedness. This refers not only to the interconnectedness of mind and body but to interconnectedness in a much wider and holistic sense.

Study tip

Be clear that you understanding the difference in philosophy between a dualist and monist approach to the mind/body question.

From this perspective, the nature of reality does not allow for people to think of themselves as having a wholly distinct and individual existence. One of the sections in *Full Catastrophe Living* is entitled 'World Stress'. Here Kabat-Zinn underlines his perception that since we all live in an interconnected world, 'our individual well-being and health, and that of our families and descendants, will depend on these larger ecological and geopolitical forces'. Therefore, mindfulness has to be 'writ small' on the individual level but also has to be 'writ large' in terms of the human species: 'whatever unfolds from here out in human history, given the condition of our fragile planet and its ecosystems and homeostatic cycles, mindfulness will of necessity be an important, potentially critical factor'.

This monistic approach is further explained in an interview in 2017 when Kabat-Zinn stated: 'the human mind, when it doesn't do the work of mindfulness, winds up becoming a prisoner of its myopic perspectives that puts "me" above everything else. We are so caught up in the dualistic perspectives of "us" and "them". But ultimately there is no "them". That's what we need to wake up to.'

Whilst it is possible to make some sense of the philosophical understandings of the nature of reality within the contemporary Mindfulness Movement, it is much more difficult to address what it has to say with regard to religious experience. For example, Kabat-Zinn has been at great pains to divest the movement of any overt connection with Buddhism as a religion per se. In the same 2017 interview he stated of MBSR: 'I bent over backwards to structure it and find ways to speak about it that avoided as much as possible the risk of it being seen as Buddhist.'

Perhaps an insight into what might be termed religious experience can be gained from one anecdote in *Full Catastrophe Living* where Kabat-Zinn relates how someone approached the Buddha to ask whether he was a God. To this, the Buddha replied, 'No, I am awake'.

That idea of being 'awake' is key to understanding Henry David Thoreau (1817–1862). Thoreau – who is often referred to by Kabat-Zinn – has been described as being one of the key American transcendentalists of the 19th century. This group of thinkers had a loose affiliation to Christian belief, the ideas of Kant, and the poetry of the English Romantic tradition.

Whilst they are hard to categorise, one of the concepts which the transcendentalists shared was the idea of religious experience transcending the intellectual and rational. Such experience could be found particularly in the beauty of nature; however, this was not nature in its extraordinary form but much more in its everyday guise as could be experienced in any rural location. The proviso being, however, that people were fully aware and fully alive to what was around them.

Thoreau's most popular work published in 1854 is *Walden: or Life in the Woods*. In this he gives an account of the two years he spent in simple living at Walden Pond near Concord, Massachusetts. Whilst not the typical religious experience per se, what Thoreau describes is an increased awareness of and greater attentiveness to nature around him – of seeing the ordinary with new eyes and greater insight.

Thoreau explains: 'I went to the woods because I wished to live deliberately, to front only the essential facts of life, and see if I could not learn what it had to teach, and not, when I came to die, discover that I had not lived.'

Living moment by moment, as it were, gave Thoreau what might be termed a sustained religious experience in terms of a greater sense of the otherness of things. 'In eternity there is indeed something true and sublime. But all these times and places and occasions are now and here. God himself culminates in the present moment....'

In *Wherever You Go, There You Are: Mindfulness Meditation for Everyday Life* (1994) – the book which brought the contemporary Mindfulness Movement

Key quote

Science is now searching for more comprehensive models that are truer to our understanding of the interconnectedness of space and time, matter and energy, mind and body, even consciousness and the universe, and what role the human brain, by far the most complex, interconnected, specialised, and ever-changing organisation of matter in the known-by-us universe, plays in all of it. (Kabat-Zinn)

Henry David Thoreau (1817–1862), a key figure in the American transcendentalists.

Key quote

The millions are awake enough for physical labor; but only one in a million is awake enough for effective intellectual exertion, only one in a hundred million to a poetic or divine life. To be awake is to be alive. I have never yet met a man who was quite awake. How could I have looked him in the face? (Thoreau)

quickfire

4.11 What does Kabat-Zinn mean by the term 'catastrophe'?

to the attention of the wider general public – Kabat-Zinn often uses quotations from Thoreau. He suggests that Thoreau's approach of simple living and living deliberately is key to understanding mindfulness. He describes 'Walden' as being 'a rhapsody to mindfulness' because, above all, Thoreau was awake to his surroundings. For Kabat-Zinn, mindfulness is essentially about being 'fully awake'. Thoreau wrote: 'We must learn to reawaken and keep ourselves awake, not by mechanical aid, but by an infinite expectation of the dawn, which does not forsake us in our soundest sleep'. In the last lines of 'Walden', Thoreau asserts: 'Only that day dawns to which we are awake'.

Kabat-Zinn suggests that whilst people might not have the opportunity to do what Thoreau did in his simple living in the woods, they can follow his example in other ways: 'But you don't have to go out of your way or find someplace special to practise mindfulness. It is sufficient to make a little time in your life for stillness and what we call non-doing, and then tune in to your breathing. All of Walden Pond is within your breath.'

Study tip

To gain a greater sense of the contemporary Mindfulness Movement, research and read Thoreau's 'Walden'.

Walden Pond, where Thoreau experienced simple living in the woods.

Specification content

The use of mindfulness in health care, education and business – examples drawn from pain management, treatment for stress, depression and anxiety, cancer-management, addiction treatment, mindfulness in schools, mindfulness in large corporations and businesses.

The use of mindfulness in health care, education and business

One significant area for the application of mindfulness in health care is connected with pain management. Kabat-Zinn distinguishes between acute pain – as caused, for example, by accidentally hitting your thumb with a hammer – and chronic pain – pain which persists over time and which is not easily relieved. In both cases the purpose of mindfulness (building on the commitment, self-discipline and intentionality of the patient and using the seven attitudinal foundations) is to enable a change to take place in the way in which the patient looks at their body and thus at their pain.

Kabat-Zinn suggests that people tend to see their body in the same way that they might see a car – as a separate entity. If the car is damaged in any way, or if part of it stops working then it is taken to the mechanic to fix. By extension if a person feels pain in their body they then go to the doctor to treat the pain through medication.

However, building on the monist understanding, the body which feels pain is not separate from the mind; it is the 'higher cognitive and emotional functions' of the brain which interpret the body's sensory impulses and which then register that what is being felt is painful.

Through mindfulness it is believed that the higher cognitive and emotional faculties can be developed over time in ways which mean that pain is re-interpreted. Thus, rather than thinking in terms of being frightened of the pain, fighting the pain or doing everything possible to avoid the pain, mindfulness is about 'putting out the welcome mat' to pain. Mindfulness encourages the person to carry out their own body scan as they breathe slowly to re-connect with their body. This means that the pain is recognised and accepted in a non-judgemental way. Pain is therefore seen as being a monolithic thing which the body experiences but as something which moment by moment is made up of a variety of sensations, emotions, thoughts and feelings. This shift of understanding can then enable a person to come to terms with their pain, 'to make room for it, to befriend it, to live with it'.

This monist approach to the human person is one which is also the basis of treatment for stress, depression and anxiety, cancer-management and addiction treatment. In these cases, Kabat-Zinn suggests that what happens is that the person is subject to both external **stressors**, which might be physical, social or environmental and internal 'stressors' which might be caused by thoughts, emotions or pain. Confronted with such stressors, Kabat-Zinn suggests that the body's built-in mechanisms maintaining **allostasis** – a term which means remaining stable by being able to change – are put under pressure.

Typically, the body responds to such stressors with an automatic stress reaction of fight or flight – work against or flee from stressors. This might cause increased blood pressure and heart rate. The stress might then be internalised leading to a range of symptoms including panic, inflammation, headaches, sleep disorders, etc. The lack of normal regulation in the body's system then leads to increased demands on the body's allostatic mechanisms.

Depending on the individual patient and their condition, what normally happens is that ways of coping with the effects of the external and internal stressors are then sought out. In some cases – such as when addiction is involved – substance dependency may become the norm as the person turns to illegal drugs. In other cases – such as in depression – overeating may become the norm and the person turns to food. Again, in some cases – for example, when cancer is diagnosed or there are high levels of anxiety – the response might be one of hyperactivity or its opposite, extreme lassitude. In each case, these ways of coping might help, if only in the short term, and they therefore become the fixed way of responding to external and internal stressors which is then repeated. In this way a loop system is formed.

Continually following this loop as a way of coping may – depending on the individual patient – lead to worsening symptoms such as exhaustion, burnout, and other physical conditions, based on the person's medical history, such as increased risk of a heart attack or stroke. Eventually it might be the case that the allostatic overload leads to a physical and/or mental breakdown.

Where Kabat-Zinn suggests mindfulness might have a significant role is in the immediate response to external and internal stressors. Rather than following the route of fight or flight and internalisation of stress, a mindfulness-mediated response might be adopted.

Key quote

So, if a doctor suggests that meditation might help you with your pain, it does not mean that your pain is not 'real'. It means that your body and your mind are not two separate and distinct entities and that, therefore, there is always a mental dimension to pain. (Kabat-Zinn)

Key terms

Allostasis: the body's ability to remain stable by being able to change

Stressors: internal or external factors which cause a person stress

Building on the commitment, self-discipline and intentionality of the patient, and using the seven attitudinal foundations, the patient is encouraged to carry out their own body scan as they breathe slowly and live moment by moment to re-connect with their body. This leads to an awareness of thoughts, emotions and sensations. With cancer-management, for example, it might lead to a sense of greater acceptance of the condition.

In general, patients might then develop a greater awareness and fuller appreciation of themselves and the whole picture of who they are and then of different strategies and options in dealing with the external and internal stressors rather than the potentially destructive responses usually adopted.

Study tip

Work out your understanding of the phrase sometimes used of pain and stress that 'it is all in the mind'.

It is *very* important to note that Kabat-Zinn does *not* suggest that the mindfulness-mediated approach is somehow a replacement or alternative to formal medical or psychiatric treatment. Indeed, he argues that standard treatments might often be the most helpful in terms of preventing the negative effects of external and internal stressors from developing into a destructive loop.

However, he does argue that, for example, when the body displays symptoms of one kind or another, such as those in relation to external and internal stressors, the immediate response of suppressing or eliminating those symptoms via drugs (both legal and illegal) or other ways of coping is in reality a way of silencing the body. Instead, it is quite possible that the body is sending a message that something is out of balance and unregulated and that the underlying cause of the symptom needs to be looked at and given an appropriate response.

MBSR is regarded by some as being a significant tool in a wide area of health care ranging from helping to treat patients with breast cancer through to those with hypertension.

In the specific area of depression, Mindfulness-Based Cognitive Therapy (MBCT) is accepted as another tool for those working in the area of significant and recurring depression. The UK National Institute of Clinical Excellence (NICE) has endorsed MBCT as an effective treatment for prevention of relapse of depression. The MBCT website states: 'Research has shown that people who have been clinically depressed three or more times (sometimes for twenty years or more) find that taking the programme and learning these skills helps to reduce their chances that depression will return.'

The MBCT programme is adapted from Kabat-Zinn's MBSR programme and includes ways of combatting what he terms depressive rumination: 'when your unexamined thought processes wind up generating increasingly persistent feelings of inadequacy, depression, and helplessness'.

MBCT encourages the person with this condition, for example, to calmly observe the processes of their mind, to live in the present moment, to be non-judgemental of themselves, and to – in a sense – 'put out the welcome mat' for their depressive rumination without battling them. In this way, as explained on the MBCT website, a person may 'discover that difficult and unwanted thoughts and feelings can be held in awareness, and be seen from an altogether different perspective – a perspective that brings with it a sense of compassion to the suffering we are experiencing'.

quickfire

4.12 What is meant by the fight or flight response?

Key term

MBCT: Mindfulness-Based Cognitive Therapy

Key quote

Most people come into the program with a relatively high number of symptoms. The average number of symptoms is 22 out of about 110 possible ones. That is a lot of symptoms. When people leave, they are checking off on average about 14 symptoms, or 36 percent fewer symptoms than when they started. This is a dramatic reduction in a short period of time, especially for people who have that many symptoms in the first place and have had them for quite a long time. (Kabat-Zinn)

Outside of health care, mindfulness has also found its way into education. In the UK in 2009, MiSP (Mindfulness in Schools Project) was founded by two teachers and mindfulness practitioners Richard Burnett and Chris Cullen. The MiSP website explains that as a charity it has now trained over 4,100 teachers to provide classroom-based curricula teaching mindfulness-based skills. Through the work of these teachers, mindfulness is then taught both to young people in schools and those who work with them.

MiSP runs through three types of programme: 'Paws b' for 7–11 year olds, '.b' ('dot-b' which stands for stop and be) for 11–18 year olds and '.b Foundations' for school staff and those working in education. Overall, the programmes teach the same type of mindfulness as that espoused by Kabat-Zinn except that it has been adapted for delivery in schools.

This can be seen in the curriculum for '.b'. Amongst the ten lessons are ones focused on 'Being here and now', which teaches how to live moment by moment and to respond, rather than react to situations. Another focuses on 'Stepping back', which suggests a new way of relating to thoughts so that they do not take control and lead young people to places they were would rather not be. Another lesson focuses on 'Taking in the Good' and is concerned with 'gratitude and the heartfulness of taking in and savouring what is good in life'.

However, the foundation of the lessons remains that of developing the skills of meditative awareness, of living moment by moment, through focusing on breathing and through carrying out a self-body scan. One method taught here rather than being called 'meditation' is called 'beditation' – essentially mediation whilst lying down – although the process of stilling, being calm, focusing on the breathing and carrying out a self-body-scan is the same. Some schools encourage the use of 7/11. The 7/11 technique is a breathing exercise where the person breathes in for a count of 7 and out for a count of 11. It is used to help in calming and centring. All of this links back to Kabat-Zinn's initial concept of the importance of switching from a 'doing-mode' to a 'being-mode'.

The possible benefits of mindfulness in education are still under review. MiSP refers to the report written by Professor Katherine Weare (1950–) entitled 'Evidence for the Impact of Mindfulness on Children and Young People'.

In Weare's executive summary of her findings, she notes that mindfulness in education can:

1. Improve the mental, emotional, social and physical health and well-being of young people.

2. Reduce stress, anxiety, reactivity and bad behaviour.

3. Improve sleep and self-esteem and bring about greater calmness, relaxation, the ability to manage behaviour and emotions, self-awareness and empathy.

4. Contribute directly to the development of cognitive and performance skills and executive function.

5. Help young people pay greater attention, be more focused, think in more innovative ways, use existing knowledge more effectively, improve working memory, and enhance planning, problem solving and reasoning skills.

6. Accompany more positive emotions, greater popularity and having more friends, and less negative emotion and anxiety.

Mindfulness may also be found in businesses and large corporations. Kabat-Zinn outlines a general approach for employers and employees in a chapter entitled 'Work Stress'. For many people, work and all it involves can be a significant external stressor. There are of course different types of external stressors depending on whether a person is a manager in the head office or an operative on the factory floor. Whatever the case, Kabat-Zinn suggests that everyone in the field of work can experience 'job stress, insecurity, frustration, and failure'.

Key term

MiSP: Mindfulness in Schools Project

Key quote

Amongst adults there is reasonably strong evidence for the positive impact of mindfulness on a wide range of mental and physical health conditions, on social and emotional skills and well-being, and on learning and cognition. (Weare)

quickfire

4.13 For what is NICE an abbreviation?

Key quote

We are a global community
making mindfulness and emotional
intelligence practical and
accessible. Together, we're working
toward a more peaceful world in
which all people feel connected
and act with compassion. (**Mission
statement of SIYLI**)

quickpire

4.14 What is meant by 'beditation'?

The response of mindfulness is to argue that people need to find ways of renewing their energy, attention and focus. This may mean not overworking to the detriment of overall well-being, not been perpetually distracted at work and not trying to multi-task. It might mean re-thinking breaks and lunch at work by spending time exercising, carrying out a self-body-scan or just breathing. Kabat-Zinn suggests, for example: 'Try to stop for one minute every hour and become aware of your breathing. We waste far more time than this daydreaming at work. Use these mini-meditations to tune in to the present and just be'.

A major work-place issue might be other colleagues and here Kabat-Zinn suggests that people are mindful of their daily communications: 'Be aware of people who tend to relate to you in a passive or a hostile mode. Think about how you might approach them more effectively. Try seeing your fellow employees with eyes of wholeness.'

There are examples of businesses which have invested time and money into bringing mindfulness to the workplace. For example, in 2007 a team of experts in mindfulness, neuroscience and emotional intelligence worked to design a course suited for those working at Google. The 'Search Inside Yourself' course includes many exercises taken from contemporary mindfulness. Guided moments of meditation include, for example, 'Being Present', 'Body Scan', 'Breathing' and 'Simply Stopping'. The course covers topics such as emotional intelligence and self-awareness, self-regulation and motivation, empathy and social skills.

In 2012 the Search Inside Yourself Leadership Institute (**SIYLI**) was founded and, their website states, 'Search Inside Yourself has become a globally recognised program and SIYLI continues to work with Google, as well as other corporate, non-profit and government organisations around the world'.

One case study is that of the German multinational SAP, which is one of the world's largest software and programming companies. In 2018 it was reported that following a trial programme, SAP had introduced mindfulness training to its German staff as a way of enabling them to pay attention to the present moment and to tune into thoughts, feelings and surroundings. Moments of stillness at the start of meetings, mindful eating and walking during breaks were all practical outcomes of the course.

The guiding principle for SAP and other businesses and corporations is that staff who engage in mindfulness may be less stressed, have a greater sense of well-being and a more balanced approach to life. This being the case, the belief is that the staff will then be better at their jobs in terms of motivation, focus and attendance.

Statistics given by SAP suggested that a 1% increase in employee engagement at work translated into a rise of 50 to 60 million euros in operating profit. The mindfulness initiative was seen as providing a 200% return on investment, with the training leading to a rise in employee engagement and a fall in absenteeism.

Study tip

Research ways in which businesses today are using mindfulness for their employees.

One significant counter-argument to the contemporary Mindfulness Movement and its use in businesses and corporations is based on the rationale used by those very same businesses and corporations. As noted above, the evidence from SAP suggests that workers who engage in mindfulness become *better at their jobs* in terms of motivation, focus and attendance. Again, amongst the seven attitudinal foundations of mindfulness are non-judging, patience, acceptance and letting go. Here too, businesses and corporations might benefit since, arguably, the results of mindfulness would be more compliant and less dissatisfied staff. Staff would be more accepting of the level of their wages, the senior management structure and the overall status quo in the work place. Most importantly, staff would be less challenging in terms of any demands made.

Such considerations might well be behind the arguments of the contemporary Slovenian philosopher and commentator Slavoj Žižek (1949–) in an article from 2001 entitled, 'From Western Marxism to Western Buddhism'. He argues that in the post-modern era, the Judeo-Christian legacy, which had been the 'ideological superstructure' of the West, is now threatened in its dominance by what he terms New Age 'Asiatic' thought ranging from Western Buddhism 'to different Taos'. This New Age Asiatic thought has become the new 'hegemonic ideology of global capitalism'.

Žižek's thesis is that Western Buddhism presents itself as the only vehicle for achieving inner peace and 'Gelassenheit' – calm composure – in the face of future shock. The term 'future shock' he explains as meaning how people are 'no longer psychologically able to cope with the dazzling rhythm of technological development and the social changes that accompany it'. Since things move so fast in today's world people increasingly lack the ability to grasp fully in their minds what is happening – they are no longer able to carry out even 'the most elementary cognitive mapping'.

Western Buddhism can then be seen as a solution to this problem because it appears to suggest that people should *not* try to cope with technological development and social changes. Instead, as it might be said mindfulness suggests, they should exercise non-judging, patience, acceptance and above all letting go. Technological development and social changes can then just be seen as further examples of anicca at work in the world; they are 'a non-substantial proliferation of semblances that do not really concern the innermost kernel of our being'.

The 'meditative stance' of Western Buddhism – which would include the contemporary Mindfulness Movement – works perfectly for global capitalism since it enables workers 'to fully participate in capitalist dynamics while retaining the appearance of mental sanity'.

Study tip

Explain how the process of breathing is key to applications of mindfulness.

AO1 Activity

Explain how mindfulness changes human behaviour.

Explain your answer using evidence and examples from what you have read.

Slavoj Žižek (1949–)

quickfire

4.15 Why does Žižek criticise the fact that the contemporary Mindfulness Movement aims to create Gelassenheit?

Key quote

It [Western Buddhism] enables you to fully participate in the frantic pace of the capitalist game while sustaining the perception that you are not really in it; that you are well aware of how worthless this spectacle is; and that what really matters to you is the peace of the inner Self to which you know you can always withdraw. (Žižek)

Key skills Theme 4

The fourth theme has tasks that consolidate your AO1 skills and focus these skills for examination preparation.

Key skills

Knowledge involves:

Selection of a range of (thorough) accurate and relevant information that is directly related to the specific demands of the question.

This means:

- Selecting relevant material for the question set

- Be focused in explaining and examining the material selected.

Understanding involves:

Explanation that is extensive, demonstrating depth and/or breadth with excellent use of evidence and examples including (where appropriate) thorough and accurate supporting use of sacred texts, sources of wisdom and specialist language.

This means:

- Effective use of examples and supporting evidence to establish the quality of your understanding

- Ownership of your explanation that expresses personal knowledge and understanding and NOT just a chunk of text from a book that you have rehearsed and memorised.

AO1 Developing skills

It is now important to consider the information that has been covered in this section; however, the information in its raw form is too extensive and so has to be processed in order to meet the requirements of the examination. This can be achieved by practising more advanced skills associated with AO1. For assessment objective 1 (AO1), which involves demonstrating 'knowledge' and 'understanding' skills, we are going to focus on different ways in which the skills can be demonstrated effectively, and also, refer to how the performance of these skills is measured (see generic band descriptors for A2 [WJEC] AO1 or A Level [Eduqas] AO1).

▶ **Your new task is this:** you will have to write a response under timed conditions to a question requiring an examination or explanation of **the main features of the contemporary Mindfulness Movement**. This exercise can either be done as a group or independently.

1. Begin with a list of indicative content as you may have done in the previous textbook in the series. This may be discussed as a group or done independently. It does not need to be in any particular order at first, although as you practise this you will see more order in your lists that reflects your understanding.

2. Develop the list by using one or two relevant quotations. Now add some references to scholars and/or religious writings.

3. Then write out your plan, under timed conditions, remembering the principles of explaining with evidence and/or examples. Then ask someone else to read your answer and see if they can then help you improve it in any way.

4. Collaborative marking helps a learner appreciate alternative perspectives and possibly things that may have been missed. It also helps highlight the strengths of another that one can learn from. With this in mind, it is good to swap and compare answers in order to improve your own.

When you have completed the task, refer to the band descriptors for A2 (WJEC) or A Level (Eduqas) and in particular have a look at the demands described in the higher band descriptors towards which you should be aspiring. Ask yourself:

- Does my work demonstrate thorough, accurate and relevant knowledge and understanding of religion and belief?

- Is my work coherent (consistent or make logical sense), clear and well organised?

- Will my work, when developed, be an extensive and relevant response which is specific to the focus of the task?

- Does my work have extensive depth and/or suitable breadth and have excellent use of evidence and examples?

- If appropriate to the task, does my response have thorough and accurate reference to sacred texts and sources of wisdom?

- Are there any insightful connections to be made with other elements of my course?

- Will my answer, when developed and extended to match what is expected in an examination answer, have an extensive range of views of scholars/schools of thought?

- When used, is specialist language and vocabulary both thorough and accurate?

Issues for analysis and evaluation

The extent to which the contemporary Mindfulness Movement can be considered to be Buddhist

Whether or not the contemporary Mindfulness Movement has its origins in Buddhism is, in some ways, a controversial question. Kabat-Zinn appears to go out of his way to distance the Mindfulness Movement from Buddhism. Thus, in '*Wherever You Go, There You Are: Mindfulness Meditation for Everyday Life*', he cites the American transcendentalist Thoreau as a key figure in mindfulness.

In the opening chapter of the book, where he defines mindfulness, Kabat-Zinn writes that whilst Buddhists have been exploring the nature of consciousness for thousands of years, their view 'is neither particularly Eastern nor mystical. Thoreau saw the same problem with our ordinary mind state in New England in 1846 and wrote with great passion about its unfortunate consequences.'

As we have noted, one of the concepts Kabat-Zinn highlights from Thoreau's 'Walden' is that of being awake. He quotes one of the last lines of 'Walden' where Thoreau asserts: 'Only that day dawns to which we are awake'. This links into the very definition of the word 'Buddha', which, according to Kabat-Zinn, simply means 'one who has awakened to his or her own true nature'.

Kabat-Zinn's presentation of Buddhism is therefore in terms of 'being in touch with your own deepest nature and letting it flow out of you unimpeded'. Essentially this means that he is content to conclude that mindfulness in itself 'will not conflict with any beliefs or traditions – religious or for that matter scientific – nor is it trying to sell you anything especially not a new belief system or ideology'.

Looking back at Kabat-Zinn's interview in 2017, the interviewer notes that whilst there is a lot of talk about Dhamma, Kabat-Zinn states that 'he's not a Buddhist'. Furthermore, he states that, 'to insist mindfulness meditation is Buddhist is like saying gravity is English because it was identified by Sir Isaac Newton'.

In the very popular 'for Dummies' guide, Shamash Alidina – a mindfulness trainer, lecturer and coach for fourteen years – writes about mindfulness and describes the statement that 'Mindfulness is only for Buddhists' as one of the ten mindfulness myths to expose. Whilst he notes that the Buddha and Buddhists investigated mindfulness, 'Buddhists don't have the exclusive rights to mindfulness'.

The separation of mindfulness from Buddhism has created what some have called 'McMindfulness'. This term is used to explain that in order to make mindfulness palatable and acceptable for the many, it has to be rebranded to maximise its selling potential. Part of that rebranding might mean that mindfulness describes itself as 'Buddhist-inspired' since this adds to its cachet as a tested and perhaps 'on trend' concept. However, at the same time, it has to be severed entirely from its Buddhist origins and linked to non-religious and non-spiritual areas such as neuroscience. In this its marketability and mass-appeal are maximised. As a brand, 'McMindfulness' then combines mindfulness with topics such as parenting, eating and teaching and can be found in its place alongside innumerable other self-help manuals. Mindfulness is now a significant part of the whole global 'well-being' industry.

Despite the secular assertions of the contemporary Mindfulness Movement, arguably there is in the end no escaping its Buddhist origins. For example, the foreword to Kabat-Zinn's *Full Catastrophe Living* is written by Nhat Hanh. It is acknowledged that after Kabat-Zinn was introduced to meditation, Nhat Hanh was one of his teachers. In the 2017 interview already noted, Kabat-Zinn explains how he came to meditation in 1965 through the 'Zen door'. From that time onwards, he has meditated every morning at 5 am.

This section covers AO2 content and skills

Specification content

The extent to which the contemporary Mindfulness Movement can be considered to be Buddhist.

Key quote

Mindfulness, or a mindful awareness, is a universal human attribute and skill, a fundamental quality of being alive, just like the eyes, ears and a stomach are part of a human body. To be mindful is to be aware, and awareness is not and cannot be attributed to any one religion. **(Alidina)**

quickfire

4.16 What is meant by McMindfulness?

AO2 Activity

As you read through this section try to do the following:

1. Pick out the different lines of argument that are presented in the text and identify any evidence given in support.

2. For each line of argument try to evaluate whether or not you think this is strong or weak.

3. Think of any questions you may wish to raise in response to the arguments.

This activity will help you to start thinking critically about what you read and help you to evaluate the effectiveness of different arguments and from this develop your own observations, opinions and points of view that will help with any conclusions that you make in your answers to the AO2 questions that arise.

Key questions

Can mindfulness be separated from its Buddhist origins?

To what extent is mindfulness any different from simply slowing down?

Is mindfulness more difficult today because of the distractions of social media being so readily available on mobile phones, tablets and other electronic hardware?

Key quote

Mindfulness is the miracle by which we master and restore ourselves.... It is the miracle which can call back in a flash our dispersed mind and restore it to wholeness so that we can live each minute of life. Thus, mindfulness is at the same time a means and an end, the seed and the fruit. (Nhat Hanh)

Thich Nhat Hanh (1926–) author of The Miracle of Mindfulness!

AO2 Activity

List some conclusions that could be drawn from the AO2 reasoning from the above text; try to aim for at least three different possible conclusions. Consider each of the conclusions and collect brief evidence to support each conclusion from the AO1 and AO2 material for this topic. Select the conclusion that you think is most convincing and explain why it is so. Try to contrast this with the weakest conclusion in the list, justifying your argument with clear reasoning and evidence.

It might be argued that Kabat-Zinn's success was in reality built on the fact that Nhat Hanh had already introduced the concept of mindfulness to an international audience through his best-selling book published in 1975 *The Miracle of Mindfulness! A Manual on Meditation.*

'The Miracle of Mindfulness' can be regarded as part of the contemporary Mindfulness Movement but it does not distance itself from Buddhism. The many anecdotes and illustrations given by Nhat Hanh are invariably drawn from his experience as a Buddhist or from Buddhist literature. Whilst secular examples might be given, these too are then linked back to Buddhism.

In one example, Nhat Hanh writes about washing dishes using ashes, rice husks and coconut husks – as there was no soap – when he was a novice at Tu Hieu Pagoda. 'Whilst washing the dishes one should only be washing the dishes, which means that while washing the dishes one should be completely aware of the fact that one is washing the dishes.' He explains this as an example of mindfulness – that a person should be focused on what they are doing: not washing the dishes in order to have clean dishes, but washing the dishes in order to wash the dishes. By focusing completely on the task at hand rather than what happens next, a person avoids 'being sucked away into the future' and thus shows that they are capable of 'actually living one moment of life'.

Elsewhere in the book, Nhat Hanh describes walking and sitting in a mindful way and the importance of 'taking hold of one's breath'.

Study tip

It is vital for AO2 that you actually discuss arguments and not just explain what someone may have stated. Try to ask yourself, 'was this a fair point to make?', 'is the evidence sound enough?', 'is there anything to challenge this argument?', 'is this a strong or weak argument?' Such critical analysis will help you develop your evaluation skills.

Ultimately it might be argued that the contemporary Mindfulness Movement is Buddhist because the key term 'mindfulness' is in itself a translation of the technical Pali term 'sati'. In *The Mind Illuminated: A Complete Meditation Guide*, Culadasa, Immergut and Graves suggest that 'sati is 'the optimal interaction between attention and peripheral awareness which requires the overall conscious power of the mind'. Similarly, Batchelor describes mindfulness as being 'aware of what is happening as opposed to either letting things drift by in a semiconscious haze or being assailed by events with such intensity that one reacts before one has even had time to think'. Both definitions fit in very much with Kabat-Zinn's understanding.

A key Buddhist text here is the Anapanasati Sutta – 'Anapana' refers to breathing. In this sutta – perhaps one of the most widely used in Buddhism with regard to meditation – the Buddha describes a monk going to the 'shade of a tree, or to an empty building' who then sits in the lotus position with mindfulness to the fore of his mind. All that happens next is that the monk breathes. The Buddha describes the monk breathing in and out and observing this process: 'Breathing in long, he discerns, "I am breathing in long"; or breathing out long, he discerns, "I am breathing out long". Or breathing in short, he discerns, "I am breathing in short"; or breathing out short, he discerns, "I am breathing out short".' Whilst breathing, the monk then focuses on the body, emotions, mind and the objects of thought. In the monk's practice the Buddha states that during mindfulness, apart from breathing and observing his breathing, the monk should prevent any thoughts that lead to 'greed or distress with reference to the world'.

Arguably, all of this is very much in keeping with Kabat-Zinn's contemporary Mindfulness approach. In the process outlined by the Buddha one can note Kabat-Zinn's seven attitudinal foundations, the commitment, self-discipline and intentionality required, and the seven 'qualities of the mind and heart' of a practitioner.

The extent to which the contemporary Mindfulness Movement offers an antidote to suffering

One of the key suttas devoted to 'sati' is the Satipatthana Sutta. Satipahttana may be translated as 'foundations of mindfulness'. Four such foundations are usually identified as the body, feelings, consciousness and mental objects. However, the key point here is that the Buddha states that mindfulness is: 'the only way, monks, for the purification of beings, for the overcoming of sorrow and lamentation, for the destruction of suffering and grief, for reaching the right path, for the attainment of Nibbana....'

This makes it clear that mindfulness was seen as the antidote to suffering as is also apparent from its inclusion as the seventh aspect of the Eightfold Path. Here what is taught is 'samma sati' or 'right mindfulness'. Right mindfulness is linked with all the other parts of the Eightfold Path with the goal of developing skilful attitudes and actions which will counter the Three Poisons of ignorance, greed and hatred all of which are linked to tanha and are thus the cause of dukkha or suffering.

Traditionally, in itself mindfulness is not seen as an antidote to suffering since the Eightfold Path also consists of the way of wisdom (prajna) and the way of sila (morality). The teaching of the Buddha indicates that all of these are interconnected and one way cannot be separated from and be given a greater importance than another way. Some might argue that this is a key example of pratitya samutpada – dependent origination. From this perspective, since the way of sila includes right action, right speech and right livelihood a person cannot isolate mindfulness and find in it alone an antidote to suffering whilst ignoring the other aspects of the Eightfold Path.

In a commentary on the contemporary Mindfulness Movement becoming 'McMindfulness' Ron Purser and David Loy, suggest that problem of the Three Poisons which are the cause of suffering is not addressed. From this perspective, what is offered by the contemporary Mindfulness Movement is simply a form of self-help therapy which focuses on enhancing attention and reducing stress and which thus enables a person to be a less problematic and more productive citizen. However, this does nothing to directly address the Three Poisons of ignorance, greed and hatred. As a consequence, tanha is not addressed and therefore suffering remains.

From one perspective, the contemporary Mindfulness Movement does not pay sufficient attention to mindfulness as 'samma sati' – right mindfulness. This means that what is being promoted could be regarded as 'miccha sati' – wrong mindfulness. In a commentary on the Satipatthana Sutta, Analyo notes that in order to be 'samma sati', mindfulness is required to be more than just 'a general mental factor'. The necessary combination of mental qualities is required 'supported by a state of mind free from desires and discontent, and directed towards the body, feelings, the mind and Dhammas'. Only this creates 'samma sati'. As we have noted, the contemporary Mindfulness Movement tends to stress that it is not Buddhist and therefore there would be no reflection directed to Buddhist Dhamma. In this way, no real or long-lasting antidote to suffering is being offered.

'Miccha sati' might also be considered using a more extreme example. As we have seen, Kabat-Zinn's seven attitudinal foundations which are required of all participants in addition to commitment, self-discipline and intentionality are non-judging, patience, beginner's mind, trust, non-striving, acceptance and letting go. From one perspective, training based on these foundations alone would be precisely what is required for a person committing a carefully thought-out pre-meditated crime, which would clearly not be an antidote to suffering. Purser and Loy comment that 'the mindful attention and single-minded concentration

Specification content
The extent to which the contemporary Mindfulness Movement offers an antidote to suffering.

Key quote
Uncoupling mindfulness from its ethical and religious Buddhist context is understandable as an expedient move to make such training a viable product on the open market. But the rush to secularise and commodify mindfulness into a marketable technique may be leading to an unfortunate denaturing of this ancient practice, which was intended for far more than relieving a headache, reducing blood pressure, or helping executives become better focused and more productive. (Purser and Loy)

AO2 Activity

As you read through this section try to do the following:

1. Pick out the different lines of argument that are presented in the text and identify any evidence given in support.

2. For each line of argument try to evaluate whether or not you think this is strong or weak.

3. Think of any questions you may wish to raise in response to the arguments.

This activity will help you to start thinking critically about what you read and help you to evaluate the effectiveness of different arguments and from this develop your own observations, opinions and points of view that will help with any conclusions that you make in your answers to the AO2 questions that arise.

Key questions

Given the complexity of the human person, is it too simplistic to state that mindfulness presents an antidote to suffering?

Could 'miccha sati' produce more rather than less suffering in the world?

Should teachers of mindfulness be giving classes to the military?

Key quote

In active military cohorts who received Mindfulness-Based Mind Fitness Training before deployment, working memory capacity was preserved after deployment and … it degraded in soldiers who did not receive the mindfulness intervention. In addition, perceived stress levels decreased among military cohorts who received the intervention compared with controls. (Brewer)

Study tip

It is vital for AO2 that you actually discuss arguments and not just explain what someone may have stated. Try to ask yourself, 'was this a fair point to make?', 'is the evidence sound enough?', 'is there anything to challenge this argument?', 'is this a strong or weak argument?' Such critical analysis will help you develop your evaluation skills.

AO2 Activity

List some conclusions that could be drawn from the AO2 reasoning from the above text; try to aim for at least three different possible conclusions. Consider each of the conclusions and collect brief evidence to support each conclusion from the AO1 and AO2 material for this topic. Select the conclusion that you think is most convincing and explain why it is so. Try to contrast this with the weakest conclusion in the list, justifying your argument with clear reasoning and evidence.

of a terrorist, sniper assassin, or white-collar criminal is not the same quality of mindfulness that the Dalai Lama and other Buddhist adepts have developed'. This is because 'samma sati' must be 'guided by intentions and motivations based on self-restraint, wholesome mental states, and ethical behaviours — goals that include but supersede stress reduction and improvements in concentration'.

The contemporary Mindfulness Movement's whole approach is non-judgemental regarding any individuals who wish to become practitioners – mindfulness is for all. This includes military personnel. In an article in the American Journal of Psychiatry, Dr Judson Brewer describes the work of Dr Elizabeth Stanley, ninth-generation US Army, who has developed Mindfulness-Based Mind Fitness Training specifically for military environments. As we have already noted with regard to pain management, the key issue is of how external and internal stressors are managed. Stanley's programme trains soldiers to both observe their stress and manage it more efficiently. This helps soldiers to deal with PTSD and to be more effective in combat.

That the contemporary Mindfulness Movement has found a place in the military might be regarded as controversial amongst Buddhists since the clear goal is making soldiers more resilient in combat, better able to cope with stress and thus more skilful overall in terms of their operational ability. Since soldiers in combat are likely to be involved in actions which injure and kill, this would directly counter the Buddhist approach of 'ahimsa' (non-violence) and it would also go against the first of the Pancha Sila, non-harming. Here too it might be stated that an antidote to suffering is not provided.

In *The Miracle of Mindfulness*, Nhat Hanh retells the story of the Emperor's Three Questions by Leo Tolstoy (1828–1910). In the story, these questions are: What is the right time to begin anything? Who are the most important people to work with? What is the most important thing to do at all times?

Nhat Hanh summarises the answers which the Emperor receives as being: 'the present moment is the only time over which we have dominion. The most important person is always the person you are with…. The most important pursuit is making the person standing at your side happy, for that alone is the pursuit of life.'

For Nhat Hanh these answers provide 'meaning and direction' for life but if the question is asked as to how these things are achieved, he responds: 'The answer is this: we must practise mindfulness. The principle that Tolstoy gives appears easy. But if we want to put it into practice we must use the methods of mindfulness in order to seek and find the way.' In this way it could be argued that mindfulness provides an antidote for suffering.

Nhat Hanh points to mindfulness as having concerns for others and not just for the practitioner alone. Purser and Loy pick up on this: the danger of 'McMindfulness' is that it compartmentalises mindfulness: 'There is a dissociation between one's own personal transformation and the kind of social and organisational transformation that takes into account the causes and conditions of suffering in the broader environment. Such a colonisation of mindfulness also has an instrumentalising effect, reorienting the practice to the needs of the market, rather than to a critical reflection on the causes of our collective suffering, or social dukkha.'

Culadasa, Immergut and Graves reinforce the same point: through mindfulness a practitioner loses their sense of being a distinct self who is suffering and instead can 'act more objectively for the good of everybody…. Then we will have discovered the true source of happiness, and the end of suffering'.

AO2 Developing skills

It is now important to consider the information that has been covered in this section; however, the information in its raw form is too extensive and so has to be processed in order to meet the requirements of the examination. This can be achieved by practising more advanced skills associated with AO2. For assessment objective 2 (AO2), which involves 'critical analysis' and 'evaluation' skills, we are going to focus on different ways in which the skills can be demonstrated effectively, and also, refer to how the performance of these skills is measured (see generic band descriptors for A2 [WJEC] AO2 or A Level [Eduqas] AO2).

▶ **Your new task is this:** you will have to write a response under timed conditions to a question requiring an evaluation of **whether the contemporary Mindfulness Movement can be considered Buddhist**. This exercise can either be done as a group or independently.

1. Begin with a list of indicative arguments or lines of reasoning as you may have done in the previous textbook in the series. It does not need to be in any particular order at first, although as you practise this you will see more order in your lists, in particular by way of links and connections between arguments.

2. Develop the list by using one or two relevant quotations. Now add some references to scholars and/or religious writings.

3. Then write out your plan, under timed conditions, remembering the principles of explaining with evidence and/or examples. Then ask someone else to read your answer and see if they can then help you improve it in any way.

4. Collaborative marking helps a learner appreciate alternative perspectives and possibly things that may have been missed. It also helps highlight the strengths of another that one can learn from. With this in mind, it is good to swap and compare answers in order to improve your own.

When you have completed the task, refer to the band descriptors for A2 (WJEC) or A Level (Eduqas) and in particular have a look at the demands described in the higher band descriptors towards which you should be aspiring. Ask yourself:

- Is my answer a confident critical analysis and perceptive evaluation of the issue?
- Is my answer a response that successfully identifies and thoroughly addresses the issues raised by the question set?
- Does my work show an excellent standard of coherence, clarity and organisation?
- Will my work, when developed, contain thorough, sustained and clear views that are supported by extensive, detailed reasoning and/or evidence?
- Are the views of scholars/schools of thought used extensively, appropriately and in context?
- Does my answer convey a confident and perceptive analysis of the nature of any possible connections with other elements of my course?
- When used, is specialist language and vocabulary both thorough and accurate?

Specification content

The reasons for the development of
Socially Engaged Buddhism.

Key quotes

Thich Nhat Hanh and his fellow
Buddhist activists sided neither
with the Communist north nor the
anti-Communist south. Nor did they
harbour any desire for political
power for themselves. They sought
understanding instead of conflict.
(Batchelor)

In the 1960s South Vietnam
endured a long and bloody
struggle.... The Unified Buddhist
Church and the Buddhist Struggle
Movement inspired a historic
campaign of mass non-violence
for a third way that could bring an
end to war and establish a neutral
Vietnam.... The movement for
peace was linked with action for
social justice and social revolution.
(Jones)

Study tip

The Specification makes reference to
'receives high media coverage', for
example, the protest suicide of Thich
Quang Duc and the Dalai Lama's Nobel
Peace Prize. Throughout this section
there are many further examples for
you to use.

F: Socially Engaged Buddhism: liberationist traditions

The reasons for the development of Socially Engaged Buddhism

One of the problems with any interpretation and discussion of Socially Engaged Buddhism is that of definition. This is explained by Phil Henry in his *Adaptations and Developments in Western Buddhism* (2013): 'scholars and practitioners alike are divided as to where, when and how a politically or Socially Engaged Buddhism actually first began....'

Some recent scholarship tends to see what might be termed '*engaged* Buddhism' as having its roots in Vietnam. The history of Vietnamese Buddhism is complex but from being introduced from China in the 2nd century BCE it grew and became increasingly popular. Vietnamese Buddhism included Zen, Theravada and Pure Land Buddhism all of which absorbed, adopted and adapted the indigenous folk religions. In addition, Daoism and Confucianism were influential.

Catholic missionaries came to Vietnam from the 16th century onwards and Catholicism became an increasingly significant force. This was further enhanced by the imperial designs of France in that part of the world so that by the end of the 19th century Vietnam was a French colony. Whilst an over-simplification, it might be said that Buddhism in Vietnam began to reassert its identity in the 20th century in response to the French colonial power and to the dominance in some circles of the Catholic Church.

Following civil war which was aided and abetted by world powers, in 1954 Vietnam split into two countries: North and South. The leader of North Vietnam was the communist Ho Chi Minh (1890–1969) and the leader of South Vietnam was the Catholic Ngo Dinh Diem (1901–1963). War between the North and South was in many ways inevitable and began in 1959 with the USA backing the South and the then Soviet Union backing the North. The war finally ended in 1975 when the army of North Vietnam captured Saigon in the South. After this the country was reunited.

It was against the turbulent background of the chaotic complexities of the Vietnam War, that some would argue a form of engaged Buddhism was born. In an introduction to this topic, Kenneth Kraft describes how in the mid-1960s Vietnamese Buddhist monks and nuns 'began working in a non-violent and nonpartisan way to aid their suffering countrymen'. In one incident, 18 Buddhist monks and nuns helped to lead about 200 civilians out of a war zone in the midst of shooting and rocket fire. Kraft notes, 'on that day and on many others, Vietnamese Buddhists parted the red sea of blood that was flooding their land. They displayed the equanimity, the courage, and the selflessness of true peacemakers.'

'Engaged Buddhism' in Vietnam at this time was not, however, a passive approach. What is termed the Buddhist Crisis of 1963 was in effect a movement led by Buddhist monks. They were protesting against what were regarded as the oppressive and discriminatory anti-Buddhist policies of the Catholic President Ngo Dinh Diem. The Buddhist Crisis was marked by civil disobedience, rallies and demonstrations led by monks. The 1963 crisis culminated in a military coup which overthrew President Diem who was then assassinated. Three years later in 1966, the Buddhist Uprising took place where again a leading role was taken by Buddhist monks in struggles against the then military dictatorship and against the continuation of war against North Vietnam. There was more violence at this time with Buddhist militants fighting to defend places of worship as well as rioting.

On 11 June 1963, the Buddhist monk Thich Quang Duc (1897–1963) burned himself to death in Saigon surrounded by 350 Buddhist monks and nuns. The photograph of what happened received huge media coverage. From one perspective it might be regarded as a profound expression of 'engaged Buddhism'. Sallie B. King in her book *Socially Engaged Buddhism* (2009) writes: 'Thich Nhat Hanh has explained that the self-immolations were an effort to communicate the sufferings of war. They were an effort to reach the hearts of those who were prosecuting the war and to touch something there that would make them unwilling to continue to prosecute the war.'

'Engaged Buddhism' might therefore be seen as developing in Vietnam in response to a particular set of historical circumstances which challenged Buddhists with regard to their faith and their way of life. It required Buddhists to become involved and committed in exceptional times of confrontation, injustice and violence. In particular Buddhists were confronted with human suffering on a huge and often personal level and a response was necessary.

Stephen J. Laumakis in his *Introduction to Buddhist Philosophy* (2008) regards Nhat Hanh as fundamental in understanding the 'engaged Buddhist' movement. He interprets the ordination name 'Nhat Hanh' as meaning 'one action' and that it is the 'one action' of founding the 'engaged Buddhist' movement upon which Nhat Hanh's reputation in the West is based. On the one hand, what is upheld is the meditative practices of the monastic contemplative life; on the other hand, what is also upheld is the practical demands of compassionate action in the world. Laumakis concludes, 'one could ... best characterise his life as the "one action" of promoting peace and human rights through "the union of meditative practices aimed at inner transformation and social action for the benefit of society"'.

Part of the 'compassionate action' supported by Nhat Hanh was the founding of the School of Youth for Social Services (SYSS) in 1964 as a programme of the Van Hanh Buddhist University, which he helped to found and where he taught. As Laumakis explains, the students were sent to help anyone suffering from the war. This meant helping villagers with 'their educational, health and economic needs'. Those helping in this way were meant to understand that theoretical wisdom and knowledge found in the Dhamma must eventually lead to enlightened service and compassionate action.

Nhat Hanh joined with others in the SYSS teaching during the week and working in neighbouring villages during the weekends carrying out what was in many ways a form of social work in terms of practical assistance to those in need. It is perhaps this understanding of compassionate action which has found its way into what is now called *Socially* Engaged Buddhism (SEB).

A very different way of understanding the development of SEB is to consider what is regarded as the largest and most successful Buddhist movement devoted to economic development in the world. This is the Sarvodaya movement in Sri Lanka, which started in 1958 through the work of Dr A. T. Ariyaratne (1931–). Sarvodaya is the largest NGO in Sri Lanka and its philosophy and approach is based on the teaching of Mahatma Gandhi (1869–1948) and on Buddhist beliefs. Today over 15,000 villages out of Sri Lanka's approximately 24,000 have adopted aspects of the Sarvodaya movement's teaching. King explains how Sarvodaya rejects Western capitalism and aims to meet only people's needs rather than what might be termed people's desires – their 'greeds'. In this way the Buddhist Middle Path is followed since 'desires are the foundation of dukkha, and they are inherently insatiable'.

Sarvodaya aims to 'awaken' villagers as individuals and then 'awaken' the village as a whole. The ten basic needs include a clean environment, a clean and adequate water supply and simple housing. One of the basic needs is cultural and spiritual development. King argues that this is the 'concretisation of the Buddha's

Key quote

You know in Vietnam, when you sat during the war, when you sat in the meditation hall and heard the bombs falling, you had to be aware that the bombs are falling and people are dying. That is part of the practice. Meditation means to be aware of what is happening in the present moment – to your body, to your feelings, to your environment. But if you see and if you don't do anything, where is your awareness? Then where would your enlightenment be? Your compassion? (Nhat Hanh)

Buddhist monk Thich Quang Duc who burned himself to death in 1963.

quickfire

4.17 Which country was Vietnam a colony of by the end of the 19th century?

Key terms

Sarvodaya: 'Awaken' movement in Sri Lanka started in 1958

SYSS: School of Youth Social Services

Thich Quang Duc: Buddhist monk who burned himself to death in 1963

Key quotes

Because material needs are means and not ends and because the true end is a spiritual condition that includes contentment and what is sufficient, Sarvodaya opposes the usual economic assumption that continuous unending economic growth is both necessary and good. (King)

[SEB] brings a liberal Buddhist perspective to a variety of contemporary issues, from gender equality to euthanasia. It aims to combine the cultivation of inner peace with active social compassion in a practice and lifestyle that enrich both. (Jones)

Key term

Shramadana: giving labour

quickfire

4.18 Why is the name 'Nhat Hanh' significant?

understanding that a hungry man must eat before he can listen to the Dharma'. Villagers then unite in working towards meeting these needs through practical measures such as building roads. This process of working together is called Shramadana, which means 'giving labour'. Again, this is linked to the Buddhist understanding of dana – generosity – which is one of the Six Perfections.

Pratitya samutpada and interdependence are also recognised in that each villager's contribution is as valuable as any other villager's and, likewise, meeting each of the ten basic needs requires work in addressing the others. The multi-faceted approach includes recognising and celebrating the different religious traditions to which each of the villagers belong.

Overall King summarises the work of Sarvodaya as being 'a radical and visionary rethinking of economic theory and extensive practical accomplishments in development and economic empowerment, which 'emphasises the well-established Buddhist values of the Middle Path, moderation and contentment'.

Some have argued that a major reason for the development of SEB has been the growth of Buddhism in the West. Here, SEB has become increasingly accepted as just another aspect of living the 'convert' Buddhist life – whichever Buddhist tradition is being followed – whilst being fully involved and active in society. One example is that of the Buddhist Welsh activist and Marxist Ken Jones (1930–2015).

At various stages in his life he was involved with the Communist Party, the Labour Party, Plaid Cymru and the Green Party. He was a member of the Buddhist Peace Fellowship and the founder of the UK Network of Socially Engaged Buddhists. In his *The New Social Face of Buddhism* (2003), he defined SEB as extending, 'across public engagement in caring and service, social and environmental protest and analysis, non-violence as a creative way of overcoming conflict, and "right livelihood" and similar initiatives towards a socially just and ecologically sustainable society'.

Western influence might also be noted with regard to Nhat Hanh. For example, he was very familiar with life in the USA in the 1960s. During much of that decade he lived and lectured there. He had studied at Princeton University and had lectured at Columbia University. Nhat Hanh therefore knew all about the Civil Rights movement led by Rev Dr Martin Luther King Jr (1929–1968). In some of its aspects this movement might be characterised as being based on socially engaged Christianity given its combination of Christian belief, the pursuit of social justice and the attitude of ahimsa – non-violence.

Nhat Hanh corresponded with Martin Luther King and the two first met in 1966. It was then that he persuaded Martin Luther King to speak out against the Vietnam War. His speeches against the Vietnam War all over the USA led Martin Luther King in 1967 to nominate Nhat Hanh for the Noble Peace Prize. Here, the Mahayana background to SEB can be illustrated by the bodhisattva vow in terms of the vow to save all beings from suffering. It was this which led Nhat Hanh to say to Martin Luther King in 1967: 'Martin, you know something? In Vietnam they call you a bodhisattva, an enlightened being trying to awaken other living beings and help them go in the direction of compassion and understanding.'

Study tip

Research the key facts about the Vietnam War and opposition to the war to gain an understanding of the complexities which led to the development of SEB as a movement.

Thich Nhat Hanh's Mindfulness Trainings and the primary drive to combat suffering

Specification content

Thich Nhat Hanh's Mindfulness Trainings; the primary drive to combat suffering (not just on achieving a positive rebirth or awakening for oneself).

In the mid-1960s, Nhat Hanh founded a new Buddhist order, the Tiep Hien Order, which was for the fourfold sangha – monks, nuns, laymen and laywomen. Its centre is now in Plum Village in France. The Tiep Hien Order provides a very useful way of understanding what is meant by SEB as can be seen in the name given to the Order. The word 'Tiep' can be translated as 'to be in touch with/continuation'. This combines the idea of being in touch with the reality of the world and the mind and continuing to extend the way of enlightenment. The word 'Hien' can be translated as 'making it here and now/realising'. This refers to the way in which compassionate action must take place in the present moment – be realised here and now.

Nhat Hanh translated Tiep Hien by coining a new word: '**Interbeing**'. In the West therefore, the Order is known as the Order of Interbeing. The term 'Interbeing' brings together key Buddhist concepts, particularly that of anatta – the absence of a separate self – pratitya samutpada – dependent origination whereby everything is dependent upon and connected to everything else – sunyata – emptiness – and anicca – everything being part of a continuum of perpetual change.

Nhat Hanh illustrated what might appear to be the complex concept of Interbeing through the example of a sheet of paper, stating that a person could be able to see a cloud floating on the sheet of paper. 'Without a cloud, there will be no rain; without rain, the trees cannot grow: and without trees, we cannot make paper. The cloud is essential for the paper to exist. If the cloud is not here, the sheet of paper cannot be here either. So, we can say that the cloud and the paper inter-are.' In the same way, sunshine can be seen in the sheet of paper. Nhat Hanh concludes: 'And if we continue to look we can see the logger who cut the tree and brought it to the mill to be transformed into paper. And we see the wheat. We know that the logger cannot exist without his daily bread, and therefore the wheat that became his bread is also in this sheet of paper. And the logger's father and mother are in it too. When we look in this way, we see that without all of these things, this sheet of paper cannot exist.'

The point made by this analogy is that nothing can just 'be' due to everything being connected with everything else. For that reason, everything can only 'inter-be'. This provides the foundation for Nhat Hanh's approach to SEB. Each person cannot just 'be' since all people 'inter-be'. This means that the suffering of any person is connected to every person. More than that, the inner world of the mind and the outer world are not separate but are all part of the same reality – they 'inter-be'.

It is against this background that Hanh's **Fourteen Mindfulness Trainings** can be understood. These are based on the dasa sila (five precepts) and are aspirations which help to guide the lives of members of the Order of Interbeing so that through mindfulness training they can create less suffering in their own lives, which will necessarily result in less suffering in the lives of others and less suffering in the world.

The Fourteen Mindfulness Trainings are recited regularly and members of the Order of Interbeing use every opportunity to bring themselves into a state of mindfulness about themselves internally and an awareness of suffering externally. Mindful breathing might therefore be prompted in a variety of ways – by striking a bell at a Mindfulness Centre, by breathing mindfully when the traffic light is red or when the phone rings.

Key terms

Fourteen Mindfulness Trainings: precepts followed by the Order of Interbeing

Interbeing: the absence of a separate self and everything being linked as a part of perpetual change

Key quote

The Order of Interbeing does not consider any sutra or group of sutras as its basic Scripture(s). The Order of Interbeing seeks to realise the spirit of the Dharma in early Buddhism, as well as in the development of that spirit through the history of the sangha, and its life and teachings in all Buddhist traditions. (**Nhat Hanh**)

Key quotes

Practising ethical behaviour can lead to a quietness of mind, seen as essential for understanding and compassion. The ... Fourteen Mindfulness Trainings are intended to deliver a stability of mind and an awareness of suffering, which cultivates compassion to protect people, animals, plants and minerals. (Henry)

Breathe, and bring yourself wholly into the present moment. It is possible that you may experience yourself as part of a continuum, part of the natural world. You may lose your usual sense of any separate self. It is this experience which is wisdom. (Nhat Hanh)

The First Mindfulness Training rejects religious fanaticism and an approach which clings 'to any doctrine, theory or ideology, even Buddhist ones' because this creates suffering. In the second, 'attachment to views and wrong perceptions' is rejected since this too causes suffering. Instead what is stated is that 'the knowledge we presently possess is not changeless, absolute truth'. In the third, imposition of views on others – 'even on children' – is rejected since this too causes suffering. Instead 'fanaticism and narrowness' are to be approached 'through compassionate dialogue'.

An explicit reference to the primary drive to combat suffering can be found in the Fourth Mindfulness Training. This states: 'Aware that looking deeply at the nature of suffering can help us develop compassion and find ways out of suffering, we are determined not to avoid or close our eyes before suffering. We are committed to finding ways, including personal contact, images, and sounds, to be with those who suffer, so we can understand their situation deeply and help them transform their suffering into compassion, peace, and joy.'

The Fifth Mindfulness training focuses on the need for simple and healthy living whilst the sixth is about dealing with anger and the need to look with 'the eyes of compassion' at those causing anger.

The Seventh Mindfulness Training is focused on the importance of mindfulness itself and describes how living in the here and now facilitates 'the work of transformation and healing'. This leads on to the eighth, which considers the importance of communication, since without it there is always 'separation and suffering'. A key point here is the importance of being able 'to listen deeply without judging or reacting and refrain from uttering words that can create discord or cause the community to break'. The Ninth Mindfulness Training refers to truthful and loving speech, and the tenth to the importance of protecting the sangha.

The concept of Interbeing and SEB can be found in the Eleventh Mindfulness Training, which concerns right livelihood – part of the Eightfold Path. This states: 'Aware that great violence and injustice have been done to our environment and society, we are committed not to live with a vocation that is harmful to humans or nature. We will do our best to select a livelihood that helps realise our ideal of understanding and compassion. Aware of global economic, political and social realities, we will behave responsibly as consumers and as citizens, not investing in companies that deprive others of their chance to live.'

Leading on from this, the Twelfth Mindfulness Training is about reverence for life and non-violence, whilst the Thirteenth refers to the importance of generosity. This concludes with the words, 'We will respect the property of others, but will try to prevent others from profiting from human suffering or the suffering of other beings'. The Fourteenth Mindfulness Training concerns right conduct for lay members of the sangha and focuses on sexual relations. To avoid 'suffering, frustration and isolation' these should not take place 'without mutual understanding, love, and a long-term commitment'.

Nhat Hanh's teaching is that each person has the Buddha-nature within them. Through developing mindfulness and living in the here and now, moment by moment, the qualities of love and understanding emerge and thus the Buddha-nature is revealed. Mindfulness, in particular, prevents the person from entering into a negative cycle by dwelling on regrets of the past or on anxiety about the future. Thus, mindful living engenders peace in the individual. By developing peace in themselves, members of the Order of Interbeing are effectively creating peace in the world.

All of this means that a different understanding of achieving a positive rebirth has developed. Nhat Hanh's teaching is that since human beings 'inter-be' with everything else, they cannot be born and they cannot die and they cannot be reborn. Human beings are part of the endless continuum of changing forms. The five skhandas (elements that make up a human being) are like five rivers flowing together: form, sensation, perception, mental formations and consciousness – none having a separate existence and none being identifiable as the self because there is no self. Attachment to the ideas of being and non-being, of the self and the other, of birth and death, of coming and going in rebirth, is attachment to wrong ideas and wrong perceptions.

For Nhat Hanh, it is the removal of attachment to these ideas that brings about nirvana or enlightenment for oneself: 'Nirvana is the capacity of removing the wrong notions, wrong perceptions, which is the practice of freedom. Nirvana can be translated as freedom: freedom from views. And in Buddhism, all views are wrong views. When you get in touch with reality, you no longer have views. You have wisdom. You have a direct encounter with reality, and that is no longer called views.'

Nhat Hanh quotes the words of the French scientist Antoine Lavoisier (1743–1794) as someone who by observing reality around him was able to let go of wrong views and wrong perceptions: 'In nature, nothing is created, nothing is lost, everything changes'.

Once wrong views and wrong perceptions have been removed through the practice of mindfulness, only then can a person become engaged with the world as someone who listens, who responds and who becomes compassionate to the suffering of others. For Nhat Hanh, this is being truly awakened: 'Buddhism means to be awake – mindful of what is happening in one's body, feelings and mind and in the world. If you are awake you cannot do otherwise than act compassionately to help relieve suffering you see around you. So, Buddhism must be engaged in the world. If it is not engaged it is not Buddhism.'

Support for Socially Engaged Buddhism from the Dalai Lama (non-violent protest with regards to Tibet)

As is explained on the office of the current Dalai Lama's official website, 'Dalai Lamas are believed to be incarnations of Avalokitesvara or Chenrezig, the Bodhisattva of Compassion and the patron saint of Tibet. Bodhisattvas are believed to be enlightened beings who have postponed their own nirvana and chosen to take rebirth in order to serve humanity.' The compassionate nature of Avalokitesvara is often symbolised by depictions showing her with many heads and eyes which can see the suffering in the world and with a thousand arms to assist those who are suffering.

The current Dalai Lama – Tenzin Gyatso – has shown through his life, example and teaching, his support for SEB. This has been particularly evident in his non-violent protest with regards to Tibet. As Laumakis notes, since his exile in 1959, the Dalai Lama has 'worked tirelessly to protect the lives of his people, to preserve Tibetan culture, and to promote peace and happiness throughout the world'. His ongoing efforts to promote a non-violent resolution to the political situation in Tibet were recognised in 1989 when he was awarded the Nobel Peace Prize.

In teaching, which is very similar to that of Nhat Hanh, the Dalai Lama has put forward the view that a person can only establish within themselves peace of mind through love, compassion and kindness. This can never be done through the use of anger. In his Nobel Peace Prize Lecture in 1989, he stated: 'As a free spokesman for my captive countrymen and -women, I feel it is my duty to speak out on their behalf. I speak not with a feeling of anger or hatred towards those who are responsible for the immense suffering of our people and the destruction of our land, homes and culture. They too are human beings who struggle to find happiness and deserve our compassion.'

Specification content

Support for Socially Engaged Buddhism from the Dalai Lama (non-violent protest with regards to Tibet).

The Bodhisattva of Compassion Avalokitesvara. The Dalai Lama is believed to be an incarnation of Avalokitesvara or, as known in Tibet, Chenrezig.

Key quote

Therefore, although attempting to bring about peace through internal transformation is difficult, it is the only way to achieve a lasting world peace. Even if it is not achieved during my own lifetime, that is all right. More human beings will come – the next generation and the one after that – and progress can continue. (Tenzin Gyatso, 14th Dalai Lama)

quickfire

4.19 What does Tiep Hien mean?

The Dalai Lama uses the example of a married couple where if one of them establishes peace of mind there will be 'happiness between parents and children; fewer quarrels between husband and wife; no worries about divorce'. This can then be 'extended to the national level' where such an attitude based on peace of mind in individuals can bring 'unity, harmony, and cooperation with genuine motivation. This can then be extended further to the international level where 'mutual trust, mutual respect and friendly and frank discussions can lead to join efforts to solve world problems.'

Whilst the Dalai Lama recognises that this approach to SEB and to establishing world peace is very difficult, he believes that there is 'no alternative'. Everything must begin with each individual's peace of mind based on love and compassion. It is in the mind that a person can cultivate less anger, more respect for the rights of other people, a clearer realisation of the interconnectedness of all human beings and the environment, and an awareness of the suffering of others.

One response to the approach advocated by the Dalai Lama is that it can appear to be a form of passive inaction – the person does not actually 'do' anything as such to bring about peace apart from establishing peace in their own mind. Nhat Hanh responded to this criticism by stating: 'Peace work means, first of all, being peace.... It is not going out for a demonstration against nuclear missiles that can bring about peace. It is with our capacity of smiling, breathing and being peace that we can make peace.'

The Dalai Lama concluded his Nobel Peace Prize Lecture by quoting a prayer he often uses from *The Way of the Bodhisattva* written in the 8th century CE by the Buddhist monk Shantideva. Here again can be seen the bodhisattva vow to relieve all beings from suffering:

'For as long as space endures,

And for as long as living beings remain,

Until then may I, too, abide

To dispel the misery of the world.'

Study tip

Investigate some of the many articles written by Thich Nhat Hanh to extend your understanding of what SEB means for him.

The Dalai Lama receiving the Nobel Peace Prize in 1989.

Socially Engaged Buddhism and its links to supporting organisations: Sakyadhita and the Buddhist Peace Fellowship

Specification content

Socially Engaged Buddhism and its links to supporting organisations: Sakyadhita and the Buddhist Peace Fellowship.

The Sakyadhita International Association of Buddhist Women was formed under the patronage of the Dalai Lama in 1987 by three Buddhist nuns. SEB is linked to Sakyadhita because the association is not one that confines itself to scholarly discussion of the Dhamma or to taking a background supporting role to males within the sangha.

Instead Sakyadhita – which means 'daughters of Buddha' – focuses on enlightening Buddhist women through researching Buddhist women's history and through giving practical assistance in supporting Buddhist women's initiatives. These include education projects, retreat facilities for women, training centres for women, shelters for women who are victims of abuse and women's social welfare projects. The overall goal is to create equitable opportunities for women in all Buddhist traditions.

Sakyadhita lists amongst its objectives:

- To establish an international alliance of Buddhist women.
- To advance the spiritual and secular welfare of the world's women.
- To work for gender equity in Buddhist education, training, institutional structures, and ordination.
- To promote harmony and dialogue among the Buddhist traditions and other religions.
- To encourage research and publications on topics of interest to Buddhist women.
- To foster compassionate social action for the benefit of humanity.
- To promote world peace through the teachings of the Buddha.

> **Key terms**
>
> BPF: Buddhist Peace Fellowship
>
> Sakyadhita: 'Daughters of Buddha' organisation advancing the place of women in the Buddhist world

An example of how Sakyadhita links with SEB can be seen in *Time to Stand Up: An Engaged Buddhist Manifesto for our Earth – The Buddha's Life and Message through Feminine Eyes* (2015) by the Buddhist teacher Thanissara. In this she argues that 'androcentric' Buddhism has tended to disregard the environment and the world by instead focusing on 'personal salvation and the transcendent'. The androcentric approach has to be rejected in favour of 'engaged compassionate action' which is what she believes Buddhist women in particular can bring. Thanissara writes: 'As we face a burning world that needs proactive and effective response, we have to evolve beyond our tendency toward introversion and narcissism as Dharma practitioners – which is often justified by a cynical ethos that sees the world as samsara, and therefore not overly worthy of redemption.'

The Buddhist Peace Fellowship (BPF) was founded in 1978 by Robert Aitken (1917–2010), his wife Anne (1911–1994), and others interested in Buddhism including the Western Zen Buddhist author Nelson Foster. It arose out of group discussions in Hawaii and San Francisco amongst like-minded Buddhists regarding the need for global disarmament. It is linked to SEB perhaps more than any other Buddhist organisation since it sees itself as 'a catalyst for Socially Engaged Buddhism'. Membership of BPF is not limited to any single Buddhist school but includes those from Theravada, Mahayana and Tibetan traditions. Basing its vision on the Buddhist concept of pratitya samutpada, the BPF aims to cultivate positive conditions for peace within those who belong to BPF, within communities in which they live and within in the world in general.

The BPF defines its purpose as: 'to help beings liberate themselves from the suffering that manifests in individuals, relationships, institutions, and social systems. BPF's programmes, publications, and practice groups link Buddhist

> **Key quote**
>
> A Buddhism that removes itself from direct engagement with the struggles of ordinary people will struggle to send roots into the soul and culture of its surrounding community. (Thanissara)

teachings of wisdom and compassion with progressive social change'. The BPF might be seen as the Buddhist representatives in many demonstrations such as those supporting action on climate change or in those opposing military action.

In order to forward what is termed the mandala of 'progressive social change' the BPF overall practice involves a threefold approach:

1. Learning: to build socially engaged Buddhist communities.
2. Speaking: to communicate Buddhist teachings to address situations in the world.
3. Doing: to collaborate with other groups to cultivate peace.

In pursuing the mandala of progressive social change, the BPF leadership training has a threefold approach:

1. Block – which refers to blocking harm and oppression which cause suffering.
2. Build – which refers to constructing relationships, communities and structures as alternative approaches to issues building on Buddhist wisdom.
3. Be – which refers to engaging in society 'in alignment with the dharma' by incorporating the spiritual values of 'wisdom, compassion and freedom'.

Overall, the BPF has what might be termed a left-wing approach. For example, one of its courses is entitled 'What's My Role in the Revolution?' This reflects on the struggle to bring about 'true social and spiritual transformation' in society and suggests that this cannot be done without a new approach. The words of the black, lesbian feminist writer Audre Lorde (1934–1992) are quoted to support this view: 'The master's tools will never dismantle the master's house. They may allow us temporarily to beat him at his own game, but they will never enable us to bring about genuine change.'

The views of Joanna Macy and Damien Keown on Socially Engaged Buddhism

Joanna Macy (1929–) combines her background as a Buddhist in the Theravada tradition with developing psychological programmes in terms of overcoming despair and apathy with regard to ecological global concerns, and reconnecting with constructive and collaborative action. As with other perspectives on SEB, she stresses the importance of pratitya samutpada: 'that law is such that every act we make, every word we speak, every thought we think is not only affected by the other elements in the vast web of being in which all things take part, but also has results so far-reaching that we cannot see or imagine them'.

Macy's reference to the 'vast web of being' builds on a metaphor from Mahayana Buddhism: **Indra's Net**. This is found in a commentary on the Avatamsaka Sutra attributed to Tu-Shun (557–640 CE). It can be summarised as follows. In the heavenly abode of Indra there is a net which stretches out to infinity in all directions. At every connecting point of the net there is a highly polished jewel. Since the net is infinite so too are the number of jewels. If any single jewel is selected and examined, it will be discovered that in its polished surface there are reflected all the other jewels. It will also be discovered that each one of the jewels which are reflected in that one jewel are also reflecting each of the other jewels. In this way the process of reflection is infinite. All things are part of Indra's net which includes all sentient life and all non-sentient life. This holistic view of reality emphasises the point that, for example, what happens to one part of the world in which people live must have an impact on every other part.

This approach is the basis for Macy's interest in ecology. Earth as a planet and all it contains in terms of flora and fauna is part of Indra's Net. From this perspective, issues such as depletion of natural resources, global warming and climate change should be things with which a Buddhist identifies in terms of the suffering which is caused and which can be stopped. Macy's latest work involves looking at the environment in terms of people living at present through the global scenario of 'Business as Usual' in which industrial growth society, extractive economies and speculative financial markets dominate. However, the impact on the earth of this approach is so damaging in terms of environmental degradation that it is unsustainable and could well lead to what she terms the 'Great Unravelling'. Living at this moment, however, there is the opportunity for like-minded people to reject the 'Business as Usual' scenario and argue for something better. Hence this could be the age of the 'Great Turning' in which care for the environment, peace and social justice take the global centre-stage through a Global Citizens' Movement. Here she refers back to Indra's Net so that 'once competitive elements begin to form an exquisite mosaic' and a whole is created that is 'larger than the sum of its parts'.

From the perspective of social concerns, Macy argues that Buddhism has never been 'other-worldly' and cites the example of the Emperor Ashoka 'who in his devotion to Dharma built hospitals and public wells and tree-lined roads for the welfare of all beings'. Here, Macy regards the Sarvodaya movement as illustrative of what SEB can be in terms of combining the Dhamma with social development. For example, the movement has adopted the four abodes of the Buddha as fundamental to its philosophy: metta (loving kindness), karuna (compassion), mudhita (joy of living from making others happy) and upekkha (equanimity). These are translated into daily behaviour and approaches to life in the village.

In this way the focus can be on suffering and an end to suffering in both the psycho-spiritual plane and the socio-economic plane. Macy writes: 'you are not diluting or distorting the noble truths by applying them to conditions of physical misery or social conflict. Their truth lies in the contingent nature of suffering, however you view it. Because it has a cause, it can cease. Because it co-dependently arises, it can be overcome.'

One of the implications of Indra's Net for Macy is that those involved in SEB can choose to focus their energy more precisely on just one aspect of concern regarding what she terms the 'global crisis'. This is because – as with the jewels in Indra's Net – everything is inter-connected. This approach is one that avoids 'burn-out' in terms of those involved in SEB trying to do too much. Thus, for example, the question of whether a Buddhist should try to protect whales or try to stop strip-mining of natural resources becomes redundant: 'If you simply stick with trying to stop the strip-mining, you're helping to save the whales, because it is all interwoven'.

For Macy, the foundation of SEB has to be acting as the Buddha declared using the saying found in the Rig Veda: 'bahujana hitaya, bahujana sukhaya' which means acting 'for the happiness of the many, for the welfare of the many'.

Damien Keown (1951–) presents a very different approach to SEB compared to that of Macy. As an academic, he has published a number of books on Buddhist ethics and is a co-founding editor of the *Journal of Buddhist Ethics*. As he also explained in a series of lectures in Hong Kong in 2010, he would not regard himself as a Buddhist and certainly not as an engaged Buddhist. His approach to SEB is therefore necessarily a cautious one.

Keown indicates that one of the problems in discussing Buddhist ethics in general is the tendency to simplify and to suggest that there is a single Buddhist approach to any given topic such as abortion, euthanasia, politics and social engagement. He writes: 'Just as there are divisions among Christians on fundamental issues, we can expect to find Buddhists occupying diametrically opposed positions on many questions'. However, in discussing the Buddhist approach to ethical issues, Keown argues that a Buddhist view can be established based on criteria such as whether or not the approach can be found and supported in Buddhist sacred texts and whether or not it is one shared by most Buddhists whether Theravada or Mahayana.

Key quote

In the last analysis, what we are and what brought us into being is the Jewel Net of Indra. Co-arising and inseparable, we can never fall out of the web of our reality/home. Opening to its presence and resilience, we can now trust. Moving beyond ego fears, we can risk, we can act. (Macy)

quickfire

4.20 What is meant by 'bahujana hitaya, bahujana sukhaya'?

Key term

Cultural misappropriation: views in the West being read back into the Asian tradition of Buddhism

Key quote

As the momentum of modernisation gathers pace, moreover, it is increasingly difficult, even in traditional societies, to maintain an ostrich-like attitude and hope that the problems of modernity will simply 'go away' and allow monks to resume an untroubled medieval pace of life. (Keown)

quickfire

4.21 What is meant by 'Block, Build, Be'?

Study tip

Check your notes on pratityasamutpada and explain in your own words its significance with regard to SEB.

AO1 Activity

Explain what is meant by Socially Engaged Buddhism.

Explain your answer using evidence and examples from what you have read.

In stressing the complexity of Buddhism, particularly in terms of its early historical development, Keown challenges the view which sees some form of authentic Buddhism as a rejection of ordinary daily life in which the sole focus is on meditation and one's own enlightenment. Peter Hershock writing about Buddhist ethics in the modern era comments: 'Although some have been tempted to see the rise of socially engaged forms of Buddhist thought and practice as a relatively recent development, in Asia as well as in the West, Keown's work compels recognition that Buddhism emerged and evolved not only within, but also in response to, complex social milieus.'

With regard to SEB, Keown recognises the approach taken by some Buddhists which would be to say that such topics are 'not the kind of thing a monk should be concerned with'. However, this view cannot survive for Buddhists in the West. Here, rather than the focus being on the monastic sangha, convert Buddhists are much more likely to be found in a wide range of lay organisations. Keown notes that in such contexts, 'group members discuss their understanding of Buddhist teachings in a free and informed manner, and are more ready to challenge, criticise and reform notions that seem outdated or mistaken'. For Keown, SEB is essential because 'if Buddhism does not rise to the challenge of the modern world it will atrophy and die'.

In addition, Keown sees engagement with the world as very much building upon the example of the Buddha himself whose 'lifetime's work was directed towards the well-being of the world and was carried out in a social milieu'. Keown argues that when the Buddha is seen as a teacher, it should be recognised that he was 'neither evasive nor equivocal, and seemed to have held the view that solutions to moral dilemmas existed and could be found'. The Dhamma as an eternal moral law can be applied in any situation – what is required is 'reason, analysis, reflection and meditation'. In this sense the Buddha is 'a moral realist'.

With regard to SEB and the ethical issues Keown writes about, such as cloning, there is often no clear statement from the Buddha or from Buddhist sacred texts. This can make the work of those involved with SEB complicated – 'a bit like assembling a jigsaw'. References in sacred texts, stories, parables, commentaries all need to be examined and put together to form a coherent pattern. Quite often this might present a whole new perspective on a topic dealt with by SEB. The key point here is that often what is required is not just acceptance of previously held teaching but 'imagination and creativity' and 'active engagement' with what has been passed down.

At the same time, Keown sounds a note of caution which can be applied to SEB. He uses the term 'cultural misappropriation' to refer to the situation when views held in the West today are 'read back' into what is essentially an Asian tradition. This process can happen when 'convert' Buddhists who are themselves 'open-minded, rational, eco-friendly, kind to animals, pacifist and neither authoritarian nor doctrinaire' find in Buddhism a mirror of their own views. Keown terms this type of conception 'liberal Buddhism' and suggests that this is a construct based on the reaction to certain dogmatic Christian beliefs and on Western culture. He concludes: 'Buddhist sources ... reveal a much more untidy and at times contradictory picture made up of different strands. To select only those which are in harmony with fashionable trends in Western society is to treat Buddhism superficially, and fail to engage seriously with its views.'

However, it might be argued that for Keown SEB is essential since it involves itself in the world of politics, economics and medicine and challenges an approach which would be entirely secular. This keeps Buddhism relevant. In many ways without SEB, 'as the status and authority of the secular world grows' it might happen that 'there will soon come a time when the monastery is so divorced from the daily life of ordinary folk that it has no more relevance than a museum exhibit or historical theme park'.

AO1 Developing skills

It is now important to consider the information that has been covered in this section; however, the information in its raw form is too extensive and so has to be processed in order to meet the requirements of the examination. This can be achieved by practising more advanced skills associated with AO1. For assessment objective 1 (AO1), which involves demonstrating 'knowledge' and 'understanding' skills, we are going to focus on different ways in which the skills can be demonstrated effectively, and also, refer to how the performance of these skills is measured (see generic band descriptors for A2 [WJEC] AO1 or A Level [Eduqas] AO1).

▶ **Your new task is this:** It is impossible to cover all essays in the time allowed by the course; however, it is a good exercise to develop detailed plans that can be utilised under timed conditions. As a last exercise:

1. Create some ideal plans by using what we have done so far in the Theme 4 Developing Skills sections.

2. This time stop at the planning stage and exchange plans with a study partner.

3. Check each other's plans carefully. Talk through any omissions or extras that could be included, not forgetting to challenge any irrelevant materials.

4. Remember, collaborative learning is very important for revision. It not only helps to consolidate understanding of the work and appreciation of the skills involved, it is also motivational and a means of providing more confidence in one's learning. Although the examination is sat alone, revising as a pair or small group is invaluable.

When you have completed each plan, as a pair or small group refer to the band descriptors for A2 (WJEC) or A Level (Eduqas) and in particular have a look at the demands described in the higher band descriptors towards which you should be aspiring. Ask yourself:

- Does my work demonstrate thorough, accurate and relevant knowledge and understanding of religion and belief?
- Is my work coherent (consistent or make logical sense), clear and well organised?
- Will my work, when developed, be an extensive and relevant response which is specific to the focus of the task?
- Does my work have extensive depth and/or suitable breadth and have excellent use of evidence and examples?
- If appropriate to the task, does my response have thorough and accurate reference to sacred texts and sources of wisdom?
- Are there any insightful connections to be made with other elements of my course?
- Will my answer, when developed and extended to match what is expected in an examination answer, have an extensive range of views of scholars/schools of thought?
- When used, is specialist language and vocabulary both thorough and accurate?

Key skills Theme 4

The fourth theme has tasks that consolidate your AO2 skills and focus these skills for examination preparation.

Key skills

Knowledge involves:

Selection of a range of (thorough) accurate and relevant information that is directly related to the specific demands of the question.

This means:

- Selecting relevant material for the question set
- Be focused in explaining and examining the material selected.

Understanding involves:

Explanation that is extensive, demonstrating depth and/or breadth with excellent use of evidence and examples including (where appropriate) thorough and accurate supporting use of sacred texts, sources of wisdom and specialist language.

This means:

- Effective use of examples and supporting evidence to establish the quality of your understanding
- Ownership of your explanation that expresses personal knowledge and understanding and NOT just a chunk of text from a book that you have rehearsed and memorised.

Specification content

Social justice as a requisite for the observance of Buddhist teachings.

Key quote

Besides being cloistered, [Zen] became esoteric and elite – doubly estranged from the surrounding community. Concerned with the preservation and elaboration of its genius, it devoted its resources to the enlightenment of its members and growth and improvement of its monasteries. Building its institutions became the dominant means of promoting the Dharma, and in pursuing this course, many abbots made the mistake of forming unholy alliances with the wealthy and the powerful. **(Foster)**

AO2 Activity

As you read through this section try to do the following:

1. Pick out the different lines of argument that are presented in the text and identify any evidence given in support.

2. For each line of argument try to evaluate whether or not you think this is strong or weak.

3. Think of any questions you may wish to raise in response to the arguments.

This activity will help you to start thinking critically about what you read and help you to evaluate the effectiveness of different arguments and from this develop your own observations, opinions and points of view that will help with any conclusions that you make in your answers to the AO2 questions that arise.

Issues for analysis and evaluation

Social justice as a requisite for the observance of Buddhist teachings

From one perspective of Buddhism overall, the Ten Ox Herding Pictures, which depict stages of practice in Zen Buddhism, illustrate what for many is their understanding of Buddhism in general. Namely that it is concerned with a person being detached, remote and other-worldly as they proceed on their individual quest for some form of personal enlightenment.

As the Buddhist scholar Kenneth Kraft (1949–) noted: 'In the early stages of spiritual seeking … most of a practitioner's attention and energy are devoted to the path that leads inward'. Only in the last picture is there a return to society depicted as entering the market place with helping hands. As Kraft comments, of these ten pictures 'which trace the stages of deepening insight into True-nature … only the last points back out to the world'.

Reflecting on the Ten Ox Herding Pictures, it might be argued that since the thrust of Zen Buddhism is on personal enlightenment, then issues such as social justice cannot be seen as a requisite. Writing on the theme of Zen and entering the market place with helping hands, Foster noted in his earlier writing that 'it is remarkable that Zen lacks a clear tradition of social action'. He acknowledges that there are 'isolated examples of people striking out on independent paths of social service' and writings on bodhisattva vows and the precepts which 'address life's largest ethical issues in ways that are congenial with social service'.

Overall, however, Foster typifies Zen of the past as 'confining the sangha's vitality within monastery walls'. Within the 'hothouse conditions' of the monastery setting, much was created which is still appreciated today, such as the tradition of Zen gardens, haikus, tea ceremonies, calligraphy and austere tranquillity. However, this came at the cost of Zen being engaged with what was going on outside the gates of the monastery. In other words, the need to enter the market place with helping hands was seen to be of very limited and marginal interest and use.

Foster characterises the development of Zen in China, Korea and Japan as being a steady process of introversion during which social constraint and social conformity became the pattern and indeed the goal. Thus, the requisite for the observance of Buddhist teachings was certainly not social justice but rather obedience to social norms. Foster seems to suggest that in this process, Zen Buddhism somehow lost part of what it was to be authentically Buddhist in following the Dhamma and the example of the Buddha.

In his presentation of Zen, Foster argues that it is only 'as Zen moves West' and becomes free of its past restrictions that it is able to engage with what he terms the politics of prajna – 'the values orientation inherent to the experience of wisdom'. For him, the politics of prajna are a simple recognition of the reality that 'merely by living and thinking, we are involved in intentional political activity'. American sanghas 'can be seen shattering some of the strictures that have bound Zen in Asia'. Now, 'American Zen seems free to develop according to the lights of prajna'.

Reflecting on Foster's presentation of Zen Buddhism is a helpful way of looking at what is a controversial area with regard to Buddhism and social justice in general. The fundamental question here is as to whether the Buddha himself would have regarded social justice as a requisite for the observance of his teaching. For example, Jones quotes the Buddhist scholar Christopher Queen, who concludes that 'after eighty years of new research, many specialists are inclined to agree … that in its essence primitive Buddhism was not based on service to others, but on the quest for individual enlightenment'.

Some might support this view since in the Four Noble Truths and the Eightfold Path there is nothing which indicates an explicit concern with what Foster calls the politics of prajna. Thus, social justice and the concept of entering the market place with helping hands does not appear to rank highly, if at all, in the concerns of the Buddha and early Buddhism.

For example, anicca (impermanence) applies to everything including the structures of the society in which people live. That being the case, it might be seen to be a misuse of time and effort to focus on tinkering with such structures given that they will – by the nature of things – change over time regardless of what any person does. This might be seen to be even more the case given that everything including concerns about social justice has about it the quality of sunyata (emptiness). Such a view might be reinforced by the viewpoint that the world is part of samsara and that the Buddhist goal is to escape from samsara rather than to change it.

That the Buddha only taught how an individual can achieve their own enlightenment through freedom from dukkha is the conclusion of the Buddhist scholar Richard Gombrich. He argues that the Buddha was concerned with this 'pure soteriology' and that he was not some kind of 'social reformer' even though 'as an unintended consequence of his teaching' some might argue that the Buddha 'made life in the world more worth living'.

Study tip

It is vital for AO2 that you actually discuss arguments and not just explain what someone may have stated. Try to ask yourself, 'was this a fair point to make?', 'is the evidence sound enough?', 'is there anything to challenge this argument?', 'is this a strong or weak argument?' Such critical analysis will help you develop your evaluation skills.

Arguably, the Ten Ox Herding Pictures might suggest that the purpose and goal of the individual quest for personal enlightenment is only to be found in the Tenth Picture – entering the market place with helping hands. Thus, the whole process of looking inwards is undertaken in order that this can lead to looking outwards and seeing reality as it truly is. Only when this is done can social justice as a requisite for the observance of Buddhist teachings be recognised.

It might be noted that one of the main goals of any Buddhist who meditates is to identify and remove from themselves the three poisons of ignorance, greed and hatred. It is these three poisons which are the centre of samsara and which are the cause of individual tanha and consequently of individual dukkha. The Mindful Awareness lecturer Diane Winston argues that it is through this process of looking inwards that those structures of external reality which cause the three poisons can be recognised. Compassion for those who perpetuate the three poisons can only then be invoked along with 'insight into understanding just how and why those structures work, and what could be done about them'.

Overall the point made by Keown above is worth restating – that 'imagination and creativity' alongside a deep understanding of Buddhist sacred texts is required to gain an insight into the Buddha's teaching on social justice. For example, it might be argued that economic welfare is the cornerstone of social justice. In this context Walpola Rahula (1907–1997) refers to the conversation between the Buddha and the banker Anathapindika. Here, four kinds of happiness are explained: that caused by economic security, that caused by being generous with wealth, that caused by being free from debts and that caused by the spiritual happiness of living a blameless life. Thus, it can be argued that social justice as exemplified by material progress is encouraged by Buddhism but that what happens externally can only be truly progressive if it is based on the internal 'development of the moral and spiritual character'.

Key questions

What is meant by 'social justice'?

To what extent can social justice be important to a person seeking their own Awakening?

Is everyone, through kamma and through simply living and breathing, caught up in the recognition and pursuit of social justice?

Key quote

The primary goal of Buddhism is not a stable order or a just society but the discovery of genuine freedom (or awakening) for each person…. Even the vocation of the bodhisattva is not as social reformer, but as the catalyst to personal transformation within society. (Buddhist scholar Bardwell L Smith)

AO2 Activity

List some conclusions that could be drawn from the AO2 reasoning from the above text; try to aim for at least three different possible conclusions. Consider each of the conclusions and collect brief evidence to support each conclusion from the AO1 and AO2 material for this topic. Select the conclusion that you think is most convincing and explain why it is so. Try to contrast this with the weakest conclusion in the list, justifying your argument with clear reasoning and evidence.

Specification content

Social engagement as a distraction on
the path to Awakening.

Social engagement as a distraction on the path to Awakening

In discussing Buddhist social engagement, Jones presents the following parable: 'Once upon a time there was an enlightened king who wished to relieve all his subjects of suffering. Everywhere, there were thorns and sharp stones underfoot. His chief minister suggested carpeting the kingdom in leather, wall to wall. But the finance minister objected that it would be impracticable. Then the king had the bright idea that each of his subjects should tie their own piece of leather to their feet. With sandals they could each "be a refuge" unto themselves.'

What this parable suggests is that the normative approach of Buddhism has been that there could be no change to those harsh circumstances of life such as widespread poverty and disease which contributed to dukkha in the world 'out there'. To use Jones's analogy, 'wall to wall' carpeting was never a realistic option. That being the case, the focus of Buddhism has been on giving individuals the means to follow the spiritual path to enlightenment through teachings such as the Four Noble Truths. Again, to use Jones's analogy, each person makes their own sandals. Only in this way can dukkha be overcome.

Today in the West, in particular, the world 'out there' has changed completely. Advances in science, technology, medicine, education, sanitation and communication – alongside an increase in personal wealth and standards of living – have improved many of the harsh circumstances of the world 'out there'. Thus, the 'wall to wall' carpeting approach to suffering seems to be an increasing possibility.

That being the case, should the priority for Western Buddhists now be focused on the remaining problematic areas of the world 'out there' such as tackling all forms of discrimination? Again, should it be on providing affordable housing, supporting anti-globalisation campaigns and marching for nuclear disarmament? Or, should it be upholding the rights of non-human sentient life forms and protecting the integrity of Gaia – Mother Earth – from human-caused global warming and climate change?

Arguably the problem with focusing on the world 'out there' in this way is that there is nothing particularly Buddhist about it. In some ways there might therefore be very little to distinguish between the concerns of Buddhists, Humanists, Atheists and those belonging to any and all of the world's religions as they campaign for a better world. All could equally share the dictum of the Dalai Lama: 'There is no need for complicated philosophies, not even for temples. Our own brain, our own heart is our temple. The philosophy is kindness.'

From one perspective, such focus on social engagement can become a distraction from personal enlightenment. As the 11th-century CE Tibetan Buddhist Milarepa observed: 'Even without seeking to benefit others, it is with difficulty that works done even in one's own interest are successful. It is as if a man helplessly drowning were to try to save another man in the same predicament. One should not be over-anxious and hasty in setting out to serve others before one has oneself realised Truth in its fullness; to be so, would be like the blind leading the blind.'

One response to Jones's parable is to reflect that the 'wall to wall' approach to removing dukkha from the world 'out there' is a Western colonisation of Buddhism which emerged following the 1960s. This type of social engagement is seen as political and secular, and is so focused on acting, doing, changing, challenging, demonstrating and protesting that it presents nothing but distractions on the path to personal enlightenment. Such a response might be supported by arguing that social engagement as understood in the West is not consistent with the teaching of the Buddha. The words of the Dhammapada (167–8) might be cited: 'Don't associate with wrong views. Don't busy yourself with the world. Get up! Don't be heedless. Live the Dhamma well'. Thus, social engagement might be regarded as

Key quote

The challenge of social activism is a valuable opportunity to further our practice of the Dharma, as mindful action, mindful service. This is so because it is our root existential condition that is primary. It is from this that our social condition originates, and the radical remedy for the ills of that social condition depends on a no less radical change in the kind of person we typically are. [Jones]

AO2 Activity

As you read through this section try to do the following:

1. Pick out the different lines of argument that are presented in the text and identify any evidence given in support.

2. For each line of argument try to evaluate whether or not you think this is strong or weak.

3. Think of any questions you may wish to raise in response to the arguments.

This activity will help you to start thinking critically about what you read and help you to evaluate the effectiveness of different arguments and from this develop your own observations, opinions and points of view that will help with any conclusions that you make in your answers to the AO2 questions that arise.

no more than 'busying oneself with the world', being heedless and not 'living the Dhamma well'. Furthermore, seeing social engagement in the Dhamma might be considered to be the result of looking at it through a modernised and Western lens which has distorted its authentic message.

An alternative response to Jones's parable is to reflect that Buddhists *should* embrace the 'wall to wall' approach to removing dukkha from the world 'out there'. Arguably, such social engagement is not a distraction on the path to personal enlightenment because it is rooted in the mission of the Buddha. He declared: 'Both formerly and now, it is only suffering that I describe and the cessation of suffering'. It might be said that rather than providing a distorting lens, Western Buddhism has uncovered through textual studies the authentic Dhamma and Buddhism's commitment to social engagement. In addition, it might be argued that Western Buddhists are not heedless in busying themselves with the world, because social engagement is built on practice such as meditation. It might be said that the whole purpose of personal enlightenment is to follow the Buddha's example. Once awakened at Bodh Gaya, he left that place *not* to find an isolated spot for meditation but to engage with people in villages and towns so they might 'live the Dhamma well'.

Study tip

It is vital for AO2 that you actually discuss arguments and not just explain what someone may have stated. Try to ask yourself, 'was this a fair point to make?', 'is the evidence sound enough?', 'is there anything to challenge this argument?', 'is this a strong or weak argument?' Such critical analysis will help you develop your evaluation skills.

Thomas Yarnall's categorisation of Buddhist social engagement suggested in 2000 remains controversial. He argues that there are two approaches.

Traditionist Engaged Buddhists are those who believe that there is *no* split between the other worldly/spiritual/soteriological dimension and the this worldly/social/political dimension to Buddhism. For a Traditionist, to be Buddhist means to be active in social engagement because this continues the Buddhist tradition traced back to the Buddha himself. Arguably this approach is present in, for example, the teaching of Nhat Hanh: 'So, the Buddha is not in the mountain. He is considered to be in everyone, so that the peace and well-being of the whole people require that every Buddhist should fulfil his responsibility to the community while not neglecting his inner life.'

Modernist Engaged Buddhists are those who believe that the this worldly/social/political dimension to Buddhism was latent but not realised in Buddhist beliefs and teachings. It only became manifest and realised when Buddhism encountered the West in modern times. The resulting movement of social engagement has some of the traditional features of Buddhism, but because it is engaging with the modern Western world there is much in it that is new. For a Modernist, to be Buddhist means to be active in social engagement in a different way because the complexities of dukkha today are unique. Thus, there is an inevitable discontinuity between Buddhists today and Buddhists belonging to the pre-modern era. It might be said that this approach can be found in the observations of Foster: 'The ancient teachers did not live in a world as ruined and miserable and precarious as ours. We cannot know how they would have responded had they felt the urgency of the atomic age.'

The debate is ongoing. Is Buddhist social engagement simply the application of the politics of prajna as an inevitable part of being on the path to personal enlightenment? Or is Western Buddhist social engagement so unprecedented that it should be seen as a standing alongside Theravada and Mahayana as a Navayana – a new Buddhist vehicle for the West?

Key questions

To what extent is suffering so great in the world 'out there' that Buddhist social engagement can never make any difference?

Should Buddhist social engagement ever involve violent confrontation?

How far should social engagement be seen as taking place before or after personal Awakening?

Key quote

Buddhism means to be awake … mindful of what is happening…. If you are awake you cannot do otherwise than act compassionately to help relieve suffering you see around you. So, Buddhism must be engaged in the world. If it is not engaged it is not Buddhism. (Nhat Hanh)

AO2 Activity

List some conclusions that could be drawn from the AO2 reasoning from the above text; try to aim for at least three different possible conclusions. Consider each of the conclusions and collect brief evidence to support each conclusion from the AO1 and AO2 material for this topic. Select the conclusion that you think is most convincing and explain why it is so. Try to contrast this with the weakest conclusion in the list, justifying your argument with clear reasoning and evidence.

Key skills Theme 4

The fourth theme has tasks that consolidate your AO2 skills and focus these skills for examination preparation.

Key skills

Analysis involves:

Identifying issues raised by the materials in the AO1, together with those identified in the AO2 section, and presents sustained and clear views, either of scholars or from a personal perspective ready for evaluation.

This means:

- That your answers are able to identify key areas of debate in relation to a particular issue

- That you can identify, and comment upon, the different lines of argument presented by others

- That your response comments on the overall effectiveness of each of these areas or arguments.

Evaluation involves:

Considering the various implications of the issues raised based upon the evidence gleaned from analysis and provides an extensive detailed argument with a clear conclusion.

This means:

- That your answer weighs up the consequences of accepting or rejecting the various and different lines of argument analysed

- That your answer arrives at a conclusion through a clear process of reasoning.

AO2 Developing skills

It is now important to consider the information that has been covered in this section; however, the information in its raw form is too extensive and so has to be processed in order to meet the requirements of the examination. This can be achieved by practising more advanced skills associated with AO2. For assessment objective 2 (AO2), which involves 'critical analysis' and 'evaluation' skills, we are going to focus on different ways in which the skills can be demonstrated effectively, and also, refer to how the performance of these skills is measured (see generic band descriptors for A2 [WJEC] AO2 or A Level [Eduqas] AO2).

▶ **Your new task is this:** It is impossible to cover all essays in the time allowed by the course; however, it is a good exercise to develop detailed plans that can be utilised under timed conditions. As a last exercise:

1. Create some ideal plans by using what we have done so far in the Theme 4 Developing Skills sections.

2. This time stop at the planning stage and exchange plans with a study partner.

3. Check each other's plans carefully. Talk through any omissions or extras that could be included, not forgetting to challenge any irrelevant materials.

4. Remember, collaborative learning is very important for revision. It not only helps to consolidate understanding of the work and appreciation of the skills involved, it is also motivational and a means of providing more confidence in one's learning. Although the examination is sat alone, revising as a pair or small group is invaluable.

When you have completed the task, refer to the band descriptors for A2 (WJEC) or A Level (Eduqas) and in particular have a look at the demands described in the higher band descriptors towards which you should be aspiring. Ask yourself:

- Is my answer a confident critical analysis and perceptive evaluation of the issue?

- Is my answer a response that successfully identifies and thoroughly addresses the issues raised by the question set?

- Does my work show an excellent standard of coherence, clarity and organisation?

- Will my work, when developed, contain thorough, sustained and clear views that are supported by extensive, detailed reasoning and/or evidence?

- Are the views of scholars/schools of thought used extensively, appropriately and in context?

- Does my answer convey a confident and perceptive analysis of the nature of any possible connections with other elements of my course?

- When used, is specialist language and vocabulary both thorough and accurate?

Questions and answers

Theme 1: DEF

AO1 answer: *An answer examining the importance of the Heart Sutra.*

A weak answer

The Heart Sutra is a famous Buddhist scripture used by monks in Buddhism. It was written thousands of years ago and contains advanced wisdom and insight into the Four Noble Truths. It is called the Heart Sutra because it is the most important Buddhist teaching ever. [1]

The teachings it contains are very much about emptiness. There is nothing that really exists and so Buddhists do not therefore have to follow the Eightfold Path but instead take bodhisattva vows. [2]

The Heart Sutra outlines the importance of the bodhisattva vows and stages and perfections. It is usually meditated on because it is so odd to read out loud but this encourages and inspires Buddhists to take the path of the bodhisattva. [3]

Back to emptiness, there is a belief that emptiness makes everything possible and so Mahayana is very different from Theravada. This is why the Heart Sutra is significant because it separates the two types of Buddhists. [4]

Having said that, Theravada Buddhists also accept anatta and emptiness but they do not really make a big thing about it. It is what Mahayana Buddhists do with the emptiness teaching in the Heart Sutra that makes it more important. This is why it is a focus of meditation every day. [5]

Commentary

1. The introduction is quite vague and needs to be more precise. There is more to be said about why it is the 'Heart' Sutra. The immediate focus on emptiness is missed but then remembered for the second paragraph.

2. This paragraph is confused and not specific enough. First of all, the understanding of emptiness is incorrect and secondly although the bodhisattva path may be significant, it is not a focus of the Heart Sutra and so does not address the question set.

3. This paragraph suddenly jumps to a focus on bodhisattva. This is just information that is not required in this answer.

4. This paragraph is actually starting to hit something of relevance but it is so poorly explained and developed that the result is little more than observing Theravada and Mahayana do not both use the Sutra. A pity because the line 'a belief that emptiness makes everything possible' is significant and could have been developed.

5. This paragraph contains some new information but needs to be expanded upon. It is a weak summing up of its significance.

Summative comment

This is a weak answer with a very basic level of understanding and accuracy. The explanations or examples are often too vague or just incorrect. There are some aspects of the answer that are not properly explained, so their value is missed. The answer needs to be improved by being much clearer about the points being made and explaining their significance in terms of the focus of the question, which is the importance of the Heart Sutra.

AO2 answer: *An answer that evaluates whether the Heart Sutra is realistic.*

Strong answer

One line of argument could be that the teachings about reality found in the Prajnaparamita, for example the Heart Sutra, are in fact representative of reality because it is consistent with what the Buddha taught. The notion of emptiness involves an empirical view of the 'self' as mere conventions and that ultimately reality is subtler involving anatta – not-self or an absence of own being (svabhava) as the Heart Sutra explains. Indeed, many who practise Buddhism use a more conventional analysis of reality but do acknowledge that, in the final analysis, everything is empty. [1]

However, it could be argued that an analysis and true realisation of everything as empty is quite an advanced level and that following the Four Noble Truths, the Eightfold Path and practices such as dana and metta bhavana are more realistic for the majority of Buddhists. Really, it all depends upon whether we equate 'real' with 'true'. I would prefer to see the real in terms of philosophically viable and practical. In terms of 'practical' then, it could be argued that the realism of emptiness may not be for those not at an advanced stage. [2]

In terms of philosophical viability, from a scientific perspective the discovery of 'quarks' in physics confirmed that reality may not be quite what we think it is. Indeed, Brian Greene and his books, for example his exploration of parallel universes in *The Hidden Reality*, suggests parallel universes and multiverses. He argues that this may appear strange but it is firmly grounded in science: 'all of the parallel universe proposals that we will take seriously emerge unbidden from the mathematics of theories developed to explain conventional data and observations'. Therefore, the Heart Sutra's explanation that emptiness creates infinite possibilities such as Pure Lands or Buddha Fields, is consistent with a scientific understanding of reality and the notion of multiverses. As Nagarjuna states: 'All is possible when emptiness is possible. Nothing is possible when emptiness is impossible'. ³

However, the philosophical viability may not stretch as far as to describe the nature of such 'universes'; the Mahayana Sutras portray a universe of demons, kings, asuras, devas, celestial bodhisattvas and multiple realms, which is not representative of reality as understood in the scientific paradigm. Although this can all be demythologised or interpreted as metaphor, the possibilities the notion of emptiness opens up for Buddhists are much more speculative than those of science. ⁴

Some may argue that some concept of origination with regard to the universe is required. However, the objection is flawed if both science and philosophy indicate that the notion of emptiness eradicates the need for this. ⁵

In conclusion, it appears that the notions of emptiness found in the Heart Sutra are in fact realistic enough to be philosophically viable and also practical – albeit for the more advanced practitioner of Buddhism. The issues that are raised seem to be about the speculative nature of exactly what that realism involves. It could be argued that it is here where Buddhist spiritual reality and scientific investigation into reality part ways. ⁶

Commentary

1 A clear introduction which clearly defines what is going to be considered in relation to the Buddhist Heart Sutra.
2 A good individual point is raised that attempts to clarify what is meant by 'realistic'. The separation into practical and philosophical is a good way to tackle this.
3 This is a very strong paragraph that explores philosophical viability in relation to science and uses two good quotes. It is clear that there is some area of compatibility, established through clear use of evidence.
4 This is a very good argument that indicates that there are limits to the compatibility and that not everything can be established clearly.
5 An alternative contention is introduced and its weakness pointed out.
6 A very good personal conclusion. It returns to its original definition but also refers to the fact that the answer has demonstrated the limits of this compatibility.

Summative comment

This is a strong answer with a clear structure and has much to commend it. This answer makes reference to different points of view, uses quotations and a variety of sources, and concludes with a personal response. It could be further developed by exploring the 'practical' side of realistic more than it does.

Theme 3: ABC

AO1 answer: *An answer examining the responses of Buddhism to the challenges of science.*

A weak answer

Science is the study of many things. For example, science includes physics, chemistry, and the study of DNA and can also involve medical matters. Science is based on testing things, observing the results, re-testing things and then confirming the results. ¹

Many people might say that in the West we have a scientific approach to everything especially today. People trust science and they trust scientists rather than religion to tell the truth about how things really are. ²

Since science challenges religion, science challenges Buddhism because Buddhism is not a way of life but a religion. For example, Buddhists believe in bodhisattvas, gods and goddesses, life after death, and the existence of different realms of existence such as the god realm and the hungry ghost realm. These are all things which can be challenged by science because they cannot be proven by studying or testing things. However, Buddhists don't share a belief in a creator God and this means that they can respond to the challenges of science in a stronger way because they do not need to explain how God created the world. ³

Overall Buddhists respond by focusing on the parts of their religion which can be tested such as the effects of mindfulness and meditation. For example, the NHS uses mindfulness techniques which shows that it must be scientifically proven and therefore ok. ⁴

The Dalai Lama has been influential here because he always had an interest in cosmology from being a child. He used a telescope and this and his travels made him realise that what Buddhism taught about Mount Meru being the centre of the universe was wrong. He stated that 'if science proves some belief in Buddhism wrong, then Buddhism will have to change'. ⁵

All of this goes back to what the Buddha said when in he was in the town of Kesaputta which is in Northern India. He was there on his travels teaching the dharma to people who were interested in becoming Buddhists. He told the people in the Kalama Sutta to think carefully about what they were taught before they started to believe in it. This shows that from the time of the Buddha, Buddhism has been open to accepting different types of evidence. ⁶

Commentary

1 The opening sentences focus just on the word 'science' and state things which are unnecessary since they are obvious.

2 Whilst this appears to be relevant, it is more of an evaluative statement than a description and explanation as required for AO1 responses.

3 This is a paragraph which focuses on the question but would be much better through the introduction of specialist language and vocabulary in context. For example, rather than 'Buddhists' the response could highlight Mahayana Buddhists and rather than 'bodhisattvas' the response could provide examples such as Manjushri.

4 This is an accurate statement but with no detail or examples. For example, the use of mindfulness being clinically proven to be of use in depression, etc.

5 This is the best part of the response thus far but could be much improved by linking what is stated back to the question asked.

6 Useful material is provided here because the specification links the question of Buddhism and science to the Kalama Sutta. However, leaving this to the end of the essay means that what the Buddha taught cannot be examined in any significant detail.

Summative comment

This is a fairly weak answer because it moves from some passages which suggest limited knowledge and understanding to others which suggest mainly accurate and relevant knowledge and understanding. The response is a clear example of the need for clear thinking and planning *before* writing. The opening does not address the topic of the *challenges* of science but instead gives general points about science. Instead of this, by beginning rather than ending with the Kalama Sutta which is the key sacred text, the response would have been much better in terms of coherence.

AO2 answer: *An answer that evaluates whether there is a close relationship between Buddhism and science.*

Strong answer

In answering this question, it is important to focus on the word 'Buddhism' as much depends on the type of Buddhism which is involved and which aspects of Buddhism are being considered. For example, the beliefs of Pure Land Buddhism, which focus on the nembutsu, faith in Amida Buddha and rebirth in the Pure Land, are incapable of being scientifically proven. However, the claims of Buddhists in general that meditation has a measurable impact on how the brain functions can be and have been tested. 1

In arguing that there is a close relationship between Buddhism and science, the work of the Dalai Lama is important to consider. He founded the Mind and Life Institute in 1997, which brings together Buddhists and scientists in studying neuroscience and cognitive science. This includes a field of study called neuroplasticity, which looks at how the brain generates new neural connections as a result of deep meditation. 2

It could also be argued that there is a close relationship between Buddhism and science based on the Kalama Sutta, which is a key Buddhist sacred text from the Pali Canon. Here, the Buddha is asked about how the Kalamas clan can know which religious tradition they should follow. The Buddha advises against any reliance on tradition but instead states that they need to weigh up the evidence. The key phrase is 'when you know for yourselves'. This is seen as supporting the need for getting empirical data from evidence, which is the basis of scientific research. 3

However, it is possible to argue that with regard to most forms of Buddhism the element of the supernatural is very important and this is something which can have nothing to do with science. For example, in Tibetan Buddhism there is the belief in yidams and evil spirits. Again, most Mahayana Buddhists believe in bodhisattvas such as Manjushri or Tara and that these bodhisattvas answer prayers and give practical help. 4

Overall, I would argue that perhaps with Western forms of Buddhism, especially for secular Buddhists or convert Buddhists, a close relationship between Buddhism and science is accepted. This is mainly because Buddhism does not involve itself in the unanswered questions such as whether the cosmos is finite or infinite, eternal or not. In addition, it helps because Buddhists do not believe in a creator God. 5

Commentary

1 This is a good way of beginning because it involves questioning or highlighting a key word in the question and shows the examiner that evaluation is taking place.

2 This is a strong paragraph because it makes accurate reference to the Dalai Lama and the Mind and Life Institute. Together these provide detailed evidence.

3 Further detailed evidence is provided here through reference to the sacred texts. The response presents a confident and perceptive analysis of what the Kalama Sutta might be seen to imply.

4 The answer now introduces a clear counter-argument through an opposing line of reasoning. The evidence presented is clear and coherent. There is also clear evidence of specialist language and vocabulary.

5 This is a good conclusion which identifies and addresses the issue raised by the question.

Summative comment

The answer is generally well balanced. Perhaps more could have been written with ideas better developed regarding the counter-argument. Here, as always, working out timing for these essays is essential and is best done through practice. The answer benefits in particular from its continued focus on the topic in the question and by its reference back to the wording involved.

Theme 3: DEF

AO1 answer: *An answer examining the historical development of Buddhism in Britain.*

Strong answer

Buddhism first became known to the educated middle classes in Britain through Edward Arnold's poem *The Light of Asia* (1879). This contains key Buddhist stories and beliefs along with quotations from the Dhammapada. This poem had a major impact in bringing many of the first British converts to Buddhism. [1]

Among the first Western converts were the founders of the Theosophical Society, Helena Blavatsky and Henry Olcott. Theosophy contained many references to Buddhism as providing ancient wisdom from the East which would bring health and happiness to the West. A number of the first British converts to Buddhism were influenced by the beliefs of Theosophy.

Buddhist beliefs became part of academic study through the collection and study of Pali texts. Academics who studied these texts were behind the founding of Buddhist societies. Out of these grew the most important, which was the Buddhist Society in London which was officially founded in 1924. [2]

Although his influence is difficult to assess, one of the first people from Britain to be ordained a Buddhist monk should be noted. Charles Bennett became Ananda Metteyya and lived as a Theravada monk and wrote many articles for Buddhist publications. Anagarika Dharmapala also helped in the development of Buddhism in Britain as a Buddhist missionary from Sri Lanka. [3]

Up until the 1960s it might be stated that the Buddhist Society under Christmas Humphreys was very important in the development of Buddhism in Britain. After that period, due to the migration of Buddhists from countries such as Tibet, China and Hong Kong, Buddhism began to develop in different ways by establishing heritage Buddhists in the country. This development was also influenced by people who were often of the younger generation travelling to countries such as Thailand where Buddhism was established. They brought back with them Buddhist beliefs and practices. [4]

In Britain today, major Buddhist groups are represented. Some Buddhist schools have large monasteries such as the Manjushri Kadampa Centre in Cumbria and the forest monk tradition of Ajahn Chah in the Amaravati Monastery in Hemel Hempstead. What could be described as a British

form of Buddhism has developed through the work of Sangharakshita and the Triratna Buddhist Order. [5]

Commentary

1. Although the opening paragraph is not a typical introductory paragraph, it does not waste time but goes straight to the impact of *The Light of Asia*. This approach is often useful if there is a lot of material to get down on paper.

2. What has been done successfully here in these two paragraphs is selection of key points, key names and key concepts in the development of Buddhism in Britain. All of these contribute to the sacred texts and sources of wisdom and authority required in the assessment bands.

3. This paragraph begins with what might appear to be evaluation but it is in fact stating what scholars observe as to Bennett's influence. Again with a very complex area, highlighting just the key points is a vital skill.

4. This paragraph summarises the period from the 1960s onwards. There could be more detail included here but keeping in mind the need for careful timing, some key points are made.

5. This last paragraph gives three examples of Buddhism(s) which can be found in Britain. Perhaps it would have been useful to indicate the type of the Buddhist groups, i.e. Tibetan, Theravada and Mahayana, etc.

Summative comment

This is a strong answer because of the way in which selection of relevant material has been carried out. In this way it displays accurate and relevant knowledge and understanding. Overall the answer is well-balanced in that about half of the answer covers the period up until the 1960s and half the period afterwards. There are some simplistic points which could have been developed but much depends on timing. The one weakness is that there is no reference at all in the essay to any numerical data taken from the census as to the percentage of Buddhists in the British population.

AO2 answer: *An answer that evaluates the unique nature of British Buddhism in comparison with Buddhism found in other countries.*

Weak answer

The origins of Buddhism in Britain can be traced back to 1879 and Sir Edward Arnold's poem *The Light of Asia*. In this epic poem, Arnold describes the birth and upbringing of the Buddha. He also describes the Buddha's Awakening and his teaching to the first five monks. The poem is very interesting especially in the way in which it quotes the Dhammapada. The Buddha is described as being 'Lover! Brother! Guide! Lamp of the Law!' [1]

In Britain today there are a number of different Buddhist groups. For example, Throssel Hole Buddhist Abbey is in the north of England. It follows the Theravada tradition very closely with chanting in Pali and English. In other monasteries there is also chanting in Pali such as in the Amaravati Monastery. I would argue that it is the use of English in chanting which makes British Buddhism unique. [2]

However, British Buddhism is not unique because it shares all the beliefs and most of the types of worship which other Buddhists have throughout the world. For example, all Buddhists whether they are British or not would have a Buddha rupa to focus upon and they would also carry out the same forms of meditation. [3]

Translating Buddhist terms into English makes British Buddhism unique because sometimes the translations do not convey the full meaning of the terms. For example, the word 'dukkha' is translated as 'suffering' but it means much more than that such as 'being dissatisfied'. Being dissatisfied is different from suffering and this changes the way such an important Noble Truth is understood. Going back to *The Light of Asia*, this presented Buddhism in an English form which was unique to Britain. [4]

I would argue that a unique form of British Buddhism is the Triratna Buddhist Order which was founded by Dennis Lingwood. This goes back to the 1960s. He brought back from his training a different way of presenting Buddhism for ordinary working people in Britain. He also wrote lots of books in English about Buddhism, which helped to make it more popular. His form of Buddhism is unique because it was his version of Buddhism which was followed by people who belonged to the order. Again presenting Buddhism in the English language makes it unique compared to Buddhism in other countries. [5]

In conclusion, I would argue that British Buddhism is unique because of the mixing between convert Buddhists and heritage Buddhists. This means that convert Buddhists can worship alongside Buddhists from countries such as Tibet and Nepal. [6]

Having Buddhist ideas and mantras in the English language also makes British Buddhism unique because it would not be found outside of countries such as the US and Canada. However, looking back to the question, perhaps there is no 'unique' form of Buddhism because there are so many different types of Buddhism such as Pure Land and Nichiren. British Buddhism is therefore just another type of Buddhism. British Buddhism might be unique because there are not many monks in Britain. Another thing is that many Buddhists in Britain are women, which is not the same everywhere in the world. [7]

Commentary

1 This introduction gives subject knowledge and understanding. However, what is lacking is any sense of critical analysis and perceptive evaluation of the subject. It is not clear from the outset as to where this essay is going to go in terms of evaluation and analysis.

2 This paragraph contains a factual error because Throssel Hole Abbey is associated with Zen Buddhism – not Theravada. Making mistakes such as this is not a major issue as there is no negative marking. The response continues by making the first evaluative point as to British Buddhism being unique due to the use of the English language.

3 Using the key word 'however' suggests that evaluation is going to continue and it is an important AO2 word in responses. The points made in this paragraph are strong ones which begin to address the question.

4 This paragraph repeats the argument regarding British Buddhism being unique because of the use of the English language. It would have been better to keep this argument to one well-developed paragraph as it is only one point. The final sentence about *The Light of Asia* does not add anything which can be credited in terms of marks.

5 This paragraph begins well – 'I would argue' is entirely acceptable as it makes the argument seem to be one with which the writer is engaging. However, the paragraph continues in a somewhat random way which returns to the theme of the English language.

6 This appears to be the concluding paragraph but it is not. A problem with this paragraph is that it introduces an entirely new point which has not been alluded to elsewhere in the essay. It is also not so much evaluation and analysis as assertion of a fact.

7 After another reference to the English language, this final paragraph begins to raise some very interesting issues for evaluation and analysis such as whether any form of Buddhism is unique. The last two sentences also indicate areas which could have generated much more fruitful evaluation and analysis – the lack of a significant monastic sangha in Britain and the significant and equal role of women in British Buddhism. However, these issues should have been addressed and developed much earlier in the essay.

Summative comment

This type of answer can be frustrating as it contains elements suggesting very good understanding and knowledge which, however, have not been put to best use. Repetition of a single point – in this case the use of English language – does not necessarily make that point any stronger. Scattered references to the same point also suggest a lack of control of the material being discussed.

Presenting brief stated points as in the final paragraphs is another weakness of this essay since these points are not fully supported with good reasoning and evidence.

Theme 4: DEF

AO1 answer: *An answer that examines Socially Engaged Buddhism.*

Very strong answer

Socially Engaged Buddhism (SEB) can be defined using the words of Ken Jones as aiming 'to combine the cultivation of inner peace with active social compassion'. This means that whilst it focuses on interior Buddhist practices such as meditation, it also focuses on exterior practices such as helping the wider community. [1]

From one perspective the roots of SEB can be traced back to the work of Thich Nhat Hanh in Vietnam when, during the Vietnamese War, he encouraged young Buddhist students at the university to go out and help people with their educational, health and economic needs.

From another perspective, SEB can also be seen in the Ariyaratne's Sarvodaya movement in Sri Lanka. Founded in 1958, this aimed to awaken individual villagers and then to awaken villages as a whole in order to work together in addressing ten basic needs such as clean water and housing for all. [2]

When Buddhism became more established in the West and the number of convert Buddhists increased, SEB became increasingly accepted as an important part of being Buddhist. A good example of how this started can be seen in the way in which Thich Nhat Hanh linked with Martin Luther King in supporting civil rights and preaching against the Vietnam War.

For Thich Nhat Hanh, Buddhism had to involve removing suffering from society and not just achieving self-awakening or a better rebirth. This can be seen in the Tiep Hien Order, which he founded based on the Fourteen Mindfulness Trainings. One of these states that members of the Order should not 'avoid or close their eyes before suffering'. [3]

One example of an organisation which focuses on SEB can be found in the Buddhist Peace Fellowship. This was founded in the USA by convert Buddhists and today is involved in supporting things such as action against climate change, globalisation and military action. Another organisation is Sakyadhita, which seeks to awaken Buddhist women and to work for their spiritual and secular welfare. It is also involved in applying a feminist Buddhist approach to the environment. [4]

Overall, the approach of SEB is teaching that because of pratityasamutpada, everyone and everything is interconnected and that therefore an individual's suffering due to, for example, oppression and discrimination is linked to everyone else. Joanna Macy gives the example of all people and the whole world being 'a vast web of being' like Indra's infinite jewelled net. Therefore nobody can think about themselves and their awakening alone because no one is an island. [5]

Commentary

[1] This is very good introduction that defines the term Socially Engaged Buddhism (SEB). The quotation from Ken Jones is also an important use of a source of wisdom and authority. The definition shows both depth and breadth.

[2] This is a very good paragraph as it presents two different examples of where the roots of SEB can be found – both in the work of Thich Nhat Hanh and in the work of Ariyaratne's Sarvodaya movement.

[3] This is a very good paragraph as the example of Thich Nhat Hanh and the Mindfulness Trainings is in the specification. The link between suffering and the Mindfulness Trainings is also made explicit.

[4] Both the Buddhist Peace Fellowship and Sakyadhita are in the specification as examples of organisations working in the area of SEB. This means they are both relevant and specific to the question of SEB.

[5] This is a very good conclusion. Macy as a source of wisdom and authority is quoted along with specialist language. There is also evidence of an insightful connection with regard to Indra's Net which draws everything together.

Summative comment

Overall the answer has a very good structure: introduction with a clear definition; then dealing with the history of SEB; then referring to specific examples of SEB at work. Throughout there is good use of examples, sources of wisdom and authority, brief quotations and specialist terminology. The conclusion in particular shows very strong command of the material.

AO2 answer: *An answer that evaluates whether social engagement is a distraction from the path to Awakening.*

Weak answer

Buddhism was founded by the Buddha over two thousand years ago and is still found throughout the world today. In particular it is growing strongly in the West. All types of Buddhism can be found from Tibetan Buddhism through to Theravada Buddhism. When the Buddha founded

Buddhism he had left the palace aged 29 and after some years of asceticism he found his Awakening under the Bodhi Tree in Bodh Gaya. By then he was aged 35. But did the Buddha get involved in social engagement? **1**

The problem with social engagement is that because a person is engaged in society they do not have very much time for themselves. It is only with time for themselves that a person can achieve Awakening. For example, if a person wanted to be awakened they would need to spend a lot of time in meditating. There are different types of meditation including vipassana which require a lot of hard work and focus. This takes time but it is what the Buddha did and so it is something which Buddhists should also do. **2**

Another problem with social engagement is that it is not really Buddhist. It is mainly something which Buddhists in the West – especially convert Buddhists – are interested in. **3**

Another point I would make is that social engagement is not mentioned anywhere in the Four Noble Truths. These are about suffering, craving, the end of suffering and the Eightfold Path. This path is the Middle Way. All of this means that social engagement is not Buddhist. **4**

Some people might disagree and say that social engagement is Buddhist. After all, the Buddha was not selfish – he helped people like Kisa Gotami who was trying to find the answer as to why her child had died. The Buddha showed her compassion because she was suffering. Compassion is a very important Buddhist characteristic.

Theravada Buddhists might be described as being selfish because they just focus on Awakening. That is why Mahayana Buddhists have bodhisattvas because these are all about compassion. They are role models for Buddhists. All of this means that social engagement is Buddhist.

The Dalai Lama is a good example of social engagement. When Tibet was taken over by the Chinese, he left for India. Since being in India he has travelled the world trying to arrange for peace in Tibet. He won the Nobel Peace Prize because he did not encourage violence among the Tibetan people. He showed social engagement by encouraging peace. Thich Nhat Hanh did the same about the war in Vietnam. **5**

It all depends on what type of Buddhist you might be but I think that social engagement is important as everyone is part of the world around them and should be involved in what happens. Helping people through social engagement is good as it stops people from being selfish and I think that being selfish might stop a person from getting rid of the three poisons from within.

Human rights are a very important issue and it is important that Buddhists are involved in supporting the rights of people especially minority groups. The Buddha did good work here in teaching that women could achieve Awakening and he also ordained women as nuns. This means that the sangha is fourfold – made up of monks, nuns, men and women. **6**

In conclusion, I believe that social engagement is not very Buddhist but it is important for Awakening. **7**

Commentary

1 This type of introduction does not focus at all on the subject of the question. It already suggests that the response is going to be limited in terms of analysis and evaluation. Asking rhetorical questions in an essay is generally not helpful in presenting a discussion. When you read the essay note how if this introduction were removed, there would be no real difference to the essay.

2 In this paragraph there are some good points made. This might have been a good way to start the essay as it raises the issue of whether time would be better spent on achieving Awakening or on social engagement.

3 Very brief paragraphs such as this are not helpful because they do not lead to further development or analysis and evaluation such as is needed in this type of essay.

4 A valid point is made here which with further development could have become part of a much more effective paragraph showing evaluation and analysis.

5 These paragraphs show some good ideas in terms of knowledge and understanding. However, as they stand, they are not sufficiently linked to demonstrate analysis of the nature of connections between elements of the topic which have been studied.

6 These points may seem valid but are placed in the essay in a somewhat random manner which again takes away from any element of analysis and evaluation.

7 This not really a conclusion – it is just an assertion of a point of view without any supporting evidence.

Summative comment

This is a weak answer mainly because there has been little in the way of thinking through or planning. With more thought, the points made and ideas expressed could have been put together and developed in a much more coherent fashion. Reading this answer there does not appear to be a clear line of reasoning that links everything together.

Quickfire answers

Theme 1

1.1 The Pali Canon, a collection of scriptures, containing the teachings of the historical Buddha. Originally written on palm leaves and kept in baskets, hence the name.

1.2 227 for bhikkhus and 311 for bhikkhunis.

1.3 The four Parajikas.

1.4 The Suttavibhanga, the Khandhaka and the Parivara.

1.5 Expulsion from the monastic sangha; a meeting of the sangha to deal with the consequences; penance; forfeiture; confession or a public admission that the action has happened.

1.6 Summary of the Patimokka rules, valuable guidance on how to observe the Vinaya and used in monastic training to instruct and examine bhikkhus and bhikkhunis.

1.7 The Sutta Pitaka and Buddha-vacana.

1.8 The Dhammapada, 'path of Truth', is a collection of sayings of the historical Buddha, probably gathered directly by his closest disciples. The Dhammapada is organised into 423 easily memorised verses.

1.9 The Jatakas consist of a collection of over 500 anecdotes and fables told by the Buddha about experiences within his previous lives.

1.10 Philosophical teachings which reveal the Buddhist perspective on the world and reality.

1.11 'Perfection of wisdom' and 'Heart'.

1.12 Tibetan and Zen.

1.13 The bodhisattva of compassion.

1.14 Emptiness does not mean nothingness.

1.15 To emphasise the direct understanding of scripture, aid direct realisation of interconnectedness and awakening to the nature of reality or satori.

1.16 Conventional truth is when we see things as relative or separate and diverse. Ultimate truth is to see the absolute truth that there is no separate existence.

1.17 'The Sutra of the Lotus Blossom of the Wonderful Law.'

1.18 A term used, mostly within Mahayana Buddhism, to refer to the historical Buddha, meaning 'sage of the Shakya'. Shakyamuni of the Lotus Sutra is seen as the Eternal Buddha.

1.19 Thus I have heard.

1.20 The sravaka-yana, pratyekabuddha-yana and the bodhisattva-yana.

1.21 Order of Interbeing.

1.22 The Mindfulness Bell and Walk With Me.

1.23 For peaceful protest against the Communist regime and civil war. He has made his new home in Plum Village in the South of France.

1.24 Living mindfully following the Fourteen Mindfulness Trainings. Non-attachment from views, anicca, pratityasamutpada and upaya.

1.25 The nature of Interbeing, the reality of life, which can be experienced in the here and now.

1.26 A simple Buddhist monk. The Gelugpa school.

1.27 The State Oracle.

1.28 Chairman Mao the political leader of China and because it was the aftermath of the Second World War.

1.29 For his non-violent fight for the freedom of Tibet.

1.30 To implement the Buddhist teaching of ahimsa.

1.31 It brings them comfort, it shows their loyalty and respect. To do so is banned in Tibet by the PRC.

Theme 3

3.1   552 CE.

3.2   Enryaku-ji.

3.3   Mahakasyapa.

3.4   'Namu Amida Butsu' ('I take refuge in Amida Buddha').

3.5   Nichiren Gohonzon, daimoku, kaidan.

3.6   Pasada is 'a calm and joyful faith' and saddha is 'soundly based faith or trustful confidence'.

3.7   Told her to return to him with mustard seeds from a household where none had experienced death of family or friend.

3.8   Kesaputta.

3.9   King of the devas.

3.10 Modern science education – particularly psychology, physics and astronomy.

3.11 Malunkyaputta.

3.12 Pali Canon.

3.13 Principle of Conditionality, Principle of a Fourfold Task, Perspective of Mindful Awareness, Power of Self-Reliance.

3.14 Dharmavidya.

3.15 Sambhogakaya.

3.16 Clear perception of what is fundamental.

3.17 'Oneself is one's own refuge.'

3.18 It depends on whether the raft/Dhamma is seen as essential or disposable.

3.19 Value of growth in the essentials of all religions; importance of restraint about one's own religion; respect of other religions; contact between religions is good.

3.20 Pure, authentic form of Theravada Buddhism.

3.21 Ananda Metteyya.

3.22 0.4%.

3.23 'This is a rule to be revered and reverenced, honoured and observed, and her lifelong never to be transgressed.'

3.24 Nalagiri.

3.25 Kuan-yin.

Theme 4

4.1   Songtsen Gampo.

4.2   Everlasting.

4.3   Gelugpa.

4.4   Vajrasattva.

4.5   The state of the person chanting and their goal of Buddhahood.

4.6   One of the five skandhas or one of the five material elements.

4.7   Vehicle.

4.8   Bell.

4.9   1979.

4.10 Calmness and composure.

4.11 Experiences in life that cause us distress and pain and that promote in us an underlying sense of fear, insecurity, and loss of control.

4.12 Work against or flee from stressors.

4.13 UK National Institute of Clinical Excellence

4.14 Meditation whilst lying down.

4.15 It suggests that people should just accept passively technological development and social changes.

4.16 Branding mindfulness to make is palatable.

4.17 France.

4.18 It means 'one action'.

4.19 To be in touch with/making it here and now: interbeing.

4.20 For the happiness of the many, for the welfare of the many.

4.21 Block harm and oppression; build relationships; be in alignment with the dharma.

Glossary

Abhidhamma Pitaka: third part of the Pali Canon of scriptures made up of the philosophical discourses and commentaries of later scholars

Ahimsa: the Buddhist teaching that you should harm no living thing, non-violence

Akaravati saddha: confidence based on reason and experience

Allostasis: the body's ability to remain stable by being able to change

Amulika saddha: blind faith

Anagarika Dharmapala: regarded as the first international Buddhist missionary

Ananda: one of the ten closest disciples of the Buddha who was well-known for having a good memory and who was the Buddha's assistant and spokesman

Arahatship: becoming an arahant (arhat (Skt)), 'noble or worthy one' who has achieved enlightenment

Avalokitesvara: 'He who hears the cries of the world.' The bodhisattva of compassion

Avatamsaka Sutra: literally, 'Flower Garland' Sutra, longer than the Christian Bible, important in East Asian Buddhism, particularly the Hua Yen school of Chinese Buddhism during the Tang dynasty

Bhikkhu: monk

Bhikkhuni: nun

Bon: original religion in Tibet prior to Buddhism

Bonpos: the name given to the followers of Tibet's indigenous religion, Bon

BPF: Buddhist Peace Fellowship

Brahma: the first god in the Hindu trimurti – traditionally regarded as the creator god

Buddha Bhaishajya: the Medicine Buddha

Buddha sasana: teaching or doctrine of the Buddha

Buddha vacana: the words or sayings of the Buddha

Buddhahood: the Mahayanist concept of Awakening or Enlightenment which is available to everyone

Buddha-nature: the fundamental nature of all beings that they *are* already enlightened and essentially need to realise it

Buddhisms: a term which reflects the view that Buddhism is not one single unified belief system as with some other world religions

Buddhist Society: the most influential and long-lasting of a number of Buddhist groups formed early in the 20th century officially founded in 1924

Canon: a collection of scriptures that holds authority

Causation: the act of causing something; or the relationship between cause and effect

Charles Henry Allan Bennett: one of the first people from Britain to be ordained a Buddhist monk

Christmas Humphreys: the founder of the Buddhist Society and its president until his death in 1983

Cittamatra: the Mind Only school of Mahayana Buddhism

Conventional truth: truth that operates within the empirical world and makes sense of the emptiness teaching; a way of explaining the world around us using skilful means; sometimes referred to as 'partial' or 'provisional' or 'relative' truth

Conventional: relative

Convert Buddhists: a term defined by Bluck as referring to ethnically European people in Britain who have converted to Buddhism rather than coming from an Asian Buddhist background

Cullavaga: part of the second book of the Vinaya Pitaka containing details about the ordination of bhikkhunis

Cultural misappropriation: views in the West being read back into the Asian tradition of Buddhism

Daimoku: the central chant (or mantra) of all forms of Nichiren Buddhism

Dalai Lama: meaning 'Ocean of Wisdom' this is the title given to the reincarnated leader of Tibetan Buddhism

Dana: giving

Dasa sila: ten precepts taken by monks and nuns

Deva: supernatural god-like being living on Mount Meru

Devadatta: the Buddha's cousin who is presented as a figure of evil in Buddhist texts but who becomes a Buddha in the Lotus Sutra

Devanampiya Piyadasi: the name given to Ashoka – which can be translated as 'Beloved of the gods – He who looks on with kindness'

Dhamma (Pali)/Dharma (Sanskrit): unit of existence. It is to be distinguished from the Dhamma/Dharma which is the Buddhist teaching or truth

Dhammas: the units or components from which everything is made

Dharma name: the name given to a Buddhist during initiation into the sangha

Dharmacharya: teacher

Dharmaguptaka: one of the eighteen early schools of Buddhism

Dharmakaya: dharma body

Dharmapalas: devas who protect the dharma

Digha-Tapassi: a leading Jain ascetic and disciple of Nigantha Nataputta

Dre: evil spirits or gods in Bon

Ehi-passiko: reasoned reflection and testing the benefits of the path are what lead to the path being followed – literally means 'which you can come and see'

Ekayana: the concept of one vehicle or 'one way' which is the way of Buddhahood

Enryaku-ji: the temple/monastery complex on the top of Mount Hiei which was destroyed in 1571

Flower and Smile Sermon: the silent sermon given by the Buddha by holding up a lotus which was recognised by Mahakasyapa who smiled

Four levels of androcentrism: four ways in which androcentrism has permeated Buddhism: preservation of male texts and stories, prioritising of male texts and stories, preserving this male bias in Western scholarship, practising this male bias in contemporary Asian and Western Buddhism

Fourteen Mindfulness Trainings: precepts followed by the Order of Interbeing

Gandavyuha: 39th chapter of the Avatamsaka

Garudhammas: the eight chief rules – also known as 'heavy' or 'weighty' rules – set by the Buddha, accepted by Maha-Pajapati-Gotami and applied to bhikkhunis

Gelugpa: meaning 'virtuous way' this is a sect of Tibetan Buddhism which focuses on the Vinaya rules, monastic celibacy and scholarship

Great Renunciation: when Gotama left behind his wife, son and the palace following the Four Sights; his renunciation of the life of hedonism

Hinayana: term used in Mahayana Buddhism, seen in the Lotus Sutra, to describe Therevada Buddhist teachings

Hoben: chapter two of the Lotus Sutra, known as 'Expedient Means'

Hrdaya Sutra: 'Heart Sutra' also known as the 'Heart of Perfect Wisdom Sutra' or the 'Essence of Wisdom Sutra'

Indra's Net: metaphor used by Macy to emphasise a holistic view of the earth

Interbeing: the absence of a separate self and everything being linked as a part of perpetual change

Jain: the name given to the followers of Jainism – a religion focused on asceticism which developed under the leadership of Mahavira – also known as Nigantha Nataputta (599–527 BCE) – a contemporary of the Buddha

Jambudvipa: the continent on which human beings live

Jowo Rinpoche: statue of the Buddha in Jokhang Temple brought to Tibet in 641 CE

Kamakura period of Japanese history: the period from 1185 to 1333 which started through government by the first Shogun

Kami: the divine energy found in the natural world and divine beings, which followers of Shinto practise devotion towards

Kangyur: collection of words of the Buddha

Khandhaka: the second section of the Vinaya Pitaka containing stories about the Buddha's Awakening and rules of etiquette for the monastic sangha

Lama: guru or teacher

lha: good spirits or gods in Bon

Lhamo Thondup: the birth name of the Dalai Lama

Lineage: the type of Buddhism being taught had been handed down from, and was true to, that of the main teacher or founder of the monastery

Madhyamaka: Middle School, of Buddhism founded upon the teaching of Nagarjuna. This school is at the root of Mahayana Buddhism

Maha-Pajapati Gotami: the aunt and foster-mother of the Buddha whose life story as a bhikkuni is recorded in a variety of sacred texts

Malas: Tibetan meditation beads

Mandala: Tibetan diagram of the cosmos for meditational focus

Mani mantra: 'om mani padme hum' ('homage to the one holding jewel and lotus)

Manjushri: one of the most important bodhisattvas in Mahayana who is the embodiment of wisdom

Mantra: tool for thinking, sacred sounds

Mappo: the third of three ages following the Buddha which is the age of the decay of the Dhamma

Mauryan dynasty: dynasty which ruled much of India from c. 321 to 187 BCE – Ashoka was the third ruler of this dynasty

MBCT: Mindfulness-Based Cognitive Therapy

MBSR: Mindfulness-Based Stress Reduction

Mind and Life Institute: co-founded by the Dalai Lama in 1997 to bring together modern science and contemplative practice

MiSP: Mindfulness in Schools Project

Mother Teresa of Calcutta (1910–1997): a saint of the Roman Catholic Church renowned for the compassion in action towards the impoverished, the sick and the dying shown on the streets of Calcutta

Mount Meru: the great world mountain

Mu Koan: the koan which asks whether a dog has the Buddha-nature or not

Mudra: sign, gesture of hands made by the hands of Buddha images, ritual bodily movements

Mulamadhyamikakarikas: ('verses on the fundamentals of the Middle Way' composed by the Indian philosopher monk Nagarjuna)

Nagarjuna: the most well-known of early Buddhist philosophers (c150–250 CE)

Nembutsu: recitation used in Pure Land Buddhism

Networking monks: monks who carried Buddhist beliefs between geographical and culture centres and peripheries

Neuroplasticity: the ability of the brain to generate new nerve cells and neural connections, thereby altering emotions, behaviour, and perceptions

New Age spirituality: the name given to a non-unified set of beliefs that developed from the 1960s onwards built on wide-ranging spiritual and philosophical beliefs such as those of the Theosophical Society

Nirmanakaya: the emanation body of a Buddha according to the doctrine of Trikaya

Nyingmapa: oldest Tibetan Buddhist tradition

Order of Interbeing: Tiep Hien, is a lay and monastic sangha founded by Thich Nhat Hanh, which has its headquarters at Plum Village in Southern France

Padmasambhava: an ancient Indian tantric Mahayana Buddhist monk considered by all traditions to have introduced Tibet to Buddhism

Pali: an ancient Indian language

Parajikas: the 'defeats' or behaviour that forces disrobing and expulsion from the monastic order

Paramattha sacca: generally translated as ultimate truth or underlying reality which might be regarded as sunyata – emptiness

Parinirvana: the final passing away into nirvana from the cycle of life, death and rebirth

Parivara: the third section of the Vinaya Pitaka containing a summary of the Vinaya rules

Pasada: a calm and joyful faith

Patimokka: the 227 rules of the Buddhist community of monks to be found in the Vinaya; nuns have 311

Philosophical monism: mind and body are manifestations of a single entity

Pitaka: basket for storage of the original Buddhist texts

Plum Village: a retreat centre set up by Thich Nhat Hanh located in the South of France. The location of the headquarters of the Order of Interbeing

Potala Palace: the headquarters of Tibetan Buddhism and the home of the Dalai Lama before his exile from Tibet

Prajna: wisdom

Prajnaparamita Hrdaya: 'Heart Sutra' also known as the 'Heart of Perfect Wisdom Sutra' or the 'Essence of Wisdom Sutra'

Prajnaparamita: meaning 'the wisdom that has gone further or beyond' or 'perfection/excellence of wisdom' and is a collection of early Buddhist scriptures from the Mahayana tradition

Prasangika: a specific interpretation of Nagarjuna's philosophy that argues against the idea of accepting emptiness and yet recognising some form of conventional empirical essence or intrinsic nature. This latter view, rejected by Nagarjuna, is usually associated with the Svatantrika interpretation of the 6th-century Indian Buddhist scholar Bhaviveka

Pratekya-Buddha: literally 'a lone buddha', 'a buddha on their own' or 'a private buddha', is one of three types of enlightened beings according to some schools of Buddhism. A Buddha who reaches enlightenment and does not go on to teach

Pratityasamutpada: dependent origination

Pratyekabuddhas: those who had found Enlightenment themselves

Pratyekabuddha-yana: the yana of the solitary Buddha. This refers to someone who is outside of the monastic sangha, who does not have a teacher and who, therefore, has not been taught the Dhamma

Revalorisation: the term used by Rita Gross for both critiquing the androcentric patriarchy of Buddhist texts and stories and for then repairing the Buddhist tradition

Rinpoche: the honorary title given to a spiritual teacher in Tibetan Buddhism

Rock Edict: proclamations of Ashoka inscribed on rock which have been found in India and neigbouring countries

Saddha: soundly based faith or trustful confidence

Sakyadhita: 'Daughters of Buddha' organisation advancing the place of women in the Buddhist world

Sambhogakaya: the celestial or heavenly body of buddhas often existing in realms such as the Pure Land

Sammuti sacca: generally translated as conventional truth which is conditioned by designations

Sariputra: in Theravada one of the chief disciples of the Buddha but in some texts – such as the Lotus Sutra – presented as one who is slow to grasp the Mahayana Dharma

Sarvodaya: 'Awaken' movement in Sri Lanka started in 1958

Self-body-scan: observing in the mind each part of the body

Seven attitudinal foundations: non-judging, patience, beginner's mind, trust, non-striving, acceptance, letting go

Shakyamuni: a term used, mostly within Mahayana Buddhism, to refer to the Buddha, Siddhartha Gautama, and means 'sage of the Shakya'. Shakyamuni of the Lotus Sutra is also seen as the Eternal Buddha.

Shinto: the indigenous religion of Japan which has no single founder or sacred text and which has ritual rather than belief as its focus

Shodai: prolonged chanting of the daimoku

Shramadana: giving labour

Sima: a boundary that surrounds the temple or monastery

Sir Edwin Arnold: author of *The Light of Asia* and thereby an influential figure in promoting Buddhism in Britain and the USA

SIYLI: Search Inside Yourself Leadership Institute

Socially Engaged Buddhism: a movement many believe to have been founded by the practices of Thich Nhat Hanh (but also traced back to 13th-century Vietnam) that requires Buddhists to become involved in social issues and committed in exceptional times of confrontation, injustice and violence (it is also sometimes referred to as Engaged Buddhism)

Sravakas: hearers of the dharma, who would attain the status of arhat

Sravaka-yana: the yana of the arhat who as a disciple been taught the Dhamma of the Buddha and who is part of the monastic sangha

State Oracle: a clairvoyant monk in Tibetan Buddhism

Stressors: internal or external factors which cause a person stress

Sukhavati: the term for 'Pure Land', the Buddha kshetra of Amitabha Buddha

Sunyata (Sanskrit)/ sunna or sunya (Pali): the concept that form (physical and mental notions of 'existence') is empty of inherent existence and therefore nothing exists independently, but that conversely emptiness necessitates form

Sutta Pitaka: second part of the Pali Canon of scriptures containing stories and teachings of the Buddha

Suttavibhanga: the first book of the Theravadin Vinaya Pitaka

Svabhava: own-being

SYSS: School of Youth Social Services

Tantra: practices which provide the means for becoming enlightened

Tathagata: a term used by the Buddha to describe himself and also used by others as a title for the Buddha; its meaning is uncertain and sometimes translated as 'the one who has thus gone' or 'the one who has thus arrived'

Tengyur: commentaries on the sacred texts

Tenzin Gyatso: name of the 14th Dalai Lama

Thay: teacher

The Light of Asia: Sir Edwin Arnold's epic poem on the early life of the Buddha and on the Dhamma published 1879

Theosophy: an esoteric religious movement – the **Theosophical Society** was founded by Helena Blavatsky and Henry Olcott in 1876 with a focus is on ancient universal divine wisdom

Theravadin: an adherent of Theravada Buddhism

Therigatha: a collection of sayings and poems written by senior bhikkhunis which is in the Pali Canon

Thich Nhat Hanh: Vietnamese Zen Buddhist Master and founder of the Order of Interbeing

Thich Quang Duc: Buddhist monk who burned himself to death in 1963

Tipitaka: Pali Canon (three baskets, made up of the Vinaya Pitaka, the Sutta Pitaka and the Abidhamma Pitaka); the corpus of scripture held to be authoritative by Theravada Buddhists

Trikaya: the 'three bodies' or ways of being of the Buddha, dharmakaya, sambhogakaya and nirmanakaya

Triratna Buddhist Order: originally known as the Friends of the Western Buddhist Order, which was founded by Sangharakshita (formerly Dennis Lingwood) in 1967 in London and is a form of Buddhist modernism

Tsongkhapa: meaning 'the man from Onion Valley', the founder of the Gelugpa school of Tibetan Buddhism

Tulku: a reincarnated lama who is trained from a young age to pass on the teachings from a specific lineage of Tibetan Buddhism

Ultimate truth: an enlightened view of existence as sunyata (empty)

Ultimate: absolute

Upali: one of the ten chief disciples of the Buddha who recalled all of the rules of the Vinaya

Upaya kausalya: skilful means in Sanskrit, delivering the Buddhist Dhamma (Dharma) to people according to their spiritual capacity and needs, and also according to emotional and intellectual capacities

Upaya kosalla: literally, 'skilful means' describing the simplified way in which difficult concepts can be taught effectively to those who do not have the capacity (also known as upaya kausalya in Mahayana)

Uposatha days: days of renewed commitment to the dharma, often occurring on full-moon

Vinaya Pitaka: the first part of the Pali Canon containing the rules and regulations for the discipline of the community of monks and nuns

Visualisation practice: a form of meditation which involves creating a picture in one's mind of, for example, the Pure Land created by Amida

Yana: vehicle

Yidam: a holy being or bodhisattva

Zazen: meditation which involves just sitting in the correct posture and letting go of both mind and body

Index